THE CATHOLIC SOCIAL IMAGINATION

The Catholic
Social Imagination

ACTIVISM AND THE JUST SOCIETY
IN MEXICO AND THE UNITED STATES

Joseph M. Palacios

The University of Chicago Press :: *Chicago and London*

Joseph Palacios is assistant professor of sociology and Latin American studies at Georgetown University.

The University of Chicago Press, Chicago 60637
The University of Chicago Press, Ltd., London
© 2007 by The University of Chicago
All rights reserved. Published 2007
Printed in the United States of America

16 15 14 13 12 11 10 09 08 07   1 2 3 4 5

ISBN-13: 978-0-226-64500-1 (cloth)
ISBN-13: 978-0-226-64501-8 (paper)
ISBN-10: 0-226-64500-2 (cloth)
ISBN-10: 0-226-64501-0 (paper)

Palacios, Joseph M.
    The Catholic social imagination : activism and the just society in Mexico and the United States / Joseph M. Palacios.
        p.   cm.
    Includes bibliographical references and index.
    ISBN-13: 978-0-226-64500-1 (cloth : alk. paper)
    ISBN-10: 0-226-64500-2 (cloth : alk. paper)
    ISBN-13: 978-0-226-64501-8 (pbk. : alk. paper)
    ISBN-10: 0-226-64501-0 (pbk. : alk. paper)   1. Christian sociology—Catholic Church.   2. Christian sociology—United States.   3. Christian sociology—Mexico.   4. Catholic Church—Doctrines.   5. Church and state—United States.   6. Church and state—Mexico.   I. Title.
    BX1753.P28 2007
    261.8088′2827—dc22

                                          2006036514

CONTENTS

The motivation for writing this book goes back to my undergraduate days at the University of California at Santa Cruz, when I was given the opportunity to spend two quarters at a very exciting educational center in Cuernavaca, Mexico: the Centro Intercultural de Documentación (CIDOC). In the early 1970s CIDOC was a crossroads for Mexican, North American, and European academics, Catholic missionaries, and activists. There we took minicourses from the likes of Paulo Freire and Ivan Illich, who helped change the course of Latin American political culture through their discourses on liberation theology and conscienticization. I had my own *despertar* or "awakening" as a young Chicano political and religious activist—particularly in my involvement with a *comunidad de base* (base community) in a poor neighborhood of Cuernavaca where I was renting an apartment.

Through the years I have wondered how people, particularly those of religious faith, become motivated to become civic and political activists. Prior to my graduate studies in sociology I worked in a variety of activist positions in the private sector, the government, and the Catholic Church. When it came time to choose a dissertation topic, I decided to draw upon my earlier experiences in Mexico and my work history in affirmative action, political consulting, and religious-based community organizing. I kept thinking about the ordinary people who made a commitment to become part of the public square, the *plaza pública*. What motivates ordinary persons to become public persons? How do people move from "private" concerns of family and job into the "public" spaces of civic and political associations? And how do Catholics use various aspects of their faith—particularly the Church's social doctrine—in making these decisions?

Like many sociologists, I found that my research has been shaped by the people I have encountered and the opportunities placed before me. I started the present study in 1996, when I began fieldwork in the San Antonio neighborhood of Oakland, California, and a master's paper focused on faith-based community organizing under the direction of Ann Swidler, Margaret Weir, and Kim Voss. Later, with the encouragement of Laura Enriquez and Peter Evans, who administered the Andrew W. Mellon Foundation's Program for Latin American Sociology at UC Berkeley, I reframed my research as a cross-national study. A predissertation grant during the summer of 1997 allowed me to travel throughout the Mexican state of Michoacán. During this research trip I met a group of civic activists from Guadalajara who were in Morelia attending a national conference on Mexican migration. These people invited me to attend a year-long leadership training program offered by the Instituto Mexicano de Desarrollo Comunitario (IMDEC) during 1999. Attending this training allowed me to meet a diverse group of Mexican civic and political actors from all parts of the country. Using the snowball approach of social research, I met people who pointed me toward the many religious and civic actors and institutions that became a part of this study. I was able to conduct two years of fieldwork in Mexico with the generous aid of the Mellon Foundation's dissertation fellowship for Latin American sociology. I also received assistance from the University of California's Chicano/Latino Policy Project.

I was fortunate to have a hands-on dissertation committee, whose members have become my colleagues. My mentor in sociology and religion, Robert Bellah, helped guide the theoretical dimensions of my work and provided critical advice on how to organize chapters. He has been an inspiration to me over the years and has helped me understand my vocation as sociologist and Catholic priest. Ann Swidler served as my chair and has since encouraged me in my writing and research interests. She is an excellent editor and a tough but friendly mentor. Margaret Weir helped me with more empirical elements of doing a cross-national study of many levels of a society. She kept me focused on the logic of inquiry.

During the spring of 2000 I was a visiting scholar at El Colegio de México in Mexico City. There Roberto Blancarte helped me develop a nuanced understanding of Mexican religion and society, especially the concepts of *laicidad* and the *transición*. He also provided a new Latin American perspective on the sociology of religion. The staffs of the sociology department and the computer center at El Colegio were most gracious in giving me direction on how to use their facilities.

This study could not have happened without the many people who generously allowed me to interview and observe them and their institutions. In the United States, these organizations included St. Anthony's Parish in Oakland, Oakland Community Organizations (OCO), the Pacific Institute for Community Organizing (PICO), the Catholic Diocese of Oakland, the Catholic Campaign for Human Development (CCHD), and the United States Catholic Conference (USCC). Key groups and institutions in Mexico were the parish of San Francisco de Asís in Las Pintitas, El Salto, Jalisco; the Pastoral Social of the Archdiocese of Guadalajara; IMDEC; the Instituto Mexicano de la Doctrina Social (IMDOSOC); DEMOS; the Centro Mexicano de Filántropia (CEMEFI); and the Pastoral Social Nacional of the Conferencia Episcopal Mexicana (CEM). My contacts were engaging in interviews and conversations and willing to let me participate in their meetings, activities, and civic actions. In particular I want to acknowledge Efrén Orozco Orozco and Carlos Núñez Hurtado of IMDEC; Manuel Goméz Granados of IMDOSOC; the Rev. John Baumann, S.J., of PICO; the Rev. Robert Vitillo and Alexia Kelly of CCHD; the Rev. Eduardo Mendoza of the Archdiocese of Guadalajara; and the Rev. Alberto Athié Gallo, formerly of CEM. All these leaders provided me access to their organizations and shared many fine moments of conversation over meals and coffee with me.

I must also acknowledge the American and Mexican Jesuit communities that provided hospitality during my research. In the United States, these included Jesuits of the Murray Community in Oakland, California; the Jesuit School of Theology at Berkeley; the Gonzaga High School Community, the Georgetown Jesuit Community, and the Woodstock Jesuit Community in Washington, D.C.; the Boston College Community in Chestnut Hill, Massachusetts; the Fordham University Community in New York City; and the St. Louis University Community. In Mexico, the San Felipe Community in Guadalajara and the Coyoacán Formation Community in Mexico City were my hosts. In these houses I was nurtured with good food, comfortable rooms, and wonderful Jesuit conversation and camaraderie. The California Province of the Society of Jesus and its benefactors provided support and encouragement each step along the way of my graduate studies. I have subsequently left the Society of Jesus but am indebted to the Jesuits for supporting the early stages of my career as a sociologist.

Over the years I have come to depend on friends and family to keep me going, especially in the last months of the solitary aspects of writing and editing. My mother, Martha Escobar Palacios, and sisters Carrie Miller, Linda Neuhauser, and Vera de Artola—as well as their husbands and children—have always given me a sense of home when I really needed to take a break from my work. My friends John McAndrew, Greg Eck, Doug and Connie Kniveton, Manuel and Ofelia Garcia, Cheri Cochran, Dennis Thiessen, John Higson, Ricardo Ortíz, Christine Grisham, David Bholat, Christopher Frechette, and Alexia Kelley were sources of tremendous consolation and repartee during various stages of this project. And I must acknowledge the proprietors and wait staff of the many coffeehouses where I have done my writing—most especially Café Mondo in Guadalajara, Zebra Café in Washington, and Starbucks everywhere.

During the first phase of this work, my writing group and Berkeley sociology colleagues were not only friends but critical collaborators in the art of sociological research and writing. These colleagues include Carolyn Chen, Russell Jeung, Scott North, Jason McNichol, Harold Toro, Michelle Williams, Melissa Wilde, Philip Fucella, and Mary Charlotte Chandler. In my final writing phase I was awarded a Pew-funded research fellowship by the Center for Religion and Civic Culture at the University of Southern California in Los Angeles. While at USC I was able to workshop four of the chapters in this book and benefited from the generous advice and friendship of Pierrette Hondagneu-Sotelo, Nina Eliasoph, Paul Lichterman, and members of the Religion, Immigration, and Justice Working Group. USC's Sociology Department provided me an office and support services that helped make my work a pleasant experience, and I am grateful to Michael Messner and Patricia Adolph for making that happen.

I am grateful to my colleagues in the Department of Sociology and Anthropology at Georgetown University, particularly to my chair, Sam Marullo, and our department administrator, Hanadi Salih, for facilitating my sabbatical year. Kathleen Maas Weigert, director of Georgetown's Center for Social Justice, has always been a source of inspiration and encouragement. I am also indebted to my students at Georgetown, who have put up with many stories and anecdotes arising from this book's research. Alan Wolfe, editor of the Morality and Society series for the University of Chicago Press, gave me ongoing encouragement to complete the project and brought it to the attention of Douglas Mitchell to bring it to final publication. My reviewers provided excellent advice on how to improve the book, and I am particularly indebted to Richard Wood, who helped situate the research in the new sociology of religion. To them and the staff at the University of Chicago Press I am deeply grateful.

My hope is that this book will provide consolation and encouragement to the many American and Mexican Catholics engaged in the social justice mission of their church. As my work illustrates, it is not easy for social justice–oriented Catholics to realize justice in the world or even in the Church. Still, this work has shown me that the struggle for justice gives us much reason to hope, especially as ordinary people commit themselves to be "men and women for others."

ACORN: Association of Communities Organized for Reform Now
ARC: Applied Research Center
CCHD: Catholic Campaign for Human Development
CEB: *comunidades eclesiales de base* (basic Christian communities)
CELAM: Conferencia Episcopal Latinoamericana (Latin American Bishops' Conference)
CEM: Conferencia Episcopal Mexicana (Mexican Bishops' Conference)
CEMEFI: Centro Mexicano de Filantropía (Mexican Center of Philanthropy)
CEPS: Comisión Episcopal de la Pastoral Social (Bishops' Commission of Social Ministry)
CFM: Christian Family Movement
CIDOC: Centro Intercultural de Documentación (Intercultural Documentation Center)
CL: Centro Lindavista
CRT: Centro de Reflexión de los Trabajadores
IAF: Industrial Areas Foundation
IMDEC: Instituto Mexicano de Desarrollo Comunitario (Mexican Institute of Community Development)
IMDOSOC: Instituto Mexicano de la Doctrina Social Cristiana (Mexican Institute of Christian Social Doctrine)
ITESO: Instituto Tecnológico y de Estudios Superiores de Occidente, Guadalajara
LOC: local organizing committee
NAFTA: North American Free Trade Agreement
NGO: nongovernmental organization
OCO: Oakland Community Organizations
PAN: Partido Acción Nacional (National Action Party)
PICO: Pacific Institute of Community Organizing
PRD: Partido de la Revolución Democrática (Revolutionary Democratic Party)
PRI: Partido Revolucionario Institucional (Institutional Revolutionary Party)

SCLC: Southern Christian Leadership Conference
SOAW: School of the Americas Watch
UCLA: University of California, Los Angeles
UFW: United Farm Workers Union
UI: Universidad Intercontinental, Mexico City
UNAM: Universidad Nacional Autónoma de México
USC: University of Southern California
USCC: United States Catholic Conference

PART ONE

The Catholic Church Takes on Social Justice as Doctrine

1 ✣ The Mission and Struggle of Roman Catholics to Create a Just Society

At Christmas Midnight Mass, 1999, Pope John Paul II ushered in the second millennium of Christian history and the Roman Catholic Church's holy year with an internationally televised broadcast of the opening of the doors of St. Peter's Basilica. For the pope and the Catholic Church, these doors symbolized not only a continuation of the *aggiornamento* begun at Vatican II but also a special time of reconciliation and forgiveness for the social sins committed by Christians in the name of their faith.[1] On 12 March 2000, at a historic confessional ritual held at St. Peter's, the pope and various cardinals prayed "that contemplating Jesus, our Lord and our Peace, Christians will be able to repent of the words and attitudes caused by pride, by hatred, by the desire to dominate others, by enmity towards members of other religions and towards the weakest groups in society, such as immigrants and itinerants."[2]

The pope at the holy doors, seen by an estimated one billion people around the world, stood as the central international religious figure at the beginning of a new millennium. Because of his extensive international travels during the more than twenty years of his pontificate, Pope John Paul II was the most personally seen public figure in the twentieth century. He represented the institutional Roman Catholic Church, the world's largest nongovernmental organization body as well its largest religious institution, with more than one billion members, or 17.8 percent of the global population.[3]

Yet this international body encompasses many country-by-country contrasts. The Catholic Church in the United States and and the Catholic Church in Mexico are prime examples, even though these are neighboring countries. Being Catholic in Mexico is not the same as being Catholic in the United States, Nigeria, or the Philippines—particularly since Vatican II, as the Church has allowed itself to adapt to national and local languages and customs. Even while becoming more particular in social and cultural adaptation, the Church has become increasingly centralized internationally through its official functions in the Vatican, such as the Congregation for the Doctrine of the Faith, which governs both theological and moral doctrine, and the Sacred Tribunals, which govern canon law and the Church's internal system of due process.[4] The Church attempts to integrate local society and its realities with a universal (catholic) teaching that in the Church's self-understanding is "ecclesial" and that it is not subject to scientific scrutiny as a social organization. As any Catholic learns, the Church "is in the world but not of it."[5]

As the Church prepared for and entered into the "jubilee year" of 2000, the International Pontifical Commission of Peace and Justice charged the national churches to focus on the Church's social justice teaching, marked by key terms such as *dignity of the human person, equality, participation, association,* and *solidarity,* and organize events around it. All the national churches adopted the motto "Open wide the doors to Christ: evangelize, reconcile, celebrate"—an obvious reference to the holy doors of St. Peter's. The national churches were encouraged to initiate "social justice weeks" that would bring together social justice ministers to prepare a national agenda for the next few years. The bishops of every country were asked to reflect upon historical social sins committed by Christians of their country and issue a public call to repentance. Catholics were called to carry out a special Jubilee Year indulgence, which would involve entering the local cathedral and offering prayers for the local church, particularly for its social needs, given the biblical sense of jubilee as a year of debt forgiveness and freedom from bondage.[6] John Paul II's encyclical *Ecclesia in America,* issued during his January 1999 visit to Mexico and the United States, urged the national churches to see themselves as one Church of the Western Hemisphere. The document has since been used as a baseline for the Church's social justice objectives in the Americas.[7]

The Jubilee Year provided me a specific setting of time and space to frame an exploration of "the Catholic social imagination." I borrow this term from two sources. One is the sociologist Andrew Greeley, who in his studies of the Catholic Church and in his novels about Catholic life in the United States provides a rich sense of the complexity of sacraments, religious institutions, habits, mores, and other cultural behaviors that distinguish Catholic culture from other religious cultures.[8] My other source is Catholic theologian David Tracy, who has analyzed what he refers to as the "analogical imagination" of Christian theologians.[9]

He argues that the texts of the Christian faith have particular literary qualities that have made them classic statements of the Christian tradition. Christian theology, according to Tracy, presents religion's rational side through analogies, which provide mindscapes for the imagination. In this study I combine the insights of Greeley and Tracy to form a concept of the Catholic social imagination as a bounded cultural space that is contested by various social factors. I'm particularly interested in determining where the boundaries of that Catholic social imagination are and what happens when they are tested by Catholic social actors.[10] And I also want to see what happens at the center of the cultural space provided by the institutional church and see how Catholics maneuver within it.

The Catholic Church's observances of the Jubilee Year raise a central question: how do national churches interpret and implement Catholic social justice doctrine? This is a sociological way of addressing a more general question: what is the Catholic social imagination, and how does it get implemented? The forthcoming chapters address this question in reference to the churches of the United States and Mexico. This empirical research raises the following questions that get to the heart of this study:

- How does the international social justice doctrine of the Roman Catholic Church—the Church's international social imagination and mission—become implemented both in theological ideas and social action in different countries, particularly the United States and Mexico?

- What opportunities and constraints—challenges to the Church's social imagination and mission—emerging from national history, political traditions and culture, the institutional church, and development of civil society are shaping the implementation of social justice teaching in Mexico and in the United States?

I have chosen to examine the Catholic Church in the United States and Mexico because these neighboring countries share many interests, as evidenced in the North American Free Trade Agreement (NAFTA) of 1994.[11] Further, there is a constant flow of Catholics between the two countries, with a significant level of permanent emigration of Mexicans to the United States. Hispanics make up approximately 30 percent of the U.S. Catholic population and 13 percent of the total U.S. population.[12] Given that the Catholic Church operates with the same structures in every country (dioceses and parishes) and that it offers a common doctrinal basis for all its members, I will examine how this common structure and doctrine are interpreted, institutionalized, and implemented with a U.S. and Mexican national identity. I will ask how ideas and doctrines matter in the development of a religious and social imagination that can help or hinder Catholics to address social injustices that they and others experience.

The U.S. Context of the Jubilee Year and Social Justice Ministry

In the United States two major national events were held to implement the Vatican's decree: "Jubilee Justice" in July 1999 at the University of California's Los Angeles campus, and "Encuentro 2000" in July 2000 at the Los Angeles Convention Center. These were the first national events devoted to social justice themes in U.S. Catholic Church history. At both of these events the national staff of the Catholic Campaign for Human Development (CCHD), the key domestic social program of the U.S. church, helped direct the agenda and the management of the gatherings. They attracted three thousand and forty-five hundred participants, respectively, including leading cardinals, archbishops, bishops, priests, and laypeople responsible for the implementation of social justice teaching in the United States. When the Rev. Robert Vitillo, executive director of CCHD, welcomed the delegates to Jubilee Justice, in attendance were Cardinal Roger Etchegarry, the pope's representative, and Archbishop Francois-Xavier Nguyên Van Thuân, president of the Pontifical Council for Justice and Peace. Both events featured internationally known speakers, including 1996 Nobel Peace Prize laureate Bishop Carlos Felipe Ximenes Belo of East Timor and Sister Helen Prejean, C.S.J., author of *Dead Man Walking*.

One of the most moving moments at Encuentro 2000 was a ritual of atonement for the social sins of the institutional U.S. church, presided over by Cardinal Bernard Law of Boston. (Law, one of the country's most conservative bishops, would later be forced to resign because of his negligent handling of clergy sexual abuse cases in the Archdiocese of Boston.)[13] Catholics representing native peoples, African Americans, Latinos, women, and the handicapped gave testimonies of how the Church had sinned against them personally and against their communities. During a litany of prayers, delegates also heard a call for forgiveness of sins of clergy sexual abuse.

At both events delegates participated in plenary talks and seminars on the mission and challenge of implementing social justice in the United States and around the world. "How to" workshops were offered on community organizing, economic development, and parish educational programs. The events provided brilliant pictures of the Catholic Church's diverse membership, particularly through high-energy liturgical celebrations drawing on different ethnic and cultural traditions and powerful speeches by well-known Catholics, including political commentator Mark Shields. A high point of Jubilee Justice was an evening of entertainment in UCLA's Pauley Pavilion featuring the Latino rock group Los Lobos.

These Jubilee Year events aimed to provide both cultural experience and intellectual content to U.S. Catholic social justice actors. It would have been hard for an outsider not to get a sense that the ordinary U.S. Catholic social imagination was being culturally constructed through the interplay of liturgy, sacraments, biblical reflection, civic activism, prophetic statements, multicultural integration, and gender, racial, and ethnic inclusivity—all within the institutional and hierarchical Catholic Church.

Like many delegates, "Carolyn"[14] attended both of these events not only as a staff member of a national church social justice agency but as a progressive Catholic layperson. Carolyn believes that her Christian and social vocation is to be an agent of change in U.S. and world society. She attributes her social activism to examples of voluntarism in her family, particularly her Quaker father. She holds an advanced theological degree from a leading East Coast divinity school. While she cannot become an ordained minister of the Church, she exercises her "ministry"[15] in program development and providing positive, energetic spiritual presence in a national church organization. Active in a multicultural parish in Washington, D.C., she serves on the board of one of the parish's outreach ministries to the poor. Like many very socially active American Catholics, be they liberal or conservative, Carolyn maintains a high degree of optimism regarding the Church's social justice goals, yet she is a strong critic of the Church's present positions on the role of women in the Church and the slow pace at which laypeople are being empowered to serve in leadership roles.

Carolyn's commitment to social justice has been inspired by an American social justice theology that addresses social, cultural, political, and economic obstacles faced by immigrant and working-class Catholics as a minority community in the United States. Catholic social justice theology in the United States has historically been oriented toward issues related to poverty, employment, immigration, discrimination, education, participation, and inclusion.[16] Theoretical and practical theologians—such as social ethicists J. Bryan Hehir of Harvard Divinity School and David Hollenbach, S.J., of Boston College, feminist theologian Lisa Sowell Cahill of Boston College, noted preacher Walter Burghardt, S.J., of the Preaching the Just Word Program of the Jesuit Woodstock Center in Washington, D.C., Catholic labor union activist and syndicated columnist the Rev. Msgr. George Higgins, and biblical scholar John Donohue, S.J., of the Jesuit School of Theology at Berkeley—have helped forge a distinctive U.S. character for theological reflection and the practice of social justice. Their theological scholarship has been incorporated into the U.S. bishops' social pastorals on peace and disarmament (1983) and the economy (1986).[17] Burghardt, one of the deans of this tradition, told me, "My very salvation depends upon doing justice in the world."

A high point of the Catholic social justice tradition in the United States was the foundation in 1969 of the CCHD by the United States Catholic Conference as a response to the urban crisis of the 1960s and a culmination of Catholic involvement in the civil rights movement, labor movement, and social service programs such as Catholic Charities. CCHD has become the Catholic Church's own antipoverty program in U.S. civil society to empower poor people to find solutions for poverty and encourage education, health, and civic and political participation.[18]

Since 1969 CCHD has given over $250 million as seed money to develop more than four thousand local self-help programs to serve the poor and the marginalized. Each year in October, U.S. Catholics are asked to give to CCHD's fundraising appeal. The average collection in recent years has amounted to $15 million, with over 90 percent going to local projects. A great many of these, inspired by the social philosophy and organizing methods of Saul Alinsky, have sought to empower ordinary citizens to implement change in their neighborhoods and communities.[19] The Pacific Institute for Community Organizing (PICO), for example, was founded in Oakland, California, in 1972 by young Jesuits who had been trained by Alinsky himself in Chicago. PICO offers a training process for leadership development and recruits and trains community organizers to serve on city-organizing committees. While founded as a secular nonprofit, PICO has evolved into the premier "faith-based" organizing network in eighty-five cities in the United States.[20] Its goal is to "help reweave the fabric of American society"[21] by linking faith and values to social justice organizing that will have long-term effects in social and political institutions.

In Oakland, lay Catholics like "Manuel" look to the local PICO organizing effort, Oakland Community Organizations (OCO), to help them live out their Christian faith and values in action-oriented solutions to problems like crack houses, proliferation of liquor stores, getting a stop sign for a dangerous intersection, and improving public schools. Both PICO and OCO have received ongoing funding from CCHD and are thus connected to the U.S. church's mission to serve and empower the poor and disenfranchised to more actively participate in civil society, politics, and government.[22]

Manuel is an immigrant from Mexico City who came to the United States in the mid-1960s in order find work and support his young family. Now in his forties, he is raising two children with his wife, "Yolanda," and they have both been very involved in efforts to improve public schools attended by his children. In Oakland, OCO has been at the forefront of a school reform movement that has initiated neighborhood homework centers, "village centers" (public schools used as community centers), the establishment of charter schools, and the "small school" project of developing local control of neighborhood schools. As Manuel notes, "Without education there is no future." He is also active in parish activities such as a Hispanic choir and the Guadalupanas. His OCO announcements at the Spanish mass in his parish have inspired many of his Latino neighbors to become active in local issues, even some who are not yet U.S. citizens.

OCO's motto, "Faith in action," has real meaning for Manuel and the other immigrants of the parish and the neighborhood, who are aware that in Mexico such activities would not be allowed in the church.[23] However, Manuel and other Mexican immigrants in the parish do not have much knowledge of Catholic social justice teaching. OCO's language is largely driven by the broader Judeo-Christian ethos of equality, ending poverty and discrimination, and participation. In fact, Manuel describes his community participation using a general Judeo-Christian vocabulary developed in the United States, not the vocabulary of the Catholic social justice tradition.

Black pastors provide much of OCO's spiritual dimension, giving a highly evangelical flavor to OCO neighborhood and citywide meetings. OCO is also influenced by an Alinsky-style pragmatism, valuing results-oriented campaigns that are high on delivery of social justice goods and low on critical analysis of the structural causes of social problems, which Catholic social teaching would analyze based on principles such as solidarity, subsidiarity, common good, and human rights and dignity.

This is a complaint of "Diane,"[24] one of the most active women in the parish. As a religious catechist and public school teacher, she wants social justice organizing to have a greater Christian consciousness-raising effect in the community. "My faith matters to me," she says. "It is the foundation of my commitments." Oddly, the local organizer, "Scott,"[25] is a practicing Jew who has on his own initiative become well versed in basic principles of Catholic social justice teaching in order to better communicate religious values among his largely Latino and Catholic organizing base. At a summer institute on how to incorporate religious and biblical values into social action, he and Diane learned the "see, judge, act" process that was developed in European Catholic Action movements of the 1920s and became very popular in Latin American liberation theology.[27] In 1999 Scott introduced this process to PICO and incorporated it into the national training process for Spanish-speaking leaders. This was the first time in more than years that a theological reflection component had become a working part of the PICO model.

Manuel's parish celebrated the Jubilee Year with a multicultural Mass on the feast of Corpus Christi. The parish of Latinos (60 percent), Vietnamese (30 percent), Filipinos (5 percent), and African Americans and whites (5 percent) gathered as one community to march in a rosary procession through the neighborhood and celebrate Mass, followed by a gathering in the parish hall that featured ethnic foods and entertainment. It was a mini–Encuentro 2000 that was encouraged by the bishop of the Oakland Diocese. For Manuel and Yolanda, Diane, Scott, and the other six hundred participants, this event of the whole Catholic community highlighted the success of many years of community-organizing efforts to bring racial harmony, neighborhood security, education, and sociocultural opportunity to a previously racially tense, drug-infested, educationally underachieving, and politically dysfunctional neighborhood.

Manuel and his fellow Catholic social activists in Oakland are very much a part of the national social justice mission of the American Catholic Church and its interconnected levels of theology, CCHD and other national programs of the United States Catholic Conference, national and local faith-based organizing in civil society, and the local diocese and parish. Thus the various levels and components of Catholic social justice teaching become interpreted, institutionalized, and implemented even at the lowest level of the Church's organizational structure. Papal encyclicals, teachings, and speeches, the international social justice doctrine, the writing and reflection of U.S. theologians, the programs of the bishops, CCHD, PICO, OCO, diocese, parish, and the neighborhood all affect both the mission and the implementation of Catholic social justice doctrine in the United States.

The Mexican Context of the Jubilee Year and the "Pastoral Social"

In November 1999, the Mexican Catholic Church held its own Jubilee Year event, Semana Pastoral Social Nacional,[27] at the Catholic Universidad Intercontinental (UI) in Mexico City. After almost a century of governmental restriction of the Mexican Catholic Church, this was the first public religious event in ninety years devoted to social justice in Mexico. Like the U.S. Jubilee Justice, held in UCLA's Pauley Pavilion (past home of the Los Angeles Lakers), the Semana Pastoral Social Nacional brought together its four hundred delegates in the informality of a basketball gymnasium. It began with a solemn high Mass at the Basilica of Our Lady of Guadalupe, the Mexican church's holiest shrine, and this set the tone for a religious gathering steeped in a tumultuous national church history. The Rev. Alberto Athié Gallo, past executive director of the Comisión Episcopal de la Pastoral Social (CEPS), delivered an opening homily on the challenges the Mexican church and society face in implementing social justice teaching amid deep poverty, class divisions, violence, and political instability. This challenge continued as a theme throughout the conference, which would initiate a national agenda on social justice. The delegates were asked to engage in a democratic "listening process" that Athié Gallo had developed for the Mexican church, borrowing from listening processes that the U.S. church had used in developing the peace and economic pastoral letters of the U.S. bishops.[28] The Jubilee Year process would conclude with a major pastoral letter from the Mexican bishops, *Del encuentro con Jesucristo a la solidaridad con todos,* in March 2000.

During the conference the delegates heard a testimony by Archbishop Francois-Xavier Nguyên Van Thuân on how he survived years in a Vietnamese prison camp.[29] Other prominent speakers included Archbishop Theodore McKerrick[30] of the U.S. Catholic Conference and Mexican intellectuals such as historian Jean Meyer and social philosopher and activist Vicente Arredondo. However, unlike the class-, ethnic-, and gender-inclusive American events, the liturgies and workshop panels at the Semana Pastoral Social Nacional were dominated by middle-class urban mestizo males. During the whole proceeding there was but one talk by a woman and none by rural or indigenous people. Yet the delegates themselves reflected a highly diverse Mexican Catholic population, including poor, middle-class, wealthy, conservative, progressive, rural, urban, *urbano-campesino,* indigenous, mestizo, and European men and women.

Almost all the delegates brought a common *inquietud* regarding social justice in Mexico, and it was expressed quite deeply during the listening sessions: a pervasive critical pessimism that change seems impossible in the context of political and religious institutional bureaucracy, hierarchy, and lack of mobility for the vast majority of Mexicans. The *inquietud* of these priests, nuns, and laypeople involved in parishes, diocesan offices, human rights organizations, and social development programs was largely with the institutional church itself. Unfortunately, the Mexican bishops at the conference did not acknowledge this *inquietud,* and their pastoral letter, sidestepped the Church's role in social sins in Mexican history.[31] Thus a striking contrast was apparent between the official Mexican Catholic social imagination, reflected in the male-dominated and high church sense of the social doctrine as doctrine—ideas coming from the Vatican to be implemented in Mexico—and the *inquietud* of the diverse delegates. While in Mexico I learned a saying common among Catholic priests about their church, "más Romano que Roma," and it accurately characterizes the official Mexican Catholic social imagination: "more Roman than Rome."

The *inquietud* common among Catholic activists was reflected by "Rafael,"[32] a professional staff member of a national church agency, who helped in the planning of the Semana Pastoral Social Nacional. In his early thirties, Rafael is a child of the post-1968 generation of Mexicans who have grown up disillusioned by the system—political, religious, social, economic, educational.[33] Coming from an upper-middle-class family in Mexico City, he had attended elite Catholic schools, but his family was not religious and not at all involved in social justice activities. During his studies at the major Jesuit university in Mexico City, the Iberoamericana, he went on an immersion experience with a Jesuit priest to live with indigenous people in the state of Chiapas. He told me, "For the first time I experienced an enfleshed Christ [*Cristo encarnado*] in the poorest people of my country." This period in Chiapas and subsequent volunteer work with the poor in Mexico City transformed his *inquietud* from a negative to a positive perspective on the possibility for change in Mexico. After receiving his *licenciatura,* the Mexican professional degree, in political science, he went to work for the Instituto Mexicano de la Doctrina Social Cristiana (IMDOSOC) in

Mexico City, a leading independent lay Mexican organization that seeks to implement social justice teaching through books, magazines, workshops, radio programs, and social ministries. Now as a national church professional at the Mexican Bishops' Conference, Rafael brings his positive *inquietud* to his work in the development of social justice programs. But at the same time he brings a sadness and skepticism about the role of the laity in the Mexican church, particularly since his own parish does not provide adequate opportunities for lay participation in the liturgy, leadership, or spiritual development. Indeed, the Semana Pastoral Social reflected this dualism: Catholic social activists who were at once positive about the role the Church might play in social change and pessimistic about how the Church's clerically dominated system limits lay empowerment.

While an estimated 90 percent of the Mexican population are baptized Roman Catholic and Mexico is considered a "Catholic country," social justice theology there has not developed a particularly Mexican character. Because Catholics have been dominant, even though national devotions to Mary as Guadalupe in Mexico City and Zapopan in Guadalajara or to San Juan de los Lagos or El Santo Niño de Atoche have a distinct Mexican flavor, there has not been a strong drive to develop *mexicanidad* ("Mexicanness") in modern Catholic theology and programs. Modern Mexican religious history has been marked by the privatization of religion and religious culture, since the Mexican Constitution of 1917 forbade any religious institution from having a role in public life.[34] Yet in a country that is so Catholic, how is it that there is not a Catholic presence in public life? In the United States, names like Dorothy Day, Fulton Sheen, William F. Buckley, the Kennedys, Cesar Chavez, Mario Cuomo, Jerry Brown, Helen Prejean, and Richard Rodriguez conjure up images of the "public Catholic" who can talk about his or her faith in public, but there is no parallel in recent times in Mexico save for Vicente Fox, president from 2000 to 2006.[35] In this very Catholic country, then, there is no discussion in the media of religious values in public life, nor is there a tradition of the public religious intellectual. And unlike U.S. civil religion, imbued as it is with the Judeo-Christian ethos, Mexico's secular philosophy of *laicismo* ("layness") disallows religious content in any aspect of public life in order to keep Mexico a "lay country."[36] In fact, Mexico's constitution specifies "freedom of belief" and not "freedom of religion."[37]

From 1917 through 1992, priests and bishops of the Catholic Church were allowed to celebrate Mass in the confines of state-owned churches, but they could not vote or speak publicly about society, politics, or the state without fear of imprisonment. The church was not allowed to operate parochial schools or to buy property and construct its own churches. The saying *No se meta en la política* (Do not meddle in politics) became synonymous with a silencing of the Church on all aspects of Mexican public life. This changed only with the 1992 revision of the constitution to allow clergy citizen rights, church ownership of property, and the free operation of Catholic schools.[38]

One of the significant consequences of the privatization of religion in Mexico was the Church's turn toward Europe and Latin America for its theological and program development.[39] Thus, since Vatican II, the ideas of Latin American liberation theologians such as Gustavo Gutiérrez (Peru), Leonardo Boff (Brazil), and Jon Sobrino (Spain and El Salvador) have become dominant in social justice documents and programs of the CEM and diocesan offices of the Pastoral Social. This theology is characterized by key social justice terms used in the Latin American church such as *solidarity, liberation, preferential option for the poor,* and *conscienticization.*[40]

"Christian-inspired" lay social justice organizations such as IMDOSOC and the Centro Lindavista have sought to Mexicanize social justice teaching, but even the few Mexican social theological authors, such as Enrique Dussel, have relied heavily on international sources for understanding Mexico's social problems. Oddly religious orders known for social activism and human rights work in Mexico, such as the Jesuits and Dominicans, have not developed within their ranks social justice theologians with a distinctive *mexicanidad.* However, at a practical level the national organizational structure for pastoral ministry, the Plan Pastoral, does have a distinctive Mexican character.[41] The Plan Pastoral's three functions—*profética* (teaching), *litúrgica* (liturgical), and *social* (social justice)—are used by the CEM, dioceses, and parishes to understand theologically the baptismal dimensions of lay ministry since Vatican II: all Catholics are called to share in the priestly (liturgical), kingly (social), and prophetic (teaching) mission of the Church.[42]

Local lay Catholic social activists such as "Victor," who lives in one of the extremely poor *colonias* of El Salto, a community of urbano-campesinos[43] near the international airport of Guadalajara, have a ready international vocabulary of social justice teaching, liberation theology concepts, and a highly theologically developed parish organizational structure. As well, Victor paid close attention to the speeches of Pope John Paul II during his pilgrimages to Mexico. The pope was the most forceful voice for social justice in the Mexican church at a national level, since his visits were broadcast on television. Given that religious organizations have not been permitted much use of mainstream media, John Paul II was actually the only religious voice with full access to it.

At weekly meetings of the Pastoral Social in Victor's parish, the priests and lay leaders spend at least half of the time in learning social justice teaching from the Bible, papal encyclicals, the documents of Vatican II, and documents of the CEM. Because of the minimal development of a Mexican social justice theology, Victor tends to think as a Latin American Catholic, even though he seeks local solutions to extreme poverty, low educational opportunity, and lack of social and political access in his *colonia*. Victor is familiar with the mission of the Church, but he is often frustrated because his concern for justice is not easily implemented given the Mexican religious constraint of *no se meta en la política* and Catholics' lack of experience with participating in civic life as public Catholics.

Victor and his wife, Ana, like the majority of the social ministry activists of their *colonia,* run small businesses. Victor operates a fix-it shop, and Ana sells prepared lunches at the local junior high school. They learned their entrepreneurial skills in Los Angeles, California, where they worked for a few years in order to save money to buy property and build their home and their business base. Victor and Ana are able to adjust their schedules in order to do volunteer work, which was originally inspired through their experiences in the Christian Family Movement (CFM). In CFM, Victor had a *despertar* (an "awakening") and felt called to begin putting his good fortune as a businessman and his close family relationships to the service of his community. Like Rafael, he has been inspired by the image of *Cristo encarnado*. Victor told me, "I have been blessed by God with a wonderful wife and family and need to help others build good families so that our community can be stronger." Everyone in the *colonia* knows him as "Don Victor," an appellation of the highest respect for a man in his fifties. He and Ana have a station wagon that is put to frequent use to deliver food and clothing to the poor of their community and to transport sick people to the closest hospital, in Guadalajara, some fifteen miles from the *colonia*.

Along with Catholics throughout Mexico, the people of the *colonia* celebrated the Jubilee Year with a healing Mass for the elderly and the shut-ins of the *colonia* on the feast of Our Lady of Lourdes, 11 February.[44] The forty or so members of the parish Pastoral Social team mobilized their talents to organize a very special day of service to the needy, giving concrete expression to the Church's teachings regarding the preferential option for the poor, the dignity of the human person, and solidarity. Don Victor's station wagon and other cars were used to ferry the elderly and sick to the church, where members of a hospitality committee greeted and pinned a name tag on each person. During the Mass, the approximately three hundred "guests" were treated to liturgical music by local musicians, and special prayers, written for the occasion by members of the liturgy committee, were said. After the Mass they moved to the parish hall to enjoy a luncheon prepared by members of the Pastoral Social. A video on the miracles of Lourdes was shown on a large-screen television. Among the members of the Pastoral Social, these activities centered on the Mass and the Sacrament of the Sick were seen as the high point of social justice mission in the community.

Other Mexican laypeople such as Elena,[45] who feel that they have learned much from Catholic social justice teaching, have chosen to be activists outside the church because there is not space for them to be activists inside it. Elena, like Rafael, is a member of the 1968 generation and comes from a family in Mexico City that was influenced by the *comunidades de base* of the Jesuits who worked in their *colonia* during the 1970s. She told me, "While I am not really active in the Church, I was deeply inspired by the *comunidades de base* in their attempt to make religion responsive to the needs of the people, especially the poorest and most marginalized." Like others I met in Mexico's new civil society, Elena feels her commitment is "Christian inspired" but is not involved in religious organizations and does not see her activism as Catholic. She works for the civil society organization Instituto Mexicano de Desarrollo Comunitario (IMDEC) in Guadalajara. Founded in 1968 as a neighborhood activist group in Guadalajara, IMDEC provides empowerment and capacity-building training for nongovernmental organization (NGO) leaders in Mexico. Its program is heavily influenced by the pedagogical principles of *concientiziçao* (consciousness raising) of Brazilian educator Paulo Freire.[46] Indeed one of the founders of IMDEC, Carlos Núñez Hurtado, is one of the foremost experts on Freirian pedagogy, and IMDEC's leadership training is premised upon key pedagogical principles of Freire.[47] Elena is one of the trainers in IMDEC's national leadership program. As well, she is a civic activist in Guadalajara and helped form a coalition of social organizations into Voces Unidas in order to test the viability of the "citizen initiative" clauses of the Mexican Constitution.

At the beginning of its drive to spearhead a citizen initiative on intrafamilial violence, lay representatives from the Archdiocese of

Guadalajara became part of the collective leadership team of Voces Unidas. These lay representatives helped persuade the Archdiocesan Pastoral Social to mobilize parishes to collect signatures for the citizen initiative, and and the ensuing one-month campaign gathered thirty-five thousand signatures. This was an important achievement: the first citizen initiative in Mexican history.[48]

When the cardinal archbishop of Guadalajara read the full text of the initiative, which had been written by human rights lawyers of the University of Guadalajara and the Jesuit university Instituto Tecnológico y de Estudios Superiores de Occidente (ITESO), he became concerned that the new citizen law would alter the definition of the family in the state constitution of Jalisco to include domestic and homosexual partnerships. He removed official representation of the archdiocesan Pastoral Social from Voces Unidas. Although the Pastoral Social representatives decided to remain active in the coalition as ad hoc members, the canceling of official church participation only reinforced Elena and other lay Catholics' sense of disempowerment by the institutional church to work in civil society with a wide variety of social actors.

Laypeople like Rafael and Victor find great solace and motivation in the Church's social justice teaching as they work within the Pastoral Social of the institutional church in order to assuage their *inquietud*. But like Elena, they are frustrated in their efforts to express their religious values in the *plaza pública* (public square). While the government, the history of *laicismo,* and the slow pace of development of Mexican civil society serve as constraints on such action, they also feel a great constraint from the institutional church itself. Thus many Mexican Catholics are empowered by the Church's social justice doctrine as a clear alternative to their country's social problems, yet they are challenged by the many constraints they face in implementing social justice.

Mission and Challenge of Catholic Social Justice Teaching

Carolyn, Manuel, Yolanda, Diane, Rafael, Victor, Ana, and Elena represent Catholics in the United States and Mexico committed to the mission and the challenge of social justice ministry in the Catholic Church at the beginning of the third millennium of Christianity. They exercise their international Catholic faith in local and national contexts, but they all are affected by what I will refer to as the *social opportunity structure* that either opens or constrains implementation of the mission. This study's accounts of these actors and their work for social justice are based on four years of participant research (involving ethnographic studies of two poor communities and five civil associations, nearly one hundred interviews with theologians, church leaders, and lay activists, and consultation with scholars of religion and society) that I conducted in the United States and Mexico.

In part 1, I provide the reader with an overview of the sociological context of Catholic social justice doctrine. Chapter 2 highlights the political and ecclesiological evolution of the social doctrine and considers it in relation to the social sciences, the development of modern civil society, and the emergence of a global society. Chapter 2 includes a review of the social encyclicals and documents of the Church and, based on them, a list and typology of Catholic social principles.

The end of chapter 2 presents a cultural construction model for analyzing the Catholic social imagination and case studies of participant-observation research in the United States and Mexico. Here I develop the model that I will use to analyze the two national churches. I also sketch the social theory that has influenced my analysis. I use social movement theory (framing, resource mobilization, and political opportunity structures) to analyze my empirical research.[49] This theory helps us understand how social actors come together and sustain their associational life, particularly in informal kinds of solidarity. But I believe that social movement theory fails to account fully for how an institution like the Catholic Church can function as a culture that forms social actors. Therefore I will use the idea of *social opportunity structure* to understand how "social resources" are generated in institutional culture. A social opportunity structure encompasses the complex of ideas, values, motivating factors, habits, and mores and the repertoire of social skills involved in creating and sustaining a space for social actors to realize their aspirations through associational life in civil society.

In the national case studies that follow in chapters 3 and 4, I examine what triggers a person's movement from the private life of family and religion to become a social actor. Key here is the "social conversion" necessary to sustain long-term social commitments. I will show how the notions of social opportunity structure and social conversion, particularly for Catholic social actors, helps us understand and analyze opportunities and constraints that social actors face in terms of national history, political traditions and culture, the institutional church, and development of civil society. I ask: How is social justice doctrine moved or not moved into each country's social opportunity structure? What constraints and opportunities exist in political, church, and civil society institutions? What movement takes place among the various levels (parish, diocese, national church, Rome) of the Catholic Church to bring integration and clarity to the doctrine?

In chapters 3 and 4, I tell stories of how Catholics seek to translate social justice ideas and activity from the local parish and neighborhood, the diocese, and the national church into local and national civil society. My ethnographies illustrate the opportunities and constraints these actors face in trying to realize social justice as empirical social goods. In both chapters I provide a sociological sense of what can be called the bounded and contested space of each country's Catholic social imagination.

Finally, in part 3 I present my research findings. Chapter 5 shows that within the two national churches there are at least four organizing approaches for implementing social justice doctrine, based on normative and strategic continuums that intersect. I analyze these approaches as cultural systems that may or may not connect with the world and the social structures that social justice requires if it is to be actualized. The Mexican church has both internal and external constraints, based on an uneasy if not hostile historical relationship between church and state, as well as a deeply conservative and ultramontane theological orientation. Thus, while within the Mexican church there are actors taking all four approaches, the ecclesial approach largely emphasizes the educational and spiritual formation of social actors, promotes a system based on charity, and does not allow strategies to address the structural issues of social injustice. The U.S. church, on the other hand, has a long history of developing an independent laity within a pluralistic society. The U.S. church has a sense of "public Catholicism," permitting Catholics to act on their faith in civil society and politics without encountering legal or cultural problems. Like the Mexican church, the U.S. church includes actors who take all four approaches, but the majority of its activity lies in the Catholic social justice ministry approach. Especially through local programs supported by the Catholic Campaign for Human Development and many Catholic-oriented justice groups, this approach attempts to address structural issues of injustice. However, many of the social actors taking this approach are not well versed in the doctrine itself and have difficulty connecting the doctrine to the larger U.S. political culture.

I conclude that for the Catholic social doctrine to be *social,* the ideas emerging from the general Catholic social imagination must correspond with social opportunity structures that allow the doctrine to be implemented freely in civil and political spheres. I argue that sociology itself, which Catholic social actors use as an analytical framework, functions as a normative social science that describes injustice and through its analytical categories—equality, freedom, solidarity, democracy, fairness, etc.—helps social actors to move toward critical resolution of unjust behaviors and attitudes. For ideas to become social reality in both the U.S. and Mexican churches, their advocates must grapple with the endemic conundrum of using philosophical precepts from natural law to guide the resolution of empirical social problems—the inductive-deductive problematic. That is, the social teaching of the Catholic Church cannot be truly *social* unless it can actually resolve social problems as experienced by social actors. In the end I raise the question, can a faith do justice? From a sociological perspective, the Catholic Church provides many means of thinking and acting that can deliver social justice goods, but its internal logic can limit justice to its ecclesial mission and objectives, thus placing constraints on its discourse and action and—limiting empirical social justice for its members and the larger society.

In the following chapters I hope that I myself "do justice" to Carolyn, Manuel, Yolanda, Diane, Rafael, Victor, Ana, Elena, and other social activists and their organizations that struggle to generate solutions within very complex social contexts.

2 ⊹ Political and Cultural Construction of the Catholic Social Doctrine

When Carolyn, Manuel, Yolanda, Diane, Rafael, Victor, Ana, and Elena go to Mass on Sunday, attend Bible studies, or work on a church committee related to the liturgy or charity, it is easy to see them as religious actors. But how are they *social* actors in relation to their Catholic faith and its social justice teaching? Intrinsic to the very idea of Catholic social justice is the sense that these religious actors will want to exert their faith outside the Church itself. This sense of faith outside its religious institution or space—and in the space to realize social aspirations—is the core sociological context of Catholic social justice teaching. In almost every interview I conducted with Catholic social activists in the United States and Mexico, this core impulse to move their faith and its values into an arena where they could help bring social change presented the fundamental challenge for the doctrine's becoming social.

In the United States Carolyn, Manuel, Yolanda, Diane, and Scott are accustomed to translating their religious values into a social sphere, particularly the very large arena of nonprofit organizations that often rely on religious values to promote social goods such as education, health care, employment training, and advocacy. Americans are accustomed to results-oriented programs with bottom lines measuring how many clients have been served, meals served, jobs filled, or bills passed in Congress. In fact, since the 1990s the idea of "religious capital" has been incorporated into U.S. public policy, with faith-based initiatives emerging as part of American political and civic cultures.[1] But in Mexico, because of political and civic cultures that severely limit religion in public life, the process of moving faith to action has undergone a very different history.[2] While Rafael, Victor, Ana, and Elena have great desire to translate their Catholic faith into action, they have encountered only limited opportunities to do so outside of the institutional church. Thus they cannot develop fully as Catholic social actors. This dilemma of moving faith to action arises from a historical problematic involving the social construction of Catholic social justice teaching and the Church's understanding of what *social* means in relationship to nonchurch society.

This chapter addresses two related issues in analyzing Catholic social justice teaching and the cultural construction of the Catholic social imagination. First, I will present the historical context of the Church's social justice teaching within a general theory of the political cultural construction of the doctrine. I will refer to the teaching as *doctrine,* not only because this is how the official Church refers to it but also to convey its serious and mandatory nature.[3] To accomplish this I will inventory papal encyclicals, addresses, and exhortations, the documents of Vatican II, and other doctrinal documents taking up social issues to generate a list of principles that make up the general body of the social doctrine. I will highlight the dialectical nature of the development of the doctrine as a set of reactions to unjust social situations that are formulated as positive principles. From this inventory I will develop a typology of social doctrine to indicate the distinctive approaches involved in the various principles. This theoretical analysis is grounded in an understanding of the Church's doctrine as a discourse that promotes an ethical perspective for its members. The discourse of doctrinal principles helps to form a religious imagination that provides opportunities and sets constraints for members' promotion of social justice. I will also analyze the influence of natural law philosophy that is embedded in the logic of the social doctrine.

A special field of social ethics has developed within the broader field of Catholic moral theology. But these studies of the social doctrine are largely limited to analyses of the historical development of the doctrine and disputes within the Church regarding how to interpret and implement it.[4] Social ethics theologians have not analyzed the sociological problems within the doctrine and how the doctrine is expressed in public life. Prior studies of the social doctrine have been largely theological in nature; here I will provide a comprehensive sociological framework to analyze the situation faced by Catholic activists who seek to strategically implement their religion's teaching within their society. Recently sociologists of religion have analyzed specific issues related to the social doctrine, such as abortion, homosexuality, birth control, HIV/AIDS prevention, and faith-based organizing, but there has not been an systematic attempt to survey the range of issues and modes of action that the Catholic social imagination organizes for Catholic social actors.[5]

If the doctrine were addressing only internal problems of charity or justice in the religious institution, then the sociologist would limit his or her analysis to the institutional culture of the Church. But the social doctrine encourages Catholics to move into the public sphere. Therefore, the sociologist must analyze how the religious institution connects with the public sphere and address what allows or constrains religious actors to develop their Catholic social imagination and put their faith into action in the public sphere.

Historical Context of Social Justice and the Catholic Church

The Catholic Church has been a historical latecomer to the philosophical ideas of the autonomous social actor and society as an independent sphere. Prior to the mid-nineteenth century, the Church thought of democracy as a process of destroying what had been a mutually beneficial relationship between the state and religion, particularly where the state recognized the Catholic Church as the official religion. The Enlightenment and its predominant liberal philosophy were condemned because it considered human meaning not in theological terms but in political and social terms.[6] Liberals saw religion as one of many human interests but not as the integrating factor for human identity and national purpose. As the Catholic Church of the eighteenth and nineteenth centuries witnessed the collapse of European monarchies and the rise of the autonomous citizen through the democratic state, such ideas as "freedom of religion" and "liberty" became threats to a Catholic worldview grounded in medieval communitarianism.[7] In this period the Catholic Church stood against the aspirations of new classes of people (the middle class, townspeople, the lower secular clergy, and the working class) as they sought their own social space in a society moving away from feudalism, monarchism, and static Catholic doctrine and moving toward industrialism, social mobility, democracy, and freethinking.[8]

Ostensibly the Church's opposition to the Enlightenment and liberalism came in reaction to modernity's concept of the human person as an individual in an independent society, freed from ecclesiastical authority. For the traditional Catholic imagination, this shift toward the individual ran counter to the body of Christ imagery of the New Testament—"we, who are many, are one body in Christ" (Romans 12:4)—and led to a fear that Catholics might come to see themselves as citizens of a sociological and political Church and demand rights and freedoms outside the Church. Church leaders feared that people viewing themselves as autonomous agents might sever the ties that bind a community together, particularly the ties of family, the local parish, national culture, and the monarchies that had given the Church special privileges. The liberal economic theory of Adam Smith and his followers was particularly alarming to the Catholic Church, since liberalism identified the human being with his or her labor and saw freedom as the exchange of that labor, whereas for the Church the person had intrinsic worth and freedom was identified not in temporal terms but in terms of spiritual salvation.[9]

As the Catholic Church reacted to modernity, it did not know how to integrate the aspirations of its members from the new classes into a judicious interpretation of the "signs of the times," as Vatican II would later put it. In the Church's previous great upheaval, the Reformation, the enemies were fellow Catholics who had revolted against the Church's theology and ecclesiology. The new heretics of modernity were likely to be non-Catholics or apostate Catholics outside of the Church's institutional jurisdiction. The last ecumenical council had been held at Trent from 1545 to 1563. The church fathers thought that Trent would settle for all times matters of liturgical, biblical, ecclesiological, priestly, sacramental, theological, and pastoral reformation.[10] By the time of the great political revolutions of France, the United States, and Latin America, more than three hundred years had passed, and the Church had retained a relatively static theology.[11] Amid the ferment of the revolutions of the late 1700s, the Jesuit order, which had led the Counter-Reformation and provided key theologians for the Council of Trent, was suppressed in 1773, thus eliminating an intellectually and culturally renewing element within the Church.[12]

It was within this liberal and democratic evolution of world society Pope Pius IX (1792–1878) convened the First Vatican Council in 1869. Ironically, its major achievement, the doctrine of the infallibility of the pope, became a watershed *modern* event: it began a slow process of internationalization and politicization of the Church and the papacy, as well as a process of making the Church into a modern political state.[13] As a result of Vatican I, the popes of the nineteenth and twentieth centuries have increasingly emphasized papal primacy and centralized church functions in the Vatican state. By the beginning of the twenty-first century, the papacy under John Paul II and then Benedict XVI had become not only the central image of the Catholic Church but also an international social and political actor in itself.[14]

For the average Catholic wishing to implement social justice doctrine, the tension between the Church's historic contestation with modernity and its drive to be international, modern, and a powerful sociopolitical actor remains an internal challenge, reflecting the Church's stance of being "in the world but not of it" (see John 17:14–15).

The Social Construction of Catholic Social Justice Teaching

The great papal architects of Catholic social justice teaching—Leo XIII (*Rerum Novarum,* 1891), Pius XI (*Quadragesimo Anno,* 1931), John XXIII (*Mater et Magistra,* 1961, and *Pacem in Terris,* 1963), Paul VI (*Populorum Progressio,* 1967), and John Paul II (*Laborum Exercens,* 1981, *Sollicitudo Rei Socialis,* 1987, and *Centesimus Annus,* 1991), as well as the world Catholic bishops who gathered to write the pastoral constitution of the Church at Vatican II (*Gaudium et Spes,* 1961–63)—did not address fully how Catholics were to be developed as "social actors" within and outside of their church. In contrast, a remarkable institutional structure has been developed for the sacraments and the liturgy, in which Catholics are trained to be religious actors. Indeed the institutional church has created a Catholic culture through its catechesis, spiritual preparation, rituals, renewal processes, organizations to prepare for religious festivals, and the like.[15] Thus it is ingrained in the Catholic imagination that one should attend Mass every Sunday, get married in the Church, baptize one's children, receive ashes on the forehead on Ash Wednesday, abstain from eating meat on the Fridays of Lent, not have an abortion,—and so on. This set of beliefs and practices provides a distinctive Catholicity to members' Christian lives, often setting them apart from their Protestant and Orthodox brethren. Such a sense of Catholicity can be enhanced by cultural factors in the so-called Catholic cultures of Spain, France, Portugal, and Latin America. My study examines whether and how the social doctrine enters this world of Catholicity.

Each of the major documents has key social themes, and these can be traced to provide a sense of the development of the social doctrine.[16] Each document, that is, can be seen as a "building block."[17] But this means that as of the time of my research, the doctrine not been systematized or given an internal logic, which means it was not as readily internalized by the Catholic faithful as moral, sacramental, and biblical theology has been.[18]

Beginning with Leo XIII's reaction to unjust working conditions and his declaration that workers should have a fundamental right to organize labor unions, Catholic social justice teaching could be characterized as having a two-step social construction of negative reaction to social problems and positive declaration of a new teaching: (1) *reactive* to social events of the time and (2) *declaratory* of the Church's understanding of the events.[19] The social doctrine developed, then, into a reactive-declaratory menu of principles and ideas. Until 2005, when the *Compendium of the Social Doctrine of the Church* was published, Catholic social actors had not been presented with a systematic social theology and could thus be characterized as "pick and choose" Catholics, emphasizing different principles or interpretations.[20] The social doctrine thus has a dynamic sense, which I will analyze through case studies in chapters 3 and 4.

I will argue that because of this pattern of development, the teaching has not evolved dialectically with modern social science, social movements, and political change. The teaching often appropriates the language of the times but defines it differently, particularly in the case of solidarity—a key concept in John Paul II's social theology.

More than any other modern pope, John Paul II developed the social doctrine as a distinctive branch of theology and doctrine. His understanding of social justice teaching is stated clearly in *Sollicitudo Rei Socialis* (1987):

> The Church's social doctrine is *not* a "third way" between *liberal capitalism* and *Marxist collectivism,* nor even a possible alternative to other solutions less radically opposed to one another: rather, it constitutes a *category of its own.* Nor is it an *ideology,* but rather the *accurate formulation* of the results of a careful reflection on the complex realities of human existence, in society and in the international order, in the light of faith and of the Church's tradition. Its main aim is to *interpret* these realities, determining their conformity with or divergency from the lines of the Gospel teaching on man and his vocation, a vocation which is at once earthly and transcendent; its aim is thus to *guide* Christian behavior. It therefore belongs to the field, not of *ideology,* but of *theology* and particularly of moral theology.[21]

His interpretation of the doctrine as a part of moral theology places the doctrine in conflict with a scientific understanding of society as dynamic—contracting, expanding, devolving, evolving, etc. As understood in the social sciences and throughout the history of social philosophy, society and the human person are not static. The Church, however, relies on the deductive method of natural law in its development of moral theology and its understanding of society and the person, and thus produces static definitions.[22]

The natural law basis of Roman Catholic moral theology, particularly as applied by John Paul II and the theologians of his Congregation of the Faith, headed by Cardinal Joseph Ratzinger (later Benedict XVI), has emphasized "eternal verities" in ethics, particularly sexual ethics.[23] According to the writings of John Paul II, the Church's social justice theologians and other social actors must use the natural law's deductive method. The *Compendium of the Social Doctrine of the Church* was a fitting conclusion to the papacy of John Paul, for the introduction and part 1 of the three-part "catechism of Catholic social justice doctrine" provide a new systematic social theology within the natural law, as he advocated. This work conceptualizes a natural law understanding of society as an organic body, with members whose roles and functions proceed from this understanding. The introduction of the *Compendium*, titled "An Integral and Solidary Humanism," lays out the Church's claim that the social doctrine is "to propose to all men and women a humanism that is up to the standards of God's plan of love in history, an integral and solidary humanism capable of creating a new social, economic and political order, founded on the dignity and freedom of every human person, to be brought about in peace, justice, and solidarity." In part 1, article 53, this claim is given a philosophical justification based on the natural law tradition: "This inspiration is given to the community of Christians who are a part of the world and of history, and who are therefore open to dialogue with all people of good will in the common quest for the seeds of truth and freedom sown in the vast field of humanity. The dynamics of this renewal must be firmly anchored in the unchangeable principles of the natural law, inscribed by God the Creator in each of his creatures (cf. *Rom* 2:14–5), and bathed in eschatological light through Jesus Christ."[24] I will return to the problems that this claim generates.

The actual history of the construction of Catholic social justice teaching shows that, in fact, it has evolved more diversely, often inductively and pragmatically, as the Church has reacted to issues related to human rights, war, the death penalty, international debt of poor countries, property rights, the role of the state, and the development of civil society. For example, the discourse promoted by the United Nations regarding human rights prompted John XXIII to deliver his 1963 encyclical *Pacem in Terris* in the context of a changing world order—the end of colonialism and the rise of new independent states. Where was the human rights item on the Church's social justice menu back when Catholic European nations such as Spain, Portugal, and France colonized Africa, Asia, and Latin America? Surely church theologians could proof-text biblical references, prior encyclicals, and the natural law to legitimize human rights as a theological principle. But the introduction of human rights into the doctrine can be seen in the reactive-declaratory process: as a reaction to human misery and violation of fundamental "rights" affirmed in liberal political philosophy and a declaration of the Church's stance vis-à-vis human rights violations and the aspirations of social actors. The very idea of the rights of human beings did not emerge without violations of those rights as experienced by social actors. An experience of injustice leads inductively to a formulation of a principle of justice that then seems to operate deductively.[25]

German sociologist Jürgen Habermas provides a way of understanding this dynamic process as "communicative action" in which ethical principles are constructed through "discourse":

> Only in theoretical, practical, and explicative discourse do the participants have to start from (the often counterfactual) presupposition that the conditions for an ideal speech situation are satisfied to a sufficient degree of approximation. I shall speak of "discourse" only when the meaning of the problematic validity claim conceptually forces participants to suppose that a rationally motivated agreement could in principle be achieved, whereby the phrase "in principle" expresses the idealizing proviso: if only the argumentation could be conducted openly enough and continued long enough.[26]

It is my argument, then, that modern Roman Catholic social justice doctrine has been socially constructed in a process of communicative action, what Habermas calls "discourse ethics,"[27] through a reactive-declaratory two-step process that has allowed the Church's doctrine to evolve in relation to a dynamic society. Because the Church lays claim to an internal moral logic reliant upon natural law methodology, however, it is constantly faced with a need for "bridging the logical gap in *nondeductive* relations."[28] Since the Church resists a truly dialectical process that would allow the teaching to become integrated with other social ideas and forces, the social justice doctrine is increasingly restricted to an internal ideology generating theological principles that active Catholics may find hard to make sense of or implement within external social spheres. I will illustrate these problems in the case studies to follow. It remains to be seen how the 2005 *Compendium of the Social Doctrine of the Church,* with its systematic social theology grounded in the natural law, will restrict the previously dynamic model of doctrinal construction.

In this work I take it for granted that social justice is distinct from moral theology, as well as moral philosophy. The very idea of "social" implies that social relationships and principles regarding the social good are worked out on an ongoing and experiential basis in public processes and social structures and institutions. Analyzing Habermas's discourse ethics, social philosophers Jean Cohen and Andrew Arato summarize how discourse ethics translates into practical justice:

> The analytic starting point of discourse ethics is not a conception of sovereign, disconnected, disembodied individuality but rather the intersubjective communicative infrastructure of everyday social life. Individuals act within relationships of mutual recognition in which they acquire and assert their individuality and their freedom intersubjectively. In the dialogue process, every participant articulates his or her views or need-interpretations and takes on ideal roles in a public, practical discussion. This provides the framework in which the understanding of others' need-interpretations is made possible through moral insight and not only through empathy. It is here that the presence of commonalities is tested and respect for difference is potentially affirmed.[29]

When we approach social justice in this way, we see that there is something intrinsically sociological about the "social" of social justice. Social justice principles emerge from the experiences of everyday life, and people articulate their everyday experience of "injustice" as a discourse of their social facts and aspirations—a process that has an *inductive* logic. As political theorist David Miller suggests regarding the scope of social justice, "If we do not inhabit bounded societies, or if people's shares of goods and bads do not depend in ways we can understand on a determinate set of social institutions, or if there is no agency capable of regulating that basic structure, then we no longer live in a world in which the idea of social justice has any purchase."[30] Social justice is driven inductively and contextually to derive its principles, while Catholic moral theology principles are derived from sacred scripture and the natural law tradition, so that moral doctrine is given an immutable sense.[31] Yet in the pursuit of social justice, Catholic social actors must enter into discourse with other spheres of justice beyond religion and moral philosophy—with the law, the economy, and other institutions embodying social and moral life. Catholics seek to integrate the social values of their faith with the social institutions, in both the church and the world, that will bring about social justice.

As a sociologist, I analyze the Catholic Church's social justice doctrine as the source of ideas and values for Catholic social actors to enter into the public sphere with other social actors such that, in the words of Cohen and Arato, "the presence of commonalities [can be] tested and respect for difference is potentially affirmed."[32] Thus there is not a "Catholic social justice" but a social justice to which Catholics contribute their faith, ideas, and values in a common social sphere, most commonly referred to today as civil society.[33] This has become known as the "faith-based" sense of religious actors acting as public actors. The case studies will show how Catholic social doctrine provides a specifically Catholic imagination for social justice.

Since the nineteenth century, then, Catholic social justice doctrine has been constructed contextually within a changing world. As social aspirations arise in civil society, the Church has reacted pastorally to these "need-interpretations" and mobilized its own ideas (biblical, theological, and traditional) and values (faith, spirituality, natural law philosophy, etc.) to declare its position regarding a social problem and advance a social good or principle and provide Catholics with a faith-based legitimation for their activity in civil society. Given that this process has been reactive and not proactive, the Church's institutional voice generally has not been ahead of people's aspirations or social needs. That is, the institutional Church has not been prophetic, despite its own theological tradition of prophecy. For example, only as modern Western democracies began to allow legal abortions did the Church begin to react to abortion issues and nourish Catholic-inspired civil associations to build prolife and profamily social movements.[34] Similarly the anti–death penalty movement in the Church has arisen only after social actors have shown the immorality of the death penalty, based not so much on natural law as on social facts—how it has been administered, whom it has affected, and its failure to deter capital crime.[35]

An Evolving Social Justice Doctrine Menu

The Catholic Church began its construction of social justice doctrine in 1891 as an evolving menu of doctrinal declarations. The term *menu* is used to refer to the set of principles because in my reading of official social justice documents and their interpretation by Catholic social justice theologians, I have found eclecticism to its construction, as Catholic leaders and members focused on particular social issues related to the injustices they were dealing with at the time. The principles have been emphasized in different ways; some have been ignored or discarded, others added, and they have never been applied as a coherent whole. Until the issuance of the *Compendium,* there had not been a systematic social theology. This allowed popes, Vatican congregations, national church bodies, and dioceses to pick and choose from the menu to address social problems.[36]

The Catholic Church's doctrine has a hierarchical structure: degrees to which teachings are required of all Catholics or highly recommended. At the highest and first level of doctrine is sacred scripture and "tradition"—that is, theological beliefs that do not have scriptural reference, such as the doctrine of the immaculate conception of Mary (1854), the bodily assumption of Mary into heaven (1951), and papal infallibility (1870). The elevation of these three doctrines into the official "tradition" reflects the Roman Church's need to heighten its distinctive doctrinal control in a world of philosophical and religious speculation.[37]

The second level of teaching, also obligatory for all Christians, is the doctrine developed at ecumenical councils. The third level, obligatory as well, is the papal encyclical, in which the pope speaks ex cathedra on matters of faith and morals in the name of the whole Church. Apostolic exhortations, addresses, and official statements issued in the name of the pope are not considered mandatory teaching but are highly recommended. The fourth level of teaching emanates from the Vatican's congregations, such as the Congregation for the Doctrine of the Faith and the Pontifical Council for Justice and Peace, which are responsible for the development, dissemination, and enforcement of the social justice doctrine. The documents issued by the congregations are mandatory in effect, functioning as permissions or punishments issued by a regulatory agency. The fifth level of teaching is generated by local bishops and national conferences of bishops and is not mandatory. The sixth level of teaching is nonmandatory theological reflection—books, articles, homilies, and instruction—by bishops, theologians, priests, and laypeople.[38]

Another level of teaching, which operates at all levels of the teaching structure, is the *sensus fidelium* ("sense of the faithful"). This is the idea that teaching is either received by the people or it is not, as the Holy Spirit is at work in the reception of a teaching. If a doctrine is not received, its credibility is called into question. An example is the ongoing negative reception of Paul VI's 1967 encyclical *Humanae Vitae,* which dealt with sexual and reproductive ethics and declared that no Catholic may use artificial means of contraception.[39]

While the modern idea of "social teaching" in the Church begins with *Rerum Novarum,* this teaching is predicated upon a long history and tradition of concern for the common good. In the New Testament, the emerging church sees itself as the center of community, distribution of goods, and works of mercy and charity. This tradition includes the communitarian practices of the early Christians, the writings of church fathers such as St. Augustine, the monastic movement of the Middle Ages (Benedictines and Carthusians), the advent of the great religious orders (Dominicans and Franciscans), and the development of scholastic philosophy and its use of the natural law (Thomas Aquinas, Bonaventure, et al.). The tradition developed key forms of social organization such as monasteries, guilds, and fraternities to distribute charitable goods in a Christian society, following a theology derived from the Beatitudes of Jesus (Matthew 5) and the evangelical virtues of poverty and love of neighbor.[40] The natural law tradition of the Scholastics, who had retrieved Aristotelian logic and Platonic concepts for theological use, brought a philosophical orientation to the scriptural and pastoral traditions, particularly ideas regarding the law and the common good, commutative and distributive justice, the role of political authority, duty, responsibility, and "the natural order of things."[41] Thus the social justice principles initiated with *Rerum Novarum* are predicated upon the Bible (both Hebrew scriptures and the New Testament), the writings of the early church fathers on morality and justice, the traditions of charity and the works of mercy, and the natural law—all of which are seen by Catholic theologians as constituting the social tradition of the Church.

The primary social justice principles generated by papal encyclicals and Vatican II are considered mandatory doctrines of the Church. Below each social encyclical is listed by year, the pope or council that wrote it, the title of the document, the negative reaction that motivated its creation, and the positive declarations generated as social principles. (See appendix 1 for doctrinal sources of each principle.)

- 1891, Pope Leo XIII, *Rerum Novarum.* Written as a reaction to industrialization, urbanization, child labor abuse, labor syndicates, and the rise of communism and socialism. Leo XIII declared the following principles:
   1. common good
   2. association

3. participation

4. workers' rights to organize

5. just wage as family support

6. dignity of work

7. private property rights

8. reasonable intervention of the state in the economy

9. application of Church's teaching to the temporal order

10. friendship[42]

- 1931, Pope Pius XI, *Quadragessimo Anno*. Written as a reaction to the effects of World War I, the rise of totalitarian and fascist dictatorships, and the worldwide economic depression. Pius XI declared the following principles:

11. social justice

12. dignity of the human person

13. subsidiarity, the proper role of government, the value of intermediary associations

14. social order as a corporatist occupational group system of mediating structures between the person and the state, from which the principle of solidarity is derived

- 1961, Pope John XXIII, *Mater et Magistra*. Written as a reaction to the growth and threat of communism, the effects of the cold war, the collapse of European colonies in Africa, Asia, and Latin America, the rise of liberation movements, and a growing interdependent world economy; John XXIII declared the following principle:

15. economic development and justice as parity between rich and poor nations

- 1963, Pope John XXIII, *Pacem in Terris*. Written in reaction to the global arms race and the threat of nuclear war, as well as the Church's understanding that it cannot remain isolated in the world; this is the first papal letter written to the whole world. John XXIII declared these principles:

16. human rights

17. social responsibilities that Christians must exercise

18. peace

19. disarmament

- 1965, Vatican II, *Gaudium et Spes* (Pastoral Constitution on the Church in the Modern World). Written as a reaction to the "signs of the times," particularly disillusionment with traditional values, the changing shape of the family, changing societal norms, and the rise in global communication and technology; the council fathers reaffirmed or redefined the principles of the dignity of the person and participation and declared these new principles:

    20. "signs of the times" as basis of social analysis

    21. family life

    22. option for the poor

    23. solidarity

- 1965, Vatican II, *Dignitatis Humanae* (Declaration on Religious Liberty). Written as a reaction to religious intolerance around the world. The Council Fathers declared the following principles:

    24. freedom of religion

    25. government is constitutional and limited in function

    26. depoliticization of the Church so it is not dependent upon the state

- 1967, Pope Paul VI, *Populorum Progressio.* Written as a reaction to the widening gap between rich and poor countries and a growing understanding of "development" concepts in the economy, politics, and the human person. Paul VI declared these principles:

    27. *development* as a word for peace and order

    28. the laity's freedom to take initiative for social aims

- 1971, Pope Paul VI, *Octogesima Adveniens.* Written as a reaction to the rise of urban problems in the world due to migration and the displacement of peoples. Paul VI declared the following principles:

    29. option for the vulnerable

    30. local analysis and self-determination in light of the gospel and social teaching

- 1975, Pope Paul VI, *Evangelii Nuntiandi.* Written as a reaction to the growth of atheism, secularism, and consumerism. Paul VI declared the following principle:

    31. liberation based on Jesus' promise of salvation to all people via the Church's social teaching

- 1981, Pope John Paul II, *Laborem Exercens.* Written as a reaction to the plight of workers in both capitalist and socialist economic and political systems. John Paul II declared the following principle:

    32. priority of the worker's labor in economics

- 1987, Pope John Paul II, *Sollicitudo Rei Socialis*. Written in reaction to persistent underdevelopment in the world and the cold war division among nations. John Paul II declared these principles:
  33. structures of sin
  34. solidarity as a virtue

- 1991, Pope John Paul II, *Centesimus Annus*. Written as a reaction to the collapse of communism in Eastern Europe and the ongoing sociocultural problems arising from consumerism. John Paul II declared the following principles:
  35. workers' participation in the life of their industries
  36. the proper and legitimate role of the market economy
  37. economic aid to poorer countries by wealthier ones[43]

- 1992, Pope John Paul II and the Congregation for the Doctrine of the Faith, *Catechism of the Catholic Church*. Written as a reaction to the plurality of theologies and methodologies that developed after Vatican II and the Vatican's desire to maintain a universal theological orthodoxy and hegemony of the natural law and Thomistic methodologies. The Cathechism serves as a "directory" of all Catholic doctrine, including social justice teaching; there are no new declarations in it.[44]

- 2005, Pope John Paul II and the Pontifical Council for Justice and Peace, *Compendium of the Social Doctrine of the Church*. Written as a systematic moral theology of all previous encyclicals, congregational documents, and papal statements related to the social doctrine. It serves as a catechism of social doctrine, particularly as articulated by John Paul II and the Congregation for the Doctrine of the Faith under the leadership of Cardinal Joseph Ratzinger.[45]

The social justice principles of *Rerum Novarum* have remained the basis for the ongoing construction of the teaching and the primary logic of the social theology. They are rooted in a natural law understanding of the family as the first societal organism. The family's survival depends on a living wage derived from dignified labor. Leo XIII began constructing the social justice teaching in reaction to attacks upon the family arising from industrialization, migration, urbanization, and abuses of workers (especially children) by an unfettered capitalism. However, at the same time, he considered that the socialist and communist philosophies that motivated the formation of the first labor unions were also threats to the family, since they treated human nature in terms of labor rather than upholding the intrinsic worth of the human person and family relations. Further, according to Leo XIII, the socialists advocated class divisions and violence against rightful owners of businesses and property.

Families connect with one another and build an organic society upon which the idea of solidarity is predicated, a society that establishes the common good. As an organic body, society can be viewed as healthy or sick. The principles established in *Rerum Novarum* were seen as remedies to assist a body that had become chronically ill. The Church, as the body of Christ, is the only true remedy to establish a good and healthy society, according to *Rerum Novarum,* and Catholics are called to implement these principles in the world.[46]

The thirty-seven social justice principles listed above are the primary premises of the tradition cited in this study. They can be sorted into at least six functional types that indicate a division of labor, as it were, for the doctrine's development. Importantly, these functions are not fully systematic, providing strict logic or consistency for the doctrine. They illustrate the doctrine's evolutionary and complex composition in response to various social issues.

1. *Organizing principle*—organizes Catholic social actors both in the Church itself and in the world: church; solidarity; subsidiarity; social order as corporatist; association; participation; family life; state intervention in the economy; economic development; market economy

2. *Philosophical principle*—conceptualizes social issues within philosophical traditions: natural law; commutative and distributive justice; social justice; common good; private property rights; dignity of the human person; dignity of work; human rights; freedom of religion; government is constitutional and limited; solidarity

3. *Moral norm*—develops the social issue in a normative orientation within a social structure and also in terms of the Catholic's responsibility when facing a social injustice: charity; duty; responsibility; just wage; social responsibility; peace; disarmament; family life; development; liberation; economic aid; priority of workers' labor in economics

4. *Virtue*—orients the individual to inculcate the principle in her or his personal life: friendship; option for the poor; solidarity; option for the vulnerable

5. *Social role*—provides a Catholic social actor specific position (as a role function) to act upon the doctrine: role of laity; worker participation; solidarity

6. *Analytical framework*—connects a social justice principle or the doctrine in general to empirical methodologies of the social sciences, political processes, and theological logics: "natural order of things" of the natural law; signs of the times; local analysis; structures of sin; solidarity

When these premises and principles are organized by functional types, we can see the complexity of the doctrinal principles and the overlaps among various types. While these principles are the "key words" of Catholic social justice teaching and discourse, there are other important social concepts that the documents connect to the various principles—the state and the economy, the modern world, ecumenism, etc.—and join them with larger social, political, and economic categories related to social justice. However, analysis of Catholic social justice theology and commentaries has made it clear to me that the "menu" reflects the scholarship and conversation in which the Church engages when it reflects upon the doctrine, and that this is a highly selective process of engagement. Such selectivity is reflected in lists, put together by various theologians and the conferences of bishops, of "building blocks" or "essentials" of the teaching and in how the principles are applied. (I will analyze this issue in chapters 3 and 4.)

John Paul II's predecessors had developed their social principles largely as moral norms intended to serve as antidotes to social problems. The doctrine took a philosophical turn with his development of a Christian humanism influenced by his understanding of phenomenology and existentialism.[47] John Paul II's contribution to the doctrine was his analysis of the principles of solidarity and options for the poor and the vulnerable—particularly in his articulation of these principles during his addresses around the world—with a functional emphasis on the philosophical principles, moral norms, and virtues necessary for the social doctrine. He summarized these ideas in a thematic discourse using the phrases "culture of death," "culture of life," and "civilization of love."[48]

In presenting the doctrine, the Church has yet to offer a spirituality of social justice that would help the Catholic put the menu together for a balanced diet: a way to integrate prayer, liturgy, the sacraments, the teaching, and social practice into a way of being Catholic in the social world.[49] For the vast majority of Catholics, ongoing religious education comes from Sunday homilies by their priest and from sacramental preparation programs for baptism, confirmation, Eucharist, and marriage. Given that since Vatican II, priests are required to receive only one course in the social teaching of the Church, the clergy have little knowledge of the doctrine and are not prepared to integrate the principles into their homilies and sacramental preparation, much less incorporate it into pastoral programs and action. (I will address how the U.S. and Mexican churches incorporate the teaching into their training programs in chapters 3 and 4.)

Case Study: The Principle of Solidarity

Of thirty-seven key doctrinal principles, those articulated in the post–Vatican II papal encyclicals and exhortations and the *Catechism of the Catholic Church* function as a working vocabulary for Catholic social justice discourse. Particular principles have been emphasized in official Vatican documents and national bishops' conferences and by theologians. The following principles have become primary motifs of the Catholic social imagination: (1) the common good, (2) dignity of the human person, (3) solidarity, (4) human rights, (5) peace, (6) development, (7) preferential option for the poor, (8) family life, and (9) participation and association.[50] These nine principles were the key items in the social discourse of John Paul II, the *Catechism,* and the *Compendium.* Meanwhile, the principles of workers' right to organize, subsidiarity, corporatist social organization, disarmament, "signs of the times," self-determination, liberation, structures of sin, and worker participation in their industries have been deemphasized.

During the course of my research, particularly during the pontificate of John Paul II, no other concept among the social justice principles was more developed than *solidarity.* This is no real surprise, given that John Paul II and the Polish church assisted the Polish labor union Solidarity morally, organizationally, and intellectually. When Solidarity was founded in 1975 by Lech Walesa and others, the union's name signaled a resurgence of one of the oldest principles of social justice, developed by socialists and labor activists beginning in the mid-1800s. Solidarity had become part of the Catholic Church's first-level social justice menu with John XXIII's 1962 encyclical *Pacem in Terris.* Given the prominence of solidarity as a social justice principle since the 1960s, especially in John Paul II's encyclicals, exhortations, and speeches, and given solidarity's prominence in the social sciences, I highlight the concept as a primary organizing principle for the Catholic social imagination.

I am particularly interested in how solidarity is used to frame social justice issues in the Catholic Church and how it is used as an organizing principle both within the church and outside it. Further, I will compare how solidarity has been understood sociologically, politically, and philosophically since the 1800s to the Church's understanding. Given solidarity's long history as a social justice principle and its use in diverse contexts, it presents a very good comparative case study of the challenges the Catholic Church faces in translating its social justice principles into the social-civil sphere.

Solidarity has become an essential part of the vocabulary of social philosophy in the early twenty-first century. From trade unionists to feminists to liberation theologians, the word has common meaning drawing from the experience of struggle, suffering, inequality, and oppression. Solidarity points to both the problems faced by various communities and groups and their hopes and aspirations for collective action to overcome injustice.

At least five approaches to solidarity have been developed since the late 1800s. The first, a sociological and political understanding dating from the French and German corporatist movements, was developed systematically in the sociology of Émile Durkheim. The second is related to Catholic social teaching per se. The third type is related to trade union organizing and collective action. The fourth developed from various twentieth-century liberation movements. And the fifth comes from late-twentieth-century philosophical ethics and the revival of civil society studies. Below I will examine how the principle of solidarity in Catholic social doctrine has evolved as the Church has engaged with various discourses. Do these various understandings of solidarity find common ground? How do they diverge? Is it possible to integrate the various meanings of and approaches to solidarity? Is solidarity simply a heuristic instrument? Or is it more constitutive, such that it acts as a symbolic sign that moves analysis to that which it represents?[51] These questions motivate this review of the history of solidarity as a primary element in Catholic social justice teaching.

Émile Durkheim (1858–1917) formulated the enduring sociological concept of solidarity in his doctoral dissertation of 1893, titled *The*

Division of Labor in Society. The concept underlies his primary questions regarding society:

> The question that has been the starting point of our study has been that of the connection between the individual personality and social solidarity. How does it come about that the individual, whilst becoming more autonomous, depends ever more closely upon society? How can he become at the same time more of an individual and yet more linked to society? For it is indisputable that these two movements, however contradictory they appear to be, are carried on in tandem. Such is the nature of the problem that we have set out for ourselves.[52]

We see that Durkheim starts with the assumption that the individual in society is gaining in autonomy, in individuality. There is a progressive nature to this sense of self and society.

Steven Lukes, in his biography of Durkheim, notes that his use of solidarity, while quite familiar with the "middle way" between "*laissez-faire* liberalism and revolutionary socialism, between 'individualism' and 'collectivism,'" is quite distinctive from the position of the French Solidarists, with whom he shared solidarist political values such as "social pacifism and desire for social solidarity through reconciliation."[53] The French Solidarists held ideas that were fairly similar to those of the German Solidarists and Catholic corporativists. Durkheim's analysis of moral beliefs led him to assert that a mere realignment of the political structures (a kind of straddling of solidarism and socialism) would not be sufficient to regenerate French society. He did not hold sacrosanct the concept of private property, nor did he have faith in mere legislative reform.[54]

For Durkheim, the division of labor is a serious matter that has moral implications: as society changes social structures and institutions, especially the law, it changes its morality. Morality functions as a social glue binding people together—the normative sense of a social structure. Durkheim distinguishes between two types of social solidarity: mechanical and organic. Mechanical solidarity "binds the individual directly to society."[55] In terms of the law, mechanical solidarity is expressed in repressive laws such as the penal codes and those imposing social and collective stigma.[56] Within mechanical solidarity, individuals are judged as equals who are absorbed into the collectivity. On the other hand, in organic solidarity individuals are distinctive organs having their own "special characteristics and autonomy."[57] This type of solidarity arises from the division of labor. In terms of the law, organic solidarity is reflected in positive and cooperative laws related to "resti-tutory sanction determining different relationships."[58]

Durkheim sees mechanical solidarity primarily in primitive societies that are characterized by segmentation, while organic solidarity devel-ops in more organized and complex societies that are characterized by differentiation. The division of labor, because of its organic nature, is characterized by differentation. This aspect of social solidarity is criti-cal, for in differentiation we see that individual identity is derived from the whole (the society) and not vice versa. Durkheim's sociology is a critical turn away from standard liberal theory, which states that the individual makes the society. For Durkheim, society makes the indi-vidual. The individual has no real identity outside of the organic whole, yet at the same time the individual maintains a moral autonomy.[59]

Durkheim's two types of social solidarity have a paradoxical quality. For example, in mechanical solidarity the individual is joined to a com-mon whole through resemblances of one individual to another, particu-larly through the concrete and specific repressive sanctions of the so-called primitive society; yet there is an elevated collective sense of the sacred or the religious, and high value is placed on society and the inter-ests of society as a whole. Meanwhile, in organic solidarity, wherein the individual is joined to the common whole through differentiation in the division of labor, the prevalence of cooperative law (civil, commercial, procedural, administrative, and constitutional law) reflects a high col-lective sense of the secular, emphasizing individual dignity, equality of opportunity, the work ethic, and social justice.[60] Thus social solidarity is defined by a collective sense, what Durkheim calls the *conscience col-lective*,[61] of a whole. This shows "the irreducibility of the social entity to the sum of its elements, the explanation of the elements by the entity and not of the entity by the elements."[62] But because in organic solidar-ity the common conscience is becoming more secularized, the division of labor and its differentiation are taking on the role of the conscience collective.[63]

Moving beyond a sense of social contract as the basis for society, particularly since "contract" implies the construction of society by individuals and not vice versa, Durkheim sees that society is mor-ally constructed via "an institutionalized system of enforcing good faith and the avoidance of force and fraud in contract. It requires, in a word, justice."[64] And "we can be sure that this need [for justice] will become more exacting if, as every fact presages, the conditions dominat-ing social evolution remain the same."[65] Robert Bellah notes that for

Durkheim the increasing autonomy of the individual demands justice, a justice necessarily evolving out of organic solidarity. Thus justice becomes "the essence of organic solidarity."[66]

The U.S. sociologist Talcott Parsons (1902–72) further developed the idea of social solidarity in his functionalist sociology, which owes much to Durkheim. For Parsons, the primary function of solidarity is the integration of norms and values in the social system, what Durkheim saw as the correlative nature of mechanical and organic solidarity. Mechanical solidarity is related to norms of "primordial solidarity," while organic solidarity is related to values of "societal solidarity."[67] The distinctiveness of Parsons' understanding of solidarity lies in his idea that modern society relies on it for a foundational moral life. Leon Mayhew reflects thus on Parsons' understanding of solidarity:

> The daily process by which people ask for each other's trust through the exercise of influence is the process whereby groups are formed and sustained. To doubt the real solidarity underneath the rich associational life of a modern society is to participate in the deflation of the stores of influence by which its manifold diversity is articulated in the social relations between groups. To insist that only primordial and warmly emotional solidarity is real is comparable to claiming that only gold is money.[68]

This understanding of solidarity leads Parsons to identify a third type of solidarity that mediates mechanical and organic solidarity: "diffuse solidarity" as "the common matrix out of which *both* the others have emerged by a process of differentiation."[69] Furthermore, Parsons advances Durkheim's thinking by showing that institutional formation is the actualization of the conscience collective. Viewed in this way, institutions carry forth not only structural norms but also communal values.[70] With diffuse solidarity, institutions can be seen as "mediating institutions" that are continually mediating norms and values. Parsons is careful to note that primordial solidarity is always present; it does not become obsolete in some kind of evolutionary process as Durkheim believed it would.

The sociological approach to solidarity has its foundation in Durkheim's distinctions of mechanical and organic solidarity. In social philosophy, the concept countered the prevailing liberal notion of the individual as the locus of societal construction. Rather, solidarity places the individual within society: society forms the individual. The innovative and enduring aspect of Durkheimian solidarity is its ability to account for the individual and society as correlative in the formation of community. Particularity is accounted for in mechanical solidarity, while universalism is accounted for in organic solidarity. The individual is not swallowed up in corporate statism. With increasing differentiation of the division of labor, individuals grow in autonomy and other values that must emerge to maintain individual dignity and freedom. For Durkheim, the increasing differentiation in organic solidarity demands justice. This kind of justice is always communal and cannot be individualistic or atomistic. Thus while not speaking of "social justice" per se, Durkheim's sociology gives a comprehensive account of how social justice develops from the organizing principle of social solidarity.

Durkheim's sociological formulation of the concept of solidarity emerged in the same historical period as the Church's construction of its social doctrine. As previously noted, the key moment for the creation of Catholic social thought was the publication in 1891 of the encyclical *Rerum Novarum* by Leo XIII. Using Thomistic principles to address social questions regarding labor, property rights, and industrialization, Leo XIII set the stage for ongoing Catholic intellectual exploration of questions related to society as society. For Leo XIII, "man precedes the state." The encyclical was a critique of economic liberalism and its defense of capitalism, yet it did not embrace a socialist perspective. Rather, it set the course for what can be called a corporatist approach to economy and society based upon the principle of subsidiarity, i.e., that "government intervention is justified when it truly provides help [*subsidium*] to the persons and smaller communities which compose society." Small communities such as the family, neighborhood, the church, and professional and labor groups "all have a dynamic life of their own which must be respected by government," since they have "legitimate claims rooted in the dynamics and structure of these groups."[71] In terms of social philosophy, "corporatism makes the supposition that the problem of conflict will be solved by integrating the different kinds of communities and associations [corporations] into an organically structured social system."[72]

This Catholic approach to solidarity is closely connected to the corporatist approach to societal analysis. The corporatist economic theory of the late nineteenth century was essentially a response to "reactionary, medieval romantics who rejected capitalism hook, line, and sinker and [it] incorporated a Catholic version of the labor theory of value."[73] Sociologist John Coleman refers to the first solidarists as the "reluctant capitalists, . . . reformers who accepted capitalism as a system while rejecting its abuses."[74]

The key figure in building the Catholic social movement was a German Jesuit, Heinrich Pesch (1854–1926). In a sense solidarity as corporativism navigates a middle way between capitalist and socialist theories of society. For Pesch and others, corporativism had two key points: "a spirit of change and a change of structures."[75] In terms of "spirit," the Catholic approach to solidarity is a critique of liberalism "with its individualism, selfishness, and materialism."[76] And in terms of a "change of structures," solidarity offers an organic view of society that "recognizes the different functions of people and the need for hierarchical ordering." Thus solidarity does not allow the "flat equality" that liberalism champions, yet it does not adhere to socialism's claims for the socialist state, since the state apparatus limits personal and small community liberty.[77]

The solidarist position gained further ground in Catholic social thought with the 1931 publication of Pius XI's encyclical *Quadragessimo Anno,* in which he sets the corporatist model of society within the principle of subsidiarity: "This is a fixed and unchangeable principle most basic in social philosophy, immovable and unalterable. The reason is that all social activity, of its very power and nature, should supply help to the members of the social body, but may never destroy or absorb them."[78] This position can be traced to St. Paul's organic model of the Church found in 1 Corinthians 12:12–14: "For just as the body is one and has many members, and all the members of the body, though many, are one body, so it is with Christ. . . . Indeed, the body does not consist of one member but of many." The solidarist position protects a sense of individual integrity of persons and small groups within the corporatist body, which defines the concept of subsidiarity. These aspects of corporatism, subsidiarity, and solidarity are defining markers of the modern Catholic approach to social philosophy, which can be seen in almost every papal social encyclical up through those of John Paul II.

The classical Catholic approach to solidarity can be seen, then, as a middle way between liberal capitalism and state socialism. In its positive sense it views society as a corporate whole (like a body) that has many parts, each having a distinct integrity. The Catholic approach allows for particularity and differentiation of individuals and various communities, such as the family, neighborhoods, ethnic groups, and various associations and organizations, as they construct society. But because it is born out of reaction to both liberal capitalism and socialism and has a natural law orientation that envisions the immutability of the social order, the Catholic approach has an inherent distrust of such liberal concepts as liberty, equality, and individualism; these are seen as undermining Catholic solidarity's hierarchical premises. It draws on an almost literalist sense of the Pauline doctrine of the Church, thus transmuting ecclesiology into sociology.

Having arisen as a reaction to capitalism and socialism, the Catholic approach appears to be seeking to establish a distinctive voice in modern social philosophy, but it is reactive and not proactive. Indeed it can seem to straddle the two conflicting theories of society. A "wider solidarity" that "calls out for a conscious acknowledgment of and commitment to our *moral* interdependence" would take into account the "technological, political, and economic interdependence" that modern complex society demands.[79]

Catholic social ethicist David Hollenbach has observed that this tradition is based on an understanding of the corporate body as having an intelligence of its own, a rational order reminiscent of the medieval guild order. But this image of society as "harmonious and changeless system of group and role relations" probably did not exist then and certainly does not exist in modern times.[80] Papal social encyclicals since John XXIII have moved on from this medieval image to articulate a greater sense of society's complexity, yet they retain the ideal of a medieval organic stasis or "harmony." For Hollenbach, particularly in the practical application of solidarity to issues of human rights, the defect in the Catholic analysis is that solidarity has an organic premise that can deny the reality of social conflict. As Hollenbach suggests: "An acceptance of a social model which envisions conflict and community as dynamically interrelated would be a major source for the renewal of the Roman Catholic approach to the implementation of human rights."[81]

Interestingly, church council documents, papal encyclicals and other writings, and documents from official church offices have never cited references other than from the tradition: scripture, the church fathers, and church documents (encyclicals, council documents, etc.). Therefore, it is difficult to identify concepts from social philosophy or social data that may have influenced the teaching or doctrine.

For example, John Paul II's understanding of solidarity takes a turn from the corporatist approach to one that is more oriented to spirituality and moral philosophy, particularly in the elevation of solidarity as a virtue. In *Sollicitudo Rei Socialis* he defines solidarity thus:

It is above all a question of interdependence, sensed as a system determining relationships in the contemporary world, in its economic, cultural, political and religious elements, and accepted as a moral category. When interdependence becomes recognized in this way the correlative response as a moral and social attitude, as a "virtue," is solidarity. This then is not a feeling of vague compassion or shallow distress at the misfortunes of so many people, both near and far. On the contrary, it is a firm and persevering determination to commit oneself to the common good; that is to say to the good of all and each individual, because we are all really responsible for all. This determination is based on the solid conviction that what is hindering full development is that desire for profit and that thirst for power already mentioned. These attitudes and "structures of sin" are openly conquered—by a diametrically opposed attitude: a commitment to one's neighbor with the readiness, in the Gospel sense, to "lose oneself" for the sake of the other instead of exploiting him, and "to serve" him instead of oppressing him for one's own advantage (cf. Mt. 10:40–42; Mk. 10:42–44; Luke 22:25–27).[82]

While not a sociologist, John Paul II comes close to a sociological understanding in this early interpretation, particularly in developing solidarity as a organizing principle with at least three constitutive parts: (1) interdependence, (2) human dignity, equality, and mutuality, and (3) the common good. He views society as developing. But societal development is hindered by "structures of sin" that generate exaggerated profit and power and must be corrected through the moral virtue of solidarity. For John Paul II, solidarity is integrally tied to a Catholic understanding of "salvation history" that sees human nature as marked by the common sin of Adam and Eve, a sin that is at once personal and communal. Unlike Durkheim and other sociologists, who take the positivist view of morality as theologically neutral—meaning that society becomes better via legal and empirical social change through its citizens—the Catholic approach assumes that solidarity will always be imperfect until the final solidarity of the reign of God.[83] However, while sin is always present, Catholics work with each other and others of good will to promote solidarity in the world, particularly by building, as John Paul II writes in *Centesimus Annus,* "real communities of persons that strengthen the social fabric, preventing society from becoming an anonymous and impersonal mass."[84]

For John Paul II, sin has social consequences reflected in "alienated" social structures:

The concept of alienation needs to be led back to the Christian vision of reality, by recognizing in alienation a reversal of means and ends. When man does not recognize in himself and in others the value and grandeur of the human person, he effectively deprives himself of the possibility of benefiting from his humanity and of entering into that relationship of solidarity and communion with others for which God created him. Indeed it is through the free gift of self that man truly finds himself. The human person's essential "capacity for transcendence" makes this gift possible. Man cannot give himself to a purely human plan for reality, to an abstract ideal or to a false utopia. As a person he can give to himself to another person or to other persons, and ultimately to God, who is the author of his being and who alone can fully accept his gift. A man is alienated if he refuses to transcend himself and to live the experience of self-giving and the formation of an authentic human community oriented towards his final destiny, which is God. A society is alienated if its forms of social organization, production and consumption make it more difficult to offer this gift of self and to establish this solidarity between people.[85]

Solidarity for John Paul II is constructed first through the virtuous person who transcends his or her sinful nature to have an "experience of self-giving" to others, to build a community where there has been societal alienation—effects of the structures of sin on social organization, production, and consumption.

Prior to becoming archbishop of Krakow, Poland, John Paul II had been trained in the philosophy of Martin Heidegger and had taught philosophy for many years at the University of Lublin. He was a noted philosopher of "Christian personalism," a philosophy that emphasizes existential dilemmas and the human capacity to transcend them. The Christian is called to enter existential reality and look for possibilities to be fully human through self-donation, to find hope, to risk for the other. This philosophical approach, which is evident in the many encyclicals of John Paul II, accounts for his development of solidarity as a virtue, the recognition of the human capacity to act for others in the face of the deepest alienation (sin).[86] This corresponds to Thomas Aquinas's understanding of the naturalness of the virtues in giving the conscience its fundamental orientation toward goodness. As U.S. theologian Marie Vianney Bilgrien notes in her study of solidarity: "Virtues are the skills which strengthen us to decide how to act in a manner which is good for our very being. They must be learned and practiced if they are to be effective, especially in those situations which are new and difficult."[87]

This view of solidarity as a virtue is reflected in the summary of the teaching on solidarity in the *Catechism of the Catholic Church*. Article 1948 reads: "Solidarity is an eminently Christian virtue. It practices the sharing of spiritual goods even more than material ones."[88] This spiritualizing tendency in the *Catechism* flows from the sense of solidarity as "friendship" or "social charity" as a "direct demand of human and Christian brotherhood."[89] Article 1940 fleshes out how the virtue of solidarity is practiced: "Solidarity is manifested in the first place by the distribution of goods and remuneration for work. It also presupposes the effort for a more just social order where tensions are better able to be reduced and conflicts more readily settled by negotiation."[90] This article expresses the close connection between solidarity and the principles of subsidiarity, the social order as a corporatist occupational group system of mediating structures between the person and the state, the dignity of work, workers' rights to organize, human dignity, and the common good.

Thus the principle of solidarity, as expressed in the *Catechism of the Catholic Church* and the encyclicals of John Paul II, has become—along with a general concept of a "culture of life" and its corollary "culture of death"—a key organizing principle for the social justice doctrine. Article 1941 of the *Catechism* expresses this summation: "Socio-economic problems can be resolved only with the help of all the forms of solidarity: solidarity of the poor among themselves, between the rich and the poor, of workers among themselves, between employers and employees in business, solidarity among nations and peoples. International solidarity is a requirement of the moral order; world peace depends in part upon this."[91] The Christian, then, is called to spiritual friendship with her or his neighbor, and this friendship requires a material dimension (just wages and just distribution of goods) and just social relations for the sake of a peaceful local, national, and international moral order.

This sentiment of the *Catechism* is more fully doctrinally articulated in article 193 of the *Compendium of the Social Doctrine of the Church,* as it emphasizes moral norms and philosophical attributes of solidarity:

> *Solidarity must be seen above all in its value as a moral virtue that determines the order of institutions.* On the basis of this principle the "structures of sin" that dominate relationships between individuals and peoples must be overcome. They must be purified and transformed into structures of solidarity through the creation or appropriate modification of laws, market regulations, and juridical systems.
>
> *Solidarity is also an authentic moral virtue,* not a feeling of vague compassion or shallow distress at the misfortunes of so many people, both near and far. On the contrary, it is a *firm and persevering determination* to commit oneself to the *common good.* That is to say to the good of all

and of each individual, because we are *all* really responsible *for all*. Solidarity rises to the rank of fundamental *social virtue* since it places itself in the sphere of justice.

In summary, the Catholic discourse related to the principle of solidarity as a virtue is quite distinct from a sociological understanding that focuses on the organization of society. However, there is an implicit sense of social organization within the traditional Catholic corporatist (body of Christ) understanding of society, particularly as related to a conservative subsidiarity, i.e., a society organized along occupational and sectoral lines with a distribution of rights and obligations pertinent to the group or sector. In these terms, a just society is one in which there are fair wages, distribution of goods, and social relations but where political and economic power itself may not be necessarily equally distributed. Thus, in a just Catholic society the liberal standards of individual equality and equality of opportunity may not be required for social justice. An "inequality by design" can result in this type of society, for while the Catholic view affirms that the "equality of men concerns their dignity as persons and the rights that flow from it,"[92] it asserts that "talents are not distributed equally."[93] This theological and philosophically essentialist understanding of equality and inequality can be remedied only by the virtue of solidarity, which allows the Christian to see that "differences encourage and often oblige persons to practice generosity, kindness, and sharing of goods; they foster the mutual enrichment of cultures."[94]

For Catholics, the virtue of solidarity is to be integrated into a spiritual and social life of association and participation in religious and civic social justice organizations, particularly Catholic trade unions, civil associations, and political parties. This understanding of solidarity was at the heart of the history of Catholic Action organizations inspired by the 1920s French Jocist movement, which flourished in Europe and Latin America up through Vatican II.[95] The virtue of solidarity with its stress on personal relationships (friendship and social charity) can serve as an antidote to the assumption that only legal and institutional mechanisms can provide social justice.

However, as the Church recognized at Vatican II, modern democratic life fosters expectations of equality of "sex, race, color, social conditions, language, [and] religion."[96] Add to this the more contemporary demand for equality among those of differing sexual orientations. In such a context, the Catholic understanding of solidarity presents church members with the problem of how to imagine and implement a corporatist approach to social organization that might be inconsistent with democratic expectations and structures. The traditional liberal principles of universal equality of individuals, equality of opportunity, freedom, and human and civil rights have acquired normative status in almost all democratic societies—yet the Church has had a historically contentious relationship with these principles and has not been reconciled to them.

Furthermore, the corporatist model employed by the Church relies on a natural law logic that understands the "natural family" to be the first cell of society. The primary solidarity, then, inheres in male and female conjugal relationships. Article 246 of the *Compendium* states: "The social subjectivity of the family, both as a single unit and associated in a group, is expressed as well in the demonstrations of solidarity and sharing not only among families themselves but also in the various forms of participation in social and political life." Thus it is not surprising that as the pontificate of John Paul II ended and that of Benedict XVI began, the Church moved from the organizing and analytical attributes of solidarity—particularly its historic relationship to workers' rights—to a solidarity of virtues, moral norms, and philosophical principles focusing on family and the related issues of family planning, stem cell research, in vitro fertilization, homosexual rights, etc. This is highlighted in the way article 582 of the *Compendium* connects John Paul II's "culture of life" to solidarity: "Only a humanity in which there reigns the 'civilization of love' will be able to enjoy authentic and lasting peace. In this regard the Magisterium highly recommends solidarity because it is capable of guaranteeing the common good and fostering integral human development: love 'makes one see neighbor as another self.'"

In contrast to this Catholic approach to solidarity, the context in which liberationist solidarity emerged in the 1960s paralleled the context of the earlier Catholic approach, with the Catholic Church caught between opposing forces of international capitalism and socialism. The new context, however, was not Europe but the Third World countries of Latin America, Asia, and Africa. In this period, especially during the rise of the U.S. antiwar movement of the late 1960s, solidarity became an organizing principle for various movements and groups seeking to support the causes of oppressed peoples. Liberationist solidarity was heralded as a "middle way" through the cold war and its players, First World capitalists and Second World socialists and communists.

The theology of liberation in Latin America had its beginnings in the 1968 meeting of Latin American bishops in Medellín, Colombia.[97]

There the Latin American bishops provided a stunning critique of the theology of mission and development that had been guiding the Latin American Catholic Church. According to Mexican philosopher Enrique Dussel, the idea of development was rooted in the functionalist ideology that such programs as the U.S. Alliance for Progress were bringing to Latin America, a kind of "state's grace" for the development model that presumed a North American goal of capitalist and democratic outcomes. At Medellín the bishops spoke in the language of development ("human promotion," "development," "liberation," etc.), but the theologians present, such as Juan Luis Segundo, José Comblin, and François Houtart, brought a new type of social analysis to add to the theological discussion of Latin American realities. All these theologians were strongly influenced by the social theology of the Catholic Action movement, which emerged out of Belgium and France and had predated Vatican II by some thirty years. Almost all the bishops at this meeting had recently been delegates to the Second Vatican Council (1962–65) and were aware of the newest theological and ecclesiological developments. While the Latin American theological scene was deeply steeped in European models, these theologians and bishops had developed their own centers, particularly in Santiago, Chile, Cuernavaca, Mexico, and Quito, Ecuador, which had been training a new generation of pastoral workers in both theology and the social sciences.

Medellín became a symbol of a new thrust to address the "Latin American challenge." Following the bishops' meeting, theologians began to set a new agenda to challenge the now discredited theology of development. As these dialogues grew, the term *theology of liberation* became the emblem of the mixture of theology, social science, and politics that generated liberation movements around the world. In 1971 the Peruvian theologian Gustavo Gutiérrez published the pivotal work *Teología de la liberación,* which established a vocabulary for liberation theology. This theology was to appropriate socialist ideals of society and economy (a withering away of class conflict and the division of labor) so that socialism would "generate new values which [would] make possible the emergence of a society of greater solidarity and brotherhood in which the worker assumes with dignity the role which is his."[98] Gutiérrez moved the traditional Catholic value of solidarity to the side of socialism, and there it has stayed as a "major symbol in liberation theology."[99]

While the liberationist approach to solidarity shifted from the Catholic middle way to an expressed affiliation with socialism, it held on to what can be termed the Catholic approach's ontology of the unity of the human race. The liberationist approach embraces solidarity within an ontological universalism based on ideal "concrete and historical forms"[100] culminating in a new heaven and new earth. Without such an eschatological solidarity, liberation theology and liberationist ethics would end up as strictly empiricist movements. Having a transcendent and ontological grounding, solidarity in the liberationist approach can account for the primordial needs of human relationships and the more organic complexity of social structures.[101]

Further, while liberationist solidarity is firmly on the side of socialism, it is not always Marxist. Rather, "this alternative vision of the world provides deeper grounds for commitment to the process of liberation than, for example, a Marxist view of reality, in its idea of a solidarity with other human beings that is also a union with God."[102]

As liberation theology developed, the idea of solidarity took on greater significance, particularly through the writing of the Salvadoran Jesuit Jon Sobrino. For Sobrino solidarity means "communion," a "bearing one another."[103] Writing from the Salvadoran perspective of a civil war that became ensnarled in cold war maneuvering, as well as from the trauma of having his Jesuit brothers and female coworkers murdered by the Salvadoran military in 1989, Sobrino sees solidarity as an existential spiritual and political philosophy that "begins at the bottom of history, in the cross of the peoples. That is the source of the historical power that unleashes radical solidarity."[104] He elucidates a virtue sense of solidarity as well as giving solidarity an analytical framework:

> Solidarity then means putting together two fundamental Christian dimensions: the willingness to give, transformative praxis in technical terms; and the willingness to receive, grace. That is how true and Christian ecclesial communion is created. This communion continually widens to become truly ecumenical communion, with other churches, and truly human communion with all men and women of good will. This is not all relativizing, but simply a way of honoring those who generated the movement of solidarity: the crucified peoples.[105]

Suffering, oppression, exclusion, and alienation is for liberationist solidarity the common experiential ground of humanity. Liberation, freedom, inclusion, healing, and reconciliation are transcendental referents for a common ontology of what it means to be human. For Segundo, as a Christian liberationist, there is particularity in local churches and base ecclesial communities. As these churches and communities work together in a struggle for liberation, the universal sense of humanity evolves. This universalism is a "wide solidarity" that can encompass other particularities such as feminist and gay solidarity, as well as the solidarity found in political and social movements. The mark of this wide solidarity is "co-responsibility." While Sobrino writes within the context of the Church, it appears that his sense of solidarity is "catholic": "Catholicity understood as co-responsibility is not an obstacle to the universality of the church, but rather helps to build it up. If this co-responsibility penetrates to the level of faith, the catholicity of the church is simply the building up of the faith of the church in history, a faith made up of pluriform and different faiths."[106]

Sobrino's distinctive contribution to our understanding of liberationist solidarity is the way solidarity seems to work as a mediating space to move personal need to public good and vice versa. Solidarity in this sense is similar to Parson's diffuse solidarity. What distinguishes liberationist solidarity from both the Catholic and sociological approaches is its faith in human liberation per se and its ontology of common humanity.

As Canadian feminist theologian Patricia McAuliffe notes, "There is a close connection between the epistemological priority of ethics to religion and theology and its causal priority."[107] Within the history of solidarity, this is a paradigm shift that "is very connected with the more general shift from an ahistorical to a historical perspective because both centrally involve our fundamental relatedness."[108] McAuliffe stresses:

> An ethic of social solidarity, an ethic that stresses our social conditionedness and connectedness, acknowledges limitations in our personal knowledge, power, freedom, and responsibility not recognized by the tradition. But it also gives ethics a broader scope. Conditions which were thought to be "natural" or "divinely ordained" and outside the sphere of our moral concern are now recognized as humanly caused, revisable, and at the center of moral concern. But this is to extend our knowledge, free our freedom, exercise our power to liberate, and take responsibility for our context. It is to recreate our conditions for existence, that is, in part, to recreate our humanity.[109]

Because of this paradigm shift, it is possible for liberation theology and liberationist solidarity to become more than an ecclesial theology and ethic. According to U.S. philosopher John Pottage, the liberationist approach to ethics may provide a "reconvergence of social values and social science." He sees liberation theology as a philosophical movement that "attempts to solve the problem of how the modern era can properly overcome its most debilitating characteristic: the dichotomy between *facts* and *values*."[110] This is the problematic that Durkheim wrestled with in his initial framing of social solidarity. But the history of social science and ethics shows that many theorists have not overcome the obstacle inherent in a "value-free" epistemology, i.e., the assumption that somehow social mores can be studied freed from the values that are implicit in social science. Liberationist solidarity allows faith to be determinate. But this faith is not theologically determined; it is historically determined by reading "the signs of the times" and their realities.[111] This kind of faith is deeply realistic, since it identifies itself with victims of oppression; it does not follow liberal development theory or Enlightenment evolutionism in an expectation of progressively better societies.[112] Rather, liberationist solidarity emphasizes that people come together in the midst of struggle.

Liberationist solidarity overcomes the middle way of the Catholic corporatist approach through its new conceptualization of faith and human freedom, a wider approach that can accommodate all of humanity and not just those of Roman Catholic faith. It attempts to overcome the modern dilemma of the separation of fact and value by locating both in a hermeneutical circle of praxis and hermeneutics, a method that integrates scripture, social analysis, political action, and critical reflection.[113] For those in the Third World, this became a radical procedure in the struggle for social and political change.

Liberationist solidarity encounters problems in its analytical framework. It can be seen as an ideological program tied to a political apparatus, as in Nicaragua under the Sandinistas. Does it have the capacity to continue to be self-critical (as demanded in the process of the hermeneutical circle) when those in solidarity assume political, economic, and social power? Based on the work of Segundo, it would seem that liberationist solidarity must always exert the virtue of humility, a virtue not resonant with the domains of power. So how is this to be institutionalized? Herein lies the primary weakness of the liberationist approach: its suspicion of institutions, since institutions carry out institutionalized violence, repression, and oppression.[114] While liberation theology recognizes the role of social space in permitting solidarity, a positive theory of institutional life would help liberationist solidarity overcome its inherent suspicion of institutions.[115]

The use of solidarity as a Catholic theological principle in either the Catholic corporatist or liberationist approach can be understood by

Catholic social actors in modern democracies only in the framework of its many understandings, interpretations, and usages. This is to say that a high-discourse concept such as solidarity (or for that matter, human rights, liberation, or freedom) cannot be isolated as a theological principle apart from the ways Catholics actually use it in the interplay of public discourse, particularly in pluralist societies such as the United States and Mexico.[116] Like many concepts with multiple interpretations and definitions, *solidarity* can be fastened to a distinctive theological definition, but as can be seen above, the term has interplay with various approaches and social movements. The suggestion of U.S. theologian David Tracy is thus appropriate for this study: "The theologian should in principle use a correlation model for relating sociological and theological understandings of the reality of the church in the same way one uses a correlation model for the more familiar relationships between philosophy and theology."[117]

Here, then, I will analyze how U.S. and Mexican Catholics engage with the principle of solidarity in different political cultures and in relationship to the evolving understanding of solidarity as a doctrine. Thus, I am comparing Catholics who are engaging with a particular doctrine of the Church within different national political cultures. My research will show that national political culture makes a different in the reception, understanding, articulation, and exercise of a common doctrine of the Roman Catholic Church.

The Catholic Social Imagination as a Basis for Social Action

While I have noted that John Paul II did not view Catholic social doctrine as an ideology, from the standpoint of the social sciences it serves as an ideology since it functions as part of the Church's comprehensive conceptual and ideational program for social justice.[118] And given that doctrine in the Catholic Church is a primary requirement for "being Catholic," it is not optional teaching; it is a functional ideological requirement for membership, even if not all Catholics are cognizant of the doctrine or practitioners of it. Catholic social justice doctrine has historically provided a piecemeal framework, a sort of menu, for understanding and practicing social justice. Members of the Church are required to base their social action on church teaching, which means they must engage with the doctrine and develop a Catholic social imagination, though it may be only rudimentary. Such "Catholicity" may be expressed not only in language but also in rituals, art, music, drama, architecture, clothing, and other manners of conveying a Catholic imagination to the larger world.[119]

The case studies of the U.S. and Mexican churches give rise to a basic question: what does the social doctrine produce? The Church's teaching about social justice is supposed to motivate Catholics to take action in their local communities, their countries, and the world. Presumably this requires a member's personal engagement with the doctrine in at least three contexts: the personal, the local parish and community, and the larger church and society. In my fieldwork in both countries, I found that ideas often have a significant role in shaping people's social commitments. Active Catholics are constantly learning—from homilies, parish bulletins, diocesan newspapers, classes, parish meetings, group activities, and even gossip—what the Church teaches about sacraments, the Bible, piety, family life, and social issues. Thus other questions arose in the course of my research: What is the local church really conveying about social justice teaching? How is it conveyed? What motivates Catholics to become socially engaged? How do they get socially engaged? What do they accomplish? What "social goods" are generated by the social doctrine?

The Church can be analyzed as a "religious sphere" that operates independently of other spheres in Catholics' lives, such as the economy, the state, public institutions, and civil society associations. To understand how the religious sphere functions in relation to other spheres, I follow the theoretical emphasis of Max Weber, who defined value spheres as orientations and structures. In this light, religion plays a particular role in the internalization of religious ethics, in this case social justice doctrine, and the externalization of religious ethics in action in a secular, pluralistic world.[120]

To understand Catholic social justice doctrine as a value sphere, it helps to draw on what sociologists refer to as "the social construction of religion." This method distinguishes between the internalization processes of religious ideas and values among church members and the externalization processes that move religious ideas and values into other value spheres such as the economy, the state, and civil society.[121]

Further, in the next chapters I will analyze interpretations of the teaching by theologians, national bishops' conferences, and Catholic associations; programs developed at various levels to teach, implement, and develop the doctrine; the internal structure of the Church and opportunities for social learning and practices within church government and organizational life; liturgical and ritual life; and the motivations, understandings, and commitments of Catholic laity, priests, religious, and bishops themselves. All these dimensions make up the religious sphere in which Catholics live and act. Clearly, Catholics have a large and complex space in which to develop their social imagination.

The Cultural Construction of the Catholic Social Imagination

During the Jubilee Year of 2000, the city of Rome became a crossroads of cultures, professions, interest groups, lay organizations, and religious institutions as Catholics came on pilgrimage to the Eternal City. The Vatican had prepared a detailed calendar of events for all these groups, particularly for summer events involving more than a million young people from throughout the world.[122] Seen as a whole, the Jubilee Year in Rome presented the image of solidarity that the Church wanted the world to see: the body of Christ made up of many functions yet all united in "the "mind of Christ" through the papacy.

Only two years after this major display of solidarity, the clergy sexual abuse scandal erupted in the United States, Ireland, Canada, Australia, Germany, and other countries. Now the Catholic Church faced a dilemma: how could the Church be a leader of social justice, building social solidarity in a pluralistic, complex global society, if the Church itself must come under the rule of law? Further, in each national context the Catholic Church faces other sorts of contestation as it attempts to communicate and implement its doctrine, particularly as national social aspirations come into play.

Here I present a sociological model of the Catholic social imagination as an ideal type. I will use this ideal-typic model to examine how the U.S. and Mexican Catholic churches develop the Catholic social imagination within the social opportunity structures that each inhabits. We will see how international doctrine becomes contextualized, so that we can speak of a "U.S. Catholic social imagination" and a "Mexican Catholic social imagination."

THE SOCIOLOGICAL IMAGINATION AND
CATHOLIC SOCIAL JUSTICE DOCTRINE

As noted in chapter 1, I have borrowed ideas of the imagination and social justice from Andrew Greeley and David Tracy. In sociology, the idea of "sociological imagination" was developed by C. Wright Mills in *The Sociological Imagination*.[123] In this classical analysis of the sociological mission, he notes that social issues come to light through the woes of people—really the experience of personal injustice that becomes "social" once the individual understands private woes as public issues. Sociologists are always researching and analyzing social injustices, using inductive methodologies that uncover pieces of the puzzles of public issues involving poverty, crime, family, gender, race, and so on. Even sophisticated quantitative sociological studies require collecting data on a specific public issue and aggregate and disaggregate data describing and analyzing public issues. The "findings" of sociologists' research result from the analysis of empirical evidence collected to shed light on questions arising from public issues—the woes of human experiences. Mills says in regard to sociological work, "In brief, I believe that what may be called classical social analysis is a definable and usable set of traditions; that its essential feature is the concern with historical social structures; and that its problems are of direct relevance to urgent public issues and insistent human troubles."

When sociologists develop theories, then, they are providing imaginative possibilities for understanding findings culled from empirical evidence. These imaginative possibilities—social theories—help social actors think through their situations and provide possible solutions to injustices. Social theory has a vision, but it is not deductive in nature: the theoretical possibilities are generated by data organized into thought experiments, what sociologists often call ideal types.[124]

Thus I develop the ideal-typic theoretical concept of "Catholic social imagination" to explore Catholics' distinctive ways of understanding, developing, organizing, and analyzing public issues of social injustice based on their social doctrine. The Catholic sense of social injustice is as old as the Jewish prophetic tradition of the "cry of the poor," articulated and practiced by Jesus in his Sermon on the Mount, his miracles, and his social relations with women, the poor, the sick, and the marginalized, and continued in the long history of the Church's charitable works. This tradition most certainly provides an ideational imagination of social justice—a vision that acts deductively as a set of principles that guide Catholics. My study recognizes the power of this religious and ethical imagination that comes "from above." But since this is a sociological and not a theological study, I necessarily orient my analysis toward the lived experiences of social actors who develop their issues "from below," i.e., from their inductive sense of experiences of social injustice that may or may not connect with the "from above" Catholic imagination. Yet because the social actors in this study are motivated by the doctrine of the Church, I must use an analytical model that handles both the deductive side of doctrine and the inductive side of lived experience. My model of the Catholic social imagination—is highly dynamic as it attempts to handle both sides of a Catholic's public life.

DEVELOPING A SOCIOLOGICAL MODEL OF THE CATHOLIC SOCIAL IMAGINATION

The Catholic social imagination is bounded by the various principles of the Church's social doctrine and the ways the doctrinal elements can be enacted in social space. I use the idea of cultural space as a dynamic terrain of imaginative possibilities, what Pierre Bourdieu refers to as "habitus":

> the durable, transposable dispositions, structured structures predisposed to function as structuring structures, that is, principles which generate and organize practices and representations that can be objectively adapted to their outcomes without presupposing a conscious aiming at ends or an express mastery of the operations necessary in order to attain them. Objectively "regulated" and "regular" without being in any way the product of the organizing action of a conductor.[125]

Understood in this way, the international social doctrine has a limited capacity defined not only by the doctrine itself as a set of ideas or ideology of the institutional Church but also the set of Catholic normative and structural "things"—organizational structures of parish and diocese, official and para- liturgical rites, customs, habits, language, gestures, and so on—that constitute the "Catholicity" of the social doctrine's imaginative possibilities.[126]

From an analytical perspective, the habitus and Catholicity of social doctrine moves in a normative continuum between an "integral"[127] sense of Catholic Church-oriented things—particularly its social doctrine, organizational life, rites, devotions, language—related to social justice and a "structural" sense of public things related to the institutionalization of social justice. With the term *integral* I am trying to convey that Catholics have the capacity to incorporate scripture, principles, liturgy, prayer, rituals, works of mercy, and the like into a Catholic life complete unto itself, irrespective of public life. However, the social doctrine recognizes unjust structural realities and calls Catholics to be involved in social change, and this necessarily pulls the Catholic away from an all-inclusive church life and into involvement in structural and institutional public life. Based on the ideal-typic formulation, we will see that this pull can be dynamic and not necessarily contradictory.

Ann Swidler's "Culture in Action" model with its threefold strategic character of cultural construction has also influenced me: (1) the "image of culture" expressed as a "tool kit" of "symbols, stories, rituals, and world-views," (2) "strategies of action," and (3) "cultural components that are used to construct strategies of action."[128] Thus, in addition to a normative analysis, the Church's social justice doctrine can be analyzed on a culturally strategic construction continuum of church and world. Again, in a commonsense way Catholic social justice actors can be identified by their strategic standpoints both within and without the Church. A diversity of standpoints is possible within the range of bounded possibilities of the Catholic social imagination. Social actors moving away from a church-oriented strategy and into toward a world orientation help us see where and what the boundaries of the Catholic social justice imagination are.

This study explores two dynamic continuums of the Catholic social justice imagination: (1) a *church and world continuum,* expressing where social justice is enacted—(its more strategic sense), and (2) an *integral and structural continuum,* expressing the kind or type of social justice to be realized—(its more normative sense). The Catholic social justice imagination, because it seeks the creation of social justice through structures and institutions in the world, has both strategic and normative dimensions that work together positively or negatively. Note that a continuum need not have an adversarial sense between two opposing tendencies but that the tendencies may simply reflect the tensions inherent in a complex cultural space. Figure 1 shows these orientations of the doctrine on intersecting axes.

Earlier in this chapter, I developed a functional typology of the principles of Catholic social doctrine. These six functional types—organizing principle, philosophical principle, moral norm, virtue, social role, and analytical framework (see p. 36)—can now be located according to their logical orientation in the cultural construction of the Catholic social imagination. The *strategic axis* encompasses organizing principles, philosophical frameworks, and social roles. At one end of it, the church orientation focuses on the institutional church's structures, doctrines, liturgy, etc., while at the other end, the world orientation focuses on contexts and situations outside the Church, such as public culture, politics, economics, the media, and the social sciences. The *normative axis*

Church

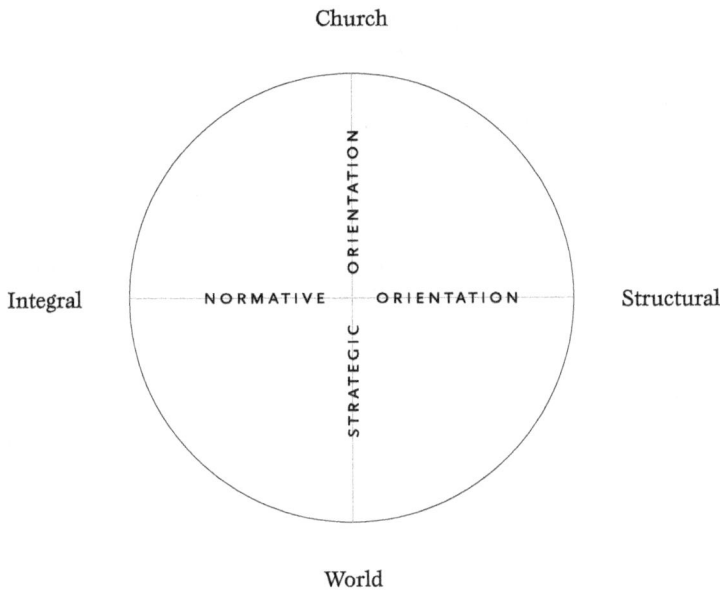

Integral — NORMATIVE — ORIENTATION — Structural

ORIENTATION

STRATEGIC

World

Figure 1. Functional orientations of the Catholic social imagination

has virtues, moral norms, and organizing principles within the integral orientation, which stresses charitable programs either within or without the institutional church; spiritual growth practices such as prayer and meditation; maintenance of ethnic and cultural identities; and ritually oriented activities. At the structural orientation end of this continuum we find analytical frameworks and organizing principles, since this orientation stresses institutions, structures, and social and behavioral sciences involved in their analysis).

My theoretical model thus organizes the church-world and integral-structural continuums as interconnecting orientations that are steered by opportunities and constraints emerging from their intersection. For example, the integral orientation can be opened or constrained by either the church or the world orientation—or by a tension between the two. In its ideal-typic sense, the Catholic social imagination has all four orientations, mediated in a centric direction as figure 1 shows, thus illustrating its dynamic nature.

My ethnographic studies show that social issues such as women's reproductive rights and gay rights pull the Catholic social activist away from the centrist position that the official Catholic social imagination requires. A structural-world orientation is often compelling in response to these issues. Conversely, social activists wishing to promote structural change such as a constitutional amendment to ban abortion but not wanting to contest the Church's authority are pulled toward a church-structural orientation. In my case studies I found that activists wish to resolve social injustices through various public institutions, not merely within the confines of the integral-church orientation that officials of the Church routinely emphasize. When Catholic activists leave the Church's cultural space to seek social justice, they do so because they have been unable to resolve social justice issues within the bounds of the centrist Catholic social imagination.

Solidarity, more than any of the other Catholic social justice principles, can be studied as an organizing principle of social opportunity, as well as an analytical framework incorporating concepts from social movement theory such as framing, resource mobilization, and transnational network advocacy.[129] Chapters 3 and 4 assess how the principles of social justice—particularly solidarity—function as key elements of the Catholic social imagination and orient it in several dimensions. We will look at how the Church understands solidarity as an important social justice principle—even though it is not of the "first order" natural law–based principles—and how theologians in the United States and Mexico understand solidarity in relation to other understandings of solidarity. I also want to analyze the principles as a second-level discourse, an example of how the ideas of theologians help form the normative orientation of Catholic social activists and move them to effect social justice along the integral-structural continuum. Further, we will consider how the principle of solidarity is "structured" in terms of national church programs sponsored by the U.S. and Mexican bishops' conferences.

We will explore further what social principles the Church brings to the table and how it steers these principles in a pluralistic social-civil space. This will illustrate the enactment of social justice within the church-world continuum. I will also analyze the constraints and opportunities the institutional Church faces in steering social principles toward the actual delivery of social justice goods in particular U.S. and Mexican contexts. All these points of analysis will serve to flesh out my theoretical model of the strategic and normative dynamics of the Catholic social imagination.

PART TWO

One Church, One Border, Two Justices

3 ✣ The U.S. Case: Pragmatic and Practice Oriented

The two U.S. Jubilee Year events, Jubilee Justice in July 1999 and Encuentro 2000 in July 2000, displayed the multicultural and dynamic dimensions of the post–Vatican II American Church. More than two thousand men and women of all races and nationalities gathered at UCLA's Pauley Pavilion and worshiped together as a cultural mélange of jazzy liturgical music, brilliant Afro-inspired vestments, Spanish and English, and informal communication between the official celebrants and the congregation.

In many ways these events contrasted to major Catholic events that I experienced as a child growing up in 1950s Los Angeles—most notably the annual "Mary's Hour" at the Los Angeles Coliseum. More than 100,000 people would gather each May, Mary's month, to recite the rosary and sing traditional hymns in Latin and English. Mary's Hour was vast and formal: all the priests of the archdiocese in cassock and surplice, a living rosary with beads represented by seminarians in clerical garb, and the honor guards of Knights of Columbus in their medieval knights' gear.

Such grandeur was replicated all over the United States in Marian celebrations, eucharistic congresses, and Corpus Christi processions through the late 1960s. But after Vatican II, the U.S. church struggled to redefine what had once been a secure and confident identity—albeit one set apart from the American mainstream. The process of redefining the U.S. church's identity involved many factors: the move to English in the liturgy, other liturgical and architectural innovations, the resignation of priests and nuns from their religious vocations, the disillusionment of many laypeople with church authority after the release of Pope Paul VI's encyclical on birth control (*Humanae Vitae*), ethnic and racial groups' demands for their own liturgies and organizations, and the feminist movement within the Church.[1] The Vietnam War and the American cultural revolution would also greatly affect the Church's identity.[2]

The year 2000 at Pauley Pavilion was not 1958 at the Coliseum. A radical shift in what it meant to be a U.S. Catholic had taken place, particularly in the social factors identifying American Catholicism: race, ethnicity, income, class, education. The national events of the Jubilee Year, at the very least, provided snapshots of the issues underlying these social factors, through the actors seeking to implement the social justice principles of their faith.

At both Jubilee Justice and Encuentro 2000, I met the various actors and groups of this study: social justice officials from Vatican congregations, bishops involved in social justice national policy, professional staff of the Catholic Campaign for Human Development (CCHD), social justice theologians, officials from the social justice ministries of the Diocese of Oakland in California, national staff of the Pacific Institute for Community Organizing (PICO), and community organizers from faith-based organizations such as the Oakland Community Organizations (OCO). All these groups seemed quite interconnected in the social justice mission of the U.S. Catholic Church—in commitment, passion, struggle, hopes, and even disillusionment. Each of the groups had a stake, at least a professional one, in that mission. Thus these events provided a historic glimpse of the long development of the U.S. Catholic social imagination and what makes it distinctive in the worldwide church.

The only group missing from the Los Angeles events was the grassroots, the people of neighborhoods and parishes. I found myself reflecting on the four years of field study in the San Antonio district of Oakland: how do the people I met there fit into this national picture and the U.S. Catholic social imagination?

In this chapter I will use the analytical model of the Catholic social imagination developed in chapter 2 to examine and analyze how the various groups focused on the social justice mission of the Church function in a national context and form the basis for a U.S. Catholic social justice milieu, particularly at the grassroots level where social justice is experienced. In particular I will highlight how their use of the community-organizing model initiated by Saul Alinsky has transformed it into a distinctive faith-based community-organizing model consonant with key principles of Catholic social teaching. Once a pre–Vatican II countercultural institution facilitating ethnic and immigrant socialization into U.S. life, the U.S. Catholic Church as an institution now works to facilitate long-term social justice in public life. The post–Vatican II U.S. Catholic Church has created a social imagination steeped in many of the principles of the social doctrine, as well as the civic values and principles of U.S. political culture.

The Development of a U.S. Catholic Social Imagination

Historians of the Roman Catholic Church in the United States emphasize three different historical lenses to view the Church's development: the "American," which begins with the foundation of Catholic life in Maryland in 1634; the "Spanish," beginning with the first Catholics in Florida in 1521; and the "Southwest Mission," beginning in 1581 with the founding of missions in New Mexico. For the purposes of this study, since it is a study of the institutional church, what is most important is the foundation of the "American" Catholic perspective, which became part of the larger U.S. historical record. This perspective is marked by a set of distinctive characteristics:

1. a Catholic population that from its beginning has been a *minority religious group* in a country that values religious pluralism[3]

2. a legacy of a semidemocratic religious organization—priests elected their bishops until the mid-1800s; bishops met in plenary councils from 1783 to 1884 to create a national policy and identity; parishes elected vestry members—reflecting an *American congregational model of lay-clergy collaboration*[4]

3. an organizational model—the parish church as a hub for a parochial school, priest rectory, nun's convent, and often a Catholic cemetery—that has provided a distinctively *neighborhood Catholic institutional life for U.S. Catholics*[5]

4. high emphasis on catechetical instruction to create a *religiously educated laity,* taught by nuns, priests, and laypeople both in a Catholic school system (elementary and secondary schools as well as colleges and universities) and in programs for public school children and continuing education for adults, especially through the Baltimore Catechism, which served as a distinctively U.S. Catholic text up through Vatican II[6]

5. a vast array of *Catholic lay and religious organizations* fulfilling social, economic, cultural, and professional needs of a largely immigrant population[7]

6. an *American orientation* to the Catholic Church as part of U.S. civil society that has evolved through the interplay across time of religious organizations, government, politics, and civil society[8]

These factors have contributed a particular socioinstitutional context for U.S. Catholics to pursue charitable and structural social justice aims of the Church, particularly through major institutions such as hospitals, schools, Catholic Charities, religious orders specializing in service to the poor and marginalized, and organizations supporting the rights of workers, racial and ethnic minorities, immigrants, and the poor. This social habitus developed as a parallel Catholic social world because of religious and ethnic discrimination experienced by U.S. Catholics, particularly following the Civil War, up through the 1960 election of John F. Kennedy as president of the United States.[9] This socioinstitutional context has provided most U.S. Catholics, especially those from areas of the country with high concentrations of Catholics, with a very strong Catholic American social ethos (rather than an *American Catholic* ethos).[10]

During the course of my U.S. field research, I was struck by the depth of the Catholic American social ethos in the lives of my informants, particularly among highly educated Catholics who were very involved in the "secular" worlds of education, business, and politics. Catholics who experienced the post–World II (1946), pre–Vatican II (1965) church of the twentieth century witnessed Catholic institutional life at its peak, with booming Catholic schools, hospitals, colleges, seminaries, religious vocations, magazines and periodicals, and lay organizations, all of which constituted a parallel society for U.S. Catholics.[11] Yet while Catholics were building their religious society, they were at the same time becoming more fully incorporated into almost all aspects of the larger U.S. business, social, civic, and political worlds. The 1960 election of Kennedy, the first and only Catholic president, was a symbolic marker of this "Catholic American" integration of U.S. and Catholic experiences.

This historical development of U.S. Catholicism is captured in responses I received to questions regarding the formation of social justice commitments. My U.S. informants became motivated to be involved with social justice ministry for the following reasons: (1) influence of a parent in a practical work of charity or justice motivated by such Judeo-Christian principles of civil rights, racial equality, ending poverty, providing opportunity; (2) influence of activities with the poor, such as immersion experiences, while a student in a Catholic school or as a member of a religious order; and (3) influence of the civil rights, antiwar, feminist, and other liberation movements dominant in the 1960s and 1970s, when the majority of my informants were beginning their adult lives. Without exception they became committed to social justice through a Catholic social world of institutions and activities—through the normative orientation of the Catholic social imagination in the United States.

Yet my informants do not have a particularly Catholic theological discourse regarding their commitments, even though they are motivated by their Catholic intellectual and cultural contexts. Rather, two dominant patterns were evident among them: (1) an American Judeo-Christian discourse of civil rights, equality, opportunity, and ending poverty and discrimination; and (2) a pragmatism and practicality of being involved and "doing the right thing." These two patterns, along with the overall U.S. Catholic socioinstitutional ethos, can be summarized as a pragmatism that orients the U.S. Catholic social imagination toward the structural-world quadrant in figure 1.

American Catholic Social Justice Theology

Jesuit priest David Hollenbach, holder of the Flatley Chair of Theology and professor of Christian social ethics at Boston College, has been highly influential in the formation of a distinctively American social justice theological discourse. Born in 1942, Hollenbach grew up in Villanova, Pennsylvania, in a Catholic middle-class household that participated as a matter of course in the neighborhood parish and Catholic schools. His father was a "dyed-in-the-wool Republican" businessman, a "person of integrity" and "honesty." Of great influence in his formation was his mother, who had a high concern "for the well-being of people." He told me how his mother wrote an article titled "What It Would Be Like to Be Black" for the local newspaper, in response to an incident of racial discrimination at the local public swimming pool in 1962. That was two years before his entrance into the Maryland Province of the Society of Jesus in 1964, after he graduated from college.

As part of his early Jesuit training, Hollenbach worked for a summer program in the inner city of Philadelphia, an immersion experience which he said "changed my political perspective." While studying philosophy at St. Louis University from 1966 through 1968, he became involved in both the civil rights and antiwar movements, and he was energized by the candidacies of Eugene McCarthy and Robert Kennedy for the Democratic presidential nomination for 1968. During this period he began his intellectual formation in social ethics, which he then taught at Georgetown University during his Jesuit "regency" years.[12] In Washington, D.C., he continued his involvement in the antiwar movement, a commitment that resulted in his being jailed three times for civil disobedience. After his ordination to the priesthood in 1971, he continued his education at Yale University, where he specialized in Christian social ethics and studied under James Gustafson, the dean of U.S. Christian social ethicists. His dissertation was on human rights and became the basis for his influential book of 1979, *Claims in Conflict: Retrieving and Renewing the Catholic Human Rights Tradition.*[13] Hollenbach told me he realized "that intellectual work in the promotion of justice" is where he "could make some difference in terms of writing." As well, he said, "a teacher can be influential" in the formation of people working for a just society. Justice is deeply rooted in a spiritual dimension, because "it's tied up with the Good News. . . . Grace sets us free to be just."

Hollenbach's story was typical of the eleven theologians I interviewed in the United States—all published authors on social justice–related theological themes.[14] Their families were first- or second-generation European immigrant, middle-class practicing Catholics who attended Sunday Mass, enrolled their children in local parish schools, held educational achievement in high esteem, but were not strongly religious or devout. Their parents were not social activists per se, but they did set an example for their children by being involved in parish and community charitable causes. In the context of this study, parental social democratic such as equality, ending racial discrimination and poverty, honesty, and civic participation had been very high and had a positive impact on their children. They learned that social justice is "the right thing to do." As these men grew up, their commitment to social justice was generated from immersion experiences of being with the poor while in college or in seminary, being engaged in the civil rights and antiwar movements, and the social teachings of the Church that emerged from Vatican II, particularly from the sense that being Christian requires a commitment to the transformation of society.

These church intellectuals received their professional or doctoral education at leading U.S. graduate schools and have been engaged in critical sociopolitical debates with their secular contemporaries. While these men emerge as "liberal" or "progressive" Catholics, they are deeply committed to being part of the mainstream Church, and this is evidenced by the type of work they do—teaching theology in Catholic universities or seminaries, writing for Catholic theological journals and magazines, consulting for Catholic and civic lay organizations, rendering service to local bishops and the Catholic hierarchy, and even celebrating Mass on Sundays at local parishes.

Hollenbach's life and work as a social justice theologian have been highly influenced by the Jesuit commitment to "faith and justice" that emerged in the international General Congregations of the Jesuits following Vatican II.[15] In the mid-1970s, Father General Pedro Arrupe requested that the U.S. Jesuits undertake a concerted effort to develop the theological foundations of the "faith and justice"—what many Jesuits call "F & J"—policy. To that end, the Woodstock Theological Center based at Georgetown University recruited Jesuits to work in a collaborative effort that produced a 1979 handbook for social justice: *The Faith That Does Justice: Examining the Christian Sources for Social Change.*[16]

Hollenbach contributed two essays to this work: "Modern Catholic Teachings concerning Justice" and "A Prophetic Church and the Catholic Sacramental Imagination." In the first essay he emphasizes that justice always deals with the regulation of relationships. He distinguishes three types of justice: commutative, distributive, and social. For Hollenbach, social justice is a political virtue that involves "the institutionalized patterns of mutual action and interdependence which are necessary to bring about the realization of distributive justice." Distributive justice "specifies the demands of mutuality and interdependence in those relations which determine the opportunity of every person to share or participate in essentially public goods."[17]

The basic concepts of social justice in *The Faith That Does Justice* have become the foundation for U.S. Catholic social teaching, particularly the contribution by biblical scholar John R. Donohue. At the time of my interview, Donohue was professor of biblical studies at the Jesuit School of Theology at Berkeley, now the Raymond E. Brown Distinguished Professor of New Testament Studies at St. Mary's Seminary and University in Baltimore. His essay "Biblical Perspectives on Justice" in *The Faith That Does Justice* provided the term "biblical justice," which has since found its way into the primary discourse of U.S. Catholic social justice activists. Before joining the team of scholars at the Woodstock Center for a four-month sabbatical, Donohue had been a professor of scripture at Vanderbilt University. He did not consider himself a social justice theologian but a biblical scholar, yet while doing his research he experienced a "shifting [of] my own perspective." He realized he could contribute to social justice theology by examining *sedaka* and *mishpat,* Hebrew scriptural words that mean "righteousness" and "right," respectively, and taken together suggest "right relationships" or "fidelity to the demands of a relationship."[18]

The theologians of *The Faith That Does Justice* articulated the following key concepts that have taken hold at the many levels of the U.S. Catholic community, particularly in various catechetical texts and scholarship produced by theologians since the 1970s: common good, social justice, biblical justice, right relationships, concern for the poor, the humanness of Jesus, and the Christian faith as social.[19] In a sense they amplified and contextualized the principles of common good, solidarity, social justice, and option for the poor from the international social justice doctrine. Their major contribution was in the linkage of scripture to social justice principles to generate the principles of biblical justice, right relationships, the humanness of Jesus, and the Christian faith as social. The principles themselves are not new, but the way these scholars approached their task helped to give them currency: high concern for the retrieval of biblical warrants for social justice (biblical justice and right relationships) and an orientation toward integrating social facts with theological investigation (humanness of Jesus and the Christian faith as social) to create a social justice-oriented theological anthropology.[20]

The Social Contribution of the U.S. Catholic Bishops

Many of the scholars from Woodstock group were invited by the U.S. bishops to provide theological contributions for their two major social pastoral letters, the 1983 *The Challenge of Peace: God's Promise and Our Response, a Pastoral Letter on War and Peace* and the 1986 *Economic Justice for All: Catholic Social Teaching and the U.S. Economy.*[21] In my interviews with theologians David Hollenbach, John Donohue, Avery Dulles, and John Langan, it was clear that their theological contribution in *The Faith That Does Justice* became the basis for these social pastoral letters and that the role of theologians—particularly emerging from the Woodstock Theological Center project—in the U.S. Catholic Church was regarded with high esteem among the bishops with whom they worked on these letters.

Jesuit social philosopher John Langan, Rose Kennedy Professor of Christian Ethics at Georgetown University, told me that "consulting has had a pastoral side—which provides for many of these professional theologians a very rewarding way to contribute in a priestly way to the Church." *The Challenge of Peace* and *Economic Justice for All* were written in a fully collaborative manner that became a template for writing pastoral letters in the United States, Canada, Europe, and Latin America: consultation with Catholic laity, input by scholars and theologians, theological debate, drafts of letters critiqued by the bishops, publishing of the letter, and a national educational program to integrate the letter into the life of the Church.[22]

The U.S. social pastoral letters emphasize issues that emerged from the post–Vietnam War era, the arms race of the cold war, and the economic recessions and problems of the late 1970s and early 1980s. In that sense the letters are reaction oriented, much like the international teaching itself. Yet the bishops and their collaborators provided a new process for listening to Americans, Catholic and non-Catholic alike. While drawing on the traditional trove of Catholic social teaching from the early church through modern encyclicals and the documents of Vatican II, the letters are marked by an American tone expressing what the late "labor priest" and syndicated columnist Monsignor George Higgins (1914–2002) told me was the "pastoral sense" of the U.S. bishops. The bishops are often "ahead of" U.S. Catholics in terms of social issues, particularly regarding the economy, rights of farm workers and laborers, military issues, the death penalty, concerns of the poor and marginalized, and foreign policy regarding the Third World.[23]

The writers of the letters drew upon the thinking of Vatican II's *Gaudium et Spes,* which signaled the Church's support of classical just war theory and the growing untenability of the use of nuclear arms. However, the council fathers did not specify a policy regarding the arms race.[24] Thus the U.S. bishops decided to provide specific moral guidance for U.S. Catholics: (1) condemnation of the use of strategic nuclear weaponry; (2) condemnation of the use of nuclear weapons as a threat to civilian populations; and (3) a "qualified acceptance of a certain type of deterrence as a device for stabilizing superpower relations while arms control and disarmament proceeded."[25] In particular, the bishops stated that they saw no possibility for a "first use" of nuclear weapons on the part of the United States, and they called for halting the production of nuclear weapons.[26]

Significantly, *The Challenge of Peace* was finalized and approved by the U.S. bishops the very week in May 1983 that the U.S. Congress voted to approve a nuclear "freeze." Despite the popularity of President

Ronald Reagan and his aggressive promilitary posture, the American people had become ready to halt the nuclear arms race.[27] *The Challenge of Peace* shows that at the highest level of the U.S. Catholic Church there was willingness to forge an Catholic American social justice public policy drawing upon Catholic moral tradition, biblical studies, and doctrine contextualized for U.S. public issues. I suggest that while *The Challenge of Peace* does not provide new concepts or language for social justice teaching, it does provide a *strategic American* orientation for Catholic social justice teaching based on a historical and cultural pragmatism and practicality that characterize both U.S. Catholics and Americans in general.[28] The dominant frames of this social letter are just war (in relation to nuclear war, deterrence, arms control, and conflict resolution), nonviolence, peace, and development—all to be effected in the world and inspired by Catholic social teaching.[29]

Building upon the public relations success of *The Challenge of Peace,* the U.S. bishops initiated a new consultation process regarding the U.S. economy. While *The Challenge of Peace* drew largely upon the Catholic moral tradition with its philosophical premises, *Economic Justice for All* incorporated a stronger biblical tone, based on scholarship on biblical justice.[30] Chapter 3 of the 1986 letter contains a detailed account of the U.S. economy, an analysis that surveys a vast array of social research and is documented with ample footnotes. The bishops read "the signs of the times" through the data available to them as well as listening to social scientists, economists, businesspeople, and ordinary citizens. They proceeded to make specific recommendations flowing from a biblical and moral theological foundation: (1) full employment, (2) expansion of job training and apprenticeship programs, (3) direct job-creation programs to decrease long-term unemployment, (4) removal of barriers to full and equal employment for women and minorities, (5) support of self-help programs for the poor, (6) an evaluation of the tax system to determine its impact upon the poor, (7) commitment to education of the poor, (8) program support for the strength and stability of families, (9) reform of the nation's welfare and income-support programs, (10) public assistance programs designed to assist recipients to become employed and self-sufficient, (11) support for the family farm, (12) farm workers' right to unionize, and (13) a preferential option for the poor as a determinative factor in U.S. economic foreign policy.[31] The letter provided a large theological context for a strategy for Catholic social action in the world and a definitive sense that only through structural changes in the economy, particularly through the Catholic Campaign for Human Development, can social justice be realized. (I will analyze the CCHD below.)

Economic Justice for All is the most comprehensive social letter written by the U.S. bishops to integrate biblical and moral norms, social and economic data, scholarly input and reflection, and both Catholic and public opinion. The dominant frames of this letter are biblical justice, economic justice, option for the poor, participation, economic rights, full employment, poverty, agriculture, and the global economy.[32] Donohue believes that this pastoral letter demonstrates "the best use of scripture" in any of the national pastoral letters.

The social justice principles of *The Challenge of Peace* and *Economic Justice for All,* particularly the idea that the transformation of society is integral to and constitutive of the gospel, are similar to those expressed in Vatican II's *Gaudium et Spes,* the first "pastoral constitutional" document of an ecumenical council. However, except for a new preface for *Economic Justice for All* issued by the bishops in 1997, these letters do not incorporate the concept of solidarity as an integral organizing principle for either American or global society.[33] Rather, the bishops use the more utilitarian concepts of "partnership" and "teamwork" for conveying the cooperation required among different societal interest groups.[34] The letters have provided an American context for the U.S. church's social programs, particularly Catholic Charities, the Catholic Campaign for Human Development, and Development and Peace. Later in this chapter I will consider how the CCHD actually takes theology to heart in the development of its mission, selection of social justice programs in civil society to support, and evaluation of its mandate.

The U.S. Sense of the Social Doctrine as a "Teaching"

Part of the "Americanness" of Catholic social teaching is that it is conveyed as a "teaching" and not a "doctrine" in all the documents of the U.S. Catholic Church. The discourse of "social justice teaching" has a pragmatic and contextual sense. While the U.S. church has an extensive record of achievement in contextualizing social justice doctrine and supporting church social programs, it does not treat the doctrine as a required and integral part of the American Catholic imagination, say at the level of moral theology or basic tenets of the faith. Put bluntly, there is no litmus test for social justice as part of the essential life of the U.S. Catholic. Thus it is not surprising that seminaries require only one course in Catholic social justice doctrine for the training of future clergy.

Catholic parishes are not required to have a social ministries component or make social justice an integral part of parish life. Even though parishes provide many social services, these programs do not incorporate a high theological content. Rather, there is a practical and pragmatic sense of the delivery of social service goods to a community within the American Judeo-Christian social discourse of equality, civil rights, and ending poverty and discrimination.[35] Of course one can articulate such principles as option for the poor, the dignity of the human person, and solidarity within the Judeo-Christian frames, but U.S. Catholics do not seem to understand these principles as part of their doctrinal responsibility, even though religious faith is a strong motivator for Catholic social justice theologians and activists.

I became aware of this situation when the Jesuit biblical scholar Walter Burghardt conveyed to me how social justice as a doctrinal requirement might sound: "My very salvation depends on my fidelity to just relationships."[36] Or as Jesuit social historian John Padberg reflected: "There is a need for a mystique of social justice in the American church."[37] That is, while U.S. Catholics and their bishops are committed to works of social justice, this commitment is not part and parcel of their overall Christian faith commitment as other doctrinal elements are. One telling sign would be whether and how social justice doctrine emerges in the practice of confession: how many Catholics confess sins related to social injustice, particularly viewed as "right relationships" with God and neighbor? While there are no surveys that would give us data on this—after all, due to its confidential nature the confessional cannot be researched—informal conversations with priests have communicated to me that there are few confessions with social justice content.[38]

There are further complicating dimensions of the discourse of U.S. Catholics as they attempt to integrate their faith into the discourses and practices of U.S. civic and political cultures. Historically, as noted earlier, a "rights discourse" has been used for U.S. social justice issues, focusing upon individual and aggregate claims for justice and often overshadowing broader themes of the common good and solidarity.[39] In American civic and political life, the rights discourse has been a way to legitimize the aspirations expressed in social movements. Meanwhile, the term *solidarity* was expunged from the U.S. labor movement after

World War I, because of its association with the rise of socialism and communism. *Solidarity* was not resurrected by U.S. activists until the 1990s, when the Polish Solidarity Movement gave the term an anticommunist as well as prolabor orientation.[40] While *solidarity* now has a certain legitimacy among Americans, my respondents and the social actors in my ethnographic work did not use the Church's discourse of solidarity in their articulations of their social justice principles. My conclusion is that U.S. Catholics do not appropriate solidarity as a principle and do not know how to incorporate it into their normative sense of social Catholicity—even though they use more pragmatic discourses of collaboration, networking, partnering, and the like. Certainly the idea of solidarity as virtue does not emerge; it probably would have emerged quite naturally had the concept of solidarity been a rallying cry of the U.S. labor movement.

U.S. Political and Religious Cultures and U.S. Catholic Social Teaching

The classic example of the legitimation of social justice discourse in American life—and thus in the life of U.S. Catholics—has been the civil rights movement, which resulted in the Civil Rights acts of 1964 and 1966 and affiliated affirmative action executive orders and legislative amendments. These processes brought a legal end to racial, ethnic, gender, religious, and marital status discrimination in the United States. Catholic activists in the civil rights movement, who were by and large African American Christians, were able to actualize their faith in terms of Catholic principles of the dignity of the human person, human rights, participation, association, solidarity, friendship, social justice, social responsibility, and "signs of the times." The organizing arm of the civil rights movement, the Southern Christian Leadership Conference (SCLC), led by the Rev. Martin Luther King Jr., while strategically advocating civil rights for the advancement of African Americans, was at the same time focused on the sociopolitical process that would shape African Americans as moral citizens.[41]

In the process, a social justice theology functioning as doctrine built on the foundations of the American social gospel movement was becoming increasingly integrated into the faith life of the various Protestant congregations and churches affiliated with the SCLC.[42] Today this doctrinal perspective on social justice—that social justice is part and parcel of a Christian's life—persists in the black Protestant churches affiliated with the legacy of the SCLC and is actualized by their members through high voter turnout, participation in civic associations, and involvement in community organizing.[43] Interestingly, these churches do not have what one might call a "high theology" of social justice, parallel to the theology generated by the Catholic Church—no systematic theology of justice evidenced in a core theological logic and theological documents, books, and professional outlets for social justice discourse.[44] However, these churches offer a *practical* social justice theological structure of sermons, Bible study, social justice programs, civil associations, and political involvement based on a biblically oriented prophetic tradition rooted in the pain and history of slavery. Thus the African American religious culture rooted in the memory of slavery, the struggle for emancipation, the civil rights movement, and the more recent emergence of black identity politics has generated a tradition of religious social justice within liberal black Christianity in the United States.[45]

Combining the African American religious culture with the social justice theological structure, liberal black Protestantism provides a faith-based social justice culture for its members. Thus, liberal black Protestantism provides a distinctive religious habitus for the training of a moral citizenry that is both practical, with hands-on experiences to effect social justice, and theological, with religious and spiritual meanings. For the liberal black Christian, living out one's faith commitments in the civil and political spheres is not only the "right thing to do" but a requirement for salvation—of building the kingdom of God in the present time. To adapt a phrase of Cornel West: religion matters.[46] Furthermore, this tradition provides an opening for "secular" Americans to enter the discourse of religious social justice ethics, particularly through religious leaders such as the Rev. Jesse Jackson, the Rev. Al Sharpton, Cornel West, and pastors of large urban congregations.[47] No other religious tradition in the United States has provided such an opening.

In contrast to the liberal black Protestant social justice tradition in the United States, the Catholic Church has provided a high degree of delivery of pragmatic social programs (Catholic Charities, hospitals, schools, prison and military chaplaincies, cemeteries, legal advocacy, etc.) grounded in a broad sense of charity and the corporal works of mercy: educating the ignorant, feeding the hungry, clothing the naked, visiting the sick, burying the dead, comforting the sorrowful, and visiting the imprisoned, based upon Jesus' discourse on the requirements for entering heaven found in Matthew 25:31–46. We could say that the

Catholic approach to charity based on Jesus' injunction developed out of the need of the pre-Kennedy and pre–Vatican II era of the U.S. Catholic community to develop a "separate but equal" institutional world of schools, hospitals, organizations, and charities.

"Catholic Moments" in U.S. Political Culture

Thus the American Catholic Church has built a broad institutional framework to respond to sacred scripture's call for works of charity. Unfortunately, however, the Church's approach has faltered in its response to and framing of broader social justice themes such as racism, sexism, and the abortion and death penalty debates within its social justice principles. Its institutionalized charity has not been able to develop the average Catholic's social justice faith commitments within a critical intellectual framework drawing on the Church's own traditions (evidenced in the U.S. bishops pastoral letters and social justice theologians). In short, it has not generated a Catholic social justice culture extending beyond charitable programs.

For example, the Catholic "right to life" discourse of the abortion debate has been generally subsumed into a moral theology framework of the moment of conception, growth of the fetus, murder of the fetus, etc.—all elements of a natural law argument regarding the life of the fetus. Thus, while the dignity of the person is a primary tenet of social justice doctrine, that principle has not been clearly applied to address the social conditions of the pregnant woman and the responsibilities of the male. As a result, the abortion issue has been made a largely personal issue of moral choice and responsibility and not a social issue per se for the U.S. Catholic Church—even though the Catholic hierarchy strongly supports the prolife movement and an overturn of *Roe v. Wade*.[48]

In fact, the vast majority of U.S. dioceses have an office for their prolife program that is separate from the office for their social justice program. Such a distinction between "moral" and "social" concerns follows the United States Catholic Conference, which organizes the social apostolate in the following offices: Pro-Life Activities, Social Development and World Peace, Catholic Campaign for Human Development, Migration and Refugee Services, and Hispanic Affairs—as well as the independent organizations Catholic Charities U.S.A. and Catholic Relief Services.[49] This belies the "seamless garment" rhetoric of the theology of the late Cardinal Joseph Bernardin of Chicago, who sought to unite the issues of the death penalty, abortion, and disarmament into a broader prolife social justice theology.[50]

While I believe it is a "Catholic moment" in U.S. political culture since Catholics dominate its leadership and mass base, the prolife movement within the Catholic Church does not have a charismatic figure who inspires its agenda. Rather, laity, clergy, and bishops reiterate the Church's moral teaching in a doctrinal discourse that does not readily link with any of the elements of the historic U.S. social justice movement discourse grounded in the broad Judeo-Christian ethos. Its most powerful metaphor, "American holocaust," not only offends Jews and other Christians but also fails to evoke a distinctive sense of abortion as a social injustice, particularly as it affects poor and minority communities.[51] I find it fascinating that the prolife discourse does not take advantage of the broader human rights discourse of the Church or society but remains reliant on the natural law. The prolife movement within the Church has its own section on the Web site of the United States Catholic Conference, "Pro-Life Activities." This is its stated mission: "We proclaim that human life is a precious gift from God; that each person who receives this gift has responsibilities toward God, self and others; and that society, through its laws and social institutions, must protect and nurture human life at every stage of its existence."[52] Catholic prolife activists have few connections with the broader structural-world social justice agenda of the Church. They tend to see their activity within an integral-world orientation of protecting life but do not connect it to the social, economic, or structural causes of abortion, euthanasia, the death penalty, in-vitro fertilization, or stem-cell research.

In contrast to the abortion question, the death penalty debate in the United States poses a particularly complex problem for social justice doctrine, because the debate turns on the rights of victims over and against the right to life of the offender, particularly in murder cases. In the case of abortion, the rights of the fetus become paramount with the application of natural law logic of human development; oddly, a similar argument for the fundamental human right to life of the offender is not made. Rather, opponents of the death penalty focus on (1) its discriminatory effects, with a disproportionate number of blacks, Latinos, and poor people on death row, (2) wrongful convictions, (3) lack of evidence that the death penalty acts as a deterrent to capital crime, and (4) the high costs of keeping an inmate on death row—particularly given the expense of ongoing appeals.[53]

The role of Sister Helen Prejean, C.S.J., as a Catholic social justice activist against the death penalty can be seen as parallel to the role played by the Rev. Martin Luther King Jr. and the Southern Christian Leadership Conference (SCLC) in the civil rights movement. Her book *Dead Man Walking* and the movie and opera of the same name have helped give the anti–death penalty movement a prophetic sense, moving it beyond the statistical claims used to bolster civil rights–based arguments.[54] Sister Prejean's talks and written works are marked by a deeply theological and biblical discourse that focuses upon friendship, solidarity, the dignity of the human person, human rights, social justice, and the "signs of the times." She has been a keynote speaker at the two official Jubilee Year celebrations of the national Catholic Church, as well as at the 2001 National Social Ministries Conference, thus establishing the aims of the anti–death penalty movement within the official national church.

The "new" anti–death penalty movement[55] has been one of five "Catholic moments" in the history of social justice in the United States, as it is shaped by a distinctive Catholic social justice imagination regarding human rights, dignity of the person, and option for the vulnerable. The other singular "Catholic moments" for U.S. social justice were sparked by Dorothy Day and Peter Maurin in the establishment of the Catholic Worker, Cesar Chavez in the development of the United Farm Workers' labor union (UFW), and the annual School of the Americas Watch (SOAW) protest, founded by a former U.S. naval officer, Maryknoll Father Roy Bourgeois. I will explore how these social movements have helped generate a Catholic social imagination that is both strategic and normative, not only fulfilling the obligation to practice charity but also helping the Catholic become a moral citizen, equipped to work for structural change in the world.

Over the years Dorothy Day (1879–1980) has emerged as an icon of Catholic social justice because of her integrity in serving the poor and her Catholic orthodoxy. The Catholic Worker movement, founded in 1927, has roots in the anarchist tradition, which distrusts government and public institutions as agents for justice. Day and Maurin felt that a Christian's duty is direct personal service to the poor and marginalized. From the beginning, the spiritual centers of the Catholic Worker movement have been the "house of hospitality" and the farm. The house serves as a place for the urban unemployed and poor to receive food, clothing, and shelter, and the farm produces the food for the urban table and serves as a place for retreat. Of all Catholic magazines and periodicals, the *Catholic Worker,* the New York–based newspaper of the movement, has since its founding in 1933 provided what is probably the most faithful dissemination of Catholic social justice teaching in the United States. Catholic Worker is not a membership-based organization, but its growth can be measured by the number and distribution of houses of hospitality and farms in the United States and Canada. By 1995 the Catholic Worker movement had grown to 134 communities.[56]

During the years of the Vietnam War, Catholic Worker leaders were at the forefront of nonviolent resistance to U.S. foreign and military policy. They linked this nonviolent resistance to Catholic social justice teaching regarding human rights, human development, self-determination, world peace, and disarmament. They helped frame the theological justification for Catholic conscientious objectors to resist the draft or seek alternative service. Day's prophetic voice during the Vietnam War was quite bothersome to her friend and supporter Cardinal Francis Spellman, archbishop of New York and military vicar. Yet Spellman admired Day's devout Catholic faith and her integrity in serving New York City's poorest in the Bowery.[57] Catholic Worker activists were founders of the Catholic Peace Fellowship and many local antiwar activities around the United States. Without the Catholic Workers and their development of a Catholic antiwar discourse based on theological orthodoxy and interpretation, Catholic contributions to the antiwar movement would more than likely have been minimal.

Many Catholic intellectuals received their justice training at Catholic Worker houses and were able to integrate Catholic theology with social justice concerns. These intellectuals, most of them laypeople, included Eileen Egan, Robert Coles, and James Forest. They helped popularize the Catholic Worker ethos and its integration of Catholic social justice teaching in the Catholic press by contributing to leading Catholic magazines, particularly *Commonweal, America, Salt, U.S. Catholic,* and *National Catholic Reporter.*

Since the rise of community service programs in U.S. Catholic high schools and colleges in the 1980s, many a young Catholic has visited a House of Hospitality to serve food to the poor. For many this has served as an entry into Catholic social justice culture, particularly at the movement's primary locus of social justice theology, with works of mercy in the world that are radical but oriented to integral and not structural change. While not part of the institutional church per se, Catholic Workers pride themselves on weekly masses, celebrated by local clergy. By integrating corporal works of mercy with social justice doctrine, the Catholic Worker Movement provides a cultural milieu for Catholic social justice, virtually a school or training center for the Catholic moral citizen.

Apart from their ongoing ministry to the poor, homeless, and unemployed at houses of hospitality, Catholic Workers were and are in leadership roles in more structurally oriented movements such as the anti–death penalty movement, the ongoing peace movement, the sanctuary movement during the 1970s and 1980s civil wars in Central America, and defense of immigrants and the poor. In this sense the Catholic Worker movement has been a continuing primary cultural nexus for the development of a U.S. Catholic social justice culture and imagination, particularly in its integral-world orientation.

In founding the United Farm Workers Union (UFW), Cesar Chavez followed the model of the civil rights movement with its focus upon the sociopolitical formation of the moral citizen. Thus the UFW pursued farm workers' legal rights for collective bargaining, benefits, and occupational protections and at the same time sought to form a nonviolent movement and build social solidarity with the U.S. labor movement and the American people. The UFW became a prophetic voice within the U.S. Catholic Church as church leaders integrated the aims of the union in social justice teaching, particularly drawing on the principles that Leo XIII's *Rerum Novarum* had set forth: common good, association, participation, workers' rights to organize, just wage as family support, and the dignity of work.

From its inception, the UFW has made connections with the ethnic and religious imaginations of its largely Mexican and Filipino American membership base. Its first nationally publicized action was a three-hundred-mile pilgrimage alongside Highway 99 in California, from its Central Valley headquarters in Delano to the state capital of Sacramento in March 1966. At the head of the march, the American flag and the banner of Our Lady of Guadalupe—as well as a number of clergy and nuns in their distinctive religious garb—signaled the Catholic and American civic-spiritual dimensions of the UFW.[58] The national church's positive response to the UFW's claims, out of its long tradition of prolabor public policy,[59] became the basis for a larger drive to advance the interests of U.S. Latinos and Hispanic immigrants. The U.S. hierarchy's support of the national Hispanic Encuentro Process was important in bringing the concerns of Hispanic Catholics to the attention of the national church.[60]

The UFW has provided a cultural site since the mid-1960s for the development of a Catholic social imagination within the U.S. Latino community, the Catholic Church, and the labor movement. Like the Rev. Martin Luther King Jr., Chavez was able to inspire a social justice discourse around civil rights, solidarity, participation, association, nonviolence, and social justice—as well as labor rights, immigrant rights, health care, and the common good. He stood as a prophetic figure, particularly during his fasts. While the Roman Catholic Chavez was trained in the liberal Protestant social gospel tradition, he integrated this formation with Catholic social justice teaching, Hispanic-Filipino religious piety, and the pragmatic social organizing methods of Alinsky.[61] Participants in the UFW—particularly those who were not farmworker union organizers—developed a citizen morality highly influenced by Chavez's moral vision of building the kingdom of God. Many UFW labor organizers have gone on to become leaders in the U.S. labor movement and have helped revitalize the movement with the social justice ethos of the UFW, embedded as it is in the Catholic social justice principles of solidarity, participation, association, labor rights, human rights, dignity of the human person, and liberation.[62]

It might be said that just as liberal black Protestant churches provide a moral and prophetic tone to the ongoing civil rights movement, the influence of the UFW upon the U.S. Catholic Church has done the same for the protection and advancement of the Hispanic, farm worker, and immigrant communities—particularly by local bishops and pastors, state bishops' conferences, and the National Conference of Catholic Bishops. For example, Cardinal Roger Mahony of Los Angeles, who had been a close collaborator with Chavez when he was auxiliary bishop of Fresno, California, from 1975 to 1980 and bishop of Stockton, California, from 1980 to 1985,[63] provided national leadership—alongside Cardinal John O'Connor of New York City—in advocating the protection of immigrants and the advancement of the labor movement, particularly among urban immigrant service workers.

Msgr. George Higgins, who had been an adviser to Chavez and the UFW while serving as a staff member of the U.S. Catholic Conference, told me that the UFW's positive relationship to the Church gave "Cesar a certain coloring" that permeated the organization's culture, even though the UFW was not a Catholic union in the mold of European and Latin American Catholic labor organizations. Cardinals Mahony and O'Connor both epitomized the concept of "doctrinally conservative but socially progressive." That is, for the vast majority of U.S. bishops, social justice doctrine warrants liberal and progressive public policy on social and economic issues, yet they remain conservative on issues of faith and personal morals, particularly the Church's positions on abortion, family planning, and medical ethics derived from the natural law.[64] Furthermore, the bishops have historically understood that labor unions and other appropriately lay-led organizations should remain as free associations in civil society. Higgins told me that his concern regarding social justice in the post–Vatican II era is that it has become a "social ministry" within religious structures that siphon off energies from Catholic laypeople's involvement in lay civic organizations such as labor unions. Referring to the head of the AFL-CIO, he said, "I would hate to see John Sweeney become a minister of the Church."

Catholic social activists involved in the UFW and its support system within the Church are primarily oriented toward the strategic world-structural direction of the Catholic social imagination. However, they are also highly developed in the integral orientation, given the UFW's emphasis upon ethnic celebration and religious rituals such as fasting, pilgrimages, music, and dramaturgy—a very strong development of the spirituality of the habitus. They have been careful in cultivating the hierarchy of the Church and using various offices of the Church for lobbying and networking.

Held annually in November, the School of the Americas Watch has become an extensive networking event for Maryknoll, Jesuit institutions, solidarity organizations, and other Catholic and faith-based peace and justice organizations. Father Roy Bourgeois founded SOAW in 1990 in order to initiate a long-term movement to shutdown the U.S. Army's School of the Americas at Fort Benning, Georgia. The School of the Americas (now called the Western Hemisphere Institute for Security Cooperation) has been the primary center for training military officers from seventeen Latin American countries, including officers who have been traced to U.S. military involvement in El Salvador, Guatemala, Nicaragua, Bolivia, and Chile during the 1970s and 1980s—and accused of using torture techniques learned at Fort Benning.

Father Bourgeois is a member of the Maryknoll order of priests, sisters, brothers, and laypeople—a distinctively American Catholic institution founded in 1911 to serve the missions of the Catholic Church. He was ordained a priest in 1972 and worked as a missioner in Bolivia from 1972 to 1977 during the dictatorship of Hugo Banzer. He was arrested and imprisoned for his human rights work and was expelled from the country. He has spent more than four years in U.S. prisons, serving time for a variety of antiwar protests. Since 1990 he has worked full time as the organizer of the SOAW.[65] The SOAW website notes:

> Over its 59 years, the SOA has trained over 60,000 Latin American soldiers in counterinsurgency techniques, sniper training, commando and psychological warfare, military intelligence and interrogation tactics. These graduates have consistently used their skills to wage a war against their own people. Among those targeted by SOA graduates are educators, union organizers, religious workers, student leaders, and others who work for the rights of the poor. Hundreds of thousands of Latin Americans have been tortured, raped, assassinated, "disappeared," massacred, and forced into refugee by those trained at the School of Assassins.[66]

SOAW and its extensive network of Catholic and other faith-based organizations has developed a particular U.S. Catholic social imagination, borrowing from the cultural strategy of the UFW, the civil rights movement, and the peace movement—nonviolent organizing with a prophetic sense of witnessing for the truth. The November event always highlights the memory of Archbishop Oscar Romero of San Salvador and the Jesuit, Ursuline, and Maryknoll martyrs of the Salvadoran civil war, as well as hundreds of other victims of military atrocities in Central and South America. Jesuit high schools, colleges, parishes, and social ministries now use the November event as an occasion to organize an Ignatian Family Weekend, which brings together the institutional resources of the Society of Jesus and the spiritual exercises of St. Ignatius. Other Catholic groups such as the Catholic Workers, Pax Christi, Catholic Peace Fellowship, the Maryknoll Family, and other religious orders use the event to network and promote the Catholic peace and justice habitus of prayer, ritual, liturgy, social justice teaching, music, drama, and nonviolent protest. For many activists, making the decision to be arrested at Fort Benning during the annual event becomes a high point of their justice commitment. The arrest has a sacramental significance, encompassing a complex dramaturgy of political, spiritual, and religious meanings. Arrest at the SOAW protest represents a radical embodiment of a U.S. Catholic social imagination with an integral-structural-world dynamic and a new understanding and retrieval of the principle of solidarity as an organizing instrument for right relationships.[67]

The cases of the Catholic Worker movement, the anti–death penalty movement, the UFW, and SOAW reveal that the Catholic contribution to U.S. social justice has not been a direct doctrinal contribution but rather a matrix of "Catholic moments" developed within a larger Catholic social imagination. Each of these movements incorporates charismatic leaders who identify themselves as Roman Catholic; identification of a clear social injustice; highly committed religious activists; religious dramaturgy such as pilgrimages, liturgies, demonstrations, gatherings, and arrests; institutional linkages between the social movement and the official church; and a spiritual and devotional sense of a moral high ground to inspire the activists and make the movement's message religious in nature. Rather than directly enunciating social justice theology as doctrinally prescriptive, such a matrix evokes principles of the dignity of the person, human rights, solidarity, participation, association, social justice, and so on in a Catholic social justice culture. And it is within these religiously oriented and prophetic social justice movements that Catholic social justice theologians and church leaders have been most motivated to pursue their theological and social policy agenda.

Social Justice Teaching and Ministry within the Institutional Church

In addition to the prophetic cultural sites for justice, I need to note three other cultural sites for social justice that are part of the mainstream church institution: pre–Vatican II social organizations, post–Vatican II lay ministry development, and intensive immersion experience organizations. Prior to Vatican II, a number of lay associations provided venues for the corporal and spiritual works of mercy, notably the St. Vincent de Paul Society, an international organization founded in France that organized direct service aid in local parishes, and the Irish-based Legion of Mary, which provided a spiritual formation for service to the poor and hospitality in the parishes. In these organizations ordinary Catholics not only provided charitable service to those in need but also learned organizational skills and Catholic principles. These two organizations, as well as some of the activities of the Knights and Ladies of Columbus, the Catholic Daughters of America, and the Knights and Ladies of St. Peter Claver, remain a source of support of charitable activities in many parishes today.[68] The international leadership has attempted to make them more responsive to social justice teaching. They have not become known as social justice organizations per se, but they function as charitable organizations that help orient ordinary Catholics to their social responsibilities. The hierarchy of the Church can rely on the members to respond to both national and international crises.

Since Vatican II, the U.S. church has experienced a tremendous growth in lay ministry, as the roles of clergy and religious in church life has undergone change. Amid decline in the numbers of clergy and religious, the laity have become necessary for the maintenance and growth of the Church. The work of teachers, administrators, liturgical ministers, and volunteers has been dramatically developed or professionalized. Almost all Catholic colleges and universities offer certificate or degree programs for various areas of social justice ministry, such as Catholic social justice teaching, ethnic ministry, and lay leadership development. Many dioceses and parishes have appointed a social justice minister to coordinate charitable services and organize prophetic witness and activities.

For example, the Archdiocese of Los Angeles has a full-time Office of Justice and Peace that coordinates an annual appeal for the Catholic Campaign for Human Development and Catholic Relief Services, organizes seminars and training for diocesan personnel and laity, and promotes education programs to disseminate social justice teaching. Every year it holds a week-long Social Action Summer Institute at Loyola Marymount University.

Lay ministers have developed extensive networks linking mainstream social justice church functions with the more prophetic activities of the Catholic Workers, the anti–death penalty movement, and the UFW. I include in "lay ministry" the activities of faith-based community organizing, involving about one million U.S. Catholics, which develops citizen disciples at the parish level to link the principles of Catholic social teaching with community issues such as crime, education, urban renewal, and housing. I found that social justice ministers see themselves as struggling to live out principles of the option for the poor, solidarity, human rights, and the dignity of the human person within their often comfortable middle-class lives. They find solace and support in local organizations and networks. The vast majority of the three thousand delegates at the national Jubilee events in Los Angeles came from this area of U.S. church life.

Finally, the U.S. church has developed formal intensive immersion experiences to introduce young Catholics to specific communities faced with social injustice. For example, the Jesuit Volunteer Corps, founded in 1955, provides a one- or two-year opportunity for college graduates to work in poor communities as teachers, social workers, business consultants, and the like, as a way to integrate the principles of social teaching, spirituality, and direct service. The Jesuit Volunteer Corps and immersion projects sponsored by other religious orders and dioceses have developed a positive reputation among college students as a valuable way to round out their undergraduate education, particularly students from Catholic colleges and universities who want to be "men and women for others"—the social justice motto of Jesuit high schools and colleges.[69] The majority of my U.S. informants in the age range of twenty-five to forty had participated in an intensive immersion program. Through these experiences they made lifetime commitments to social justice, and they shared a sense that social justice is part of the committed Catholic's lifestyle.

Formulating an American Catholic Social Imagination

The "American" version of the Catholic social imagination is marked by distinctive theological contributions, "Catholic moments" in U.S. social justice movements, and institutionalized social justice contexts. Catholic social justice theologians in the United States participate in a well-organized and highly developed theological enterprise that features a positive role for the theologian; chairs of social justice and Christian social ethics in major Catholic and secular universities; consultative roles with local bishops and the U.S. Catholic Conference for pastoral letters and strategic planning; contribution of books and scholarly articles published by Catholic and secular presses, magazines, periodicals, and journals; theological conferences; and a place for theologians within social justice organizations. Since Vatican II, U.S. social justice theology has been highly shaped by the social justice project of the Jesuit-sponsored Woodstock Theological Center, which produced *The Faith That Does Justice* and promoted the concept of biblical justice among Catholics, as well appropriating Judeo-Christian principles for Catholic theology and the Preaching the Just Word retreat program for priests and deacons.

The major social justice letters of the U.S. bishops feature an American discourse of civic engagement and sociopolitical concepts. These letters have served to legitimate a structural-world direction for the Catholic social movements that I have analyzed. The Catholic Worker movement, the United Farm Workers Union, the anti–death penalty movement, and the School of the Americas Watch have provided cultural sites for the formation and training of moral citizens imbued with Catholic social justice teaching and ethos.

Overall, the "Americanness" of U.S. Catholic social justice teaching is constituted by the following: openness to the U.S. secular culture;

ecumenical outlook and cooperation; institutional embeddedness of theological contributions; and theology that is both pragmatic and practical, both professional and grassroots. Furthermore, Protestant theology and Catholic theology in the United States have a positive history in the formation of social movements that worked for the abolition of slavery, suffrage of women, temperance, civil rights for blacks and other minorities, the farm workers' movement, and abolition of the death penalty. The Catholic social justice theological enterprise works in an American tradition of "public theology" that has both a religious and a secular audience in the United States, particularly in the discourse calling for social change.[70]

In the United States, the Catholic social imagination has the capacity to incorporate the above elements and tendencies because the hierarchy and clergy are themselves educated and active in U.S. political culture; they do not see themselves as apart from or above the U.S. culture, and they are capable of integrating principles of the social justice doctrine with the structural and normative nature of that political culture. In relation to the ideal-typic Catholic social imagination, the U.S. Catholic social imagination is marked by different orientations energized by the U.S. bishops' structural-world orientation. In the following section I will further elaborate the significance of the structural-world orientation of the American Catholic social imagination for faith-based community organizing.

The CCHD and Faith-Based Community Organizing

Community-organizing and social justice organizations in U.S. civil society have had a historic relationship with the U.S. Catholic bishops' chief social justice organization, the Catholic Campaign for Human Development (CCHD). The CCHD was founded in 1970 as the Church's own antipoverty agency, in order to provide start-up grants for groups fighting poverty in the United States. Since then, the organization has distributed hundreds of millions of dollars to civil society organizations dedicated to fulfilling the principles of human development and the preferential option for the poor that Pope Paul VI articulated in his 1967 encyclical *Populorum Progressio*.[71] The money collected through an annual CCHD appeal in every U.S. Catholic parish. The recipient organizations are all independent from the Church itself and must be legally registered as 501(c)(3) nonprofit organizations, which cannot participate in partisan political activity. Over the years grants have been given to thousands of economic development start-ups, empowerment groups, and community organizing national and affiliate organizations.[72]

The Pacific Institute for Community Organizing (PICO) and Oakland Community Organizations (OCO)—organizations that I will analyze in the next section of this chapter—have received grants in almost every CCHD funding cycle. In addition to PICO, other Alinsky-method community-organizing networks—in particular, the Industrial Areas Foundation (IAF), the Association of Communities Organized for Reform Now (ACORN), and the Gamaliel Foundation—have been successful in receiving CCHD grants. The CCHD stamp of approval says, in effect, "The Catholic bishops think this is a good organization, so it must be legitimate and sound." In 1999 CCHD distributed $7.1 million (47 percent of its operating budget of $15 million, collected in the annual appeal) to 238 community-organizing projects throughout the United States and another $1.3 million to sixty-two economic development projects. Only 8 percent of CCHD's budget goes to administrative costs.[73] In fact, CCHD has been the primary financial backer of community organizing in the United States, and local affiliates use their CCHD funding to leverage other funding and support in their communities.[74]

CCHD emerged from the pastoral work and concerns of a group of priests and bishops from around the country who had over the years worked together on interracial and poverty issues and had organized themselves in 1967 as the Catholic Committee on Urban Ministry:

> Monsignor Geno Baroni of the Archdiocese of Washington's Urban Office; Father Eugene Boyle of the Archdiocese of San Francisco, active with the United Farmworkers of America; Father Patrick Flood of the Archdiocese of Milwaukee, active in race matters; Father P. David Finks of the Diocese of Rochester, active in Alinsky's FIGHT organization; Father John McCarthy who was assistant to labor priest George Higgins; Father Phil Murnion of New York who was to direct the National Institute on Pastoral Life; Father Marvin Mottet of Davenport who was to become the director of the Campaign for Human Development, and other clergy. These priests were at the forefront of Catholic activism and had experience in organizations focused on self-determination: community organizations, economic development organizations such as worker cooperatives or credit unions, housing initiatives, and neighborhood associations.[75]

In the immediate post–Vatican II stage of ministry development and the crisis of U.S. cities, these clergy wanted the U.S. bishops to commit themselves to helping solve the problems of structural poverty. Many of these priests had been involved in or exposed to the Alinsky organization in Chicago and knew that the Church could support grassroots efforts to change urban public institutions.[76] Their instinct was to move on from the charity and direct services model of Catholic Charities, the St. Vincent de Paul Society, and the Legion of Mary to assist laypeople to influence organizations in civil society. The Church could become a mediating institution, moving its resources to civil associations dedicated to fighting poverty and getting people civically engaged. This idea had been developed in the "Cadre Study" conducted by Catholic Charities in 1969–1970. The report affirmed the work of Catholic Charities but urged a separate organizational structure for services to empower people to do advocacy work and become the "voice of the voiceless."[77] By 1970 they had helped prepare the U.S. bishops to initiate an annual campaign to collect money from all U.S. Catholics for fighting poverty.

Until 1998 the campaign was called the Campaign for Human Development (CHD), and for many its relationship to the Catholic Church was unclear. The CCHD has never required any group receiving funding to espouse a religious purpose, although moral guidelines for funding were issued in 1972 and these were revised in 1999 to prohibit any group's receiving money that might be used to promote activities contrary to Catholic moral teaching regarding "life issues." Specifically, any program promoting abortion would not be granted funds. More recently CCHD has attempted to strengthen its religious, spiritual, and Catholic character by generating educational programs and materials promoting Catholic social justice teaching in parishes and dioceses, particularly through its Journey to Justice retreat program. One of the staff members told me that this program aims at a "conversion of heart" so that persons can "move faith outside of their parish into their everyday life." In 1999, $1.3 million (8 percent of the budget) was spent in these educational and spiritual efforts.[78]

Over the course of 1999, I was able to interview the entire professional staff of CCHD at the organization's offices, located at the United States Catholic Conference in Washington, D.C. Field representatives have a key role at CCHD, because these six persons actually go into the field to work with 175 local diocesan officials and the more than 300 civil associations funded by CCHD. They review applications for grants and evaluate the organizations for their potential in fulfilling CCHD's objectives. All of the field representatives were very clear that their fundamental objective is to assist the bishops and the Church in fulfilling the principle of the preferential option for the poor. Any group making an application that would not fulfill this objective would not be funded. The second objective that was highlighted by all the field representatives, which can be summarized as empowerment, is related to the principles of association, participation, solidarity, and subsidiarity.

The field representatives had a common discourse related to those two principles. It was clear that they speak to each other on a regular basis and are very conscious of their mission in both the development of groups and the accountability attached to a CCHD grant. As one representative said about her work: "It's definitely about empowerment . . . empowerment as a discernment and development process of the Spirit present. . . . It brings on the successes of individuals and collectively [brings] more power [so that people] are not powerless." In other words, her work is about "empowering the poor" to realize that "we are all created in God's image and likeness—there is equality and oneness." All the representatives were capable of integrating theological concepts and reflection with a standard CCHD discourse on the principles of Catholic social justice teaching. For example, another representative said that getting poor people to participate in the process of social justice was a "litmus test" for CCHD because needed changes in society have to be "deeper," meaning that "human and leadership development is key. . . . They develop people's gifts and reveal the dignity of the people." People need to be "interconnected," he told me, in order to make a "transformation of sinful situations." He continued, "Salvation is about changing God's world—a total capacity for transformation." These representatives were revealing a working knowledge of the principle of the "structures of sin" that can be changed only through "institutional change."

This understanding of Catholic social justice teaching as an instrument for social structural change in the United States illustrates the difference between CCHD's mission and those of Catholic Charities and other charitable organizations of the U.S. Catholic Church. Conservative critics of CCHD, particularly the Rev. Richard John Neuhaus, editor of the journal *First Things,* have singled out CCHD's past funding of organizations having connections to prochoice projects as a prime reason to actually encourage Catholics not to contribute to the annual appeal.[79] On the left, CCHD has been criticized for falling victim to the prolife antiabortion litmus test without being equally cautious regarding other life issues such as the death penalty. In fact, Gary Delgado, a well-regarded social theorist of community organizing who directs the

Applied Research Center (ARC) in Oakland, California, helped wage an Internet campaign to discredit CCHD's 1998 moral guidelines for funding projects.[80]

During my visits to the CCHD offices throughout 1998 and 1999, I was aware that more was going on than just work. There was a strong organizational culture that emphasized the same principles that the staff was implementing throughout the United States. One day I was asked to stay for the weekly staff lunch held in CCHD's conference room. That day they were celebrating the birthday of a temporary clerk who had been working at CCHD over the past few months. Apart from the birthday cake and gifts, the lunch included an affirmation exercise in which everyone present spoke about the gifts that this clerk brought to the office "community." Having worked in a variety of office and other environments, I was struck by the naturalness and genuineness of the process—the workers' affirmations contained nothing goofy or saccharine, but communicated a sincere sense of values that they were trying to live out in both their private and public lives. My visits to the CCHD offices showed what an institutional cultural milieu can do for people, especially a social justice cultural milieu. The staff reinforced the bottom-line principles that they applied to their clients in the day-to-day milieu of the office. The executive director, the Rev. Robert Vitillo, told me that the institutional goal of CCHD is the "linking of the charity and justice sides of our work. . . . Charity sets the stage for structural change." A high degree of charity, expressing the virtue of solidarity, was palpable among all the staff, from clerical workers to managers.

Solidarity as a virtue and as an organizing principle was also demonstrated outside the office, in CCHD's fieldwork and the staff's involvement in the Jubilee Year events in Los Angeles, where they were responsible, with other U.S. staff of the Bishops' Conference, for facilitating the meetings and setting the tone for the events. Father Vitillo cochaired the Jubilee Justice event at UCLA.

Above all, I felt that the professional staff—Catholic and non-Catholic alike—involved with client agencies, educational programs, and public relations loved their work and were committed to social justice principles in their private lives as well. Many of them served on the boards of directors of various Washington-area nonprofit organizations. Each the professional workers (field representatives, education specialists, economic development specialists, program managers, as well as executive staff) told me that working at CCHD was actually the high point of their lifelong commitment to social justice causes and professional work. Most had moved to Washington to take the job after having worked in an organization affiliated with CCHD.

The significance of CCHD both in the U.S. Catholic Church and in U.S. civil society is very wide, considering that more than a million people in social justice organizations are financially and morally supported each year. No other national organization has had such direct impact on grassroots organizations seeking structural change. In addition, the national appeal held each year on the Sunday preceding Thanksgiving provides an education regarding social justice for all Catholics attending Mass. Local diocesan directors and leaders of funded organizations are often invited by pastors to speak on behalf of the appeal and are able to reflect on local social justice issues funded by the campaign—the most regular, direct, and universal provision of social justice teaching in the United States.[81] One might think of CCHD Annual Appeal Sunday as a day when more than 18 million Americans are listening to a message regarding their social and religious responsibility to assist in the alleviation of poverty and the empowerment of poor people.[82]

Through the appeal CCHD initiates and closes an annual feedback loop for supporting the work of the St. Anthony's Local Organizing Committee, Oakland Community Organizations, and the Pacific Institute for Community Organizing, which I will analyze in the next section. The CCHD is the key national institutional mechanism of the Catholic Church to move its social justice teaching from the theological levels of international and national teaching to theological reflection in dioceses and parishes and through the levels of national and local civil society. In practical terms, the work of Jesuit biblical scholar John Donohue flows through all these levels of church and civil society and ends up as the discourse of Mexican immigrants in Oakland. His social justice scholarship matters because the poor matter, and the poor are better off because of his scholarship. Because of this relationship between ideas and social action, the concepts of biblical justice, particularly "right relations," and the principles of solidarity, option for the poor, human rights, participation, association, and human development form part of CCHD's discourse to help alleviate poverty and empower poor people. More than any other group in my study, CCHD stands at the center of the Catholic social imagination.

Community Organizing in Oakland: A Case Study

ALL POLITICS IS LOCAL: LOCATING
THE GRASSROOTS SOCIAL JUSTICE MISSION

The first Sunday I attended the Spanish Mass at St. Anthony Parish in the San Antonio District of Oakland, I knew that the parish and the district would be a rich site for ethnographic research.[83] The church was packed with more than six hundred Latino parishioners from at least three generations of Mexican Americans, as well as very recent arrivals from Mexico. The celebrant was a Latino priest. An image of the apparition of Our Lady of Guadalupe was placed behind the altar in the middle of the modern sanctuary. I was struck by the spirited and well-executed liturgical music sung throughout the service. I thought, "This is a place I can come to every Sunday and leave ready to face the week ahead—as well as a vibrant place to do social research."

The next week when I arrived at the church, though, I encountered a quite different scene. Something had died, overnight. First, the image of Our Lady of Guadalupe had been moved to a side location, alongside the depiction of Our Lady of Perpetual Help, the Virgin of the Filipinos of the parish. Second, the choir was gone—for good. Third, a new pastor, a Vietnamese priest, was presiding at the Spanish Mass. And fourth, a new Mass in Vietnamese began immediately after the 9:30 AM Spanish Mass. As I watched the Vietnamese filling the pews, it seemed I was witnessing an occupation by a highly disciplined cadre of foreign troops, particularly as I saw a crack team of men redecorate the sanctuary with flowers, banners, and a statue reflecting the Vietnamese Catholic culture—all within fifteen minutes.

By the third week of my investigation, I had been scheduled to celebrate the Spanish Mass, something I would do about twice a month over the next two years. That first Mass left a lasting impression. At my Mass there was no music; however, there was a full complement of lay liturgical ministers assisting me: a sacristan, lectors, eucharistic ministers, adult altar servers, and ushers. But what I remember most was an encounter after Mass as I was greeting the people at the door of the church. A very angry and determined woman named Diane pointedly asked me: "Who are you? Were you sent here to take over this community? We've worked long and hard here to build up this community."

I was stunned, but I responded that I was a doctoral student in sociology at Berkeley and a Jesuit priest. My only interest was to do social research in the community and help the parish by celebrating Mass in

Spanish as needed. I knew that Diane felt suspicious of my answer. I did not see her again until several months later.

By this point, I thought that I made a bad choice in choosing this community for my field study. I did not want to be caught in the middle of a political storm. But as time progressed, the choice to study the San Antonio community proved a good one, allowing me to examine a community and a parish facing many changes reflective of both the Church and civil society in the United States.

My primary reason for choosing this district to observe was the fact that it had one of the oldest and continuous community-organizing efforts in the western United States. Community organizing is the largest social justice phenomenon in the United States, involving from one to three million people.[84] The San Antonio and Fruitvale districts were the first neighborhoods to form the Oakland Community Organizations (OCO) in 1973 as a network of local organizing committees. In the first few years the organizing was neighborhood centered and depended on local churches to recruit members and to loan facilities for meeting spaces. The early organizers were two California Jesuit priests who had been trained in Chicago by the key organizers of Alinsky. The California Jesuits wanted to create an organization similar to the Woodlawn organization in Chicago. The old-timers of St. Anthony's told me that in the early days of community organizing (the late 1970s) they had been concerned with the proliferation of liquor stores and prostitution along the two main boulevards of the district. By the 1980s, the liquor store and prostitution issues were replaced by new issues: crack cocaine houses in the middle of the neighborhoods and gang violence that accompanied drug dealing.

Founded in 1977, OCO has been highly successful in training local laypeople in the "Alinsky method" of pragmatically oriented civic activism based on "one-on-one" method interviewing of one's neighbors to find out their self-interests. Saul Alinsky (1909–72) believed Alexis de Tocqueville's observation, made in *Democracy in America,* that Americans can be motivated to serve their fellow citizens if one taps into their "self-interest rightly-understood," or their "enlightened self-interest."[85] The fundamental premise of the Alinsky method is that when members of a community discover their common self-interest, they can work in a concerted effort to achieve it. Self-interest becomes the common interest—the common good. For Alinsky and his followers in Oakland, the problem in the United States is that poor people, the working classes, immigrants, and minorities are not organized in such a way that their self-interests can emerge. Middle-class, upper-middle-class, and wealthy citizens are organized through their involvement in politics, business and professional associations, and a variety of other networks where their self-interests become institutionalized. OCO's mission is to organize the interests of disempowered people into an associational life and civic institutions that represent the members of the community.

Every St. Anthony and citywide OCO meeting begins with the reading of a "credential" that reflects the power of the organization: "OCO is a organization of 35,000 families in the City of Oakland in 32 churches . . ." Over the years OCO has become the largest civic organization in Oakland, and it can claim a successful track record of "victories." As one of the lay founders of OCO states: "Those were simple beginnings, the issues were less complex and local—stop signs, stray dogs, run down properties—but the seed was planted, the soil was right, and it was bound to grow. As we began working together as groups to resolve issues, first in our own neighborhood, then with others who had identified similar problems, we were, and still are, constantly challenged to move beyond, to stretch our horizons, and to develop leadership qualities we didn't even know we had!"

OCO's victories resulted from a strategy of mediating the self-interests of the parish group and the institutions of urban life, such as the police and fire departments, city council, school board, zoning boards, the Catholic Diocese of Oakland and other religious bodies, the business sector, and philanthropic foundations. This strategy places the organization as a leveraging mechanism between the people as citizens with interests and the institutional players of the community. The local organization committee and OCO inductively define the problems that emerge from one-on-ones as "issues," and these become the basis for connecting the constituency to the institutional structures, with the goal of effecting long-term institutional change. The goal is that all the players "win": the constituency gets a problem solved, and the institutional players can claim that they are not only doing their job but also working on behalf of the grassroots. OCO is not interested in running programs or building new institutions. Rather, it wishes the existing structures to work for the people they are intended to serve. The one-on-ones keep the organization current on the issues, so that once an issue is taken care of the organization can easily move to another.

During the time of my field research, I was able to participate in a major education initiative that had come about through one-on-one research regarding the plight of the Oakland Public School District. In the early 1990s, the school district had achieved national notoriety because the school board had attempted to make Ebonics a second language and also because it had gone into receivership by the state of California. Adding to the district's problems were some of the lowest scores in California on the state's standardized tests in reading and math in 1994 and 1995.[86] The one-on-ones revealed that parents felt powerless in the face of the school district's entrenched bureaucracy and the seeming obstinacy of the teachers' union. OCO leaders knew that the education agenda of its constituency would not be an easy issue to tackle, but it had to be taken on or else the children would never get a quality education in the public schools. "For the children!" became a rallying cry at OCO meetings.

Local Social Justice Teaching and Implementation

At St. Anthony's and other Catholic parishes of OCO, the appropriation of sacred symbols and the scriptures for social purposes was an essential component of "faith-based" community organizing. Indeed, the almost unconscious Catholic and religious instinct to do this was a key reason that OCO's parent organization, PICO, switched from a neighborhood-based community-organizing model to a faith-based model in the early 1990s.[87] PICO provides OCO and the other eighty-five affiliate organizing committees with their professional community organizers. Most important, PICO offers national training institutes for local clergy and lay leaders, using the principles of Alinsky.[88] The Rev. John Baumann, S.J., PICO's long-term executive director, has described the fundamental drive of the organization in this way: "In its own way, PICO too is a family—a place where people can find their own true voice. It is a place where all people are treated as individuals deserving of respect and love. And, like a family, PICO looks out for its own. We are all filled with anger when we see conditions that foster fear, hatred, and despair. We are moved to justice to make the world right for our family. And we realize that the power to change the world rests in our capacity to unite as family, as community, and as children of God."[89] For PICO, faith-based community organizing draws on a pragmatic approach of getting new members from religious congregations and a desire to integrate religious culture, social justice teaching, and the scriptures as a way of providing ongoing meaning for the disciple citizens.

In 1997 I was invited to attend PICO's national leadership training, which is held each January in Ponchatoula, Louisiana.[90] During the five days of intensive training of clergy and lay leaders of local units around the United States, I was able to observe the "classic" organizing tools and behaviors that unify all of PICO's local units and citywide community organizing efforts. In a study of PICO and OCO, Richard Wood discusses these tools and behaviors as a set of practices, beliefs, and ethos that are culturally tailored in the black and Latino communities.[91] In addition to this cultural system, I suggest that the skills developed by PICO and other Alinsky-type civic organizations have a primary orientation toward U.S. civic culture, with its normative orientation toward incorporating its members into U.S. civil society in order to promote structural change in the world. As well, this normative orientation sets the tone for what becomes the foundational cultural milieu for Catholic social justice teaching and implementation at the local level of a parish or neighborhood.

The normative orientation of PICO can be seen in its educative mission to "empower" its members to implement grassroots change in American public spaces, such as school boards, city halls, police departments, and governmental bureaucracies. In this sense, PICO training is a school for the behaviors necessary for active members of civil society. This is what Alinsky himself called "popular education," i.e., education and mutual understanding among various groups in order to gain a "new appreciation and definition of social issues."[92] PICO training represents what David Lloyd and Paul Thomas see as a cultural education in public life, nurturing what I will call, following Antonio Gramsci, "organic intellectuals"[93] for a newly constituted ethical state: "The school, in other words most effectively permits the transfer of the subject from the private domain of the family into the public world of the political, not by teaching civics but by representing representation."[94]

The educative mission for PICO is located in public meeting spaces in which people gather as participants in the public and democratic practices of "representing representation." More specifically, PICO training assists its practitioners in learning fundamental roles of trust. As Adam Seligman notes regarding the difficulty of talking about "trust" without reverting to an essentialism of attitudes: "Roles here are used as a heuristic device, as a type of analytical shorthand the better to grasp the structurally conditioned nature of trust and remove it from all philosophical abstraction or theological justification."[95]

As noted by Richard Wood, PICO teaches the following primary civic behaviors and skills:

- *one-on-ones:* the primary process for relationship building and initiating an organizational web of trust, wherein each member is important, through grassroots identification of one's self-interest and common values and interests

- *prayer:* the exteriorizing of beliefs in the public forum in order to create a "culture of belief"

- *credentials:* a review at every PICO gathering of the organization's identity, membership status, and relationship to power brokers in the community

- *research:* an inductive process of systematically evaluating one-on-ones to determine issues for the organization to address with the cooperation of other organizations, elected officials, academics, other professionals, and governmental bureaucrats

- *action:* holding a public institution or official accountable through a mass meeting at any of various levels: local, areawide, citywide, interorganizationally, regionally, statewide, or nationally

- *accountability:* the development of a challenging process for organizational discipline as both an internal activity of the organization and an outside activity of holding a target accountable

- *negotiations:* usually a behinds-the-scenes process of lay leaders and organizers meeting with targets prior to an action to forge agreements that can be ratified at the action

- *evaluation:* accountability process by leaders and organizers, at the end of every meeting of a local organizing committee (LOC), research meeting, or action, to assess the event and improve communication and critical reflection[96]

My field research in Oakland showed that these practices were carried out consistently as a method for addressing issues.

On the day-to-day level, PICO organizations employ a standard way of conducting a meeting or action. This scheme has proved critically important in the formation of disciplined leaders:

1. *Call to order:* A lay leader is selected to lead the meeting with the help of the professional organizer. Leadership is rotated on a regular basis so that there is never a sense that the organization has a "president."

2. *Prayer:* This is normally led by the pastor or religious leader of the congregation that is closely attached to the community organizing effort. Prayers tend to be denominationally oriented at the local level and more inclusive and general at larger areawide and citywide actions.

3. *Organization credentials:* The citywide organization is identified, along with how many congregations and families are involved. The mission of the organization is also stated.

4. *Opening remarks:* The leader of the meeting states the purpose for this particular meeting.

5. *Agenda items:* Each item on the agenda is addressed. People are encouraged to participate in discussion of the items. The leader keeps track of time and moves the discussion along as rapidly as possible.

6. *Action items:* If agenda items require follow-through, the leader notes what the item is, who is responsible for it, and the deadline.

7. *Commitments:* Normally at LOC meetings the participants are asked to commit themselves to doing one-on-ones. Each person is polled and commitments are made. At other meetings participants, especially non-OCO members, may be asked to commit themselves to the action items on the agenda.

8. *Closing remarks:* The leader summarizes the accomplishments of the meeting.

9. *Closing prayer:* Again, the pastor or religious leader leads the group in prayer, very often summarizing what has just happened in the meeting and asking God to bless the efforts of the group.

10. *Dismissal:* The leader adjourns the meeting.

Meetings are normally one hour in length. Finishing on time, as a verification of the social contract, is highly valued. When Spanish-speaking members are present, someone is chosen to interpret all the meeting remarks between Spanish and English. At larger citywide meetings there is also American Sign Language interpretation. At all gatherings there is a staff member or organizer present whose task is to ensure that the meeting space is set up, the leaders for the meeting have been briefed, and the agenda is clear. The professional organizer does not participate in the meeting unless a leader or member asks a question that needs to be answered or clarified.

Local and research meetings are typically organized as roundtables. Leaders often use flipcharts to illustrate their points and to record important decisions. In larger unit meetings, seating is often arranged in a semicircular fashion with a focus on a speakers' table or podium. It is not uncommon to have small group discussions of an agenda item, with sets of six to ten chairs organized in small circles. In that process, each small group will select a reporter to summarize its findings for the large group. Also at every meeting an attendance sheet is passed around so that each attender's name, address, and phone number can be recorded. This provides leaders and organizers with an update on membership, and new participants can be targeted for a personal one-on-one by a lay leader or organizer. The sign-in sheet also gives the participant the opportunity to self-identify for the record and as a sign of participation.

The picture conveyed here is of a highly structured organization dependent on numerous practices that are practiced regularly and routinely. Newcomers are folded into the organization by involvement in the practices of civic participation and are introduced to habits of the organizational culture that facilitate a well-organized and effective process. Newcomers are not given overviews of organizational philosophy as ideological formation. Rather, particularly through the one-on-one, a newcomer is given the experience of being able to articulate his or her self-interests with a willing listener who shares those interests. The leaders adhere to the Tocquevillian notion that democracy should be built upon "the principle of self-interest rightly understood."[97]

Thus, a school for civic participation is formed with a bottom-up, experiential process of participation in the cultural system of practices, beliefs, and ethos. New members are brought into the habitus of faith-based community organizing. The listed practices serve as a normative formation for civic participation that functions across lines of cultural, religious, community, political, and ideological variance among its members and local units. The normative formation generates an experiential solidarity among members—solidarity as an organizing principle, as well as solidarity in relationships or public friendships, and solidarity building the institutions of civil society. Furthermore, this cultural system functions as an "American" model of civic participation that is embedded in the public life of democracy, "making democracy work."[98] In the following section I will examine how the PICO model incorporates Mexican immigrants into U.S. civic life and into the solidarity of the local organizing committee and citywide organizing committees, allowing them to maintain their *mexicanidad* while at the same time becoming American through civic practices.

In October 1995, I began involvement in two Roman Catholic congregation–based units of PICO in Oakland, both affiliated with OCO. The two units were chosen for comparative purposes. The St. Augustine unit of three hundred families is located in a racially integrated middle-class neighborhood, while the St. Anthony unit of about a thousand families is located in a predominantly Latino neighborhood. During the time of my research, both units had very active local organizing committees that allowed me full access to meetings and interviews with local members. I also met on a monthly basis with a professional organizer, who served as my key informant regarding PICO and OCO. This organizer provided me with general overviews of citywide actions, membership lists, and contact people. My name was on the mailing list for pastors so that I was notified of special meetings and citywide issues. Here I focus on participation practices in both units as part of the construction of the cultural milieu for social justice at the parish level and consider how they help to form a Catholic social imagination.

LOCAL ISSUES, CITYWIDE ACTIONS, MULTICULTURAL SOLIDARITY

My primary observation of OCO was at the monthly parish-neighborhood meetings. Both parishes followed OCO's standard meeting format. Over a period of eighteen months, I attended six monthly meetings at St. Augustine's and fourteen at St. Anthony's. Both units dealt with citywide issues related to class size reduction in the Oakland Public School District and the development of homework centers in the neighborhoods. Information gathered at the meetings related to these issues was taken to research meetings attended by key leaders and the organizers. This led to negotiations with school officials prior to a citywide action in March 1996.

For that citywide action, more than two thousand members filled the grand ballroom of the Oakland Convention Center to capacity to gain commitments from the City of Oakland and the Oakland School Board to fund class size reduction and the proposed homework centers. This highly charged multicultural event began with music by two gospel choirs and one Latino music group. City and school district officials made public commitments to fund the two projects. The slogan "For the children!" was repeatedly used by the leaders of the meeting to raise the energy of the rally. Each time an official committed himself or herself to the projects, the audience would break out into wild applause and shout "For the children!" or "¡Para los niños!" The meeting began at 6:30 p.m.

and ended promptly as planned at 8:00. From my seat among the people from St. Anthony's, I sensed that the people around me thought the rally to be highly successful.

OCO citywide actions make visible the multicultural alliance among the primarily ethnically or racially oriented congregational units as whites, Latinos, and blacks bring distinctive culturally based elements to these gatherings. The result is that culture "from below" "moves up." At the larger actions, I suggest, OCO incorporates the cultural practices that work best for a particular cultural group in the context of a multicultural event. A large action appears to convey the solidarity of the membership. But how do these cultural practices emerge from below? Next I shall examine the distinctive cultural dynamics of St. Anthony Parish and then how the parish LOC incorporated Mexican immigrant neophytes into the organization.

CONSTRUCTION OF ETHNIC ENCLAVES AND
EFFECTS ON COMMUNITY ORGANIZING

St. Anthony Parish's approach to multiculturalism stands in marked contrast to that of St. Augustine Parish. Rather than attempting to integrate various cultural groups (race, age, ethnicity, sexual orientation, marital status) into a coherent whole while respecting each group's identity and autonomy, St. Anthony allows separate ethnic enclaves to operate in one parish plant. Walking into this modern church, built after Vatican II, one encounters a multitude of ethnoreligious images conveying the interests of the Latinos, Filipinos, whites, and Vietnamese who make up the parish. Each of the four Sunday masses caters to a specific group: the 8:00 a.m. Mass in English, with traditional music, oriented toward the remaining whites and blacks in the parish; the 9:30 Mass in Spanish, with Mexican-oriented hymns; the 11:00 Mass in Vietnamese, with traditional Vietnamese music; and the 12:30 p.m. Mass in English, with a Filipino choir that sings contemporary American church music.

At various points in the liturgical year, the Latino and Vietnamese communities, the dominant enclaves in the parish, might display their ethnoreligious emblems in the central sanctuary, such as an elaborate Virgin of Guadalupe shrine in mid-December and a special altar for the Vietnamese New Year. During the major liturgical seasons such as Advent and Easter Time, it is not uncommon to find banners with words in English, Spanish, and Vietnamese. In one nave of the church there are three different images of Mary, each reflecting Vietnamese, Mexican, or Filipino Marian devotion. It appears as if there are competing cultures vying for space. Judging by the fresh flowers placed at these various shrines every week, there seems to be regular devotional activity around these cultural-religious practices.

As I began my observation of St. Anthony's in October 1995, I was able to note a dramatic change that occurred as a Mexican American pastor was replaced by the first Vietnamese pastor, a man in his early forties, in the Oakland Diocese. St. Anthony's is the second oldest parish in the East Bay. Founded in 1871, it serves a neighborhood that reaches from Lake Merritt to the Fruitvale neighborhood. The San Antonio District of the city of Oakland is made up of about thirty-five thousand people, of whom approximately 70 percent are Hispanics, 10 percent black, 10 percent Asian, and 10 percent white. In St. Anthony's immediate neighborhood, residents are mostly immigrants from Mexico, Vietnam, and Cambodia. The housing stock of the neighborhood mirrors the demographic changes of the district: stately turn-of-the century mansions that once housed the wealthy and powerful of California but have now been cut up into apartments for the immigrant working poor; 1930s and 1940s California bungalows for Oakland's white working class, now housing Latino, Filipino, black, and white working-class single-family homeowners; 1950s and 1960s apartment complexes, housing many of the Mexican and Asian immigrant working class.[99]

St. Anthony's parish name actually determined the name of the neighborhood, San Antonio. The San Antonio District is the oldest Mexican neighborhood in Oakland, and for that reason from the 1970s until 1995 there were four Latino priests who served as pastors of St. Anthony's.[100]

When the Vietnamese pastor was assigned to St. Anthony's, the Oakland Diocese assigned Filipino American and Ecuadorian American priests to the multicultural parish. However, diocesan personnel did not consult the parishioners regarding the transition process. As I noted earlier, on the first Sunday of my observation the Spanish Mass had a vibrant folkloric choir and skilled musicians. The Sunday following the arrival of the new Vietnamese pastor, the very large image of Our Lady of Guadalupe, the patron saint of Mexican Catholics, was removed from the center of the sanctuary and placed in a side nave—again without consultation. The move of this symbol to make way for new Vietnamese decorations led the Latino music director to quit his position. What had been a very dynamic Latino liturgy became a Mass without music for more than a year. Furthermore, the parish suddenly became a

Vietnamese Catholic center, with a parish organization based on a Vietnamese model of parish cells directed by the new pastor.[101]

In the summer of 1996, the Spanish-speaking priest left the parish and was not replaced. And in the summer of 1997 the Filipino American priest, who was the chief contact for OCO in the parish, became seriously ill and went on medical leave. To say the least, the Latino sector of the parish experienced a leadership crisis. In conversations with parishioners and community leaders, I learned that the Latinos of St. Anthony's had been accustomed to clergy leadership of the traditional Mexican variety, i.e., highly authoritarian and hierarchical—"Padre gets things done."

St. Anthony's involvement in community organizing dates to the origins of the PICO organization and the formation of OCO in 1977.[102] OCO has relied on St. Anthony's to produce key Latino leaders for the citywide organization. Because of the cleavage caused in the parish Latino community with the appointment of the Vietnamese pastor, several of these leaders dropped out of the parish unit, but they continued their activity in citywide research meetings and actions. In the initial months of my observation, attendance at the monthly meetings was small, usually from four to eight women. However, whenever there was a call for St. Anthony's presence at a citywide action, such as those mentioned in the above discussion of the organizational culture, the parish could mobilize 100 to 250 parishioners to attend.

In the spring of 1996, two new members—a Mexican male, Manuel, and a Mexican American female, Silvia—were recruited by the local organizer. They helped bring a new vitality to the group. By the fall of 1996, the local group and the organizer began to strategically plan for the recruitment of new members, since it was clear that many of the old activists had changed parishes even though they had not moved out of the neighborhood. That fall one of the old activists, Diane, a white female who speaks fluent Spanish and is very Mexican in culture and style, returned. (This was the same Diane who had confronted me that Sunday on what I was doing at the parish.) The local group decided to use the liturgical year of 1996–97 to begin a process of parish renewal in the Latino community by holding parishwide meetings on Sunday mornings following the Spanish mass.

It should be noted that the pastor did not attend these meetings until 1999. However, he faithfully paid the parish dues to OCO, and the organizer kept him informed of his activities in the parish.[103] I also met with the pastor each month to keep him aware of my ongoing research and activities in the parish.[104] He never impeded OCO activity, and when he got involved in the organization in 1999, he brought new energy into the meetings by introducing multilingual music to get the people motivated. More important, by being present as the pastor he brought a new legitimacy to the organization, especially for the Vietnamese parishioners.

Scott (the lead organizer) and I had observed that on Sundays following the 9:30 Spanish mass, many parents escorted their children to the Catholic school for religious instruction, offered from 11:00 a.m. to 12:00 p.m. every Sunday during the school year, and waited in the gymnasium during this time. Scott suggested that OCO might target these parents as potential new members. With this idea, the leaders decided to offer an Advent program entitled "On the Road to Tepeyac," signifying that Latinos are *guadalupanas* on a continuous journey of faith. The idea was to connect themes of neighborhood social justice with the religious practices associated in the Mexican community with Advent, Guadalupe, and Christmas.

The Road to Tepeyac theme for the meetings was an attempt to integrate the liturgical cycle with the social justice image of Our Lady of Guadalupe that has developed in the United States, and thus to legitimate social concerns by connecting them with common religious symbols and impulses of Mexican immigrants. This type of integration is quite common in U.S. pastoral practice and planning, based on the practical question, how do we get more people to our meetings? The use of saints and feast days by Catholic pastoral workers for various social objectives, particularly in immigrant communities, is common in U.S. Catholic history.[105] The appropriation of Our Lady of Guadalupe for social purposes has been a significant development in the evolution of the meaning of the apparition. Hispanic theologians such as Virgilio Elizondo, Andrés Guerrero, and Jeannette Rodriguez have brought new meaning to Guadalupe based on her message of compassion for the natives of Mexico and her social location as an indigenous woman during the Spanish conquest.[106] Elizondo, the leading theologian of the social Guadalupe, has written: "The real miracle seems to be in the hearts of the people. Mary, as Mother, gave a meaning to the people's lives and granted them the strength and courage to undertake over and over again, what, humanly speaking, seemed impossible: for the illiterate, the powerless, the poor, and the oppressed to rise up against the powerful to bring about justice."[107]

This kind of social justice theological reflection is not at all common in Mexico, even though Mexican national identity has been historically driven by the Guadalupe story—particularly in the image of Father Hidalgo, the founding father of modern Mexico, leading the nation into independence under the banner of Guadalupe and the red, green, and yellow flag of the new nation-state on 16 September 1810.[108] The appropriation of Guadalupe for social justice objectives in the United States—also noted in my discussion of the United Farm Workers—has become part of the social imagination not only for Latino Catholics but for all U.S. Catholics. This was evident, for example, in the U.S. Hispanic church's use of Guadalupe as a symbol of social liberation for the national Encuentro processes of 1972, 1977, 1985, and 2000, conducted by the bishops' office for Hispanic affairs.[109] The Guadalupe practices demonstrate the integral orientation of the Catholic social imagination developed in the United States, particularly among Latinos.

RECRUITMENT OF MEXICAN IMMIGRANTS FOR FAITH-BASED COMMUNITY ORGANIZING

As noted earlier, one Sunday after the Spanish Mass I noticed parents in the school gym for their children. They sat in folding chairs set here and there against the walls of the gymnasium—each person keeping to himself or herself unless there were small children playing or sleeping near them. On the day of the first meeting of the Advent program, the parents gathered in the gymnasium as usual, having bypassed a registration table that had name tags and sign-in sheet. As was their habit, they gravitated towad the chairs against the walls, even though other chairs had been set up in a semicircle toward the center of the building. The parents talked with their children until the teachers took them to their classrooms.

Once the children had left, the organizer, the two leaders, and I went around the gym to personally invite the parents to sit in the chairs set up in semicircles. This took about ten minutes to accomplish. It was clear that all the parents present were primarily Spanish speaking. The meeting was conducted entirely in Spanish. There were approximately twenty-seven women and thirteen men—all Mexican immigrants, from midtwenties to about forty.[110] The meeting followed the typical OCO meeting format: opening remarks, prayer, presentation of agenda, opening talk, small group sharing, large group sharing, action items, closing remarks, prayer, and dismissal.

During the meeting, the people were asked to give their opinions on what parish priorities should be. They were divided into four small groups of ten each. This took about five minutes to organize: pulling chairs out of the semicircle, forming four small circles with them, positioning each group's facilitator so that he or she could have access to flipchart paper that was taped on the walls. Once the small groups began, most participants moved their chairs out, breaking the circle, to form a row facing the facilitator.

The facilitators attempted to elicit opinions by asking direct questions about parish and neighborhood concerns. Very few people participated. Those who did spoke directly to the facilitator and not to the other group members. The facilitators recorded the ideas of each person on the flipchart paper. There was little, if any, interaction among the participants. Each facilitator chose a spokesperson who would highlight the results of the process in the large group discussion to follow. This process lasted approximately fifteen minutes.

Following the small group time, the facilitators directed participants to rearrange the chairs similarly to the original setup. The organizer announced that he would pass around a sign-in sheet so that people could sign their name, address, and phone number. About twenty-five people did sign in. The spokespersons were invited to come forward to give their reports. The facilitator for this process recorded these summary ideas on flipchart paper that could be seen by the entire group.

Four general themes emerged from this consultation: (1) the Latino portion of the parish saw the need for a full-time Spanish-speaking priest to serve the community, particularly since during the week there was no Spanish-speaking priest in the parish to consult; (2) the youth of the parish should have programs to serve them; (3) greater outreach from the parish to the community was needed, especially offering hospitality and generating a sense of solidarity among the Latinos of the community; and (4) greater parental involvement was needed to advocate improvement in local public schools.

After this process was completed, the organizers announced that there would be a follow-up meeting to address these concerns on the following Sunday. The meeting closed with a prayer led by the priest. The people were dismissed at 12:15, as their children were released from the religious education classrooms. People departed immediately with their children; there was little small talk as they left the gym. The organizers did a quick evaluation of the meeting and assigned one member to type up the results from the flipchart papers. They also arranged a meeting to plan the next Sunday's meeting.

The same meeting process was replicated the following Sunday. Participation dynamics were similar as well: people bypassing the registration table; parents seated with their children close to the walls of the gym; the slow process of inviting people to take seats; low participation in small groups, with attention focused upon the facilitators; and the slow process of moving chairs. However, during the large group discussion there seemed to be a greater energy and participation, particularly from the men, that allowed for greater cross-fertilization of ideas. It was clear that the participants felt that having a full-time resident Spanish-speaking priest was their highest priority for getting the parish and the neighborhood more involved in the Latino community. They felt that with such a leader present, the liturgical life, outreach to youth and the community, and general pastoral life of the community would return to the state of the parish prior to the appointment of the Vietnamese pastor.

Participation in the December and January local organizing committee meetings increased, as four new members attended as a result of these two consultations. For at least four monthly meetings, these new participants sat first against the walls; at last, however, they became used to taking seats at the table. The new members often brought their children to the meetings. The other regular members were middle-aged or seniors. The meetings at St. Anthony's were conducted bilingually—if the leader for the evening spoke Spanish as a first language, the meeting would be conducted in Spanish with English translation, or if the leader was English-speaking, a Spanish translation would be done (often by the same person).

EFFECTS OF THE CONSULTATION
MEETINGS AND RECRUITMENT

Over the course of eighteen months, I participated in eight consultation processes with Mexican immigrants in the Catholic school gymnasium. I was able to witness a continuum of behaviors related to civic participation: entering the meeting room, finding a place to locate oneself, entering the meeting space, participating in a variety of consultative and democratic processes (expressing one's opinion, casting a vote, volunteering for an activity), socializing with one's peers, being helpful, etc. These behaviors may seem very commonplace in U.S. civic life, but for Mexican immigrant urbano-campesinos in Oakland these behaviors were not "natural" or easy to carry out.

At the beginning of the process, the participants were brought into the public meeting space through personal invitation by an outside leader. They were told where to sit, how to participate, and how to express themselves. They learned the civic process by *doing* the civic process. In this sense the leaders provided a basic civic education for these Mexican immigrants in the introduction of behaviors that make a meeting in the Alinsky ideal-typic model work. Furthermore, they learned by practice the Catholic principles of association, participation, solidarity, the role of the laity, and the common good.

The introduction of skilled civic participants—other Latinos involved in other parts of the parish—helped introduce the immigrants to other more "social" aspects of civic participation: chatting with one's peers, enjoying refreshments together, and being helpful in setting up and taking down chairs and tables, preparing refreshments, and cleaning up. The old-timers modeled social skills for the newcomers, who at least in this situation were uncertain, oblivious, or nervous about such behaviors.[111] Generational and immigration-status divides were crossed through this process, which is critically important to achieve before the old-timers are no longer capable of getting to meetings or actions. Furthermore, crossing these divides has become a major challenge for the future of the political culture in states like California where there often deep divides among Latinos by language capacity, immigration status, and religion.[112]

Over time the parents adapted and were able to join in, participate, and enjoy the faith-based community-organizing habitus. Not only had they learned the primary skills for civic participation, they had learned to become citizens together—that is, seeing each other as peers and becoming involved with each other's opinions, values, and commitments. They began to see and experience that they themselves can effect local change. They incorporated themselves into the U.S. parish model, in which their active membership was important. They experienced how the U.S. Catholic Church bridges the religious institution and civic life.

Specifically, they saw that to expect a Spanish-speaking priest to be hired in the parish and solve all the problems of the Latino community was not only unrealistic but did not reflect healthy expectations of the clergy's role. They began to realize that the meetings they were attending were giving them skills and voice that they could apply to needs in the parish and the community, as evidenced in the incremental changes that other Latino laity are bringing about. From a Catholic perspective, they began to see that "the people are the Church" and that their membership, participation, and social commitment matter.

THE ISSUES AND THE RESULTS

The pastor, who did not attend these meetings because he was involved in the Vietnamese mass held at the same time, supported the first proposal of trying to get a full-time Hispanic priest. Even prior to the listening sessions he had been pressuring the diocese for such a priest. But due to the clergy shortage and to the parish's reputation for having "aggressive" lay Hispanics, no priest was available to serve St. Anthony's. The bishop of Oakland actually told me about this reputation—many clergy in the diocese actually assumed it was true.

From my vantage point, I saw that a strength of the parish was a cadre of trained OCO leaders (I identified at least twelve people fitting this description) who spoke up about perceived injustices in their parish and community. They were leaders like Diane, who had put in many volunteer hours with the OCO and parish organizations. These leaders formed a permanent substructure in the St. Anthony Parish community, going back for twenty-five years. They could be counted on to be present at OCO meetings, actions, and rallies. I learned from informal discussions with diocesan priests that the "aggressive" label had been generated by priests who had served at St. Anthony's and were not accustomed to working with trained laity. The irony was that because of an empowered core Latino laity, the parish would not get a Spanish-speaking priest. Further, the people most wanting a Spanish-speaking priest had no knowledge of the parish's reputation.

As late as mid-2001, the parish had not been given a Hispanic priest. However, one of the OCO leaders, Manuel, was in training to be a deacon. Once ordained as a permanent deacon, he would be able to do baptisms, perform marriages, and preside at quinceañeras for the Latino community. Maybe this was actually a bigger "win" than getting a priest, because Manuel was an immigrant from Mexico, married with children, and had proved a real servant to the parish and OCO. He and his wife Yolanda had put their "faith into action."

The second issue, youth programs, was of personal interest to the associate pastor of the parish, Father Rick. At the time of the meetings he was already organizing a bilingual youth program that encompassed confirmation, community service, and sports and entertainment. Father Rick also became very involved in St. Anthony's grade school. He was well known among the children and youth of the San Antonio District. Thus over time this second goal of the listening sessions was being achieved through the various programs that Father Rick introduced. But

Father Rick's programs cannot be classified as "wins" for OCO, because they were strictly parochial programs that had spillover for the community. For example, the youth in the confirmation program would show up for OCO actions because Father Rick had encouraged them to do so.

The last two issues—greater outreach from the parish to the community and parental involvement in the improvement of public schools—were clearly ones that the local organizing committee and OCO could develop as "wins." Apart from the civic education that was taking place at these listening sessions, I was struck by the energy that was generated at the meetings to develop new leaders for OCO. The new participants ranged from their late twenties to early fifties, while the old-timers were largely over fifty. These younger parents were *urbano-campesino* (urban farm worker) Mexicans.[113] Sixty percent of them came from the rural areas of Michoacán in central Mexico. It was evident that for all of them the listening sessions were the very first civic activities they had engaged in since coming to the United States. Later I would learn that they had not been exposed to civic education or activities in Mexico. Thus they were completely open to U.S. civic practices and were not comparing experiences in Mexico to their new situation.

I also turned around a question that I had in mind when I started my Oakland fieldwork: "Why is it so difficult to get Mexican immigrants involved in American civic life?" became "Why is it so easy to train Mexican immigrants in American civic skills and habits?" My observation was that once these people were personally invited into each civic process, they easily learned the skill or habit attached to it. But the community organizer could not take this for granted. I also learned, as I will further explain in the next chapter, that since the early 1970s there has been very little development of civic education in Mexico, practically none in the rural areas. This means that there is not a set of Mexican civic skills that migrants carry with them from their home country. In point of fact, as I will discuss in the next chapter, the civic skills now being developed in the growing Mexican civil society are based on U.S. and European civic processes that have been brought to Mexico through the business sector and international NGOs.

Faith-Based Community Organizing and the American Catholic Social Imagination

My experience working for two years (1987–89) with another Alinsky neighborhood- and congregation-based model in Los Angeles suggested that without a faith-based integrative process, rank-and-file activists lose their commitment and enthusiasm once their social objectives have been met. And they resent their parish's "being used" by the organizing committee simply to get people to an "action," a mass event. PICO's faith-based process allows for an ongoing reintegration of social issues, parish pastoral cycles and processes, and leadership development. Basically PICO's faith-based model helps balance the pragmatism of the Alinsky community-organizing model with renewing processes drawn from the liturgy, religious education, and cultural practices.

All throughout the education campaign (1996–2000), the OCO professional community organizers, particularly Scott, worked with local leaders (priests, nuns, pastors, and laypeople) to spark "faith in action"—integrate Catholic social justice principles and processes with the social issues of the community. Scott was convinced that the faith dimension needed to be institutionalized in PICO national training, OCO issue formation, and local processes. In early 1999 he invited me to help him offer the first articulated faith component in national leadership training, which turned out to also be the first national training held for the Spanish-speaking.

Scott and Diane had attended a summer institute on multicultural ministry in 1998 at the Franciscan School of Theology in Berkeley. There he had been introduced to the biblical reflection process of "see, judge, act" of the European Catholic Action movement, which became very popular in the Latin American *comunidades de base*. The process is very easy to teach: oral recitation of a scripture passage, time to reflect on it, sharing of what it means in everyday life. Individuals or small groups may make posters to symbolize their reflections. At the national training we used the poster method. Scott asked the participants to choose a social issue that they were working on in their local units and use the scripture text of the loaves and fishes (Matthew 14:13–21) to illustrate it. Once the process was explained, the participants, working in small groups, quickly went to work using poster paper and colored markers. Later each small group leader explained to the entire assembly what the poster signified. Every group made an application of a scriptural principle to the social issue chosen.

Scott continued to make this kind of "faith-based" contribution at the local meetings and in planning large OCO actions. Conversations with him revealed that as a practicing Jew he had taken to heart the concepts of biblical justice that he had learned at a PICO trainers' meeting held in the summer of 1998—PICO's first concerted attempt at institutionalizing faith-based social justice concepts, albeit Catholic ones, in the organization. For Scott the idea of "right relationships" applied directly to how one-on-ones should be conducted and how local solidarity should be constructed. Indeed "wins" for PICO should be based on the principles of biblical justice. As an organizer, Scott realized that the "see, judge, act" exercise and other games and processes were important tools to use at meetings in order to convey these principles and experience them in the educational process itself.

A subtle but significant change became evident in the OCO citywide organization as faith-based dimensions were more integrated into the organizational culture, particularly articulated faith-testimony and faith-principle dimensions. For example, at an Oakland City Council meeting that OCO activists attended in 1999 to lend support to the building of a supermarket in West Oakland, one of the professional organizers—a black liberal Protestant pastor—actually spoke before the council about food as a fundamental human right in such a way that one council member later in the meeting echoed him in speaking of access to good food as a human right. Two years prior, OCO leaders would have framed the issue more in terms of equal access to food—a distributive justice concept—and appealed to council members' emotions with testimonies of senior citizens having to deal with the high cost and inferior quality of food sold at the small liquor-grocery stores in the neighborhood. The turn to actual social justice principles had developed its own gravitas as the language and practice of faith had become more embedded in the normative formation of OCO members.

Within the OCO professional group, over the course of three years a melding of Catholic social teaching, black liberal Protestant biblical justice emphases, and a general Christian emphasis on common prayer and discernment became increasingly evident. Interviews with these organizers revealed that they saw their work as a social justice vocation and that they, as well as OCO members, wanted "more" from community organizing—the "more" being spiritual meaning. One Catholic school–educated Latina feminist organizer in her midtwenties, who was not active in a parish, said to me, "Through organizing we're doing God's work." She felt quite comfortable finding scriptural passages to use at local meetings and told me that one of her favorite sections of the Bible was the exodus story of Moses and Pharaoh. She had used this text to help her unit see the need for research on an issue—that to "let my people go" requires footwork to prepare for the journey.

Since 1997, the PICO national organization has sought help from pastors for developing a more articulated faith-based organizational culture. According to the national PICO leaders I interviewed, Protestant pastors did not have difficulty understanding and using the principles of biblical justice and Catholic social justice teaching (solidarity as an organizing principle, dignity of the human person, human rights, association, participation, the right to organize, the dignity of human work, etc.) as the ideational foundation of PICO's evolving faith-based culture. And under the influence of black Protestant pastors, Catholic priests and women religious were learning how to express the biblical foundations of their faith in a more emotive way. At St. Anthony's, Father Rick's homiletic and prayer style often echoed the call-and-response technique of black preachers that brings people into the emotions, as well as the content, of scripture texts. My understanding of this technique is that it brings the scripture back to its origins in the oral tradition: these texts convey stories of people's real lives.

At an OCO action, the dynamism of scripture and testimonies of real people often become integrated into a common message. During the campaign for homework centers, a passage from Joshua 6 on the siege of Jericho was used to convey that the power of the people would prevail over the forces of resistance to changes in the Oakland Public School System: the people would march around the walls of the school district headquarters (Jericho) until the walls fell. At these actions, a mural of the walls of Jericho was placed behind the speakers' tables so that the members could visualize their "faith in action." Periodically during the course of the meeting, the leader, a black male in his sixties who chaired the OCO steering committee, would let out the rallying cry in both English and Spanish: "For the children! ¡Para los niños!" Everyone would respond back in kind, "For the children! ¡Para los niños!" It was a clarion call for political battle. And the politicians and school board members in attendance could certainly feel its emotive power.

But the constant references to Joshua and Jericho also conveyed a different kind of seriousness in OCO's objectives: the members not only want social change but are exercising their faith. No politician or bureaucrat has been willing to get into a public debate regarding the faith dimension of OCO, because of both the gravitas of the convictions expressed and the facts that U.S. politicians respect the religious. They know—as do the press and the general public—that OCO is an organization in civil society that draws its membership from religious congregations, though it does not represent the congregations. City council members, school board members, and even mayors of Oakland (Elihu Harris and Jerry Brown) affirmed in varying ways their respect for OCO members both as citizens and as active church members.

My research was conducted before President George W. Bush's 2002 introduction of the federal Faith-Based Initiative, which allows religious institutions to apply for federal funds to support their projects and thereby (theoretically) reduces the role of governmental social services.[114] PICO has a completely different understanding of *faith-based* in its mission to make public institutions accountable to the citizenship. It analyzes public services, seeks its members' opinions, and exerts citizen pressure on these institutions to serve the public better. PICO does not seek public contracts, nor does it promote the seeking of such contracts among its member congregations.

Furthermore, the religious dimension of social justice in these public settings comes across as a natural ecumenism of black spirituality, Catholic social justice teaching, and multicultural expressions. This is a new dimension of U.S. civic religion. At one and the same time this faith-based model can express its members' faith with integrity and respect the separation of church and state. These facets of the PICO-OCO faith-based organizing model have evolved through efforts to integrate pragmatic organizing styles to achieve sociopolitical wins, recruit and retain members, be accountable to religious congregations and other funders, and promote the development of its professional organizers. In the beginning phase of building a faith-based organization, the PICO staff did not have a strategic plan for incorporating faith dimensions into an already successful neighborhood- and congregation-based model of community organizing. However, they knew that many of their affiliate pastors and some of the most active laypeople wanted the organization's religious roots to be expressed more explicitly. This impulse is driving the ongoing evolution of PICO faith-based community organizing.

During the last few months of my Oakland research (June through December 2000), OCO was beginning to face a challenge to the meaning of faith-based organizing. It had begun to partner with other community organizations in pursuing charter and small schools initiatives. In 1994 OCO had initiated the first charter school in the Oakland Public School District and had helped set a statewide policy for charter schools in California. By 2000 there were many more organizational actors wanting to participate in charter schools. After Jerry Brown was elected mayor of Oakland in 1998, OCO was greatly encouraged, because Brown stated that the reform of the public schools was one of his top three priorities. Mayor Brown was not part of the old political machine in Oakland that had let the school district and other public institutions become mired in political patronage. Within a year of Brown's election—after at least six years of constant struggle with school bureaucrats and city hall—OCO was in a position to take the lead in all aspects of school reform initiatives in the city. However, the leaders realized that with new initiatives unfolding rapidly, new institutional players not only to distribute the labor more broadly but also to have a greater civil society infrastructure so that the changes would be realized and maintained.

OCO partnered with the local leaders of the Village Centers—it had initially gotten these off the ground, but they had spun off to form a separate organization—and with nonprofit development agencies. The new partners did not have faith-based organizational cultures, nor did they have broadly based memberships like OCO's local organizing committees in congregations. However, the partners brought expertise on educational reform issues and new people, particularly from non-Christian Asian communities and nonreligious minority professionals and artists who were moving into the San Antonio District. At stake in the integration of these groups was the faith-based focus of OCO. The new partners did not like the prayers and scriptural readings at OCO meetings and did not want them at joint meetings. However, as three OCO organizers conveyed to me, these basic faith-based behaviors could not be negotiated if OCO was to be involved—the members would not want to be involved in strictly secular social action, because they had become integrated into the habitus of faith-based community organizing. The prayers and scripture, as well as the presence of the pastors, brought a legitimacy to civic activity, especially for the Latino immigrants and the black Protestants and Catholics.

A key test of OCO's determination to maintain its faith-based orientation came at an action to promote the small schools initiative, held at a middle school in the fall of 2000. While many OCO members would attend, the crowd of more than five hundred people would be primarily students, teachers, and parents of the middle school. Prior to the action's call to order at 7:30 p.m., OCO staged a pilgrimage of about one hundred members walking from St. Anthony's Church to the school. During the one-hour procession, the members carried a statue of Our Lady of Guadalupe and made five stops at homes that had set up altars for the statue. At each stop, the members recited a decade of the rosary for the social justice intentions of the San Antonio community. The pilgrimage was a way to let OCO members give full expression to their faith outside the joint action.

When the meeting was convened at 7:30, it was conducted as a normal OCO action with prayer and a brief scriptural reflection, but the pastors involved in these prayers found it difficult to quiet the assembly—something that had never occurred at a strictly OCO action. The spirit of the meeting quickly shifted to that of a political rally without any religious dimensions. Leaders of all the partners participated. In the end it was a highly successful action because it gained commitments from Mayor Brown, the new school superintendent, city council members, and school board members to implement the small schools initiative in the San Antonio District. OCO's community organizers had made sure that all the action steps were followed, and the partners had no problem with the organizing process itself, but the faith-based culture was missing from the meeting: there was much disorder with children running around, there was talking during the speeches and testimonies, and the spiritual unity and cultural expressions that I had witnessed at the more than twenty actions I had attended in four years were lacking.

After the meeting, the OCO organizers expressed their pleasure that the goals had been achieved but also their dismay at not feeling the meaning of their action. They were not eager to be involved in planning another such event unless there were guarantees that the faith dimensions of the OCO organizational culture could be carried out with the full dramaturgy of an OCO action. They expressed concern about the disorderliness of the meeting and noted that their nonreligious partners did not understand how the spiritual elements help give moral weight to the civic experience.

Clearly, PICO has helped Catholics bridge the church-world continuum by learning how the Church can be independent yet seek justice empirically and politically through community organizing. Further, PICO's model of faith-based community organizing can also mediate the integral-structural continuum through its care to develop disciple-citizens who seek structural change to overcome social injustices as Catholic Christians who do justice as part of their faith commitment. These activists take seriously Father Walter Burghardt's statement that their very salvation depends upon doing justice.

As I noted earlier in this chapter, PICO and OCO have received financial support from the CCHD, which itself has the capacity to mediate the church-world and integral-structural continuums. Because PICO must work closely with pastors and bishops, it has developed a faith-based sense that leads to a dynamic discourse within the Church, particularly drawing upon the doctrinal principles of solidarity (both as an organizing principle and as a virtue), association, participation, human rights, self-determination, subsidiarity, common good, social justice, dignity of the person, and the right to organize. This discourse is translated into the civic and political culture both contextually and literally. PICO's multireligious, multicultural city organizations have developed a new kind of civic life that has been possible and sustainable over the years because of its normative orientations in membership development. It mediates the tensions inherent in the two continuums defined in this study, artfully moving social issues toward a structural-world orientation of "community organizing" but constantly renews its members in the integral-church orientations of "faith-based."

PICO's model of faith-based community organizing is both a distinctively American contribution to the Catholic social imagination and a distinctively Catholic contribution to American community organizing as it evolves from the legacy of Saul Alinsky. With the extensive networking of PICO's affiliates around the country, it has slowly made a dent in public culture, so much so that "faith-based" was co-opted by the Bush Administration for its own ends, which run counter to the PICO philosophy of public accountability for public schools, police, fire, social welfare, federal block grants, and the like. Indeed PICO's use of the principles of the common good and solidarity aims at helping citizens see that government should provide for the general welfare through education, health care, elder care, child care, youth programs, employment and public works—as well as the police, fire, and security departments necessary for good order.[115] For PICO, a shift to religious or private institutions to accomplish the general welfare would have the negative effects of undermining democracy and the aims of social justice and privatizing and individualizing public responsibility.

The Catholic American Social Justice Cultural Milieu

As the U.S. Catholic Church enters the second millennium, it stands as one of the most complex institutions in U.S. society. It encompasses every ethnic group and race, every language, and every social class in the United States, and its more than 59 million members face every social issue challenging the country. In the course of four years of fieldwork on how Catholic social justice teaching was reflected in the St. Anthony's local organizing committee and its relationship to OCO,

PICO, and CCHD, I encountered this complexity at each operational level. The same complexity and challenge were evident in the Jubilee Year events in Los Angeles. I encountered the actors of this study at these national events and saw how they were creating a distinctively American Catholic social imagination that was both strategic and normative in orientation. This strategic-normative capacity provides a way to both institutionally and culturally address social injustice: from the practical aspects of civic skills, education, and development that OCO and PICO address to a deepened knowledge of the the Church's social justice teaching that the theologians, bishops, and professional staff of CCHD seek to impart. PICO adds its ability to actually accomplish social justice goals and renew its members by bringing them back into a integral-church orientation.

Carolyn, of the professional staff of CCHD, could be seen as representative of the U.S. disciple-citizen that has evolved since Vatican II and filled the seats at Jubilee Justice and Encuentro 2000. She wants to live out her faith in her daily activities, not only by offering her professional skills to a national-level social justice organization but in also in her parish life and her community commitments. Her divinity school training allows her to understand the social teaching at a professional level, so that she can "translate" for the U.S. Catholic public through CCHD. She told me that she wants to help bring about a "synergy" of what CCHD does to support core civic competency, contemporary educational programs, and client programs. Carolyn is informed "from below" by her attendance at an integrated inner-city Washington parish and involvement in an immigrant rights association. She is an ardent feminist and a traditional Catholic who goes to Mass regularly, prays, and has a devotional life. She is progressive on social issues, taking positions that may not be fully in line with the Church's teaching: she believes that women should have the right to be ordained priests and that homosexuals should be allowed to have full lives, including the right to marry. Some critics might see Carolyn as a "pick and choose" type of American Catholic, but the fact is that she is as full a Catholic as any other liberal, moderate, or conservative U.S. Catholic living in a highly complex society. As sociologist Andrew Greeley has found, U.S. Catholics find themselves in the midst of "mystery," particularly in the mystery of the Eucharist as the Real Presence, and can live within the ambiguity or contradictions of dogma and faith practices.[116]

The Los Angeles events encapsulated the U.S. Catholic social justice cultural milieu that has been evolving over the past several decades. The elements of the well-planned liturgical events represented the "cultural toolkit" that the social justice cultural milieu provides the entire country.[117]

A Catholic from Reno or Duluth could go home from Los Angeles and say, "We did this at Encuentro 2000. Cardinal Bernard Law of Boston presided at a penitential service where the national Church publicly repented for the social sins of slavery, colonization of the Indians, subjugation of women, and abuse of handicapped people. The victims of these sins gave testimonies of how they and their families were affected. Everyone present, representing the whole U.S. Catholic Church—cardinals, bishops, priests, women religious, and lay men and women—asked God for forgiveness. It was the most moving experience of my life, and I want to bring this spirit home."

Another Catholic could go home and tell others, "The liturgies were so uplifting. We sang contemporary and traditional songs and hymns in English, Spanish, even Vietnamese and Tagalog. Lay people gave testimonies during the masses. All kinds of cultural forms were used for the rites of sprinkling and incensing. There were liturgical dances expressing the richness of the African American, Mexican, Polish, and Polynesian traditions. The homilies were so powerful, challenging us to live our faith in the real world and to really implement the Church's social justice teaching. I never thought I would live to see the Church so willing to struggle to be one people with so many different gifts from the diverse American community. The Holy Spirit had to be present to make all this happen."[118]

For Roman Catholics, the liturgy provides a specific cultural site to bring together the elements of its complex social structures and cultural life, not simply as an event but as part of the overall cultural fabric of the institution, its sacraments, and its public face. It is a site for teaching, cultural expression, testimony, and the enactment of a variety of skills on the part of the ministers and the congregation. In the course of this study, I found the liturgy, be it at St. Anthony Parish, a diocesan event, or the national events, to be a barometer of the larger cultural milieu.[119]

From the interviews and participation in the organizations discussed in this chapter, I have distilled a number of dimensions and characteristics of the U.S. Catholic social imagination:

NORMATIVE CONTINUUM

1. Integral orientation (religious, theological, and spiritual dimensions)

- *Faith-based:* A deeply Christ-centered and incarnational sense of religious faith; one's faith must be believed and lived out in society. Salvation is an "already but not yet"[120] event that is achieved through God's free gift of grace and the disciple's good works. These are the virtue and moral norm functions of the Catholic social imagination.

- *Theological and biblical education and reflection:* Social justice is predicated upon values from the sacred scriptures and Christian tradition. The Church has a responsibility to educate its members, and the members should develop their discipleship through knowledge of and reflection on the Church's social justice teaching. The U.S. Church has a long history of contextualizing doctrine and giving it an American interpretation and discourse. This capacity reflects the future of the organizing principle of the Catholic social imagination.

2. Structural orientation (programmatic, cultural, and intellectual development of social justice dimensions)

- *National church support of the Catholic Campaign for Human Development:* Since 1969, the U.S. Catholic bishops have explicitly supported the idea that the Church has a clear mission to change the "structures of sin" through institutional structural change to effect the principles of the option for the poor, human development, the dignity of the human person, the dignity of work, the right to organize, solidarity, subsidiarity, participation, association, and human rights. By institutionalizing this mandate in the Catholic Campaign for Human Development, the bishops have given support empowered lay Catholics to bring their values to civil organizations without the control of the bishops or clergy. CCHD provides the analytical framework and the organizing principle for implementing the Catholic social imagination.

- *Ecumenism and interfaith cooperation:* There is a widespread understanding that Catholics are to be leaders in ecumenism and interfaith dialogue and cooperation. Catholic social activists see that all people of goodwill can be involved in the cause of justice. Progressive U.S. Catholics have learned to be inclusive in their language regarding God, faith, and social justice. This capacity expands the Catholic social imagination to a broader audience, as Catholics exercise public Catholicism.

- *Ethnic culture, diversity, and multiculturalism:* The U.S. church is a church of immigrants; every ethnic group should be able to express itself liturgically, socially, and culturally within the Church through its own language, symbols, and devotions; at community-wide events, every effort should be made to be inclusive and to make use of the "gifts" that each group brings to the celebration. On any given Sunday, a parish may home to a variety of ethnic and cultural liturgical styles, which come together for the high holy days of Christmas, Easter, and Pentecost. This capacity bridges the functions of virtue and the organizing principle to allow the Catholic social imagination to be both integrally and structurally inclusive.

STRATEGIC CONTINUUM

3. Church orientation (pastoral and ecclesial dimensions)

- *Parish lay ministry and leadership development:* Key to the U.S. church's maintenance and growth is the development of laity in emerging lay ministries, including the social justice ministry, and in leadership positions within parishes, dioceses, and national church structures. There is a strong sense of collaborative ministry among the laity, religious, clergy, and bishops; there are formal programs for lay ministries and leadership development through Catholic colleges and universities, dioceses, and lay associations—in 1999 more than 330 programs in all the states, enrolling more than thirty-one thousand adult lay leaders.[121] Here the functioning of the social role and the organizing principle are allowed to flourish.

- *Participatory liturgical parish milieu:* The Catholic activist is nurtured each week in parishes that have undergone extensive parish renewal since Vatican II, particularly with active lay participation in liturgical ministries (lectors, eucharistic ministers, hospitality, music, liturgy committee, and the Rite of Christian Initiation of Adults). An American-style liturgy has developed involving contemporary Christian music, ethnic music, and traditional chant and hymnody. Priests and deacons are trained to give scripturally based homilies that include content relevant to the local community, the country, and the world. There is high participation in the reception of the Eucharist under the forms of both bread and wine—and the communicants stand and receive the eucharistic bread in their hands, as opposed to kneeling rand eceiving the bread on their tongues. Following the reception of Communion, there are announcements regarding the coming events of the parish, or often a layperson gives a testimony regarding a parish ministry or a local community organizing event. The spirit that flows from the liturgy is expressed in the social hour or hospitality following the Sunday Mass, which includes refreshments and organizations publicizing their events or services. All the elements reflect an active adult participation in the liturgy to reflect the spirit of Vatican II, which saw the liturgy as the "source and summit of the community." The liturgy in a parish that is attempting to fulfill the social justice mission expresses this commitment and activates the principles of participation and association as social functions of the Catholic social imagination.

- *Parish renewal programs:* The U.S. church has supported a variety of parish renewal programs, including RENEW, Parish Renewal Weekends, Journey for Justice, and Small Parish Renewal. Especially within large parishes, these have been important for developing small communities that serve as locations for faith sharing, Bible study, and social justice and, again, help develop the principles of participation and association for the Catholic social imagination.

- *Diocesan program development and gatherings:* Because the Catholic Church is hierarchically organized with the bishop as the local head, diocesan programs most often reflect the will of the local ordinary. Given the nature of church authority and sanctioning of ideas and programs, it is significant that all 175 U.S. dioceses have local programs to support the work of the CCHD and Catholic Charities. About 25 percent have offices specifically designated for the work of social justice. Many dioceses have initiated annual social justice gatherings, bringing together the various parishes, groups, and organizations involved in the "ethic of life." Here the functions of philosophical frameworks and the organizing principle are primarily developed in the U.S. Church.

4. World orientation (community, civil society, and political dimension)

- *Neighborhood and local community:* Catholic community life is parish-based, and parishes have specific territorial boundaries; therefore parishes must serve the needs of the local community, especially the social needs of education, charity, and culture.

This element has brought a certain tenacity to Catholic life in the United States: it is extremely difficult to eliminate a parish simply because members have left or because it is not self-supporting. Furthermore, the priests of the parish live within the neighborhood and give witness to its livability. Thus, many Catholic parishes, schools, and ministries have survived in urban cores through the financial and moral support of dioceses and twinning parishes, while many Protestant and Jewish congregations have moved from urban sites to the suburbs where the congregants have moved.[122] As well, the inner-city parishes have provided means for more affluent suburban parishioners to become active in the work of social justice and specific ways to practice solidarity as an organizing principle and as a virtue.

- *Civic skills and civil society:* All Catholics, be they legal citizens or not, should be involved in their communities and have the necessary skills and education to fully participate in civic institutions and freely associate in U.S. civil society. Catholics bring their values to civil society through active participation and association.

- *Government institutions and politics:* Catholic social activists understand the importance of the separation of church and state. However, this does not preclude lobbying for social justice issues, nonviolent resistance, and mass demonstrations and rallies. Catholics have a moral obligation to vote and participate in the political processes of their country.[123] There is a strong Judeo-Christian ethos within U.S. civil religion that allows for open dialogue among religious figures and institutions and government officials and politicians.

- *Catholic public intellectuals and intellectual freedom:* Catholics have played and are playing significant roles in a "public Catholicism" focused upon social justice and moral issues in the United States. This characteristic allows a flourishing Catholic American discourse to exist, contextualizing Catholic social justice teaching for a U.S. audience. Catholic journalists, academics, politicians, and social activists participate in civic discourses addressing social issues and may freely state that they are Catholic as well as Democrat, Republican, Green, Reform, or of any other stripe. Furthermore, Catholic journals and magazines—be they progressive, moderate, or conservative—such as *America, Commonweal,*

US Catholic, the National Catholic Reporter, the National Catholic Register, The Wanderer, and *First Things,* provide venues for independent Catholic thinking on theology, the arts, and society. Debates on even "forbidden" topics such as ordination of women and gay rights flourish in these journals without interference from the bishops. In addition, there is an independent Catholic press represented by Paulist Press, Liturgical Press, Michael Glazier, Orbis Books, Ethics and Public Policy Center, Sheed and Ward, Doubleday Image, and Crossroads Press—as well as Catholic college presses such as Notre Dame University Press, Georgetown University Press, and Loyola University Press.

These four dimensions of the U.S. Catholic social imagination have a strategic-normative sense and logic, providing a multidimensional formation in Catholic social justice in the United States. Part of the mix is the official teaching of the Church, and part is the historical evolution of social Catholicism in the United States. This gives the U.S. Catholic social imagination a post–Vatican II tone of "doctrinally conservative but socially progressive." Several factors can be said to be critical for the Americanness of this cultural system:

• the immigrant nature of the Church's membership evolution

• ongoing involvement of Catholics in U.S. civil society and its civil religion particularly, and the social movements leading to "Catholic moments" exemplified in the Catholic Worker movement, the United Farm Workers, the anti–death penalty movement, and the School of the Americas Watch, where many Catholics have been inspired and trained to become social activists

• the congregation-based parish with its various institutional components, such as the parish school, social programs, and immigrant cultural support

• the growth of a well-trained lay cadre of liturgical ministers, parish and diocesan administrators, educators, and social activists

• Catholic public intellectuals and their institutional networks for the independent distribution of scholarship and opinion

• widespread national support for Alinsky-type faith-based and congregation-based community organizing as a means for Catholics put

Church

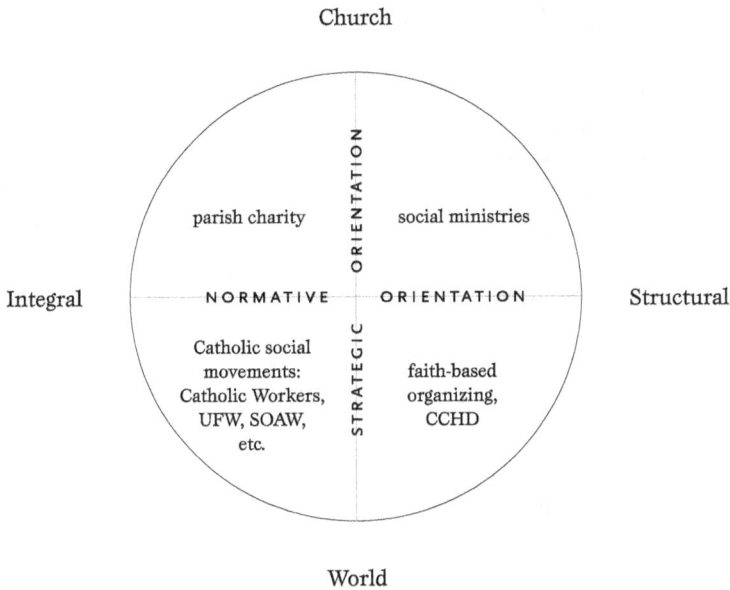

Figure 2. Dominant functional orientations of various structures and institutions of the U.S. Catholic Church

their "faith in action," effect social change in local communities, and move beyond the charity model

- the institutionalization of social justice teaching in the Catholic Campaign for Human Development as a means to effect long-term structural change in the United States through independent civil associations

Figure 2 illustrates the standpoints of specific Catholic moments and the more general national standpoints of the Catholic social imagination in the United States.

Challenges Facing the American Catholic Social Imagination

Catholic social justice teaching in the U.S. context, particularly through the community-organizing model, has been pragmatic and results driven, emphasizing the right to organize, participation, association, the signs of the times, social justice, just wage, solidarity, and subsidiarity. As community-organizing groups such as PICO and OCO have evolved as faith-based organizations, they have emphasized concepts from biblical justice, particularly building right relationships, which reflects the principles of friendship and the virtue of solidarity. CCHD, serving as the U.S. bishops' primary social justice organ, emphasizes in its mission to the nation's poor the principles of the preferential option for the poor, human development, empowerment (a conflation of participation, association, subsidiarity, and solidarity), biblical justice, solidarity, dignity of the human person, and the dignity of work. The result is an American sense of independent social spaces for Christian action or discipleship-citizenship: Catholics effect social justice in civil society, in government, and in politics because of their formation in a broadly based and institutionalized social justice cultural milieu.

However, at every level of the U.S. church one can observe the marginalization of social justice with references to "the social justice group" or "the peace and justice group" in the parish, the diocese, or the United States Catholic Conference. Social justice teaching and practice are not always a full expression of the pastoral mission or objectives of the parish, diocese, and national organizations. Because there is not a national theologically inspired pastoral model for U.S. church life that integrates social justice teaching as an essential part of the Church, this marginalization will most likely continue. Furthermore, because of the lack of a national pastoral plan, at every level an emphasis on social justice is contingent on the role of the pastor and bishop. The pastor and the bishop can be agents of empowerment or disempowerment. A parish where there had been a strong emphasis on social justice can be changed almost overnight by a pastor not wanting this as part of the parish mission.

Social justice as a "ministry" presents a further problem. Msgr. George Higgins expressed concern about internalization of justice as a ministry within the Church rather than the externalization of social justice principles in civil society through citizen-disciples active in their labor unions, in their professions, in social movements, etc. The model that CCHD provides shows the possibility for this to occur and to be solved.

More positively, my study of the U.S. Catholic Church has shown that faith-based community organizing has become the preeminent American way of implementing Catholic social justice teaching. Faith-based community organizing connects the infrastructures of the Church and civil society, and as it taps into the American pragmatic social imagination, its "wins" lead to long-term institutional changes in civil society, government, and politics. Faith-based community organizing stands as the foremost "Catholic moment" for U.S. social justice. Unlike Catholic social movements that emphasize particular issues such abortion, poverty, farmworkers, the death penalty, or U.S. military issues and have developed special interest members and supporters, faith-based community organizing is parish and neighborhood centered and by necessity connects to the institutional church as well as to the local political, business, and philanthropic communities. While not "radical" in the sense of liberation theology, faith-based community organizing seeks to achieve structural social justice that can appear to be extremely progressive, even radical, especially when the goal is to reform a school district, gain health insurance for the working class, or create affordable housing. While it may directly engage only one million Catholics of the almost forty million in the United States, its aims of empowerment of poor and working-class people within a multicultural and religiously pluralistic organization have become part of the overall American Catholic social imagination of social justice.

In the San Antonio District in Oakland, was social justice achieved through faith-based community organizing? OCO's educational initiatives have substantially improved the test scores of children in the city. For example, in 1995 second-graders had performed in the lowest quarter percentile on the Terra Nova standardized tests, but in 1998 "second-graders throughout the district showed substantial improvement in reading, language arts and math achievement on the 1998 Terra Nova student achievement tests—reading was up 18 percent, language arts up 13 percent, and math up 10 percent, with half to two-thirds of . . . second-graders performing near, at or above grade level proficiency in these content areas."[124] Improvement has come about through the new class size standard—twenty students per teacher in grades kindergarten through four—homework centers, increased parental participation, and greater willingness to discuss educational problems in the community, particularly in the school board and the teachers' union. All these things happened because of OCO's determined membership from the congregations. As of 2005, more than six new charter schools had opened in Oakland since 1995 due to OCO's efforts, and more were on the drawing board.[125] Beginning in 2002, OCO developed the New Small Autonomous School Movement in Oakland, which had been instrumental in opening fifteen small schools as of 2005. These "schools within schools" operate similarly to charter schools but without the operational burdens of buildings, administration, and salary issues that often diminish the effectiveness of charter schools. The village centers have become thriving places where parents, teachers, artists, and community activists meet on common ground to revitalize the educational and cultural life of the San Antonio District and other Oakland neighborhoods. Over the years OCO has been responsible for developing (also as of 2005) two hundred units of new housing and four hundred units of rehab housing, and it won more than $50 million in state, local and federal funds for new housing in Oakland.[126]

At St. Anthony Parish itself, I saw a profound change that OCO helped generate. On my arrival in 1996 the parish was organized into distinct ethnic enclaves and did not have common liturgical events. By 2000, the parish had institutionalized multicultural events, the most impressive being the Jubilee Year celebration when an image of Our Lady of Guadalupe, which was touring the U.S. church, was hosted at St. Anthony's for two days in October 2000. In the past, Guadalupe had been solely a Latino devotion at St. Anthony's, but now the pastor and the parish council organized a set of liturgies, processions, and events that brought the entire community together. A center shrine in the church sanctuary was built by Vietnamese craft workers and remained until the closing of the Jubilee Year on Christmas. The parish had taken to heart Pope John Paul II's exhortation *Ecclesia in America,* which named Our Lady of Guadalupe the patroness of the Americas—one common Marian devotion. The social solidarity of the local Jubilee events reflected an integration of parish organization, liturgy, and community organizing—a symmetry of lay leadership and participation. This was a major achievement of the normative sense of the Catholic social imagination, with potential to assist movement from the integral orientation of Catholic life to the more structural orientation that community organizing demands. Religious culture indeed matters in building social solidarity at the local level—and it can matter in promoting either ethnic and cultural enclaves or niches or a diverse, multicultural community. In Oakland, John Paul II's exhortation mattered, moving ideas from the very top of the Church to its lowest reaches in the San Antonio District.

More than anything, OCO has served as a location for ordinary people to be trained in social justice in order to make social, cultural, and political institutional changes in Oakland and California. OCO has built local solidarity and has achieved institutional change for the common good. As part of the national PICO network, it is "reweaving the fabric of America's communities."[127] The U.S. Catholic social imagination matters for the people of Oakland. Faith-based community organizing and OCO deliver.

4 ✧ The Mexican Case: Doctrinally Oriented

1 December 2000. This date is on a par with 16 September 1812, 5 May 1862, and 2 February 1917, which all marked turns in Mexico's political culture: independence, victory in a great battle at Puebla against the French, and the inauguration of the modern constitution, respectively. On the first day of December 2000, with the first peaceful and transparent multiparty presidential election in Mexican history, the country began the *transición* (transition) from almost seventy years of single-party rule by the Partido Revolucionario Institucional (Institutional Revolutionary Party, PRI) to a future that is as yet unclear. The winner, Vicente Fox of the Partido Acción Nacional (National Action Party, PAN), won a clear mandate in every state of the republic.

What role will religion play in Mexico's changing political and social culture? As noted in the previous chapter, for more than two hundred years the United States has permitted an open role for religion in public life; this has allowed Catholic social teaching to penetrate U.S. civil, social, and political culture without fear of religious control of public institutions. But Mexico's history has been very different. The opportunities for constructing a Catholic social justice milieu are often hidden; it is the constraints that are most apparent, particularly federal laws constraining the Church. Moreover, a very conservative Catholic hierarchy trained in Roman seminaries and universities has historically constrained the development of Mexican theological investigation, lay leadership, and social programs. During three years of travel and field study in urban Mexico I did, however, find many active Catholics, disillusioned Catholics, and even secular Mexicans trying to find openings for the Church to enter the public life of their country. This chapter will highlight these openings and analyze how the Catholic actors of the *transición* are attempting to construct a Catholic social justice cultural milieu, despite the Church's historic conflicts with the state, its social conservatism, and its ultramontane perspectives.

I was present in Mexico City on 1 December 2000 for the events of the *toma de posesión* (inauguration) of Vicente Fox. As part of my ethnographic research and in order to receive firsthand information on the campaign, I had joined the Amigos de Fox (Friends of Fox), the nonpartisan citizen group supporting his candidacy. Because of this, I received an invitation to attend the *toma de posesión*. Amigos de Fox was an extremely modern campaign organization modeled upon the principles of pyramid marketing and the use of the Internet for political networking. Its campaign techniques were clearly aimed at solidifying votes among the middle class, who had become increasingly disillusioned with ideologically driven political parties and their "pure" candidates.[1] Fox had been president of Coca-Cola Mexico and was personally familiar with the most advanced organizational technologies.[2] His team was recruited from the Mexican corporate sector and independent civil society organizations—people who made up Mexico's significant urban middle class.[3] One young PAN party member had told me before the election of 6 July 2000 that many Panistas were very upset that Fox had bypassed the party structure to organize his campaign. Actually PAN's membership rules are so strict that its actual party membership is very small compared to the votes it has won.[4] Fox and his supporters clearly understood that they needed to bypass traditional Mexican political culture, which caters to ideological interests, and generate a new direct and transparent political culture.[5]

Many facets of the new political culture were in evidence at the *toma de posesión*. Fox's activities, which were televised throughout Mexico and the United States, signaled a new political story through pictures without the incessant political chat that Mexicans had been accustomed to in television broadcasts. At 7:00 a.m. he arrived at the Basilica of Guadalupe with his four adopted children to attend Mass. He was wearing blue jeans, a white open-collar shirt, a wide leather-tooled belt with his initials on the buckle, and his ever-present cowboy boots. Never before in Mexican history had a national president entered the Basilica, much less attended Mass and received Communion. Fox made no public comments at the basilica.

At about 8:00, the Rev. Enrique González Torres, S.J., rector of the Iberoamericana, Mexico City's Jesuit university, accompanied Fox to a poor neighborhood in Mexico City. There the new president served breakfast to *niños de la calle* (street children). Important in this scene were the signals being sent. Fox was with a Jesuit priest from his alma mater. He was the first Mexican president with a Catholic education—and it was from the Jesuits, who had been vilified by recent PRI regimes. (In 1994, after the Zapatista revolt began in Chiapas, the Zedillo regime had put out misinformation that Subcomandante Marcos was a Jesuit priest, in order to discredit religious leadership in the indigenous quest for human rights and political freedom.) Further, with the breakfast event Fox was showing Mexicans and the world that real poverty exists in their country, especially affecting *los chiquillos* (the little ones). Recent regimes had tried to mask poverty in Mexico with a barrage of TV commercials showing the country's economic progress, particularly since the institution of the North American Free Trade Agreement (NAFTA) in 1992. Now Fox simply served breakfast to poor children for over an hour, chatting and joking with them. The event had one more symbolic dimension: Fox has four adopted children, and in his mind they might have very well ended up like these *chiquillos* had it not been for the adoptions. Adoption of children who are not related to the adoptive parents by blood is very rare in Mexico.[6]

At 10:00 a.m., he arrived at the Mexican Congress for the *toma de posesión*. Standing in front of the members of the Congress, the Senate, and the international diplomatic corps, he looked presidential in his sharply tailored black suit, white shirt, formal tie, and red, green, and white presidential sash. Following the official words of the *toma de posesión* (Mexico's president is not sworn in, so no one else is involved in this official act), Fox gave a speech emphasizing a new democratic and transparent direction: "We Mexicans aspire for and deserve to live in the certainty of the rule of law. The example the government gives to the legal order is a civic reality."[7]

During the speech he was booed and catcalled by PRI elected officials. The Mexican people, watching on television, saw this most uncivil display of partisanship by the old regime. Fox noted the disturbance by addressing the hecklers as *niños y niñas* (boys and girls). It was a stunning moment, an opportunity for the country to see the kinds of obstacles the new president would face as he sought to shape a different type of government and political culture.

Around 11:30 a.m., Fox arrived at the National Auditorium, where ten thousand invited guests from throughout Mexico and other countries were to hear his inaugural address and witness Fox administer an oath of ethics to members of his cabinet—an entirely new concept in Mexican political culture. When he came into the auditorium, he was greeted with tumultuous applause. These were his people—Panistas, Amigos de Fox, leaders of indigenous groups and civil society, independent academics, journalists, cultural leaders, and even clergy and bishops.[8] There was also a large contingent of Mexican American leaders from the United States, who had been invited in order to forge a cross-border alliance. Fox's speech, almost an hour long, was a thoughtful and serious exposition of Mexico's problems and the ways his administration would go about resolving them. His priority was resolution of the Chiapas conflict. Indigenous leaders from throughout Mexico, many in tribal dress, were seated in the front rows of the assembly. Speaking directly to them, Fox said that the Mexican people must accord them true freedom, human rights, and a new place in national life: "¡Nunca más un México sin ustedes!" (Never again a Mexico without you!). His second priority would be to address poverty, which had grown in the midst of economic growth and the resolution of Mexico's foreign debt problem.

Following this speech, Fox instituted a new twelve-point civil ethical code for his presidential cabinet of forty men and women from all of the major political parties, including prominent public intellectuals such as Carlos Castañeda (minister of foreign affairs) and Carlos Aguilar Zinser (minister of internal affairs). Just before he read the pledge, his oldest daughter, Paulina, came forward and silently presented him with a crucifix, which everyone in the audience saw on the big-screen monitors. The crowd spontaneously stood up and wildly cheered this eloquent action. Through it the Mexican president was acknowledging a truth about Mexican society: it is largely Christian and Catholic in spite of 150 years of religious repression.[9] Fox held the crucifix as he read the ten points. Given years of *laicidad* as a guiding civil religion, these ethical and religious symbols would be points of controversy in the press, stirring up fear that Fox's public Catholicism might signal a resurgence of Catholic political power.[10]

Fox's terminology for discussing poverty reflected his educational and spiritual formation in Catholic social justice teaching. The speech was laced with the principles of solidarity, human rights, the dignity of the human person, human development, participation, association, and the common good. As he did throughout his campaign, he employed an inclusive Spanish, always using both masculine and feminine forms of words referring to people, for example, "nosotros y nosotras"—yet another symbol of a new political culture.

Following the National Auditorium event, Fox went to the Palacio Nacional in the city's central plaza to have lunch with the foreign dignitaries. Meanwhile, two wealthy businessmen, close friends of Fox, had invited me to lunch at the San Angel Inn, an exclusive restaurant in Mexico City's wealthiest neighborhood. Friends since their days at the Iberoamericana, they were founding members of the Amigos de Fox and served on of Fox's transition team. These men came from the highest social class in Mexico and had received part of their education in the United States. The conversation was mostly about their university days and how the Jesuits had shaped their outlook on life. The Rev. Xavier Scheifler, S.J., a Basque who had been expelled from Spain and settled in Mexico during the Spanish Civil War, had particularly influenced them all. Scheifler was ordained a priest for the Mexican province of the Society of Jesus. He had been their business ethics professor and became their postgraduation mentor or *padrino* (godfather). Every year they got together with Scheifler for a reunion. They told me that they and Fox had been deeply influenced by Scheifler's constant questions about their concern for the poor and how they would help in creating a more just Mexico. Scheifler gave them what the U.S. social theologian Reinhold Niebuhr would call an "uneasy conscience."[11]

My hosts spoke of Fox's sincere religiosity, formed by Jesuits at his high school in Leon, Guanajuato, as well as at the Iberoamericana. In his autobiography Fox states, "The heart of Ignatian spirituality radiates an understanding that can only be realized in personally serving others. The Jesuit order is involved in the work of forming men and women capable of transforming reality and serving others, a philosophy that left a profound influence in my adult life and encouraged me to work to create openings for work and opportunities."[12] My hosts also gave testimony of their religious and spiritual journeys of trying to bring social change in Mexico. One of them has a daughter who has been the Mexican provincial of the Religious of the Sacred Heart of Jesus and has spent her life with the poor and involved in the progressive life of the Church (the *comunidades de base,* human rights issues, immersion among the poor). The people at the table told stories of their involvement with social justice issues—strikingly, always outside the official institutional church.

In the face of a stultifying parish life and obstacles in Mexican public culture, educated and socially conscious Mexican Catholics have sought to live out their Christian commitments in Christian-inspired civic associations, a sort of parallel church. One of the forces of change in Mexico is this parallel church of religious orders and institutes of the middle and working classes and the hidden church of Christian social activists serving the poor and the indigenous. Fox's election—the *transición*—resulted in part because of these Mexicans' *inquietud* regarding their political culture,[13] an *inquietud* that is very often faith based and that Mexican social and political analysts seem to miss. Vicente Fox represents a new kind of public Catholic, something never before seen in Mexico. The election itself was a *despertar* (awakening) for Mexico's traditional institutional powers.[14]

What role will religion play in this new culture? To begin to answer that question, let us examine the contemporary Mexican Catholic community and probe the Mexican Catholic social imagination.

Laicidad *and Catholic Identity*

Since the Spanish conquest of the Aztecs in 1511, the formation of Mexico has involved a grand struggle between religious and political interests. The Roman Catholic Church was the official state religion of colonized Mexico until the Constitution of 1857, which was particularly inspired by French liberalism. The liberal agenda of secularization and the distinctively Mexican process of laicization (*laicidad*) of Benito Juárez and his implementation of several reform laws—Ley Juárez, Ley Lerdo, and Ley Iglesias—initiated *laicidad* as Mexico's civil religion.[15] Fundamental to *laicidad* is the state's role in the moral and social formation of the Mexican citizen, particularly in primary loyalties and identity. According to the ideals of *laicidad,* the Mexican is a social citizen whose soul is "lay oriented" and not religious, which had signified colonization, antidemocratic positions, monarchical and papal loyalty, and anti-intellectual and antiscientific attitudes toward the empirical world.[16] By the time of the Mexican Revolution of 1812, almost three hundred years of tensions culminated in a process of rigid separation of church and state, epitomized by the Porfiriato (1876–1910), during which the Mexican government embraced modernism and the ideals of positivism with its slogan "Order and progress," and by the 1917 Mexican Constitution. For all intents and purposes these reforms would curtail the Church's influence in social and political life and limit the Church's role to being a liturgical, devotional, and spiritual custodian of the private lives of Mexicans.[17] Practical consequences of these legal restrictions included the following: (1) a number of Catholic schools and seminaries were closed; (2) the Church was no longer permitted to officially own buildings or land (all church structures were made government patrimony); (3) priests and nuns were not allowed to wear their religious garb outside their own houses; (4) priests were required to register with the state and were not allowed to vote; (5) the government regulated times and places for worship; and (6) the operation of religious publishing houses was severely limited, which resulted in the curtailment of Catholic magazines, periodicals, and books. These harsh restrictions remained in Mexican law until 1992 and the introduction into the constitution of article 130, which allowed the Church to purchase and own property, operate schools, and have a free press—and also permitted priests to vote and wear religious garb in public.

From 1917 through 1992, the Church promoted and made use of independent lay associations for Catholic education and cultural activities in order to fulfill its educational and doctrinal objectives outside of church buildings.[18] These lay associations have resulted in the formation of networks of "Christian-inspired" schools and civil associations, such as high schools and colleges sponsored by religious orders. Since 1992, even though restrictions of religious activities have been softened, the Church—as well as all other religious organizations—remains under the jurisdiction of the secretary of state's Subsecretariat of Legal Concerns of Religious Associations, commonly referred to as the Asuntos Religiosos. The government grants permissions for the purchase of property and materials for the construction of church properties and monitors the public activities of religious organizations.[19] In this sense the new law follows the spirit of the 1917 Constitution, which provides for freedom of belief but not full freedom of religion and its expression—meaning that Mexicans can believe anything they want but the government controls the institutionalization of these beliefs. Even though the vast majority of Mexicans are Catholics, they are content with these limitations placed on religion in public life. They are aware of the long history of church interference in the social, economic, and political development of Mexico during the colonial period and in the Cristero rebellion of 1926–29, when the Church itself forbade public masses as a protest against government restrictions.[20]

Because of the legal and political limitations placed upon religious organizations in the twentieth century, the implementation of *laicidad,* and a broad consensus that the Church should not meddle in political concerns (*no se meta en la política*), at the beginning of the twenty-first century the Catholic Church finds itself as a broad religious structure but largely lacking both infrastructure and cultural cachet in Mexican public life. Roberto Blancarte, professor of sociology at El Colegio de México and the country's leading sociologist of religion, has observed that even though Mexico is an overwhelmingly Catholic country (at least 80 percent of Mexicans claim to be Catholic), it does not have a public "Catholic culture." Catholicism was domesticated from the time of the Porfiriato through 1992 to such a degree that Catholic theology, arts, literature, and journalism have not engaged with Mexican public life. Venues to do so have been lacking, and the Church has not developed a laity or clergy able to bring faith into the *plaza pública,* the public square.[21]

The Development of a Mexican Catholic Social Imagination

Unlike the U.S. Catholic Church, whose role in public life has enjoyed a more or less continuous development, Mexican Catholicism has suffered three large shocks—the Porfiriato, the 1917 Constitution, and the Cristero rebellion—that have greatly affected the Church and limited its role in public life.[22] Rather than reviewing the Church's long history, this study will focus upon the Church's development since Vatican II, specifically within its mainstream institutions. Six major tendencies have shaped the institutionalized life of the Mexican Catholic Church:

1. *parish life tendency,* which limits ordinary religious life to liturgy, fiestas, and parish activities without influence in civil or political society[23]

2. *popular religious tendency,* including devotions to Our Lady of Guadalupe and regional Marian expressions, local saint-day fiestas, and syncretistic religious expressions combining indigenous religion and culture and Catholicism, which serve as cultural sites for local and national identity, as well as the more recent development of the Catholic charismatic movement[24]

3. *parallel Catholic organization tendency,* with the formation of "Catholic" labor unions, political parties, professional associations, and social organizations that look to priests and bishops for their actual leadership[25]

4. *religious-political fusion tendency,* with the creation of both right-wing (Catholic Action, Cristero movement, Partido Acción Nacional, Legionnaires of Christ, Opus Dei) and left-wing (comunidades de base, liberation theology) religious-political movements, often drawing upon elements of Catholic social justice doctrine[26]

5. *pastoral tendency,* emerging since the 1980s as a mainstream model for integration of the teaching, liturgical, and social (*profetíca, litur-*

gíca, and *social*) elements of the pastoral mission or plan (Pastoral Conjunto) of a diocese and its parishes

6. *"integral-intransigent" tendency,* a suspicion of liberalism and *laicidad,* a tendency to make everything "Catholic" and to look to Rome for interpretations of Mexican social life—so that Mexican Catholics often look more Roman than Catholics in Rome[27]

These six tendencies have affected the way Catholic social justice teaching has been construed in Mexico as the *doctrina social de la Iglesia,* the Church's social doctrine. *Teaching* in Spanish is translated *enseñanza,* a word that is used as in English to refer to something to be taught. The Mexican church, like most of the Spanish-speaking Catholic world, tends to prefer the term *doctrina* with its implication of a requirement of Catholic faith. In my interviews with Mexicans at all levels of the Church, I found that they spoke of a "doctrina social" in this literalist way, unlike their U.S. counterparts, who used "social teaching" with its implication of something important that may or may not be fundamental to Catholicism.

The Limited Context of Post–Vatican II Social Justice Theology

In order to locate social justice theologians in the Mexican Catholic Church, I first tried to find published Mexican authors to interview. I discovered that there were no social justice theologians who had contextualized the social doctrine for the Mexican political culture, no working theologians who had published books or articles on social justice theology in Mexico as part of a theological enterprise based in academic institutions, publishing houses, foundations, etc. Francisco López, S.J., rector of the Instituto Teológico in Mexico City (the former Colegio Máximo de Cristo Rey), believes this low level of theological production has been due to the fact that after Vatican II the chief religious orders in Mexico—the Jesuits, Dominicans, and Franciscans—dedicated their intellectual resources to pastoral services and local social development, especially *formación de inserción* (intensive pastoral experiences within poor and marginal communities), rather than the traditional intellectual enterprises of the pre–Vatican II church. An example of such a theologian is the Jesuit Jorge Manzano, professor of sociology and social ethics at the Instituto Libre de Filosofía y Ciencias Sociales in Guadalajara. Manzano uses many of his own essays and newspaper articles for teaching sociology to his students, who are mostly seminarians and women religious. He also edits a local journal that publishes articles on religion, psychology, and sociology. Intellectual resources from outside Mexico have dominated the curriculum at the institute and the contents of the journal. López felt that the turn toward the pastoral was very good for the Mexican church but that it is now time to develop a new generation of scholars who can integrate their intellectual expertise with the *compromiso social* (social commitment).

Since Vatican II, very few Mexican priests have received professional training beyond their initial priestly formation. They have not been encouraged to enter the academic career path, where theological writing has historically been most encouraged and practiced. This does not mean that there is no theological reflection on Mexican social issues but that a contextualized Mexican theology is not institutionalized in the official church, as has occurred in the United States and in many other Latin American countries. Furthermore, while the U.S. church has produced key social justice theologians noted for their books, articles, academic posts, and consultative roles in the United States Catholic Conference, there is not a like public and professional place for the Mexican social justice theologian either inside the institutional church or in public or secular institutions.

Rather, what I discovered were two types of theological activity relating to social justice: (1) broad grassroots theological reflection in national church offices, diocesan offices, and parishes, drawing on the social doctrine, texts and ideas from non-Mexican theologians, and internal documents of the Mexican bishops, local bishops, and diocesan synods; and (2) independent, lay-dominated centers of social doctrine reflection, such as the Mexico City–based Instituto Mexicano de Doctrina Social Cristiana (IMDOSOC), the Centro de Reflexión de los Trabajadores (CRT), and the Centro Lindavista (CL). Mexican Catholic theologians largely draw upon Latin American and European sources for theological reflection, particularly liberation theologians such as Gustavo Gutiérrez, Jon Sobrino, Ignacio Ellacuría, Juan Luis Segundo, and Leonardo Boff. Both types of theological activity seek to integrate a broad range of liberation themes, including preferential option for the poor and marginalized, the poor in history, the oppressed-oppressor dichotomy, solidarity, liberation, freedom, and human rights.[28] These fundamental themes were reiterated by the Congregation of the Doctrine of the Faith and Pope John Paul II in their declarations on liberation theology, which served to legitimize liberation theology themes for the Mexican church.[29]

The work of the of the Rev. Alberto Athié Gallo, a priest of the Archdiocese of Mexico City who was the executive secretary of the

Pastoral Social of the Conferencia Episcopal Mexicana (CEM) at the time of my study, is an example of the first type of theological activity. This national office of the Pastoral Social includes Caritas México, the largest provider in Mexico of emergency services and charity, and offices for human rights, indigenous concerns, refugee services, migrant services, and social doctrine education. The Pastoral Social is one of the three primary functions of the Pastoral Conjunto (Pastoral Plan). In theory, the social function of the Church is integrated with the teaching (Pastoral Profética) and liturgical (Pastoral Litúrgica) functions of a diocese or parish. The theological basis is the idea that Jesus Christ is priest, prophet, and king, three roles manifested in his transfiguration on Mount Tabor (Mark 9:2–8), and the institutional life of the Church should reflect Jesus in all three dimensions.[30] The Conferencia Episcopal Mexicana is organized along these lines, as well the major archdioceses of Mexico City and Guadalajara.

Given the Pastoral Social's range of services for the national church, Athié Gallo was the most influential priest in Mexico regarding social justice issues during his tenure as executive secretary (1995–2000). Under the leadership of the bishops' committee overseeing the Pastoral Social, he initiated the offices for human rights, indigenous concerns, refugee services, and migrant services. (The first two offices became controversial in the late 1990s.) When I met him in 1998, he was in the process of conducting national hearings regarding the social conditions of Mexico. He intended to use this information in a pastoral letter the Mexican bishops were writing to celebrate the Jubilee Year—the first social justice letter of the Mexican bishops in more than thirty years. The letter was issued in March 2000 as *Del encuentro con Jesucristo a la solidaridad con todos.*[31]

Father Athié Gallo was the closest I came to finding a working Mexican Catholic social justice theologian within an official church institution. Prior to becoming executive secretary of the Pastoral Social, he had published in 1993 *El Tratado de Libre Comercio: A la luz de la opción cultural propuesta por la doctrina social de la iglesia,* a work looking at NAFTA through the lens of Catholic social doctrine.[32] He was born in 1955 in Mexico City to a father who was a successful engineer and a mother who was a housewife; her family name, Gallo, is well known in Mexico's business circles. He attributes his commitment to social justice to the ethical examples of his father, who constantly fought against the corruption inherent in government contracts, and his mother, who showed "indignation against injustice." His father died at the age of fifty, when Athié Gallo was only sixteen. This early loss led him into a spiritual journey, which included reading works of Mahatma Gandhi and Jacques Maritain, the French Catholic social philosopher. Eventually he began to talk to a priest friend of his father, who introduced him to Mexico's poverty through immersion experiences with the poor. He thought that he could best serve people by becoming a doctor, so he entered medical studies. But his deep interest in social and spiritual matters gained greater influence and motivated him to enter seminary in order to become a priest. After completing his philosophy training in the diocesan seminary in Mexico City, he went on to Rome for theological training at the Jesuit-run Gregorian University, where he completed a doctorate in philosophy and moral science. He told me that his interest in the social philosophy of Maritain was strengthened during his graduate studies. Upon his return to Mexico City, he worked several years in a parish serving the poor. At the parish he spearheaded a center of evangelization and a social apostolate that included a credit and savings union.

Because of this pastoral work, Athié Gallo was tapped in 1983 by the initial organizers of the IMDOSOC to be a founding member, teacher, and chaplain. Other founding members were Cardinal Ernesto Corripio Ahumada, then archbishop of Mexico City, and Bishop Carlos Talavera, who was president of the Comisión Episcopal de Pastoral Social (CEPS) during the time of this study. Bishop Talavera, who had been the influential priest friend of Athié Gallo's father, now became his priestly mentor. Athié Gallo also taught classes on the social doctrine at the major seminary in Mexico City. The greatest influence upon him as a priest was his ongoing involvement in the L'Arche movement through retreats offered by Jean Vanier, the movement's founder. L'Arche is an international organization that creates Christian communal living experiences for emotionally and physically handicapped adults and capable adults.

In addition to these involvements with IMDOSOC and L'Arche, Athié Gallo became involved in the Conferencia Episcopal Latinoamericana (CELAM). At CELAM he worked for Bishop Talavera, who had assumed an elected post in the organization representing Latin America's bishops. Further, Athié began to do consulting for Caritas International, serving on international committees related to Caritas and refugee work. He was well known in Mexican academic and political circles as an open-minded and culturally literate priest—something almost unheard of in Mexican public life, particularly given that he is not a

Jesuit.[33] He has shown himself to be an applied social justice theologian, particularly in creating new spaces for the social doctrine to be institutionalized in the Mexican church.

Father Athié Gallo allowed me to interview his staff and participate in the national Jubilee process sponsored by the Mexican Bishops' Conference. His office was run with a crisp professionalism by his generally young staff of men and women heading up the different sections of the Pastoral Social. All of these staff members had obtained the Mexican professional degree—the *licenciatura.* The majority of them had attended the Iberoamericana, Mexico's largest and most respected private university, and had been inspired to work in the area of social justice because of immersion experiences with the poor in Mexico City and in the southern states of Chiapas and Oaxaca. They shared the *inquietud* of the post-1968 generation of young Mexicans but were not cynical or despairing in their work. Athié Gallo had recruited at least half of the staff from IMDOSOC. Both the Pastoral Social and IMDOSOC had developed a social justice ethos within their organizational culture. Staff members regularly shared prayer, liturgy, and critical reflection regarding their work in staff meetings. This cultural milieu was flavored by a shared *inquietud,* nurtured by the social doctrine, and energized by a common hope for the Mexican church and the political *oposición* (opposition). (Every Catholic social activist I interviewed, whether they were oriented toward the PAN or the Partido de la Revolución Democrática [PRD, Revolutionary Democratic Party], wanted an end to the prolonged PRI regime.) The milieu's spiritual glue was an amalgam of religious, social, and political hopes for a *transición* (transition) in Mexico. Athié Gallo epitomized this amalgam in his work as administrator, leader, and thinker. His staff and the diocesan directors of the Pastoral Social throughout Mexico told me that his leadership and commitment inspired them.

In late October 1999, Athié Gallo organized a *semana pastoral social nacional* as a key part of the Mexican church's celebration of the Jubilee Year.[34] The gathering would be the first public display of Mexican social Catholicism since the early 1930s. Similar to the Jubilee Justice conference held at UCLA in July 1999 and the National Encuentro at the Los Angeles Convention Center in July 2000, the event would respond to the Vatican's desire to have the Church in each country examine social justice doctrine in its national context.

As noted in chapter 1, key speakers at the Mexico City event were Cardinal Roger Etchegarry, the pope's representative for this event,

Archbishop Francois-Xavier Nguyên Van Thuân, president of the Pontifical Council for Justice and Peace, and Theodore McCarrick of the U.S. Bishops' Conference International Peace and Justice Commission, who at the time was archbishop of Newark, New Jersey, and is presently cardinal archbishop of Washington, D.C. As well, noted Mexican intellectuals such as the historian Jean Meyer and civil society theorist Vicente Arredondo addressed the delegates. Part of the four-day conference held at the Marist Order's Universidad Intercontinental was a listening process to draw out the social justice concerns of the more than three hundred delegates representing the Pastoral Social of all of the country's dioceses.

As I listened in on the discussions of various small groups, particularly those attended by representatives of the Archdiocese of Guadalajara, where I had done ethnographic research, I was struck by the intensity of the *inquietud* regarding the Church's readiness to assist in the *transición*. To a person, the delegates were positioning themselves for a major transition in Mexican public life, but they felt that the official church, as represented by many of the bishops, was not at all prepared for this change. Laypeople, nuns, and priests working at the grassroots level to address poverty, hopelessness, and out-migration expressed distress as they related how the hierarchy had placed obstacles in their paths. Such obstacles included limiting the Church's public support of the Chiapas peace process, the closing of seminaries that were training priests to serve the poor and indigenous in southeast Mexico, the hierarchy's failure to protest the government's expulsion of foreign priests who had been serving in Chiapas and Oaxaca, the closing of *comunidades de base* in various dioceses, and divisions among bishops regarding liberation elements of social justice doctrine. Other complaints included poor preparation of seminarians for homiletics and service to the poor, so that many priests did not preach about daily life themes at Sunday Mass. Again, this *inquietud* came from the most loyal and committed members of the Church—men and women who volunteered their time to end poverty through the works of Caritas, to promote human rights, and to raise public consciousness regarding the social doctrine.

The goal of the national process was to gather findings that could be included in the forthcoming pastoral letter on the state of social justice in Mexico. The findings regarding the Church itself were so negative that it was hard for anyone to imagine that the bishops would actually use them. Thus the listening-process organizers steered public discourse to more public themes—corruption, drug trafficking, the way neoliberal economic and globalization policies were widening class disparities, the privileging of capital over people, the growth of individualism, human rights violations against the country's indigenous communities (including forced *mestizaje*) upon the indigenous, the lack of educational opportunities for the poor, and emigration of Mexicans to the United States and Canada.[35] These were the issues that were incorporated into the public record of the event and that were noted by the secular press.

Three Strikes against a Contextualized Mexican Social Imagination

During the course of the meeting, a rumor floated that Father Athié Gallo had been censured by Cardinal Norberto Rivera Carrera and would be removed from office. The official reason would be the triennial *restructuración* (restructuring) by the bishops serving as president and committee members of the Pastoral Social. Indeed on 15 November 1999, the Rev. Camilo Daniel Pérez was assigned to Athié Gallo's position but without specific duties. Three months later, Cardinal Rivera, who was Athié Gallo's immediate religious superior, demanded that Athié Gallo resign his position under pain of losing his priestly credentials. Further, key staff in charge of the human rights and indigenous sections of the Pastoral Social office were fired. Cardinal Rivera did not serve on the executive committee of the Pastoral Social nor as an elected member of the executive committee of the Mexican Bishops' Conference, but as the archbishop of Mexico City he served as the primate of Mexico (a position that the U.S. church does not have). Thus he could strongly influence the direction of the Bishops' Conference, especially in this case, since Athié Gallo as a diocesan priest of Mexico City was under his juridical authority.

When Athié Gallo was removed, Cardinal Rivera did not reassign him to a position in the Archdiocese of Mexico City, which would have been the normal course of action. In fact, Father Athié Gallo went to Chicago in a kind of self-imposed exile because he could no longer work as a priest in his own diocese. In the United States, he told me that the real reason for his removal had to do with the brewing controversy surrounding revelations of sexual abuse by the founder of the Legionnaires of Christ, Father Marcel Maciel Delgollado. As Athié Gallo developed a list of "social sins" of the Mexican church for the Jubilee Year atonement, he had wanted the bishops to atone for clergy sexual abuses—and bring the well-investigated allegations regarding Father Maciel and other priests to public light.[36]

On 30 December 1999, the Mexican church also suffered the removal of the coadjutor bishop of San Cristóbal de las Casas, Raúl Vera, who was to be the successor of retiring bishop Samuel Ruiz. And in mid-February the Vatican announced that papal nuncio Archbishop Justo Müllor, who had helped steer a new course for the Mexican church on human rights and indigenous protection, would become the new head of the Pontifical Academy, the Church's school for the training of its international diplomats.[37] In a sense the names of Athié Gallo, Vera, Ruiz, and Müllor go together as leaders who were willing to open the Mexican church to "the signs of the times," especially the *inquietud* of social justice actors, the plight of the indigenous and the poor, and the consequences of Mexico's neoliberal economic policies for emigration and economic restructuring programs. However, a small group of conservative bishops aligned with the previous papal nuncio, Archbishop Jerónimo Prigione—Cardinal Rivera, Cardinal Juan Sandoval Iñiguez of Guadalajara, and Bishop Onésimo Cepeda of Ecatepec—was able to exert muscle at local and international levels to make key personnel changes and effectively disempower the Mexican Bishops' Conference and the Pastoral Social. This group has become known in the Mexican press as the "Club of Rome." When these bishops made public statements regarding the personnel changes, they invariably stated that Müllor was receiving a *promotion* to be head of the Vatican's diplomatic school in Rome and that Vera was being *promoted* to bishop of the northern diocese of Saltillo—that is, he would now be working with *mestizo* Mexicans and not with the indigenous people of Chiapas. These personnel changes at the national level validated the *inquietud* expressed by delegates to the October 1999 Semana Pastoral Social regarding the church hierarchy's view of itself as being "above justice."

In the midst of these national personnel shifts that January, I was invited to join forty members of the Pastoral Social of the Archdiocese of Guadalajara, many of whom had participated in the October national meeting, in a two-week fact-finding mission regarding indigenous rights in southern Mexico and attendance at the final mass of Bishop Samuel Ruiz in the plaza of San Cristóbal de las Casas, Chiapas. In many informal conversations with these social activists, it was clear that the firings and transfers had left them despondent regarding the official church. These activists would not describe themselves as radicals or even leftists but as part of the broadly based *oposición,* which included conservatives aligned with the PAN and liberals of the PRD. The group included attorneys, parish priests, nuns, teachers, university students, women working in feminist organizations, and leaders in Guadalajara's civil society—a spectrum of mainstream Catholics who wanted to see for themselves the situation of the indigenous of their country.

At Bishop Ruiz's farewell mass on 25 January, the "center-left" luminaries of the Mexican Catholic Church were in attendance, including the recently removed Bishop Vera, Father Athié Gallo, bishops from throughout southern Mexico and Guatemala, delegations of church social activists from throughout Mexico, and public figures such as Guatemalan Nobel Peace laureate Rigoberta Menchú, who spoke of Bishop Ruiz's generosity in providing hospitality for thousands of Guatemalan refugees. In a rare acknowledgment of the role played by Bishop Ruiz in his leadership in resolving the indigenous revolt in Chiapas, the newsweekly *Proceso* issued a special edition on his life and the situation in Chiapas.[38]

The *inquietud* of Catholic social activists regarding injustices in society and within the institutional church moves their activity and ministry toward the church-integral orientation of the Catholic social imagination. They find few avenues to connect their faith to a broader Mexican public life, largely because their social justice discourse is shaped by a highly Catholic language—of the social doctrine itself or of liberation theology—that is not used in public discourse. Catholics have not developed organizations in Mexican civil society that can function alongside other civil associations working for social justice, which means their capacity for networking and building a broader solidarity is limited. Except in the cases of IMDOSOC and national Pastoral Social offices, little attention has been paid to the spiritual and cultural development of social justice actors so as to contextualize a social justice cultural milieu for Mexicans. Almost all Catholic social justice work was oriented toward charitable services within the Church, such as food and clothing dispensaries and medical clinics—even though the activists were eager to see structural change in the larger Mexican society. Because of the long-term legal restrictions placed upon it—lifted only in 1992—the institutional church has yet to develop into a mediating institution to transmit its values and services to the larger Mexican political culture and civil society.

The Bishops Respond to the Mexican
Social Context: Solidaridad

January, February, and March 2000 proved to be critical months for the Mexican church, particularly in its public positioning of the pastoral letter issued on 25 March 2000, *Del encuentro con Jesucristo a la solidaridad con todos*[39] (hereafter, *Solidaridad*). This was the first social letter of the Mexican bishops since March 1968; following the 1968 Tlatelolco massacre, the hierarchy had been tentative in addressing social issues for fear that it might be identified with opposition groups. During those three months, mainstream magazines and newspapers closely dissected the Church's image. Editorials concluded that the Club of Rome was in firm control of the Mexican church. *Proceso,* the largest circulation newsweekly in Mexico, provided investigative reports on Cardinal Rivera's obstructions of the Pastoral Social and other social justice ministries in southern Mexico and in Mexico City.[40] But the most revealing and damaging reports focused on Bishop Onésimo Cepeda of Ectepec, the self-styled spokesman of the Mexican hierarchy, who had recently completed a multimillion-dollar cathedral—so expensive that papal nuncio Archbishop Müllor refused to attend the dedication ceremony. (However, former president Ernesto Zedillo, PRI presidential candidate Francisco Labastida, and other PRI officials close to Cepeda and others in the Club of Rome did attend.) In its defense, the Club of Rome announced that the decisions to remove Müllor, Vera, and Athié were the will and directive of Pope John Paul II.

It is important to note that none of the bishops elected to serve on the executive committee (*consejo permanente*) of the Mexican Bishops' Conference were members of the Club of Rome. As the newsmagazine *Milenio* revealed, the conference officials were moderate-to-progressive bishops looking for a broad consensus.[41] On 4 February, three key conference bishops—Cardinal Adolfo Suárez Rivera of Monterrey, Bishop Sergio Obeso of Xalapa, and the president of the CEM, Bishop Luis Morales Reyes—went to Rome to meet with Pope John Paul II to review the situation of the Mexican church. At this meeting the pope revealed that he was not aware of the changes that had been made in Mexico, particularly the transfer of Coadjutor Bishop Vera from San Cristóbal de las Casas to Saltillo—a very grave canonical problem, because a coadjutor is placed in a diocese with the right of succession unless the pope himself makes a change for the good of the Church.[42]

The change had been made, yet there was still time for the selection of a new bishop who might reflect the aims of the priests and laity of the Diocese of San Cristóbal de las Casas, particularly the preservation of the Pastoral Indígena, ecumenical relations, and the Church's general support of the Chiapas peace process recognized in the San Andreas Accords. As well, there was time to select a new papal nuncio who might continue the pastoral orientation of Archbishop Müllor, especially reflected in his nomination of moderate bishops with a pastoral focus on serving the poor and the indigenous rather the Club of Rome's orientation toward doctrinal and ecclesiological regulation.[43]

The pilgrimage to Rome proved to be enormously significant in the selection of the new bishop of San Cristóbal de las Casa and the papal nuncio. In April Bishop Felipe Arizmendi, who had been bishop of Tapachula in the neighboring state of Oaxaca, a supporter of the Pastoral Indígena, and secretary of CELAM, was named the new bishop of San Cristóbal de las Casas. Upon his nomination he told reporters, "The challenge I face is enormous, because for forty years Bishop Samuel Ruíz has left his great footprint in the diocese. We are both inspired by the gospel and above all by the spirit of the Vatican Council. In the manner of Bishop Samuel, my collaborators and I will try to be faithful to the task that God has given us. This is not just my work but that of the entire community."[44] Also that month a former papal nuncio to Venezuela, Archbishop Leonardo Sandri, was named as the new apostolic nuncio to Mexico. He was expected to continue Archbishop Müllor's policies. Both appointments signaled the immediate failure of the Club of Rome to actually carry out their intentions for Mexico and helped realign the power of the Mexican Bishops' Conference in the hands of its elected officials.

However, the Club of Rome did succeed in influencing the direction of the pastoral letter *Solidaridad* by having Athié Gallo removed and claiming that the pope himself wanted a theological and political conservative direction for the Mexican church: systematic elimination of liberation theology and indigenous tendencies from national and diocesan pastoral plans and abstention from criticizing the domestic policies of the PRI in upcoming presidential and congressional elections. *No se meta en la política* served the needs of the Club of Rome and its relationship with the ruling party.

Clearly, the Club of Rome and its supporters did not share in the *inquietud* or the *oposición* of the mainstream social justice–oriented Catholics whom I encountered in Guadalajara, Mexico City, Oaxaca, and Chiapas. The Club of Rome's political alliances in the PRI had been cultivated by Archbishop Prigione during his tenure as apostolic delegate from 1978 to 1992 and as papal nuncio from 1992 to 1996.[45] Mexican bishops were urged to support the political status quo in order to maintain the Church's status quo, especially its privileged informal relations with the PRI and the state apparatus.[46] The Club of Rome feared that any major changes in the state would bring major changes for the church apparatus. The Club of Rome represents the integral-intransigent tendency of the Mexican church, minimizing the Mexican social context and maximizing the Church's doctrines and Roman authority. This helps maintain the church-state "you pat my back, I'll pat yours" power hegemony. In a country that officially restricts religious freedoms, this is an odd subaltern reality. The Club of Rome's power plays have made it difficult for mainstream Mexicans to integrate their feelings of *inquietud* and *oposición* with the social doctrine of the Church.

Prior to Athié Gallo's removal, participants in the more than fifty local listening sessions organized by the national Pastoral Social anticipated that the bishops' letter would include vital information regarding poverty, the plight of the indigenous and their need for self-determination, and the lack of citizen participation in the political system. The process itself elicited this expectation. The published version of *Solidaridad* primarily expresses the sentiments of Pope John Paul II in his postsynodal apostolic exhortation *The Church in the Americas,* or, in Spanish, *Eclesia en América.* The pope's themes of personal encounter with Christ, Catholic identity in the Americas, conversion as both a personal and social experience, solidarity, structural sin, option for the poor, and the "new evangelization"—as well as specific issues of national debt, ecology, corruption, drugs, the "culture of death," immigration, and discrimination against indigenous peoples and those of African descent[47]—did serve as a way for the moderate bishops to provide a critical appraisal of Mexican society. As an outsider, the pope essentially provided a national template for social justice analysis that could not be achieved internally given the power of the Club of Rome.[48]

Solidaridad is organized in three thematic sections: (1) encounter with Jesus in Mexican history, particularly in the development of Our Lady of Guadalupe as a source of Mexican national identity and the role played by the Catholic Church in the cultural development of the country; (2) encounter with Jesus in the Church itself, particularly in the place of conversion, church community, and evangelical service in the life of Mexican Catholics; and (3) encounter with Christ in solidarity with the aspirations of the Mexican people. The first section attempts to offer a critique from a Catholic perspective of the official regime's reading of Mexican history, which portrays the Church as antidemocratic and power hungry, and it addresses developments arising from nineteenth-century liberalism, in particular *laicidad*. This critique becomes important in the third section, where the bishops call for a revision of national educational policy so that Catholic values can be taught in the nation's public and private schools. Social statistics are excluded from the document, as are sentiments of *inquietud* articulated in the listening sessions held in Mexico during 1999. While the bishops address the obvious social problems of poverty, disparity of income distribution, corruption, government involvement in drug trafficking, voter intimidation, and government intimidation and coercion, the greatest social need addressed by the letter is an educational system freed from the restrictions imposed by the ideology of *laicidad*. In particular, article 354 calls for an integrated education for the formation of the whole person, with values formation based on Catholic doctrine, in the public schools.

The bishops stress that the *transición* of the country is dependent upon a new kind of Mexican citizen who can exercise a values-oriented citizenship. In article 359 they state: "In the social sphere, a Christian-inspired education ought to encourage participation, dialogue, enculturation, social change, family involvement, and care for the environment."[49] The document does not delineate how the bishops actually see Catholic values being implemented in civil society or public life.

The Mexican press reported that the letter focused upon allowing the Church to play a role in public education. However, the bishops do not know how to convey a possible positive role for Catholic values in civil society, public life, and public education because they are beholden to the older integral-intransigent model of Catholicity, in which the institutional church defined values for public life and did not permit a translation of those values for use in Mexico's evolving political culture. Thus even now when "the Church speaks," it uses its own special religious language, which does not connect with modern Mexican public discourse.

Given that the pastoral letter is entitled *Solidaridad,* the reader might expect a developed Mexican context for the principle of solidarity. In the letter's section on pastoral work, the bishops focus upon the virtue dimension of solidarity: "It is time that Mexican Catholics take on the Pope's proposition to rehabilitate the idea of an integral charity, not just its immediate and superficial sense, but to understand it and live it as the highest theological gift-virtue, which God gives to the believer in Christ through the Holy Spirit as the Trinity resides in the believer."[50] The use of solidarity in its virtue sense positions the principle in the internal relations of the Church, particularly in connection to the principle of the dignity of the human person and the construction of a culture that values human life.[51] This application of solidarity to virtue, human dignity, and culture effectively limits it to addressing the cultural threats of concern to the bishops: pluralism, new religious movements, individualism, materialism, nihilism, and the "culture of death" that abortion engenders.[52]

The principle of solidarity within *Solidaridad* is stripped of its organizing, philosophical, social, and analytical dimensions. It loses its capacity for empowering Catholics to work with others of goodwill, and its heuristic power as an organizing and analytical tool for social justice is diminished. Furthermore, the pastoral letter does not engage the Mexican political or social culture: there is no attempt to enter the larger Mexican discourse of social justice of the *transición* and the *oposición* or, for that matter, the older uses of solidarity within the Mexican Constitution, Mexico's sociopolitical traditions, and the Catholic labor movement. Thus, the principle of solidarity is limited to Pope John Paul II's theological-moral interpretation of solidarity as charity and friendship. It would have been highly innovative had the bishops brought together uses of solidarity in Mexican political culture and the Church's development of the principle, but the Mexican theological community has not developed methods or theoretical frameworks for contextualizing Catholic social justice doctrine.

The letter presents a sociological dilemma for Catholic leaders and laypeople who sincerely desire to locate and help solve the social problems Mexico faces in the twenty-first century. The bishops state:

> It is the profound aspiration of millions of Mexicans to grow within a culture of life that will strengthen democratic and participative institutions, founded upon recognition of human rights and the cultural and transcendent values of our nation: a culture and institutions built upon the participation of all in solidarity, that can safeguard representative and subsidiary organizations called to create conditions that will allow a life of dignity for all people. This requires an integral education based upon respect for the human person and the culture, to increase responsibility and citizen participation.[53]

In this one paragraph the bishops seek to incorporate the principles of solidarity, subsidiarity, the dignity of the human person, association, participation, human rights, and the signs of the times. Yet as the bishops illustrate their country's problems and evoke the social doctrine, they fall back into their intrinsically Catholic discourse and set themselves against the Mexican culture and its institutions, particularly with such language as "integral education" and "culture of life." For non-Catholic Mexicans, such terms signal not only a repudiation of modern Mexican history but also the integral-intransigent tendency to seek a restoration of church dominance in history, culture, and institutions—particularly the restoration of Catholic education within the public school system. The problem of communication is symptomatic of the way the Mexican bishops convey religious ideas for the public life of Mexico. Their language speaks to the Church itself because it uses doctrinal language.

Nevertheless, the letter was a major accomplishment for the bishops, especially since they had not spoken about broad social issues in more than thirty years. With the removal of Athié Gallo and his staff, the bishops relied on the expertise of Manuel Gómez Granados, the executive director of IMDOSOC, and his staff to actually write the document. They certainly knew the parameters for shaping the letter, particularly the importance of not venturing too far into the structural and world orientations of the Catholic social imagination. (Interestingly, Gómez Granados had himself been the executive secretary of the Pastoral Social Nacional of the Bishops' Conference during the early 1980s.) So IMDOSOC personnel filled in at a critical time and crafted a letter with a broad social doctrine orientation and discourse but without a Mexican "translation," i.e., a public language connecting with Mexican political culture.[54] Thus, while the social data and mood of Catholic social activists is missing from the document, it remains an important theological statement that the Church can use to reinforce both John Paul II's perspectives, which were more critical than those of the Mexican bishops themselves, and the Pastoral Social's orientation toward liberation themes, human rights, and indigenous rights.

I have noted that the Catholic social imagination of Mexican activists has an integral-church orientation. Their desire is to move to a new structural-world orientation, but they face massive obstacles. The bishops are responsible for shaping the Church's orientation, based on their hierarchical authority and the clericalism of Mexican Catholicism.[55]

Lay Catholic Organization Attempts to Construct a Mexican Catholic Social Imagination

Founded in June 1983 as a civil association by a committee of more than one hundred key Catholic lay and religious leaders, IMDOSOC plays a critical role in the theological and pastoral development of the social doctrine in Mexico. The organization provides a civil structure for Catholics to implement the social doctrine in Mexico's civil society. The organization recognizes the problems that a largely integral-church orientation poses for post–Vatican II Mexican Catholics marked by *inquietud;* it has sought to provide a more world-structural orientation for social Catholicism even while remaining faithful to the Church's hierarchy and the social doctrine.

From its beginning IMDOSOC has been financially independent of the Church, and over the years its founders have made financial pledges to maintain the organization's financial health and independence. While it has always had representatives of the hierarchy on its board of directors, it has maintained independence in order to function in Mexico's growing civil sector. In IMDOSOC's spacious offices in the San Angel district of Mexico City, its employees and volunteers generate a lay spirituality of social justice that is modern, intelligent, and action oriented. The center provides a highly professional ambience for its publishing enterprise, seminars, research, and social projects.

The publishing arm has generated books and pamphlets on the social doctrine in general and in specific works related to Mexico and Latin America. Its Mexican authors have included Jean Meyer, Roberto Blancarte, Gabriel Zaid, Alberto Athié Gallo, and Rodolfo Soriano Núñez—a who's who of the small Mexican Catholic intellectual world. If anything, IMDOSOC has helped lay a foundation for a Catholic intellectual culture oriented toward social justice concerns. It also publishes a monthly magazine, *Signo de los Tiempos* (Signs of the Times), and a more scholarly theological journal, *La Cuestión Social* (The Social Question), dedicated to the advancement of social justice issues in Mexico. In addition, its research arm provides a news service for the bishops and nongovernmental organizations and specific social scientific studies for clients- including background research for Amigos de Fox, the independent campaign organization for Vicente Fox's successful presidential bid in July 2000. Through its Fundación Leon XIII (Leo XIII Foundation) it has sponsored social action programs for middle-class Mexicans to become involved in Chiapas and in service to the poor in Mexico City.

IMDOSOC's services have a far reach in the Mexican church because it is the primary Mexican purveyor of social justice books, games, videos, seminars, and consulting services. As well, as I noted regarding the Pastoral Social Nacional, IMDOSOC has provided a training ground for a new generation of Catholic social justice professionals and activists. More than anything, IMDOSOC serves as a cultural site for the development of a more explicit Mexican Catholic social imagination, different from a social movement but an independent habitus that nurtures citizen discipleship and promotes strategic structural change.[56]

In many ways IMDOSOC's ongoing presence in Mexico is connected to the middle-class disaffection with the old regimes of the PRI and the clerical-dominated church, meaning that *inquietud* and *oposición* have a double-edged quality. In my informal conversations with people at IMDOSOC prior to the July 2000 national elections, they conveyed respect for Fox because he was the first presidential candidate in Mexican history who publicly expressed his Roman Catholic faith, who genuinely seemed to embrace Catholic social justice doctrine, and who inspired hopes for a true *transición* that would settle their *inquietud* and *oposición*. They hoped that the candidacy of Fox as a professing and active Catholic would signal the beginning of a new public Catholicism.

IMDOSOC cultivates Catholics who are capable of being socially progressive on issues related to option for the poor and marginalized, liberation, human rights, association, participation, the dignity of the human person, and solidarity and simultaneously doctrinally oriented in their faith, particularly regarding family and natural-law moral issues. For them—unlike the bishops of the Club of Rome—it was not incongruent to support the San Andreas Peace Accords and indigenous rights and autonomy, to oppose neoliberal economic policies, and to work for full participation of the laity in the life of the Mexican church. This cultivation of social Catholicism was particularly evident at IMDOSOC's weekly staff Masses, modern and participatory liturgies that included Communion with both bread and wine, laity receiving the bread in their hands, laypeople distributing Communion, lay readers, socially conscious liturgical music, intelligent and socially oriented homilies by visiting clergy, and a sense of community. Visitors taking classes and seminars are provided a liturgical experience that they would like to take to their home parishes.

The staff told me that they could not find in their parishes the same liturgical vitality and social consciousness that they found at IMDOSOC. They felt that parish clergy do not know how to adequately connect the liturgy to daily life concerns or to empower the laity. This was borne out in my Sunday visits to middle-class parishes in Mexico City and Guadalajara, where I experienced largely passive congregations (registered by extremely low participation in singing, attention to the homily, and a lower than 10 percent participation rate in Communion) fulfilling their Sunday obligation. At IMDOSOC, as in the U.S. church, I found an interrelationship between empowerment of the laity in civic skills and participation in the liturgy.

Criticism of IMDOSOC can be heard from both the left and right wings of the Mexican church. On the left I heard that IMDOSOC's chief financial support has come from Mexican businesspeople, such as the founder of Pan Bimbo, the largest bread manufacturer in Mexico, and that this financial relationship indicates the organization's intimacy with the PAN and neoliberal economic policy. Thus, for many on the left IMDOSOC is a modern middle-class front for conservative and ecclesial interests. While IMDOSOC does have strong ties with Mexican businesspeople and its staff is middle class, it is probably more accurate to say that IMDOSOC aims to bridge social classes in Mexico in a way that has not been previously achieved: Catholic social movements have tended to be left or right wing, with very limited class integration.

On the right, meanwhile, the organization is considered to be filled with malcontents and misfits. Further, IMDOSOC is said to use church doctrine as a pretext for leftist subversion of church and state regimes, particularly in its support for the San Andreas Peace Accords, the *transición,* and indigenous and human rights—as well as the fact that IMDOSOC has provided a venue for "leftist" Catholic intellectuals such as Jean Meyer, Gabriel Zaid, and Latin American and European liberation theologians and social thinkers. Gómez Granados told me that the old-regime church has a tendency to Catholicize and bring under its authority all lay associations. It has been difficult to maintain the organization's independence as well as to show its cooperative nature in being of service to the Church. The old regime, particularly the Club of Rome, generally equates "independent" with "antiorthodox and antiauthoritarian." He showed me a letter from the retired archbishop of Mexico City, Cardinal Ernesto Corripio Ahumada, that guaranteed the independence of the organization—a letter he needs to pull out every so often when he is questioned on the basis for IMDOSOC's independence.

The Legacy of Liberation Theology: Comunidades eclesiales de base (CEBs)

IMDOSOC serves as the premier theological venue and cultural site for the development of Catholic social doctrine and a new Catholic social imagination in Mexico. But it should be noted that after Vatican II, the *comunidades eclesiales de base* (CEBs, basic Christian communities) provided another significant cultural site for social justice discipleship. CEBs have been widely studied as social settings for the implementation of liberation theology.[57] They are organized within parishes or communities as supplements to often anonymous membership in large parishes. CEBs are organized as small neighborhood units where members meet for prayer, scriptural reflection, and mutual aid. The first Mexican CEBs were formed in the early 1970s in the Diocese of Cuernavaca under the auspices of Bishop Sergio Méndez Arceo. One of the first "Mariachi Masses," the *Misa Panamericana,* was instituted at the Cuernavaca cathedral as an expression of the integration of Mexican culture, the liturgy, and the CEBs. Many Mexicans journeyed to Cuernavaca to learn how to organize CEBs in their dioceses and parishes.

In 1971 and 1972, as a college student studying at the Centro Intercultural de Documentación (CIDOC) in Cuernavaca, I participated for six months in my own neighborhood's CEB. A key practice of the CEB was the integration of biblical study with reflection upon daily life concerns. Particularly important to this practice was the introduction in 1968 of a Catholic edition of the American Bible Society's Today's Bible in Spanish translation, supported by the Mexican bishops, particularly by Bishop Méndez Arceo, who was one of Mexico's earliest ecumenists. This Bible was accessible to Mexicans with a primary school education because of its colloquial text and pictograms illustrating the Bible stories. It was a key instrument in the *conscientización* (consciousness raising) of post–Vatican II Mexican Catholics.

The Brazilian pedagogist Paulo Freire had developed the concept of *conscientización* in his *Pedagogy of the Oppressed.*[58] The book was popularized under the auspices of CIDOC and its director Ivan Illich. At CIDOC Freire regularly gave intensive seminars on critical education for the poor and the oppressed to missionaries going to Latin America and to Latin American clergy, nuns, and laypeople. Freire's ideas were integrated into the first book on liberation theology, *A Theology of Liberation: History, Politics, and Salvation,* by Peruvian theologian Gustavo Gutiérrez.[59] By the mid-1970s, the CEBs became identified with a leftist-oriented religious-political agenda for Mexico, particularly as liberation theology integrated Marxist social and economic theory into its primary discourse of oppressed-oppressor relationships in society.

For conservative bishops, this orientation could only be construed as class warfare that would lead to the polarization of Mexican society. Bishop Méndez Arceo and others became known as the "Red

Bishops" in the Mexican press—which up until the early 1990s was fully integrated into the state apparatus. For the PRI and the government, the CEBs, liberation theology, Red Bishops, and anything looking like independent Catholic social organizing were threats to the PRI regime's hegemony. Given the widespread political disaffection following the 1968 murders at Tlatelolco, the government needed to marginalize the CEB movement, and it did so in the press by painting the movement as communist and as anti-Mexican, given its foreign inspiration.[60] After Archbishop Prigione was appointed papal nuncio by Pope Paul VI in 1978, and energized by the anticommunist spirit of Pope John Paul II's papacy, which began in 1979, he worked with the government and conservative bishops toward a slow but sure elimination of the CEBs in Mexico, particularly in the Archdioceses of Mexico City and Guadalajara, as well as a marginalization of the theology of liberation in seminary training and pastoral development.[61]

By the mid-1980s, the CEBs were eliminated from diocesan parishes in Mexico's cities and survived only in urban parishes run by some Jesuits, Dominicans, Franciscans, and Missionaries of the Holy Spirit and in rural dioceses serving the very poor. Nevertheless, from the late 1960s until the mid-1980s many Mexican Catholics were introduced to Catholic social justice doctrine through the CEBs, learning the organizing principles of association, participation, and solidarity as well as the analytical framework of the signs of the times, local analysis, and structures of sin. During this period a distinctively progressive Catholic social imagination developed with a highly world-structural orientation and a church orientation that was only minimal. Many of my Mexican informants over the age of forty had been exposed to CEBs in their parish or diocese and in national movements, so they had been trained to put faith into action and had learned a hermeneutic of suspicion regarding the old regimes of church and state.

Never institutionalized as civil associations, the CEBs were not able to sustain their organizational life after the "cleansing" of the Church by Prigione and the bishops he appointed from the 1980s on. By 1996, when Müllor was appointed papal nuncio, the Mexican hierarchy consisted of almost 90 percent Prigione appointments—bishops who had been trained in Rome and had a conservative orientation. Participants in the CEBs found a place for their *inquietud* and *oposición,* but they were unable to translate their concerns into citizen action due to the weakness of the Mexican opposition in the 1970s and 1980s. By 1988 and the presidential candidacy of Cuauhtémoc Cárdenas Solórzano and the formation of a leftist opposition party, the PRD, the CEBs were largely defunct, but many of the PRD's most active members had been active in the CEBs and had become disillusioned with the Church.

Institutional Church Organization of Social Justice Doctrine within Catholic Social Movements

Another set of cultural sites for social justice in Mexico had been such international social organizations as the Movimiento Familiar Cristiano (Christian Family Movement), Encuentro Matrimonial (Marriage Encounter), the Legion of Mary, and the St. Vincent de Paul Society. The first two focus upon the renewal of families as the first units in society: good families make a good society. Both of the family organizations are Vatican II–oriented and emphasize loving relationships within the family and the virtue required to be good spouses and family members. Families are seen as a leaven for justice in the world. The Legion of Mary and the St. Vincent de Paul, as described in my survey of the U.S. church, are pre–Vatican II lay organizations founded to assist Catholics in actualizing works of mercy within a parish. In all of these organizations, which now have very little overall influence in Mexican church life due to the more recent development of the Pastoral Conjunto (Pastoral Plan), participants learned the organizing principles of association, participation, and solidarity, the virtue of friendship, option for the poor and vulnerable, and the social role of friendship and of the laity. These organizations had a strong integral-church orientation toward the larger Catholic social imagination. Many of my informants above the age of forty-five had been active in one or more of these organizations and received a discipleship formation that would move them toward civic responsibility. However, none of my informants had continued in these older organizations as they switched their commitment to the Pastoral Social or the more social justice–oriented organizations such as IMDOSOC.

Building a New Civil Society Inspired by Christian Values: The Case of the Instituto Mexicano de Desarrollo Comunitario (IMDEC)

As noted in chapter 2, the 1968 massacre of student demonstrators at Tlatelolco in Mexico City set in motion a social, religious, and political culture of *inquietud*. This *inquietud* marked all of the Catholic social activists I interviewed during my fieldwork in Mexico. The best way I can translate *inquietud* for U.S. readers is as a deeply felt disappointment with the stated aims of the modern Mexican project. Based on the socialist and solidarist principles of the 1917 Constitution and those of the PRI as an institutionalization of the Mexican Revolution—"¡Para la justicia social y el progreso!" (For social justice and progress!)—the state was supposed to provide for the general welfare of society. There was a widespread sense that the project had failed. Catholics with the *inquietud* had an "uneasy conscience" about their country's social ills, prompting them to ask, "What can I do to bring social justice to Mexico?"

I spent the summer of 1998 traveling throughout the state of Michoacán in order to better understand the Mexican immigrants of the San Antonio District in Oakland. I initially wanted to find out if there were civic skills and a civic culture that had been left behind when they came to California. To my surprise I found that in both the urban areas of Morelia and Uruapán and the rural areas of the state that I visited, there was a very low development of civic association and participation among urbano-campesinos. This was confirmed at a Mexican government-sponsored conference on migration that I attended in Morelia, the state's capital. There I encountered people from Guadalajara who were associated with a civic organization, the Instituto Mexicano de Desarrollo Comunitario (Mexican Institute of Community Development, IMDEC). They had set up an information table at the conference and were selling educational materials on community development, adult popular education, and Mexican social movements. I asked if I could visit them in Guadalajara in the fall of 1999. They suggested that I participate in their training program for civic leaders.

IMDEC's national training program for civic leaders is an intensive participatory training spread out through the year in four one-week sessions. It was developed through several years (1971–79) of experience of IMDEC's founders in the community of Santa Cecilia in Guadalajara. Carlos Núñez Hurtado, IMDEC's visionary founder and educator, told me that he and his compatriots—all Catholic-educated middle-class people from Guadalajara—had been deeply affected by the Tlatelolco massacre. These young people mostly attending the state-run University of Guadalajara were inspired by the opening of the Church following Vatican II and were being exposed to the ideas of liberation theology emerging from the 1968 Medellín conference. He said that a convergence of *inquietud* from the massacre, the ideas of liberation theology, and a desire to do something in Guadalajara brought about the Santa Cecilia organizing project in 1971.

Santa Cecilia was a very poor new community of *campesinos* who had moved to Guadalajara for urban jobs beginning in 1968. Within two years the population had grown to thirty-five thousand. This type of new neighborhood is known as a *fraccionamiento popular* (popular settlement)—a squatters' settlement without any infrastructure. By 1971, the Jesuits and the Religious of the Sacred Heart of Jesus both wanted to form immersion communities for their young members in Guadalajara and chose Santa Cecilia as their neighborhood. Santa Cecilia very quickly became a laboratory for social justice in Guadalajara. Núñez is of the opinion that the projects developed quickly because the people were accustomed to religious authority and responded readily to the authority of the priests and the nuns. The greater challenge for the IMDEC people was to get laypeople to realize their own potential as leaders and to create their own structures apart from the nuns and priests. But the IMDEC experiment persisted and developed into Guadalajara's first civil association of *colonos* (neighborhood inhabitants).

IMDEC's training program emerged through a trial-and-error process of citizen participation and adult education. The educational component was primarily influenced by the work of Freire and his idea of consciousness raising based on a "from below" education.[62] Organizationally, IMDEC was influenced by the small group processes of Bible reading and sharing about daily life that marked the *comunidades eclesiales de base* (CEBs), which the religious orders were developing in Santa Cecilia. IMDEC was one of the first groups to separate from religious affiliation. The organizers preferred to describe themselves with the term *inspiración cristiana* (Christian inspiration), reflecting the influence of liberation theology and a spirit of ecumenism. Politically they were motivated by a radical vision of a socialist Mexico. Together these elements are characterized by Nuñez as IMDEC's *visión integral* (integral vision) for its process of promotion, communication, and education.[63]

From 1971 through 1979, IMDEC activists in Santa Cecilia gained a track record of achievement in the creation of an infrastructure for the new community. Streets, curbs, water supply, sewage and trash services, electricity, and telephone service were all elements of IMDEC's initial agenda. They accomplished these victories through the mobilization of laypeople, who eventually became leaders of Guadalajara's civil society and of the opposition political parties, the PAN and the PRD. Núñez himself served as a PRD member of Congress from the state of Jalisco from 1994 through 1997.[64] The primary method of mobilization became the *taller* (workshop) through which *técnicas* (technical skills) could be taught. It should be noted that prior to attending IMDEC workshops, the participants would not have been exposed to any of these methods or this pedagogical philosophy. The workshops would provide a primary civic education and introduce civic skills to the people of Santa Cecilia.

The IMDEC organizers were imbued with the ideas of Freire: conscientization, "from below" research, and self-education, with the people's own history, experience, culture, ideas, and values being given priority. The IMDEC organizational, educational, and training process involved the following developmental steps, which over a period of six years became the IMDEC model:

- *preliminary investigation:* consult existing documentation on the neighborhood; dialogue with the women and men religious already working in the neighborhood; interview the *colonos;* assemble a preliminary synthesis of ideas from the various parties working in the neighborhood

- *physical investigation:* detail *colonos'* desires for the community's physical infrastructure; create a graphic presentation of proposed infrastructure projects including materials, costs, and personnel needs; develop a *módulo de servicios a la vivienda* (neighborhood service module, which became a kind of community hardware store); provide for emergency services.

- *dialogical investigation:* formulate conversation guides for IMDEC organizers to generate a *universo temático* (universe of themes, which included work, family, education, neighborhood, religion, and politics) and *universo vocabular* (universe of vocabulary), leading to understanding of how to build a team to work on an ongoing basis in the neighborhood

- *stage of strong promotion:* recontact the *colonos* to see if they will commit themselves to one of the themes; based on this, generate functional thematic divisions within the IMDEC organization; create an ongoing organizational structure, called the *trabajo integral* (the integrated work)

- *consolidation of the groups:* analyze overlapping functions among groups in the neighborhood and attempt to create an integrated community system; begin a more formal theoretical and methodological formation of the team; reformulate objectives; elaborate different levels of tasks; integrate different groups and areas of existing tasks in the neighborhood

- *the "assembly of representatives"*: organize a meeting of representatives of the more than eighty groups that had developed in the neighborhood; create a permanent representative organization, which in Santa Cecilia became known as the Colonos Unidos (United Neighbors); begin mass mobilization in the neighborhood

- *stage of renewal and evaluation* (a critical stage that distinguished IMDEC leaders as "professionals"): provide expertise in workshops and skills for the community to use; evaluate the *proyecto-proceso* (project-process)

- *the work of objectives and concrete plans:* form a team of promoters who will work with a methodological pedagogy that had developed within IMDEC and the community; define the role of the team coordinator as a small group facilitator; establish a permanent group leadership committed to the objectives of the community (eliminating the ad hoc leadership style that had created confusion and conflict at meetings); institutionalize IMDEC as the provider of "Workshop on Cooperatives," "Membership Workshop," "Communication and Popular Culture Workshop," etc., for the Santa Cecilia community and other neighborhood organizations forming in Guadalajara[65]

By 1979, by creating a systematic leadership-training program incorporating these elements and offering it to leaders of evolving nongovernmental organizations throughout Mexico, IMDEC had become an institutional force in Guadalajara. Within ten years, Santa Cecilia had developed into a thriving community with a good infrastructure and a vibrant civil sector that was clearly a product of the IMDEC strategy for community development based on its *visión integral*. Núñez and others in IMDEC told me that in those early days they really had not imagined that their ideas would become institutionalized. But their pragmatism and results-oriented program generated an ongoing process that the *colonos* took to. Since the early 1990s, Santa Cecilia has been part of a citywide structure of *colonos* within the municipal government that has provided a mechanism for citizen participation. This reform has been another result of IMDEC's long-term involvement in civic education in Guadalajara and the state of Jalisco.

The training program in which I participated, Escuela Metodológica Nacional Ciclo 1999 (National Methodology School, 1999 Cycle), was held at the University of Guadalajara's Hotel Primavera, located in a beautiful woodsy area south of the city. The Hotel Primavera is a full-service resort and conference center with restaurants, sports facilities, disco, and tennis courts spread out over several acres of manicured grounds. Forty students and five staff stayed in several cabañas that had kitchens and bedrooms, each housing from five to seven people. We ate our main meal at the restaurant and cooked our breakfast and late-night supper in the cabañas. The pleasant surroundings and modern facilities in a vacation location provided a needed respite for the vast majority of the students, who were working as leaders of a wide variety of civil associations throughout Mexico. Many of them told me that they had never stayed in such a nice place. The Executive Director of IMDEC, Efrén Orozco, told me that the Hotel Primavera was chosen because of the opportunity to offer their training in a first-class facility at a very reasonable cost, since the facility is subsidized by the Mexican government since the University of Guadalajara is the premier state university in Jalisco.

The tuition, room, and board for each of the four sessions came to about U.S. $100. Many participants received full or partial scholarships. Over the years IMDEC has received financial support from several European religious organizations, particularly the German Catholic Church's international social fund, which supports the development of civil society in Latin America. This international support had allowed IMDEC to survive the 1992 economic crisis and continue its annual training programs.

Over the course of the four training sessions I learned much about the state of Mexican civil society from my fellow students as I listened to firsthand accounts revealing the depth of the *inquietud* of the post-1968 activist generation. Every participant had a story of how he or she became committed to the cause of social change, usually after personal encounters with poverty, discrimination, or repression. In my cabaña three of the men had been in seminary studies and had become disillusioned with the prospects for being priests in the cause of social justice: each had a story of marginalization or repression by the Church because of his concern for the poor and human rights. Each represented a civil association (Habitat for Humanity in Mexico City, Instituto Pastoral Don Vasco in the state of Michoacán, and Servicios Para una

Educación Alternativa in the state of Oaxaca) as a way to realize his vocation for social justice. In our many late-night conversations, I realized
that these men had really wanted to become priests. They had a deeply
felt *inquietud* regarding both the Church and the PRI and were totally
committed to be part of the *oposición*—a new kind of social vocation.
Of the four Mexicans in my cabaña, two were oriented toward the PAN
and the other two were with the PRD—but they had profound respect
for each other's commitment to work for social and political change and
create a true democracy in Mexico.

The training sessions were conducted by three IMDEC educators,
including Orozco. At every session there was a secretary/recorder who
typed up notes on a laptop computer. Following each session the participants received a detailed summary of the training, called a *memoria*
(memory), including text and photos of the activities. These were the
primary elements of the training that I experienced:

- *concienticización* (consciousness raising): the "from below" perspectives of those affected by a given social problem, drawing on Freire's
  educational pedagogy

- *concepción metodológica dialéctica—proceso de pensar y transformar
  o hacer* (dialectical methodological concept—process of thinking
  and transforming or doing): generating the *visión integral* as an integrative process of analysis, critique, and action through research,
  dialogue, critical analysis, role playing, educational processes, and
  action-oriented projects; building processes for reflection and action

- *planeación estratégica* (strategic planning): creating a strategic plan
  that includes step-by-step objectives to be fulfilled within given time
  frames

- *dinámicas y técnicas* (dynamics and skills): a "cultural toolkit" of dynamic adult educational games and skills that are learned within the
  concepción metodología dialéctica for the purpose of team building

- *identidad de sujeto y transformación personal (sujeto transformador)*
  (identity of the subject and personal transformation [the subject
  transformer]): the participant, who by learning is doing the work of
  social justice transformation, as the object of the process

- *investigación participativa* (participatory investigation): research
  through participatory investigation

- *sistematización* (systematization): development of a rational schema for theory and participatory investigation that details the various elements of the project[66]

For Núñez, the primary theorist of this training program, IMDEC training is "an ontological vision or a theory of being," which strives for an educational process that is fundamentally different from the "from above" ideological education that Mexicans have received. Instead of ideology, the IMDEC process is "a range of criteria and of values placed within a context and its daily changing dynamics, which establish, re-evaluate and/or modify the norms of individual and social behavior, always maintaining the fundamental principle of putting the man or the woman at the center of social action."[67]

During the four training sessions I witnessed how this educational philosophy is played out, particularly through the use of techniques, games, and skits which prompted the participants to act out their local experiences as "from below" data, analysis, critique, and action. For example, during a process focusing on motivating a team (*equipo*), the participants were divided into groups based on a particular interest in common, such as type of organization the person represented. My group of nine was associated with faith-based social action programs. We developed a sociodrama of building a house in a local community and the obstacles we might encounter. The construction materials were the values that we brought to the project. Each participant wore a sign indicating a particular value. We constructed a house with chairs from the conference room. Once the house was built, various "ills" or obstacles arrived on the scene and tried to destroy the house of values. The house was destroyed, so the "values" regrouped and rebuilt the house strong enough to withstand the second attack by the "ills."

In this process the group employed mime, social analysis, each person's experience, and the motivating values of each. The participants were quite at ease entering the process, and they were highly cooperative in taking on the roles of "values" or "ills." The "ills" certainly had a lot of fun attacking the house. The participants who viewed our sociodrama analyzed it and thought we had presented the concept of motivation in a very understandable and impassioned way. These games could easily be replicated in each participant's organization. They were a participatory way of understanding the theoretical talks about elements of the IMDEC process.

Every year forty leaders are chosen from throughout Mexico to participate in the yearlong National Methodology School. However, IMDEC has not developed itself as a mobilizing institute like PICO in the United States. Its graduates have informal networks for ongoing contact. More formally IMDEC is connected to several national and international civil society associations: Convergencia de Organismos Civiles por la Democracia en México, Alianza Cívica, Foro de Organismos Civiles de Jalisco, and Red Alforja. The following sections of this chapter will illustrate how IMDEC's processes have penetrated both civil society and the Catholic Church.

Case Study: Bringing a Catholic Social Imagination into Mexican Public Life

During the training I met a couple from Guadalajara, Carlos and Esther,[68] who were very involved in the Pastoral Social of the Archdiocese of Guadalajara and also in independent civic groups. I decided to base my fieldwork in Guadalajara to explore the institutional church's social mission and its relationship to the emerging Guadalajara civil society. Having invited me to attend meetings and witness how IMDEC's processes were being implemented, Carlos and Esther introduced me to a variety of Pastoral Social sites: their local parish, the vicariate, and the archdiocese.

One night in April 1999, at a vicariate meeting of the Pastoral Social—about fifteen people seated in a circle in a classroom of a fairly modern middle-class parish in Guadalajara proper—I met Father Tacho, who was teaching an ongoing course on Catholic social justice doctrine. That night he spoke on the Jubilee Year and global debt. He handed out copies of a text on this issue that had been prepared by IMDOSOC.[69] Each participant read a paragraph of the text, after which there was a general discussion. I was struck by Father Tacho's and the group's critical sense of Mexican life, the institutional church, and the global economy. Probably half of the group was middle class, and the others were urbano-campesinos from the southern part of the vicariate of forty parishes. While the theme of the evening was the global economy, the participants seemed to relish the idea of the Jubilee Year as an opportunity to put Christ first and for the social doctrine to usher in a greater realization of social justice in Mexico. Indeed almost all Pastoral Social meetings that I attended in the vicariate and local parishes were marked by a "how to be more Christlike" social discourse. The meetings were organized in a participatory manner and drew upon a number of basic civic skills. Father Tacho told me he had learned these skills and processes through involvement in IMDEC programs—in the mid-1990s the archdiocese had sent leaders to IMDEC to implement the Pastoral Social's voter education campaign—and through a course at IMDOSOC in Mexico City.

That night I met three people—Victor, Ana, and Lizbette—from the *fraccionamiento popular* or colonia of Las Pintitas, in the most southern part of the vicariate and within a mile of the international airport. The next day Lizbette took the bus into central Guadalajara, where I was residing at a Jesuit student house, so she could escort me to Las Pintitas. She wanted to show me how to get to the bus stop—a task that can be confusing in a city of many public and private bus lines—and where to get off. As well, she wanted me to go on the bus during the rush hour to experience how most of the people of the colonia go to and from work. She certainly was an excellent "from below" teacher for me as she introduced me to the daily life of Las Pintitas. Lizbette was a married woman of about forty with four children ranging in age from ten to eighteen. Her husband had a good job handling baggage at the airport. As we rode the bus together, she told me her life story while pointing out the various sites along the fifteen-kilometer route from downtown to the colonia.

Over time I learned that Lizbette had many entrepreneurial skills. For example, she rented out refrigerator space and food preparation tables located in a spare room at the front of her modest house. She also rented out use of her phone, since few people in the colonia had their own. Phone service in Mexico costs more per month (about U.S. $30.00) than a minimum-wage job would allow. The minimum daily wage in 1999 was U.S. $3.50, or about U.S. $90.00 per month. People like Lizbette's husband with good jobs at the airport or in the *maquiladoras* (assembly plants) in the nearby Guadalajara "Silicon Valley" earn three or four minimum wages, which might allow a family to purchase property and build a house. But with U.S. $270 to $360 a month people are still hard pressed to buy a car, pay for tuition at a private *colegio,* have a phone, or buy new clothes and electronic goods. During the time of my research, from 1999 to 2001, not a single person in the colonia had local access to the Internet. Lizbette is like many of her smart (*listo*) neighbors, who are always scrambling to find new ways to make money.

I started a pattern of taking the bus to Las Pintitas at least three days a week. Very quickly I learned that the people were quite similar to those in the San Antonio District of Oakland: everyone was originally from Mexico's rural states and had come to the urban area in search of work following the massive rural restructuring processes of the 1970s.[70] Like San Antonio, Las Pintitas had about thirty-five thousand people. Because of these similarities, I decided to do my base ethnographic research in Las Pintitas in order to compare migrant Mexicans working for social justice with the Catholic Church.

This colonia, like Santa Cecilia, had formed in the late 1960s without a master plan. The only paved road was a massive superhighway connecting the airport to downtown Guadalajara; it divided the colonia in two parts. For the five-kilometer stretch through Las Pintitas, there is not one highway off-ramp. To catch the bus to Guadalajara, the residents on one side had to run across the six-lane highway. People told me to be careful, because at least five people had been killed each year running across the highway.

Las Pintitas had a minimal infrastructure of electricity, twice-weekly home water delivery, private public transportation, three primary schools, one secondary school, one high school, a small municipal building on one side of the freeway, and the main Catholic church on the other side. I was told that there were two Protestant groups that met in homes. No parks, recreation facilities, libraries, paved roads, drainage, public garbage service, ambulance service, or hospitals had been provided by government. Most Mexican communities are organized around a central plaza, the *zócalo,* with the Catholic church and the municipal buildings located around it. Not only did Las Pintitas not have this kind of geographical or civic central point, but it was divided by the highway.

The parish of Las Pintitas, San Francisco de Asís, was founded in the mid-1970s following the rapid expansion of the community. The parish complex reflects a post–Vatican II style of church construction in urban Mexico: classrooms, hall, a plaza most often used for parking, housing facility for the two priests, and administration offices. These offices provide space for a medical clinic and a dispensary for the activities of the Pastoral Social. The modern church is well constructed, of brick with steel reinforcement, and capable of seating six hundred people—just like the church of St. Anthony's. It has a very clean, airy feel. The doors of the church are large sliding partitions that can be completely opened to accommodate overflow in the plaza. This plaza is the only open public space in the entire Las Pintitas colonia. The events of the 4 October *fiesta patronal* (feast day of the community's patron saint) of St. Francis take place in this plaza and the unpaved streets adjacent to the parish's property.

After Lizbette and I arrived in the colonia, we went to evening Mass. Later I met several people in front of the church who would be attending the meeting of the parish Pastoral Social at 8:30 p.m. The leader of the group, Rafael, was in his late twenties and was accompanied by his pregnant wife, Cecilia. The meeting, which was held weekly on Wednesdays, took place in the church hall, which had been set up with four large rectangular tables surrounded by benches. Twenty-seven people were attendance: eighteen women, nine men. About a third were under thirty, another third from thirty to fifty, and the last third fifty and over.

The meeting got under way with a prayer. Rafael then asked participants to take out their Bibles so they could begin a study of the chosen scripture and consider how it related to their local work. Only six people had Bibles, so Rafael suggested that the group begin buying more for use in the meetings—one each week with funds from the raffle for handmade items they had at every meeting. Over time, everyone would be able to have a large-print Bible.

After the Bible study, Rafael mentioned that the group needed to inform the parish of the results of the previous Sunday's fundraising effort: fifteen hundred pesos (about U.S. $140). The ongoing fundraising of the Pastoral Social consists of selling *empanadas* (a fruit-filled pastry), raffle tickets for religious articles, and the archdiocesan newspaper, *El Semanario.* This fundraising is critical for supporting the charitable and justice works of the parish, since the Pastoral Social coordinates all these activities in the parish and the colonia. There are no other charitable organizations in the community. The parish was founded at a time when the archdiocese was implementing the integrated pastoral plan; thus the major parish functions had been organized as the Pastoral Profética, Litúrgica, and Social, as explained earlier in this chapter. When I asked about groups like the St. Vincent de Paul Society and the Legion of Mary—which are present in Mexico—none of the Las Pintitas people knew what I was talking about, which helped verify that they had come to the colonia as migrants from rural areas that have not established these more urban Catholic service organizations.

Following the fundraising topic, there was a discussion of activities for the upcoming Festival de las Madres (Mother's Day) on 9 May. They agreed that they would raffle a more expensive item for that event, a *cromo* (framed religious picture, usually with a 3-D effect). Every time there was need for money, the solution would be to have a raffle; these appeared to satisfy the need.

The pastor came into the meeting during this discussion and brought up a new topic: a ten-parish deanery-wide Escuela Pastoral Social that would be held five kilometers away in the community of Toluquilla. The planning meetings for this training effort would take place at 8:00 p.m. on Fridays at the parish of La Señora del Rosario. He said that he could not attend the meeting that Friday and wanted to know if four to six people could represent the parish. The parish would pay for transportation. Victor, Ana, Lizbette, and two others volunteered to go.

A discussion of the parish program for *útiles* (school supplies) followed. *Útiles* are purchased in bulk by the parish and then sold at the beginning of the school year at cost to the parents of the schoolchildren. The key idea discussed was making sure that the teachers in the public schools provided updated information about their classroom needs in time for the bulk purchase. Rafael said that he would be working with a stationery store in Guadalajara to buy the items.

Rafael noted that no one from Caritas Guadalajara (Catholic Charities Guadalajara) was attending the meeting as he had hoped. He had expected a report on how a census of families might be conducted to ascertain what would be needed by families for the proposed *banco de alimentos* (food bank) organized by the Archdiocese of Guadalajara. Pepe, a man in his mid-twenties sitting next to me, explained in a whisper that the census would capture primary information on family demographics for a needs assessment process.

Lizbette then spoke of a young woman who had recently miscarried. She had accumulated 450 pesos' worth of bills at the Hospital Civil de Guadalajara. There was a consensus that the Pastoral Social would pay the bill for her.

Last, there was a brief discussion, under new business, of who would sell *empanadas* the next Sunday. As well, there was talk of starting the *dispensa* (food distribution) the coming Saturday at 11:00 a.m. instead of 10:00 because of the First Communions that would be taking place at the satellite chapel close to the airport. In addition to the main church site, there are three satellite chapels served by the two priests and the Pastoral Social. After a short prayer offered by the pastor, Padre José, the meeting was adjourned at 10:05 p.m.

While Rafael had dominated the meeting, many people contributed ideas during the various discussion periods, particularly Victor, Lizbette, Pepe, and his wife, Reina. Padre José had allowed Rafael to truly run the meeting, which followed an informal adaptation of Roberts' Rules of Order. (Indeed throughout my time in Las Pintitas, I observed that Padre José trusted Rafael, Lizbette, and Victor to make judgments for the Pastoral Social; the pastor seemed to only hover in the background at its activities.) There was a lively, friendly, and joking atmosphere throughout the meeting.

Rafael had attended the college seminary of the archdiocese and had an extensive knowledge of the Bible and the social doctrine. He told me that he was involved in social justice because "it is part of the salvific plan that we learn about in the Bible and the catechism of the Church. We are called to the more human Christ of the Church's doctrine. Here we see the Christ of dignity and equality. Society and religion have to be joined, but we lack the education to know how to do this." One day I ran into Rafael on the bus coming into Las Pintitas and found out that he worked at the University of Guadalajara's Hotel Primavera, where I had been attending IMDEC training, as a janitor—a good job earning three minimum-wage salaries. He said that he spent at least ninety minutes taking three bus lines to get to work. Yet he was always at the Pastoral Social meetings and was usually accompanied by his wife.

Following the meeting, Victor and Ana drove me to central Guadalajara in their station wagon, because I had missed the last bus. They were among but a handful of couples in the community who owned a car. Seven of us jammed into the wagon, because they wanted to visit the woman who had miscarried at the hospital. When we got to the hospital at 11:00 p.m., I was struck by the amount of activity in the waiting rooms. The people from Las Pintitas had a hard time finding their neighbor, since there was no central information desk. They finally learned that she had been there that day but had checked out in the afternoon. No one had called the hospital to check ahead of time, and no one was bothered that their attempt had been unsuccessful. They simply enjoyed doing ministry together. I eventually got to my residence about 12:30 a.m. I learned to watch time on the nights of these meetings so that I could get the last bus into Guadalajara at 10:00 p.m.[71]

During the more than thirty meetings I attended in more than a year of fieldwork in Las Pintitas, I listened carefully for theological discourse utilizing the social doctrine that might emerge. At every meeting Rafael made some instructional point based on the Bible, the social doctrine, or something that Pope John Paul II had recently said. Further, in my interviews with members of the Pastoral Social, I noted that when directly asked about their social involvement, they had well-articulated knowledge of the social doctrine and biblical concepts related to social justice. In particular the people of Las Pintitas were motivated by

Cristo encarnado (incarnated Christ)—an enfleshed Jesus who served the poor and is revealed as Christ in the poor. Unlike their U.S. counterparts, who were primarily motivated to "do good works" because of Judeo-Christian principles of liberty, civil rights, and ending discrimination and poverty, these Mexican Catholics were inspired mostly by the Scriptures and the social doctrine. They freely used religious concepts such as solidarity as a virtue, human rights, and the option for the poor—and most particularly *Cristo encarnado.*

In point of fact, I could not detect a civil discourse related to social justice among the poor and working-class people of Las Pintitas, though I did encounter it among middle-class people in Guadalajara. Victor expressed well the common sentiment of the urbano-campesinos of Las Pintitas: "I am involved in the Pastoral Social because of the Word of God. We need to put the Word in all our situations—the family, our jobs, our community. We need more workers each day, because this is a big job for a few people to do. For me the defense of the oppressed worker is very important. We need to defend the rights of the worker." He reflected:

> The sacrifice of the Mass is the center of our work. We need to introduce the liturgy into all of our actions. Before we just read the scriptures; now we need to live the scriptures in our daily lives. Today we have a much more open church. Before we used to have a vicious circle, because the laity could not do anything, but today we are able to enter into the Church's ministries. We need better-formed laity. Here in Las Pintitas I remember just five years ago when only ten people would receive Communion—just women. Now more than one hundred men and women receive Communion at every Mass. This happened because the priests hear people's confessions whenever the people want to confess. We are really improving the spiritual life here. I think that the spiritual change is important, because it changes the whole environment.

Victor operated a bicycle repair shop in the front of his house. Every time I visited his home, he was extremely busy. He enjoyed the children who came in to get their bikes fixed and was a kind of father figure to many of the boys in the neighborhood. His wife, Ana, and their three daughters ran a food-preparation business from their kitchen. Every weekday morning beginning at 5:00, they prepared more than two hundred meals, which they sold at the local middle school. Victor told me that together they earned about U.S. $1,000 a month, making them one of the wealthier families in Las Pintitas. They invested their money back into the businesses and their property. They had a four-acre piece of formerly *ejido* land, on which they were constructing a home for each of their four adult children.[72] All members of the family had lived illegally in the United States at some point. They had always sent their money back to Mexico, and this was how they had been able to acquire their property. The whole family had an entrepreneurial spirit, a knack for finding opportunities and making money. This quality made it all the more interesting to me that Victor and Ana were so involved in the Pastoral Social. Victor felt that because the family was so richly blessed, being of service in his parish was the least he could do. On Sunday afternoons he supervised one of the parish mission sites, where he coordinated the people assisting at the evening Mass and organized local services of the Pastoral Social.

As already mentioned, during summer and fall 1999, the local deanery of fifteen parishes initiated a common Escuela Pastoral Social (School of Social Ministry) at the parish hall of La Señora del Rosario in Toluquilla. At the entrance of the parish, signs pointed the way to reception tables, where people were standing in line waiting to register. At the tables were bright balloons and a huge sign saying "Bienvenido a la Escuela Pastoral Social" (welcome to the School of Social Ministry). There was also a large sign with the agenda for the evening. Everyone received and put on a nametag. The participants entered a very large hall that could probably accommodate eight hundred people on the main floor and in the balconies on three sides. The twelve participants from Las Pintitas sat toward the front of the main floor. While the people waited for the meeting to begin, they sang a number of popular Christian songs—praise music—used at liturgies in Mexico. By the time the meeting started promptly at 8:00 p.m., the hall was packed. The priest leading the opening prayer spoke in an energetic voice and asked that the Holy Spirit guide the beginnings of this new era in the deanery. He then asked all the priests in attendance to join him on the raised stage. They were greeted with thunderous applause. The mood was upbeat, like that of a U.S. political rally—and very close to the spirit of OCO rallies. The keynote speaker was a psychologist from Guadalajara, who spoke of the importance of building up self-esteem of everyone in the community. She spoke in the manner of a highly charged motivational speaker and was dressed as a professional, in stark contrast to the simple garb of the largely poor and working-class people in attendance. She was an excellent communicator, and the crowd responded with applause throughout the talk.

Following her talk, the people broke into groups based on their particular social justice interest to discuss how the school might help their ministry. These groups were very large—from thirty to eighty people each—which made it difficult to have dialogue. Generally the leader ended up dominating the session. Topics of concern discussed in the groups were presumably being reported later to the organizing group of priests; reports were not made in the large assembly. The meeting concluded about 10:00 with a prayer and a hymn.

These meetings at both the parish and deanery levels of the Pastoral Social in Guadalajara revealed a variety of skills used by the religious actors:

- membership inscription: signing in, wearing of nametags

- small group dynamics: sitting in small groups, participating in dialogic discussions, facilitators, small group reporters

- integration of prayer and religious music: spontaneous prayer oriented toward the purpose of the meeting; use of religious music for group motivation

- agenda and Roberts' Rules of Order: a clear order to the meetings following an informal adaptation of Roberts' Rules; starting and ending meetings on time

- lay leadership: consistent leadership by designated lay facilitators even in the presence of clergy

- ongoing development of membership: educational materials and instruction provided on an ongoing basis

- results orientation: meetings are used to report outside activities and to help members stay accountable to the group

- open process: people freely exchange ideas and express their opinions; mutual respect

These elements demonstrated the development of democratic skills for the people of Las Pintitas parish and the Toluquilla deanery. However, during my time in the community I never saw the transference of these skills into a civil arena—even though I witnessed an opportunity for this to occur.

In fall 1999, Victor invited me to attend a meeting at the middle school where his wife sold meals. In attendance were teachers and businessmen from Las Pintitas who had formed a civic group to address the problems caused by the superhighway. Juan, the proprietor of a hardware store, was already known to me because his wife, Francesca, was a member of the Las Pintitas Pastoral Social. The group had done a great amount of research on how to coordinate efforts of the federal, state, and municipal governments to construct a pedestrian bridge at the sixteenth kilometer of the highway—which would place the steps of the bridge at one of the entrances to the parish property. The bureaucratic maze seemed overwhelming, but the group was determined to fulfill its dreams of connecting the two sides of the community and reducing hit-and-run fatalities.

These fifteen men were the only nonpartisan *colonos* I encountered in Las Pintitas. Juan later told me that he hoped they would stay together as an ongoing civic association after their goal was achieved. I mentioned that they might contact IMDEC for training programs, and he told me he knew about the organization. He and his wife, both attorneys, chose to start a business in Las Pintitas in the early 1970s; they are two of the most respected people in the community. They moved into a small house behind their store in 1997 because they decided that living in the Country Club Colonia (its actual name!) was keeping them distant from the people they saw day to day.

Francesca had had somewhat of a conversion experience when attending a Mass for the Sick and Elderly. She told me: "At the Mass of the Sick I experienced the total Eucharist, especially that to serve your brother and sister is the love of Christ, of God." She was very active in the Pastoral Social and had recruited a number of the *damas* (upperclass women) of the country club to help out the poor of Las Pintitas. She said, "If we are going to create a better Mexico, we need more consciousness about the situation of the poor. We need an awakening of conscience about human rights, about the poor, about being participants, because Mexicans are too often conformists and have a million excuses for not being involved. We are tired of all of the lies."

Juan had been thoroughly formed in the secular philosophy of *laicidad* and was not at all involved in the parish. They shared in the *inquietud* of the 1968 generation, though they had different ways of trying to resolve it. Juan asked Francesca if she could get permission from the pastor for the civic group to hold a community meeting in the parish hall to discuss the bridge. Padre José gave permission for this to occur and even allowed Francesca to make an announcement about the meeting at the Sunday masses.

Given the relationship of Juan and Francesca, I thought that a marriage between the civic group and the Pastoral Social might be in the making. But none of the participants imagined this possibility. Members of the civic group, especially the teachers, were all imbued with the philosophy of *laicidad* and the strict separation of church and state.[73] And the members of the Pastoral Social who attended the civic group's meeting did not understand that the bridge might have a social justice character, as would have emerged in the American faith-based organizing model. The opportunity was literally at the door of the church. But such an idea has not evolved sufficiently in the religious, civic, and political cultures of Las Pintitas—or Mexican political culture—to sustain the integration of faith values and civil institutions. The fact that none of the ongoing members of the civic group is religious is telling regarding the history of *laicidad* in Mexican culture: smart, intelligent businessmen, government officials, and teachers do not get involved in religious commitments. In the end, the bridge was constructed in March 2000 and brings people safely to the parish. However, the parish did not contribute to this effort.

Francesca's conversion experience at one of the Masses for the Sick and Elderly was exemplary of the powerful effects that this one activity of the Pastoral Social had on all the members. Four times a year, the full repertoire of skills and services of the pastoral team come into play for this event. It provides a quarterly communal renewal for the group, what Émile Durkheim describes as collective effervescence.[74] As mentioned in my profile of Victor in chapter 1, this event was developed in Las Pintitas in order to address the acute needs of elderly shut-ins of the parish. These Masses draw on the following elements of the Pastoral Social's cultural repertoire:

- *liturgical component:* use of the Mass and the Sacrament of the Sick in the social context of serving the elderly and sick of the community

- *teaching component:* following the Mass, a reflection on scripture and the social doctrine by a team member for those in attendance; ongoing teaching during regular meetings of the group

- *organizational component:* ongoing fundraising to pay for the meals, the *dispensa,* and other materials; clarity of roles and functions on the day of the event; accountability process via the regular meetings of the Pastoral Social

- *community-building component:* participatory processes that help build associational life both within the group and in the larger parish community

- *hospitality:* volunteer "taxi service" by members of the community who have cars, to pick up people at their homes; greeting of the elderly and sick by team members, who hug them and give them nametags; a meal served after the Mass, with youth of the parish organized to wait tables

- *dispensa (food distribution):* bags of groceries assembled for the elderly and sick by the team, from food and supplies provided by the archdiocesan food bank, plus a blanket provided once a year; the *dispensa* is also provided to all of the poor of the parish on a weekly basis at the main church or at one of satellite chapels

- *office:* an office, open five days a week and staffed by a person paid by the Pastoral Social, at the entrance of the parish near the bus stop, which dispenses medical supplies, clothes, and emergency food and coordinates other services: weekly visit by a family-planning nurse from Caritas Guadalajara, after-school tutoring services, bulletin board with job postings

All these elements contribute to the integral-church-world orientation of the Las Pintitas Pastoral Social members' Catholic social imagination. It is faith based but is inwardly oriented toward the parish community and ministry within the Pastoral Conjunto, even though many of its activities such as the *dispensa,* the *útiles,* the services offered by the office, and the Mass for the Elderly and the Sick provide social services for the Las Pintitas community. The participants do not see their activities as civil in nature, nor have they imagined the Pastoral Social as forming a civil component that can mediate the concerns of the parish and the larger community. Though many of the skills in their repertory could be transformed into civic skills, there is not a civil opportunity structure present for this to occur. Their Mexican Catholic social imagination does not have space for the possibility of structural agency on their part, nor do they see structural change as an outcome of their ministry. Their deep desires to change the poverty and infrastructure of their community does not connect to their doctrinally conditioned imagination.

The participation of the laity in liturgies at the parish church and the mission sites reflected a certain threshold of lay empowerment in the Mexican church. In Las Pintitas there were several trained lay lectors but only three eucharistic ministers, primarily because in Mexican parishes it is very rare that people receive both the bread and the wine of Communion, so cup bearers are generally not needed. While there was music at all the Sunday masses, very few people sang along with the music group. Music books or sheets were not provided for them. Interestingly, in Las Pintitas and most of Guadalajara and Mexico City, parishioners purchase a pamphlet with the Sunday prayers and scripture readings and then read along as the priest recites the Mass. Most priests do not look up from the prayer book while "reading the Mass." Unlike U.S. parish priests, who have an inviting style, step down into the congregation to preach, and punctuate their homilies with mention of current events to connect the scripture with daily life, Mexican priests are generally very formal in style and deliver their homilies from the pulpit. They tend to focus on the spiritual themes of the scriptures. During Mass at Las Pintitas, the collection often generated a bit of confusion as the sacristan tried to find people to pass the baskets. At Communion time, people rush up to the front of the church and form a haphazard line. Those going to Communion receive the bread on their tongue. The liturgical leaders in Las Pintitas truly believed they had good liturgy compared to other parishes because they had many liturgical ministers who had undergone training by the archdiocese. Based on what I saw in Guadalajara, the Las Pintitas liturgy was indeed as inviting and participatory as possible given the limitations of a highly clerical Catholic culture.

All the leaders of the parish Pastoral Social either held well-paying jobs or had their own small business. They were able to volunteer time and resources to their parish and community. The creative and entrepreneurial spirit they brought allowed them to find new ways to raise money. Their major activities, such as the Mass for the Sick and the food distribution program, were well organized and featured high-quality "social goods." Victor, Ana, and Francesca also brought their experience of living in the United States, particularly with different ways to organize parish life and ideas about how the Church can influence society. Some key features of the organization of the Las Pintitas Pastoral Social came about because of their experiences in the United States, particularly the idea of having a permanent office for the *dispensa* staffed by an employee who was paid through the funds raised by the sale of empanadas after Sunday Mass.

The repertoire of organizational skills on evidence in both Las Pintitas and Toluquilla illustrated the influence of IMDEC's training in the Archdiocese of Guadalajara, which began in the 1990s and has been replicated within the structures of the Church. However, unlike the situation in the United States, where PICO training has helped groups like OCO to develop civic actors within the Church for civil society itself, grassroots members of the Pastoral Social of the Archdiocese of Guadalajara view their work as an internal transformative experience. As presented in my analysis of the Mexican bishops' letter *Solidaridad,* this orientation reasons that what goes on inside the Church should reflect outwardly in the development of Mexico as a more Christian and Catholic nation.

Efrén Orozco of IMDEC noted that many dioceses have used IMDEC methods but do not have an organizational mechanism to link church-based social organizations to civil society. Given the difficulties of getting a free civil society to function in Mexico, the weak institutional basis for religious social outreach, and the endemic concept of *laicidad* in Mexican public life, it is easy to see why the Pastoral Social has not developed a community-organizing function in Mexican civil society. Those who have attempted to make this link within the Church have been labeled as "meddling in politics," because many priests and bishops do not have an understanding of what civil society can be in Mexico. Civil society requires the independence of the laity in directing social justice doctrine–inspired civil associations that are not "Catholic" per se.

The Complexity of Social Justice Doctrine within Mexican Civil Society

Unlike Juan and Francesca of Las Pintitas, who have not sought a marriage between faith and civil society, Carlos and Esther have struggled to integrate their involvement in the Archdiocesan Pastoral Social—more so Esther—and in the *movimiento de colonos* (citizen movement) in Guadalajara. In May 1999 they invited me to attend several meetings regarding a campaign to end "intrafamily violence," the first citizen initiative in Mexican history.[75] They were part of the core circle of leaders who had initiated the citizen initiative through their involvement with IMDEC. Esther and Carlos were primarily responsible for presenting this issue as a concern for the archdiocesan Pastoral Social. They helped gather forty-five signatures at local parishes, and these signatures became the backbone of the initiative and a sign of the "from below" concerns of the people.

Carlos and Esther are both doctors and have their own allergy and homeopathic practices. They manage their consulting hours so that they can often attend daytime meetings. They were both very close to their three children and ate their main meal every day with them at their modest home in a middle-class Guadalajara neighborhood. The family members did their own housework and did not employ the poorly paid maids who are generally ubiquitous in Mexican middle-class households. Esther and Carlos earned enough to own their own car and have cable television service, a phone, and Internet service. But unlike many of their middle-class counterparts, who send their children to the private *colegios,* they enrolled their children in public schools because they believed in them. They had traveled in Europe and the United States. Carlos told me that he lived for two years in Chicago and earned enough there to buy property in Guadalajara. Without prying too deeply, I got the impression that they had invested wisely in property as a buffer against drops in the peso. But they were modest people, particularly in their extensive relationships among the poor and the working class in Guadalajara. They were also very modest in their entertainment choices, preferring to eat in small local establishments and going to hear live folkloric and rock music in inexpensive local venues.

Their commitment to the Church and social justice had come about through their involvement in the Christian Family Movement. As they worked with other couples on improving family life, they realized that they had to begin improving their colonia as well. In the late 1980s their neighborhood had become plagued by drug dealers, so they decided to get involved in the local group of *colonos* and raise the issue of the neighborhood drug problem. Because of their active involvement in the parish, they were able to book their church's classrooms for these civic meetings. They suffered threats and violence because of their advocacy, but with hard work and vigilance they were successful in ridding their neighborhood of the drug blight. Their commitment to the *colono* movement led them to both IMDEC and the archdiocesan Pastoral Social. Carlos has become very involved in state and national civil society associations. Politically, Carlos and Esther are PRD sympathizers, although they are not active in the party. They think that the PAN is too conservative.

The meetings for the intrafamily violence campaign were held at IMDEC's facility in Guadalajara, a spacious complex of meeting rooms, large auditorium, and individual offices. This facility served as a "free space" for the formation of civil associations. The organizing committee was composed of leaders of feminist groups, an independent labor group, human rights lawyers from the University of Guadalajara and the Instituto Tecnológico y Estudios Superiores de Occidente (ITESO), and the archdiocese as an unofficial partner through the involvement of Carlos and Esther. The group's official name was Voces Unidas (United Voices). The meetings followed a consensus model incorporating the Freirian model of conscientization, participatory investigation, and systemization as developed in IMDEC's organizational model. It was highly important for the participants to feel that their concerns were being heard and discussed. My sense was that over the months of the campaign that camaraderie and sense of solidarity as friendship was very significant for them as well.

Over the several months that I participated in the activities of Voces Unidas, it became clear that this was a historically important moment in Mexican civil society, as citizen groups were beginning to generate direct legislative changes without mobilizing political party constituencies. Creating an *imaginario social* (social projection of the future self) has not been an easy task in Mexico, yet Voces Unidas was generating an *imaginario social* "as a joining of the social signs that permit and present something that is not yet, but is desirable in the future, and gives a sense of discourse, of action, and of social practices, which at the same time permits the defining of strategies and the prioritization of relations."[76] The participants had a specific legislative objective, but the process of pursuing it was just as important as winning a legislative victory. In my model of the Catholic social imagination, Voces Unidas was able to organize a normative sense of solidarity along both sides of the integral-structural continuum by building solidarity among comrades, indeed a whole culture and morality of participatory democracy, and a way of mobilizing this solidarity for structural change through the legislative process. Obviously the group had a worldly orientation, but it was quite interesting that there was due attention paid to the Church and its interests, and not only because they did not want the Church in Guadalajara to be an enemy. Most of the members of the group had developed their social activism within the post–Vatican II Mexican church of CEBs and liberation theology and had continued ties with people like Carlos and Esther. Further, they were connected to the Mexican religious culture through *compadrazgo,* the religious and spiritual system of sponsoring and mentoring that is very strong in Guadalajara social life.[77] In that sense, while Voces Unidas was entirely secular, it had an extremely religious cultural sense and was "Christian inspired" with integral and church orientations. Carlos Forment has identified a similar tendency in nineteenth-century Mexican civic culture, calling it "Civic Catholicism"—the "age-old Catholic concern for socio-moral order with the new democratic concern for self-rule."[78]

This dual normative-strategic process was demonstrated in public demonstrations that Voces Unidas orchestrated during the course of 1999 to engage the state government apparatus and political parties with its issue. It also demonstrated a new kind of citizen participation in Mexico: less shrill and demanding, more civil and demonstrative of the nonviolent principles of human rights. In observing IMDEC leaders in a variety of civic situations, I found that in distinction from other civic actors, IMDEC-trained leaders demonstrated an integral-oriented "civic spirituality" marked by nonviolence, graciousness, and mutual respect. For example, IMDEC leaders always began the public events of Voces Unidas with a spiritual exercise of quieting or gestures of hospitality, such as greeting the people nearby—something akin to the "kiss of peace" at Catholic Mass. Participants in these events were encouraged to wear white clothes as a sign of peace and tranquillity. Certainly these symbolic and spiritual efforts aimed to exemplify alternatives to intrafamily violence theme, but more generally they were part of a repertoire of civic skills evolving in Guadalajara's civic culture.

One of the leaders, a feminist educator and psychotherapist, articulated the rationale of the new civic spirituality: "I want to invoke the Spirit that accompanies us. I want people to feel the importance of their own individuality. I don't want them to feel that they are a mass. The Left often does not understand the importance of the capital that each person has and treats the people, especially from the rural areas, as a mass." This leader told me that in her youth she had been influenced by the theology of liberation, but as she became more involved in IMDEC-related civic activities, she did not see the Church responding to the changing sociopolitical environment. In particular, the Church was not positive toward the emerging Mexican feminist community, in which she was very active. "I just did not see the Church involved in the real issues of social justice that we were involved in."

IMDEC is attempting to create a civic culture that counters the traditional Mexican political culture, which is dominated by ideology, hierarchy, and *machisto* leadership.[79] While its repertoire of sociopolitical skills was not much different from that of other Mexican political movements, IMDEC's skill set is shaped by the philosophy of *senti-pensamiento. Senti-pensamiento* is the glue of this political culture. The development of an ethos for civic skills necessarily forms a new kind of Mexican public actor.[80] At an IMDEC-cosponsored conference on popular education held at Tlaquepaque, Jalisco, in February 2000, the Jesuit rector of the ITESO in Guadalajara, David Fernández (who had in the 1990s headed up the largest human rights organization in Mexico), noted that *senti-pensamiento* draws upon the aesthetic aspects of Latin American culture, particularly the literary and artistic heritage, to make change more humanistic.[81] Indeed, Carlos Núñez believes that nothing short of an ethical revolution will bring about social justice in Mexico and in Latin America. Such an ethical revolution would entail a cultural revolution, applying the rule of law to ensure people's right to realize their deepest hopes and aspirations that emerge from their cultural and religious experiences and values.[82]

In Guadalajara and the state of Jalisco, IMDEC has been able to generate a "from below" civil society by bringing into a common space diverse organizations and actors. It has been successful in fomenting civic participation within a mediating structure that has bridged grassroots organizing, the state government apparatus, the Catholic Church, and the three key political parties in Jalisco. Thus, in the context of participatory investigation it has formed leaders who have a common civic language and can wield the techniques required to create an intermediary network of actors.

Despite these strengths, however, the "from below" elements of IMDEC's model can become lost in this process of mediations, primarily because the IMDEC model does not build in a mechanism for continually generating citizen *senti-pensamiento,* as the Alinsky model of one-on-ones provides for U.S. community organizing. IMDEC's organizers seem to move from issue to issue, without an ongoing organizing model that would keep participants active once an issue has been resolved. For example, Voces Unidas had the specific goal of raising consciousness about intrafamily violence and to get legislation passed to acknowledge and address the social problem at an institutional level. Once there was legislative success, Voces Unidas had fulfilled its purpose, and it has not continued as an organizing instrument for further initiatives generated "from below." A new social issue would require a new organization.

Because of these dynamics in the civic culture, Esther and Carlos's social activism always moves on to the next evolving civic structure. However, their involvement in the archdiocesan Pastoral Social has had more continuity—even though they are often dispirited by the limitations the Church places upon lay leaders. Their religious life is always anchored in their parish and the relationships they have there. They have been important lay participants in the clergy-dominated Pastoral Social. Prior to the national elections in July 2000, Carlos and Esther were very active in the archdiocese's political education campaign, focusing upon the responsibility to vote. Carlos helped create the educational materials for this campaign. He and others with IMDEC background incorporated many of IMDEC's guiding principles in training sessions for parish leaders. (While IMDEC had helped organize the 1994 educational materials for the archdiocese, by the year 2000 the archdiocesan leaders felt that they could produce their own materials and run their own trainings.) Interestingly, some members of the PRI thought that the Church's involvement in voter education was a violation of the law and *laicidad*. This concern was ameliorated by the participation of José Waldenburg, the head of the Instituto Federal de Elecciones (IFE), at the key archdiocese-wide forum for the 2000 campaign.

During the 2000 campaign, IMDEC and other civil organizations ran their own get-out-the-vote programs and were not involved in the Church's educational processes. It seemed another indication of the bifurcated field of social justice: civil or religious, rarely the two working together, even when each influences the other. During the campaign for the intrafamily violence initiative, the Church had a nonofficial role through the participation of people like Carlos and Esther, and many clergy, one of the auxiliary bishops, and many laity were involved in the signature collection process. However, the archbishop of Guadalajara, Cardinal Juan Sandoval Iñiguez, almost derailed the campaign when he voiced concern that the new legislation might redefine the concept of family in Mexican law, since the act would treat all types of households as families, including nonmarried couples and same-sex partnerships.[83] Much time was spent at Voces Unidas leadership meetings discussing how to avoid a collision course with the cardinal. But after the intervention of key clergy, Cardinal Sandoval became convinced that fundamental family law would not be changed and decided not to hinder the legislative process. The incident reflects the fragility of Catholic social justice actors' attempts to connect the institutional church to civil society. While Catholic supporters of the act were motivated by the social doctrine's principles of the dignity of the human person, option for the vulnerable, and human rights, the public campaign did not integrate the discourse of the social doctrine with that of family violence. Furthermore, the public campaign did not incorporate any Catholic religious symbolism associated with the family, solidarity, or a biblical discourse of right relationships.

Alternatives to Institutional Constraints: Emergent Mexican Catholic Social Justice Culture

At every level of the institutional Mexican Catholic church—parish, diocese, and the bishops' conference—the social doctrine functions as part of the overall ideological superstructure through the Pastoral Conjunto. In both Las Pintitas and the Archdiocese of Guadalajara, the social doctrine was placed within the ministry of the Pastoral Social. Yet while educated middle-class Catholic social activists desired to take the social doctrine outside the Church and into civil society, they found themselves impeded by the larger Mexican political culture and by church authority.

The unofficial pilgrimage of forty middle-class Mexicans of the Archdiocese of Guadalajara's Pastoral Social, including Carlos and Esther, to Chiapas in January 2000 exemplified the kind of faith-based activity that clergy and laity initiate on their own as a parallel noninstitutional structure that draws its membership from the official structures. For many very active members, the Pastoral Social functioned as a parallel parish community, since the clergy involved were willing to celebrate special Masses with high lay participation and social justice content that their parishes did not provide. Many of the Catholic-identified participants in IMDEC's national training had a similar parallel identification and activity in human rights groups, women's organizations, and civic associations where an underground Catholic life exists served by progressive diocesan and religious-order clergy. During the time in Chiapas, the delegates participated in a Mass with Bishop Arturo Lona Reyes of the diocese of Tehuantepec. Bishop Lona, now retired, was one of Mexico's most progressive bishops and was particularly identified with the quest for indigenous rights. During Bishop Lona's Mass, there was a high degree of participation of the local laity (reception of both bread and wine in Communion, women giving testimonies, lay copresiders in the eucharistic prayer, a socially relevant participatory homily, very energetic music). The visitors from Guadalajara experienced a kind of conversion. They saw that liturgy, social action, and politics can be integrated as a Catholic *modo de ser* (way of being)—a kind of existential integral-structural balancing. And if they could, they would have tried to express such a Catholic social imagination in Guadalajara, but they realized that they faced many constraints in the institutional church.

This parallel religious-activist life was even more pronounced in Mexico City. Employees and members of IMDOSOC experienced it as a responsive religious community for Catholic social justice. One IMDOSOC employee told me, "I really want to be involved in my parish, but they don't have activities that help me spiritually or educationally. I go to Mass like all the other people, but the liturgies are not very inspiring. I get most of my spiritual fulfillment here at work, especially with our Masses and the way we work as a community." The irony is that IMDOSOC members consider themselves mainstream Catholics, but they are not empowered at the local parish level, so they identify their religious life mainly with the organization. Disillusionment with parish life on the part of the most committed social Catholics is one of the most challenging tests for the future Mexican Church.[84]

Another instance of middle-class Catholics' attempts to live out a social Catholicism is the Christian-inspired civil association. Organizations such as DEMOS and the Centro Mexicano por la Filantropía (CEMEFI) are headed by ex-Jesuits, who took their social doctrine-oriented values into the civil sphere because the urban church had been unresponsive to the *inquietud* of many of its members during the John Paul II–Prignone era. Two of these former Jesuits told me that because the Mexican Jesuits after Vatican II had become extremely ideologically left-wing, they believed that the Jesuits could not have much influence in the kinds of changes necessary for the *transición*. They felt that the institutional church was too conservative, siding with the rich, and the Jesuits were too leftist, siding with the poor, so they left both behind to be involved in a more pragmatic strategy for long-term social change: involving the middle class in civil society.

This type of organization is not parallel to the Church, because these Catholics do not look for an integration of liturgy, social activism, and politics in their civic commitment. One leader told me, "After I left the order, I kind of drifted away from parish life, because the kinds of parishes where middle-class people go are just not inspiring. You are treated like children. The parish priests do not take advantage of the education and experience of their parishioners. Being a Catholic in Mexico is mostly cultural. Just look at how we celebrate Guadalupe and our saints' days." This person and others like him still consider themselves Catholic but more than likely do not participate in a parish or other church associations. Yet they are conversant with the theology of liberation and many aspects of the social doctrine that might converge with their present progressive commitments. And those I met were very aware of Mexican church gossip, which they heard from their old clergy friends.

Both the parallel church phenomenon and the Christian-inspired civil associations reflect a growing dissatisfaction with the old traditions of religion and politics in Mexico. They seem to suggest that the educated middle classes must be utilized to mobilize long-term institutional social change. Many of the people from IMDEC, the Guadalajara and national Pastoral Social, IMDOSOC, DEMOS, and CEMEFI would be identified by Antonio Gramsci as *organic intellectuals,* necessary for the leadership of mediating institutions that will connect the aspirations of the poor and marginalized with the institutions of power in the state, the military, and the economy.[85] The Church and political parties are part of this matrix of power. By marginalizing its moderate-to-progressive social actors, the Catholic Church hierarchy limits its potential for implementing the social doctrine in Mexican associational and institutional life.

Presently in Mexico there are many civil associations that target specific social issues. CEMEFI compiles an annual directory of *asociaciones civiles* (AC), such as IMDEC and the Alianza Cívica, which are equivalent to U.S. nonprofit associations. However, in the 1999 listing of more than two thousand such associations in Mexico, there were no examples of ongoing urban community-organizing associations capable of mediating long-term social change parallel to the U.S. networks that have specific organizing methodologies, interconnecting leadership training programs, and exchange of personnel.[86] Intrinsic to this problem in Mexico is the lack of a renewable methodology that would sustain an ongoing social movement. Efrén Orozco of IMDEC noted that it is difficult to maintain organizational identity and resources on a local level. Very often local groups are competing for scarce resources and are not eager to cooperate with each other. And because of the Church's distance from lay-led civil associations, it does not serve as a structure to connect competing groups as occurs with U.S. faith-based organizing networks. Nothing like the Catholic Campaign for Human Development exists in Mexico.

There is a low development of a culture of philanthropy among the middle class in Mexico to support social change organizations. CEMEFI has attempted to bring change through its campaign to encourage middle-class people to contribute volunteer time to such organizations.[87] The leaders of CEMEFI are in agreement with Carlos Núñez of IMDEC that Mexico requires an ethical revolution to move the middle and upper classes toward a sense of social responsibility.[88] In the late 1990s the Spanish moral philosopher Fernando Savater was having a great influence in the Mexican press and among social activists with books such as *Ética para Amador* (Ethic for Amador).[89] As David Arredondo, executive director of DEMOS (Mexico's leading civil society intellectual organization), told me, "We need a citizen revolution of how 'to be a citizen' [*ser ciudadano*]."

Although Caritas México is the largest private provider of charitable funds for emergency and disaster aid, the Mexican Catholic Church does not solicit funds to support social change programs as the U.S. church does with the Catholic Campaign for Human Development. As noted earlier, IMDEC itself has been able to survive due to assistance from international religious funders. For the Church to move in the direction of supporting social change in civil society, a fundamental departure from the idea that the social is political is required. *No se meta en la política* (do not meddle in politics) is a controlling metaphor for the institutional church and is a critical constraint upon visions of a new civic culture with Christian values.

Overall, the fundamental constraint keeping the social doctrine outside the civil or social sphere is a complex political culture that has historically limited the development of a civil society that could be influenced by the religious values of citizens. When Arredondo talks about "how to be a citizen," he is not talking about voting but about citizens who would take social and ethical responsibility for the problems of society—something beyond voting. Throughout the more than seventy years of the PRI regime, Mexico's political culture was controlled by a state-party apparatus that saw itself as fulfilling the social aspirations of the people. As this political culture began to unravel in 1968, Mexico saw the growth of civil society as a way to fulfill the lost promises of the regime. Today the leaders of the new civil society acknowledge that a larger cultural revolution is required to form responsible citizens to develop and maintain free, nonpartisan public institutions—as well to address the endemic problems of corruption and violence that plague Mexican public life.

The Mexican Catholic Social Imagination: More Roman than Mexican

The Catholic Church has been very late in contributing help to shape a new public morality for socially responsible citizens. But its voter-education programs in the larger urban dioceses such as Guadalajara and Mexico City have helped in the development of an honest and scandal-free election culture and system. Education within the Church is very limited. Because of the historic government restrictions on Catholic education, Mexico does not have a parochial school system to serve the poor and working classes. Only the wealthy can afford to send their children to private Catholic schools. For most Catholics, the religious education received in preparation for First Communion at ages six and seven is the their highest level of religious training. As noted in earlier chapters, the Church has only a limited institutional infrastructure, mostly dedicated to parish life, limited diocesan services, and Caritas. Furthermore, church-related institutions such as publishing houses, training programs, and membership organizations are very few compared to such organizations in the United States. Opportunities for lay leadership in the liturgy have been very limited in Mexico. A typical Sunday Mass in Guadalajara or Mexico City provides a vertical, priest-dominated worship experience. Very few people go to Communion, few people join in the singing because music books are not provided, and the priests rarely touch upon social concerns in their homilies. Mexican seminarians do not receive courses in public speaking or homiletics. All of the priests I asked about this situation told me that they had never received training in how to prepare and deliver a homily.

During his visits to Mexico, Pope John Paul II made much of the country's being very Catholic. But what does this mean? In 1999 Mexico had a total of 12,829 priests, resulting in a priest-people ratio of 1 per 9,536, compared to the United States with 47,210 priests and a priest-people ratio of 1 per 1,037. Mexico had fewer than 600 married deacons, largely serving in dioceses serving the indigenous, as compared to 12,700 permanent deacons in the United States. There were 26,673 nuns in Mexico, compared to 84,034 in the United States. Mexican Catholics attended 5,318 parishes, while U.S. Catholics participated in 19,705 parishes. Interestingly, Mexico has fewer than 120 bishops governing 70 dioceses for some 122 million Catholics, while the United States has 410 bishops governing 191 dioceses for its 62 million members. Clearly Mexico's church, though serving a country that is highly Catholic by baptism, is very lacking in a personnel and organizational infrastructure. It has very large parishes, low development of priestly and religious vocations, and low institutional organizational development.[90] Given the very high priest-to-people ratio in Mexico, it is surprising that the laity have not been more empowered to serve in leadership capacities in parishes and dioceses.

The social doctrine is well reinforced in the Pastoral Social with its church-centered charitable function. Thus, the Pastoral Social has a strong orientation toward the clergy and bishop–dominated hierarchical structure, generating a church-integral Catholic social imagination dominated by doctrinal discourse. But moving the social doctrine to the *plaza pública*—the world-structural orientations—would require major institutional and cultural shifts in Mexican political culture, civil society, and the Catholic Church itself. Factors such as limited liturgical, leadership, and educational opportunities for the laity, a low development of Mexican contextual social theology that might bridge theological and civil discourses, and the problematic of what is appropriately in the social sphere contribute to a limited cultural habitus for Catholic social justice doctrine in Mexico. Catholics wanting to implement the "social" of the social justice doctrine face both internal and external constraints. The best they can do is to be involved in parallel church groups or independent Christian-inspired civil associations trying to implement social change in Mexico.

Parallel church groups, human rights and indigenous rights associations, and civil associations such as IMDEC, IMDOSOC, DEMOS, and CEMEFI can be viewed as a nationwide informal network of Catholics who feel the *inquietud* of their society and have experienced a *despertar* (awakening) to do something about social injustice. Many of these activists are former priests, nuns, and seminarians who bring their education and experiences into the growing Mexican civil society. While difficult to measure in numbers, such social actors hold significant leadership positions in the civil sector.[91] While their discourse does not directly echo the social doctrine, they are inspired by Christian values of justice, liberation, rights, and responsibility in the formation of Mexican civil society, which helped usher in the *transición* of Fox's presidency.

An examination of the normative and strategic continuums of the Mexican Catholic social imagination permits a complex understanding of the public face of the Church and the often latent Catholicity that permeates the culture in terms of history, family life, and social relations based on *compadrazgo*. Given that *laicidad* and anticlericalism persist in the public culture, it may seem surprising that between 2002 and 2005 Mexicans gave the Catholic Church their highest level of confidence among all public institutions (75–80 percent) and priests the highest level among public figures (63–70 percent).[92] This hidden Catholicity is exemplified in the "spiritual" activists associated with Voces Unidas, CEMEFI, and DEMOS—and even among the activists of the Pastoral Social at all levels of the Mexican church, who often feel ambivalent about the Church but remain Catholic and respectful of the Church. One can discover these kinds of hidden behaviors and attitudes only by doing ethnographic research.

My research brings to light the following dimensions and characteristics of the Mexican Catholic social imagination.

NORMATIVE CONTINUUM

1. Integral orientation (religious, theological, and spiritual dimensions)

- *Faith-based:* A deeply Christ-centered and incarnational sense of religious faith (*Cristo encarnado*); one's faith must be believed and worked out in society. Salvation is an "already but not yet"[93] event that is achieved through God's free gift of grace and the disciple's good works. This reflects the function of virtue and moral norm.

- *Theological and biblical education and reflection:* The Mexican Pastoral Conjunto provides a comprehensive sense to the kingly, priestly, and prophetic mission of the Church and assigns the Pastoral Social the task of providing a comprehensive biblical, doctrinal, and theological program of education for the social doctrine. The Pastoral Conjunto strongly carried out the function of organizing principle.

- *Spiritually and sacramentally focused:* The social actors active in the various levels of the Pastoral Social are focused upon spiritual growth through corporal and spiritual works of mercy, resulting in a charity-oriented social justice formation. This capacity fulfills the function of virtue.

2. Structural orientation: (programmatic, cultural, and intellectual development of social justice dimensions)

- *Historical governmental constraints:* The Mexican Catholic Church has not been given freedom to serve as a mediator for religious values to enter public life in Mexico. Even with the 1992 changes to the Mexican Constitution, the Church has not had the imagination to move beyond the *no se meta en la política* attitudes pervasive both in Church and society. Thus, the function of the organizing principle is confined within the Church.

- *Historical public culture constraints:* Alongside governmental constraints, the public culture of the academy, arts, sciences, television, and the press has limited the Church's voice and thus impeded the development of a public Catholicism with public Catholic intellectuals in modern Mexico. Catholic social doctrine has been prevented from fully entering the public culture and becoming contextualized with a Mexican discourse. Thus doctrinal discourse has remained "Roman." The analytical framework function, then, has remained church oriented.

STRATEGIC CONTINUUM

3. Church orientation (pastoral and ecclesial dimensions)

- *Parish lay ministry and leadership development through the Pastoral Conjunto:* Key to the Church's maintenance and growth is the development of laity in the emerging lay ministries, including the social justice ministry, and in leadership positions in parishes, dioceses, and national church structures. The Mexican hierarchy has developed an integrated pastoral plan known as the Pastoral Conjunto, which organizes national, diocesan, and parish life within three primary theological functions of the Church: priest (liturgy), prophet (teaching and doctrine), and king (charity and justice). The Pastoral Conjunto clearly provides the social role and organizing-principle functions to operate at all levels of the Church.

- *The Pastoral Social as conduit for Catholic social doctrine:* Catholic activists are nurtured each week in parishes that have undergone extensive parish renewal since Vatican II, particularly through active lay participation in the various liturgical ministries (lectors, eucharistic ministers, hospitality, music, liturgy committee, and the Rite of Christian Initiation of Adults). Mexican parishes that have developed the Pastoral Conjunto will have the Pastoral Social as the organizing instrument for social doctrine education, food and medical dispensaries, charitable works, and outreach to workers and migrants. Except in rare emergency situations, the Pastoral Social confines its work to the life of the parish community and does not network with civic associations.

- *Church renewal programs:* The Mexican Church has largely been reliant upon extraparochial renewal programs such as Cursillo, Marriage Encounter, the Christian Family Movement, and the charismatic renewal for its internal post–Vatican II renewal.

Religious orders often have their own parish renewal programs, but the national Church has not developed concerted parish renewal efforts like Renew in the United States. Instead church leaders have believed that its Pastoral Conjunto and the so-called new evangelization provide parish renewal. These programs confine the functions of philosophical frameworks and organizing principle within the Church itself.

- *Extraparochial neoconservative ecclesial communities:* Since the 1980s there has been growth in the influence of the Legionnaires of Christ's Regnum Christi, Opus Dei, Focolare, and the Neo-Catechumenate—international lay-oriented ecclesial communities that often draw active parishioners away from the local parish, particularly since Mexican parish life does not do a good job of developing educated Catholics. As the urban bishops of Guadalajara and Mexico City become more reliant upon these communities, they will inadvertently contribute to a weakening of the parish system and accelerate an elitist lay movement removed from the life of the ordinary Mexican church. These movements are identified as "neoconservative" because they are marked by an ultramontane (*más romano que Roma*) and intransigent approach to church renewal—the ideas that Vatican II "excesses have gone too far" and there needs to be a return to a "restored Church" centered in the papacy and adherence to the doctrines of the Church, particularly the moral and social doctrine based on natural law.[94] This provides the philosophical framework and organizing-principle functions with doctrinally directed church and integral orientations.

- *Comunidades eclesiales de base (CEBs):* Following Vatican II, many Mexican dioceses allowed a new form of parish development to emerge through the CEBs, which promoted small faith-sharing groups, Bible study, and community service. The CEBs became integrally linked to liberation theology themes of oppressor-oppressed relationships, human rights, and opposition to capitalism and neoliberalism. After the pontificate of John Paul II beginning in 1979 and the subsequent appointment of Archbishop Prigione as papal nuncio, the CEBs were systematically eliminated through the appointment of neoconservative ordinaries in Mexico City, Guadalajara, Cuernavaca, and Monterrey—all significant dioceses that had flourishing CEB parishes connected to religious orders such as the Jesuits, Franciscans, Salesians, and the

Missionaries of the Holy Spirit. By 2000, the CEBs in Mexico had become a relic of liberation theology except for in very few rural dioceses. As noted, many Catholic social activists had been developed through the CEBs. Because in Mexico the CEBs were never constituted as part of civil society, they provided the philosophical framework and organizing-principle functions with strong church and integral orientations.

- *Diocesan program development and gatherings:* Because the Catholic Church is hierarchically organized with the local bishop as the local head, diocesan programs most often reflect the will of the local ordinary. Given the nature of church authority and sanctioning of ideas and programs, it is significant that the Pastoral Social is a recognized function of the Church; in many dioceses, like Guadalajara, its mission has become part of the diocesan synod and inscribed into the local governance of the church. Because of the institutionalization of the Pastoral Social, many dioceses offer training programs and promote the Semana Pastoral Social, an annual weeklong parish or diocesan renewal effort that includes a spiritual retreat, minicourses, and pastoral planning. This organizational plan guarantees an ongoing development of organizing-principle and social role functions for the Catholic social imagination.

4. World orientation (community, civil society, and political dimensions)

- *Neighborhood and local community:* Catholic community life is parish based, and parishes have specific territorial boundaries; therefore, parishes must serve the needs of the local community, most particularly the social needs of education, charity, and culture. In Mexico the local parish provides a cultural center for community life through the annual *fiestas patronales,* the weeklong celebration of the patron saint of the parish, which brings together members of the community, musicians, artisans, and an organizing committee to create the event, which includes a novena of Masses, folk dancing, music, food, processions, and artisan booths.[95] The *fiestas patronales* are celebrated throughout Mexico and, along with the 12 December Feast of Our Lady of Guadalupe, may be said to be the primary civic-religious habitus in Mexican public culture. The *fiesta patronal* is not a civic association in civil society but a unique "space and time apart" from both the Church and Mexican official public life—a kind of suspension of things, what Roger Bartra calls a "floating" in Mexican culture.[96] The community devotes many resources to make the event happen, and as Octavio Paz observes in his *Labyrinth of Solitude,* the fiesta creates a burst of energy for the community but then subsides the day after with not much to show for it.[97] While there is truth to Paz's statement, I would rather stress that the *fiestas patronales* build social solidarity in the community given the extensive labor required to put it on, but there is no justice effect in terms of making education, health care, ot infrastructure better for the community. Since the 1990s, there has been a movement of Mexican emigrants to return to their hometowns during the time of the *fiesta patronal* and do a social project to commemorate that year's event.[98] Like key activists I met in Las Pintitas, Guadalajara, and Mexico City, many of these emigrants bring back the pragmatism and action-oriented strategies that they have experienced in U.S. church life and civil society. As noted, this sense of empowerment can generate conflict with traditional clergy culture at the parish and diocesan levels. The functions of social role and organizing principle can be integrated into the Mexican Catholic social imagination, but because of a level of popular religious ambivalence, that imagination tends to remain unclear.

- *Civic skills and civil society:* Since the late 1800s there has been no expectation that Catholics will bring their values or resources into Mexican public life. As noted, the Church has been severely restricted from creating anything like a public Catholicism. However, social activists who have been involved in certain Catholic organizations such as Acción Católica, the CEBs, or the Pastoral Social exhibit a latent civic Catholicism, bringing "Christian inspiration" to civil society—particularly, as noted, through Voces Unidas, CEMEFI, DEMOS, and human rights and indigenous rights organizations. Thus the philosophical frameworks function has a latent function in Mexican civil society.

- *Government institutions and politics:* Prior to Vicente Fox's presidential election in 2000, no party had fielded a "Catholic" candidate in Mexico's modern political history. Fox opened a new space for public Catholicism in Mexico by his entering Catholic churches, going to Mass, receiving Communion, and openly talking about his faith and Jesuit educational background. It remains to be seen how this new space will evolve. The Roman Catholic Church enjoys a kind of privilege through laws that restrict new religious institutions and operations, thus limiting the importation of Protestant, New Age, and other religious sects into the Mexican religious marketplace. The federal Asuntos Religiosos monitors "official religions" in Mexico and restricts religious use of radio and television outlets. Foreign missionaries must be licensed by the state, and these licenses are restricted to the already established religious organizations.

- *Catholic public intellectuals and intellectual freedom:* Prior to 1992, practicing Catholics were excluded from receiving governmental appointments, including academic appointments in state-run universities and research centers. This largely prevented intellectuals from integrating their religious lives with their public positions—or contextualizing religious values and Mexican culture. The chilling effect was reflected in books, the press, and the mass media. As noted, the only "Catholic intellectual" of the twentieth century was Gabriel Zaid. Since 1992, the Church has been allowed a new opening and is developing its colleges and universities to allow them to take a more integrated place in Mexican intellectual and public life. The educational work of the Jesuits and Marists, representing a structural-worldly educational orientation, and Opus Dei and the Legionnaires of Christ, representing a more integral-worldly educational orientation, will be important in repositioning Catholics in public life. Presently there are no national Catholic magazines or journals with a public audience. The social role function by which public Catholics might disseminate a distinctive Mexican Catholic social imagination thus remains limited.

These four dimensions of the Mexican Catholic social imagination have an integral-normative sense and logic that provide a virtually unidimensional formation in Catholic social justice in Mexico. Social justice work is perceived and experienced as a doctrine set within the institutional church's Pastoral Social and is not conceived as carried out in partnership with civil society. The more progressive reforms of Vatican II were set back in the 1980s by the papal nuncio through his appointment of neoconservative bishops who dismantled the CEBs and progressive practices within the Church's largest dioceses. The social doctrine has never been contextualized into a Mexican public discourse and has been historically reliant upon European and Latin American interpretations. Further, the official church hierarchy has become more reliant upon new neoconservative ecclesial communities that look to Rome for their direction. This gives the Mexican Catholic social imagination a post–Vatican II tone of *más romano que Roma*. Critical factors for the Mexicanness of this cultural system include the following:

- the colonial nature of Spanish Catholicism with special privileges that led to a historic church-state rift as the Church entered the 1800s

- the rise of *laicidad* as Mexican civil religion, which severely limited a public Catholicism from developing

- provisions of the Mexican Constitution of 1912 that restricted the Church to its cultic function and prohibited the the Church from owning property, schools, mass media, etc.

- the legacy of the Cristero rebellion (1927–30), which established a new attitude for Catholics, summed up as *no se meta en la política*—meaning that as long as Catholics did not meddle in politics, the government would allow the Church a certain freedom to have seminaries and open new churches, while the government maintained historic properties as the patrimony of the people

- the legacy of Acción Católica as a Catholic social movement that promoted aims similar to those of European Catholic labor unions and political parties and continued a latent civic Catholicism in Mexican public life

- the rapid development of *comunidades eclesiales de base* following Vatican II, which opened a space within the Church for the *inquietud* and the *despertar* experienced in post-1968 Mexico, flourished for more than twenty years, and stimulated the development of a generation of socially concerned Catholics who would become active in the Church's Pastoral Social and join the new civil associations that developed in 1980s and the political parties of the *oposición* (PRD and PAN)

- the rise of a neoconservative hierarchy, following the 1979 election of Pope John Paul II, marked by *más romano que Roma* attitudes—some of whom became known as the Club of Rome—and their systematic dismantling of the CEBs, liberation theology, and other progressive programs that had critiqued sexism, capitalism, neoliberalism, and the PRI's political hegemony

- institutionalization of the Pastoral de Conjunto with its social justice function, the Pastoral Social, following the demise of the CEBs and the delegitimizing of liberation theology

- the development of independent Catholic social justice organizations like IMDOSOC and Centro Lindavista, which provide materials, educational programs, and social service projects to implement the social doctrine of the Church and carry an *inspiración cristiana* into Mexican public life

These factors contribute to a complex Mexican Catholic social imagination that is highly church oriented by external public constraints and internal biases. The neoconservative ecclesial communities, such as the Legionnaires of Christ's Regnum Christi, Opus Dei, and San Egidio Community, found their way into the Pastoral Social in Mexico during the time of this study, particularly at the national Jubilee Year events. They, along with the prolife and family movement, have been gaining ground among Mexico's bishops—especially following Mexico's hosting of the International Eucharistic Congress in Guadalajara in October 2004. The Eucharistic Congress provided Cardinal Juan Iñiguez Sandoval of Guadalajara, Cardinal Norberto Rivera Carrera of Mexico City, and other members of the Mexican hierarchy an opportunity to showcase the Mexican church as a conservative and loyal national church supporting the agenda of Pope John Paul II. In the early planning stages for the congress in 2001 the planners thought that there would be a strong social justice theme in talks and workshops. The working document for the congress acknowledged the Eucharist as a primary source for "fraternal acceptance, solidarity, sharing of goods, as well as preferential care of the most needy. A fitting witness of love is an indispensable dimension of true evangelisation."[99] But the congress speakers largely emphasized the church orientation that the Eucharist provides in consolidating the Christian community and bringing new members into the Church—concepts reflected in the "new evangelization" that John Paul II encouraged during his trips to Mexico. Neoconservative ecclesial communities were strongly present in the various national delegations attending the congress. Their influence will eclipse the moderate-to-progressive forces in the Mexican church because like

Church

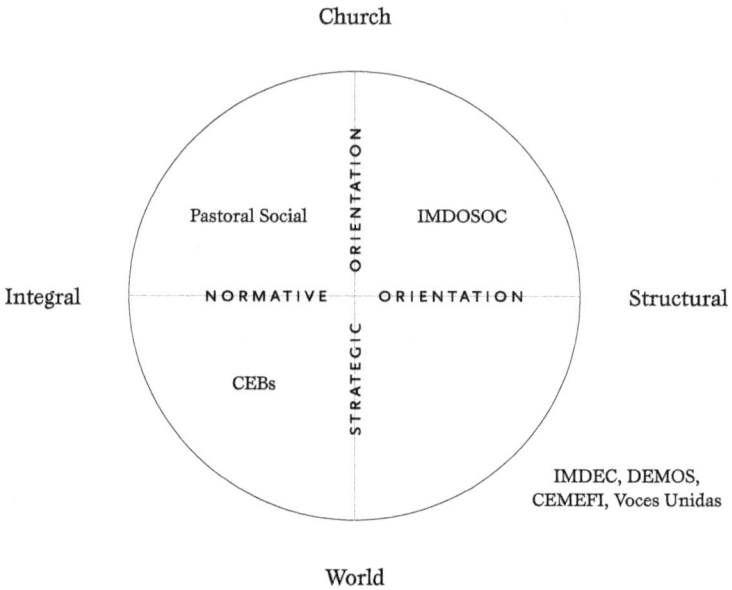

Integral

NORMATIVE · ORIENTATION

Structural

ORIENTATION

STRATEGIC

Pastoral Social

IMDOSOC

CEBs

IMDEC, DEMOS,
CEMEFI, Voces Unidas

World

Figure 3. Dominant functional orientations of various structures
and institutions of the Mexican Catholic Church

John Paul II, Pope Benedict XVI sees the new ecclesial communities as
a guiding force for the new evangelization and the restoration of Catholic culture in Latin America and Europe.[100]

The Mexican Catholic social imagination is dominated by the doctrinal discourse of the social doctrine and a strong neoconservative
hierarchy that pulls it toward an integral-church orientation. Figure 3
illustrates the standpoints of the key organizational contexts that the
Mexican Catholic Church provides for the Catholic social imagination.
In general for the national church, the Catholic social imagination—even
as a latent civic Catholicism—has not been contextualized as a mediating discourse for church and Mexican society. It has almost no capacity
to empower Catholic social actors toward a dynamic structural-world
orientation, to inspire and create social change in Mexican society,
though it does motivate these actors to provide charity through its integral-church orientation. In this sense it is a thoroughly doctrinal Roman
Catholic social imagination that is often *más romano que Roma.*

PART THREE

A Faith That Does Justice?

5 ✣ The Catholic Social Imagination as Doctrine and Practice

For many socially active Roman Catholics, the social teaching or doctrine of their church has been a means for moving their faith and values into the spaces of public life. Many such Catholics lament that this doctrine has been what Jesuit theologian Walter Burghardt calls "the best kept secret of the Catholic Church."[1] The social doctrine has served as a vehicle for them to integrate their lives as disciples and citizens, even though it is not widely practiced or emphasized in the Church.

However, as the Church enters the twenty-first century, the Vatican's Congregation for the Doctrine of the Faith has become increasingly insistent that Catholics in public life adhere strictly to all doctrinal statements if they are to consider themselves public Catholics. In November 2002 the Congregation of the Faith issued a historic directive titled "A Doctrinal Note on Some Questions regarding the Participation of Catholics in Political Life," calling on Catholic public officials to see their role in public life as defenders of Catholic moral and social doctrine. The doctrinal note clearly expresses Cardinal Joseph Ratzinger's views about "cultural relativism," which he has made a primary trope as he has begun his papacy as Benedict XVI:

> A kind of cultural relativism exists today, evident in the conceptualization and defense of an ethical pluralism, which sanctions the decadence and disintegration of reason and the principles of the natural moral law. Furthermore, it is not unusual to hear the opinion expressed in the public sphere that such ethical pluralism is the very condition for democracy. As a result, citizens claim complete autonomy with regard to their moral choices, and lawmakers maintain that they are respecting this freedom of choice by enacting laws which ignore the principles of natural ethics and yield to ephemeral cultural and moral trends, as if every possible outlook on life were of equal value.[2]

The document makes clear that its philosophical underpinning is natural law philosophy. Significantly, this doctrinal note has been incorporated into the authoritative *Compendium of the Social Doctrine of the Church*. For example, article 570 of the *Compendium* references the doctrinal note and states: "When—concerning areas or realities that involve fundamental ethical duties—legislative or political choices contrary to Christian principles and values are proposed or made, the Magisterium teaches that 'a well-formed Christian conscience does not permit one to vote for a political programme or an individual law which contradicts the fundamental contents of faith and morals.'"[3]

In this study I have emphasized that the natural law serves as the foundational philosophy for all Catholic moral and social doctrine. This philosophical foundation has fueled the Church's public campaigns (by both the Vatican and national bishops' conferences in Mexico and the United States) against civil and human rights for women in regard to reproductive issues such as artificial contraception and abortion. Further, the Church has directed the Mexican and U.S. bishops to campaign publicly against civil and human rights for homosexuals, such as marriage, adoption of children, civil unions, employment rights, and free assembly and expression.[4] In both countries the bishops have begun to work more closely with neoconservative political and religious groups such as Focus on the Family, the Family Research Council, and the Acton Institute in order to lobby national and state legislators to implement laws with a prolife orientation. A neoconservative Catholic and evangelical-fundamentalist Protestant ecumenical alliance has formed through this realignment of the social doctrine with family and life issues based on deductive natural-law logic. In the 2004 election cycle the U.S. Catholic Church was extremely prominent in public debates and legislative battles regarding gay marriage and assisted suicide, and in the run-up to the infamous Terry Schiavo feeding-tube case.[5] The Catholic Church offered legal and philosophical argumentation regarding these issues, benefiting its new conservative Protestant allies, who had been dependent upon simple biblical arguments. The alliance worked for passage of the Federal Marriage Act as an amendment to the Constitution defining marriage as an act between a man and a woman. During the 2004 election campaign, state bishops' conferences and the Family Research Council also worked closely together to put "Defense of Marriage Act" amendments to state constitutions on various ballots.[6]

This focus for the social doctrine directs attention away from structural issues related to the economy, war and armaments, the death penalty, and systemic discrimination. For example, during 2002–3 the U.S. bishops did not enter the public debate on U.S. intervention in Iraq—even after President Bush articulated his justification for "preemption," which the Church's just-war principles clearly condemn. Pope John Paul II himself had stated that the doctrine of preemption has no ethical basis.[7]

Given these political directions, as well as continuing limitations on the role of the laity in the Church's administration, we do well to ask how "social" the Church's social doctrine is. Will the Church stand by its own principles of social solidarity, the right to organize, participation, association, self-determination, peace, disarmament, etc., to address social justice issues that arise from human experience and develop as public issues through the organization of empirical data? Moreover, given the clergy abuse scandal that has surfaced throughout the worldwide church, we must go further and ask, is social justice possible in the Catholic Church itself?

How can Catholics be *social* actors in living out their Catholic faith and its social justice doctrine? Intrinsic to the very idea of Catholic social justice is the sense that these religious actors want to exert their faith, i.e., the integral-church orientation, beyond the Church itself in a structural-world orientation. This sense of faith outside its religious institution or space—the space to realize social aspirations—is, I believe, the core sociological context of Catholic social justice teaching.

Since I began doing research for this study in 1996, the Vatican and national bishops' conferences have undergone a marked transition in handling the social doctrine with a structural-world orientation and execution to giving it a more integral-world orientation. But this transition had actually begun earlier, in the 1980s, when the Vatican began to limit listening processes and evidence gathering in national churches as part of the process of generating pastoral letters. The results were evidenced in the problems the U.S. bishops faced in writing a letter on the status of women in the Church and world[8] and the Mexican bishops' exclusion of evidence and church members' responses from their 2000 letter *Solidaridad*.

Nevertheless, nearly every interview I conducted with Catholic social activists in the United States and Mexico revealed that the social doctrine has been a core impulse for their seeking social justice through structural changes in political, cultural, economic, and social institutions.[9] These Catholics respect the avowed "doctrinally conservative and socially progressive" stance of many of the Church's leaders and theologians, but it troubles them when a strict deductive logic hampers Catholics' forward movement on such issues as women's rights, domestic violence, family planning, gay rights, and due process within the Church—social issues that arise from the woes of real people.

In the United States, Catholics are accustomed to living out their religious values in the broader social sphere, given the very large arena of nongovernmental organizations (nonprofits) wherein religious values can flourish to promote social goods such as education, health care, employment training, and advocacy. Americans are accustomed to results-oriented programs with bottom lines measuring how many clients have been served, meals served, jobs filled, or laws produced. This kind of social action does not present a specific problem for the social justice doctrine, because it flows from the charitable or integral orientation toward corporal and spiritual works of mercy in Catholic tradition. However, issues related to sexual ethics and their social outcomes in the family, relationships, and public policy have proven to be extremely problematic for Catholics—most specifically for Catholic politicians and officials who see their public role as upholding the law within a pluralistic society—because of the deductive, natural law orientation of the Church's positions on sex and family.

Mexico has had a very different history regarding the process of moving faith to action. I found that Mexican Catholic activists have great desire to express their Catholic faith in action, but they have encountered only limited opportunities to move their faith and values outside the institutional church, which has severely limited the role of the laity both within the Church and without it. Thus, they are limited in being Christian or Catholic social actors in the *plaza pública*. This dilemma of moving faith to action, I suggest, arises from Mexico's historical problematic of the construction of Catholic social justice doctrine and the Church's own understanding of what *social* means in relationship to nonchurch society.

In this study I have addressed two related issues in analyzing Catholic social justice doctrine. First, I analyzed the historical social construction of the Church's social justice doctrine. Second, I provided a sociological framework to analyze the Catholic social imagination, a logic of orientations that Catholic social actors are provided in the Catholic habitus or cultural system. If the doctrine were simply addressing internal problems of charity or justice in the religious institution, then the sociologist would limit his or her analysis to the institutional culture. But the social doctrine encourages the actors to move into the public sphere. Therefore, I needed to explore the constraints and possibilities that Catholic social imagination provides religious social actors to put their faith into action in the public sphere.

Previous studies of Catholic social life in the United States have emphasized the importance of Catholic social doctrine for "faith-based" social organizing, how progressive Catholics become religious insurgents while believing they are still part of the Catholic community, and the rich sacramental and aesthetic dimensions of Catholic social life.[10] In many ways I have used these prior studies to analyze the Catholic social imagination. I believe that my research reinforces each element of this prior work yet constructs a more comprehensive theoretical understanding of the complexity of Catholic social actors and the ways they attempt to strategize the Catholic social terrain.

One of the key findings of this study is that for Catholics—particularly those without previous public experiences—to become committed to the social doctrine of their faith, their milieu must offer experiences that can trigger a social or public awakening and elicit commitment in the civic and political spheres. Carlos and Esther of Guadalajara and Manuel and Yolanda of Oakland became involved in their parishes and the civic activities of their communities because they wanted better lives for their children. They are Catholics by birth and culture, but they reached a level in their faith—a *despertar* or awakening—that pushed them into making real commitments to civil associations seeking changes in the civic and political culture of their community. For both couples, that moment of clarity about becoming civically involved was a spiritual experience emerging from their involvement in the liturgy, the sacraments, prayer, the Christian Family Movement, and parish life. They were empowered in certain ways through their religious culture—the integral-church dynamism of the Catholic social imagination—to move beyond their religious community into a larger civic community in which they assumed new roles as public Catholics. The other actors of this study all had similar spiritual moments that triggered a moment of decision, a commitment, and a long-term quest to live out the social dimensions of their faith. This kind of spiritual preparation through the integral dimension of the Catholic social imagination also serves as an ongoing renewal source for Catholic social activists: prayer, reflection, rituals, commemorations, pilgrimages, retreats, music, drama, and the like seem to be essential for the ongoing life of the Catholic social imagination.

In the communities of Las Pintitas in Guadalajara and the San Antonio District in Oakland, almost all the people I encountered were migrants from rural Mexico who had made decisions to leave their limited economic, social, and political opportunities for new cities providing jobs, education, and other possibilities. They had a common Catholic and *guadalupana* religious heritage. But once in the new environments of urban Guadalajara and Oakland, they entered parish communities with very different opportunity structures and cultural environments. Almost like blank slates, these migrants entered worlds they had to learn quickly and adapt to. They took on what they were offered in the religious and social opportunity structures of Las Pintitas and San Antonio. In Mexico these urbano-campesinos adapted readily to the Pastoral Social's integral-church orientation, while in the United States similarly situated migrants adapted to faith-based community organizing's centrist orientation while remaining quite similar in their Mexican religious and spiritual traditions. And along the way, those in Oakland became "American" as they became active in the civic and political life that faith-based community organizing demanded of them. They learned to contextualize their Catholic faith within their experiences of social injustice such as poor public schools, inadequate police protection, and lack of affordable housing and good neighborhood shopping. Their Mexican counterparts did not have this capacity to move their social doctrine into structural justice—even though they provided a great amount of charity to their community.

Within Catholic Church life in Mexico and the United States, I noted that the single key factor for mobility in the institutional structures of the Church was education. The key leadership group of the Church in both countries is the priesthood, composed of men from mostly working-class and middle-class backgrounds. Very rarely do men from the upper classes or the poor of either country become priests. The same can be said about religious women.[11] And in both countries the activists at the parish and diocesan levels, in national offices, and in civic associations had sufficient educational attainment (whether in formal institutions or through self-training) to read, write, analyze, organize, and lead. These activists thrived in settings that allowed them to grow as educated, conscious Christians and citizens, particularly in a cultural milieu in which liturgy, spirituality, training, organization, and activism were integrated. For the laity, clergy and episcopal leadership that allowed such empowerment was critical. Without this encouragement, laypeople encounter constraints upon their commitment to parish and diocesan life, and these hindrances can either curtail the commitment or propel them to seek alternative ways to live it out. Indeed, clergy and bishops can make or break opportunities for the Catholic social imagination to move from its strategic center toward the boundaries or exit points where faith enters public life.

The clergy and bishops may move in any of a variety of directions; the Vatican, for example, wishes to orient the social doctrine in a world-integral-church direction, focusing upon sexual morality and family life issues. My study shows that "being Catholic" requires moving in the direction of church authority; otherwise this same authority forces exclusion or marginalization. I found that Mexicans facing this kind of problem with authority regarding social doctrine exited the Church completely, while Americans are more ambivalent and find ways to stay "Catholic" in a variety of Catholic social movements that create their own "moments" of Catholicity.

Because Catholic life is centered on the rituals of the Mass and the sacraments, it became very clear in both countries that the ritual environment and its own social opportunity structure constituted another critical factor in the development of active laity. The level of lay participation in the liturgy itself was an indicator of the potential for social activism in the parish and the community. At the parish level in both countries, the social activists had entered the realm of the social through the exercise of skills related to the liturgy and sacraments that placed them in front of the public as lectors, eucharistic ministers, ushers, music ministers, and catechists. These roles provide a training in being public actors. This was especially true for people without prior institutional church or civic training or involvement, such as rural migrants coming to urban settings. Because the Catholic Church is an institution that migrants trust in both countries, an invitation by a priest, nun, or respected layperson involved in liturgical and catechetical ministries was a critical first step in forming social leadership in a parish and a community. In both countries, the key social activists also had liturgical roles in their parish that provided them ongoing integral development, such as prayer, devotions, and music, which energized their structural involvements at meetings, city council hearings, demonstrations, and the like. Furthermore, the key lay activists in Oakland and Guadalajara all had ongoing clergy support for their work on behalf of the social doctrine of their faith.

While many of the most interesting and articulate people of my study were involved in metropolitan and national civic associations or diocesan and national church structures, men and women at the parish level were the people who were delivering the "goods" of social justice on a day-to-day basis. The parish is where the Catholic Church reaches its membership and where ordinary people experience their religious life. Healthy parishes do not lose their members to alternative religious associations. Therefore, it was very telling that in Mexico many educated urban Catholics had found it necessary to seek out and join alternative and parallel associations to fulfill their social commitments—or had simply opted out of parish life. While there are similar cases in the United States, the tendency is less pronounced because U.S. Catholics are more mobile and feel free to join parishes that better suit their needs, "shopping around for a parish" similar to the way Protestants select a congregation.[12]

In the introduction of this work I raised the following questions:

- How is the international social justice teaching of the Roman Catholic Church—the Church's social mission—implemented in theological concepts and social action in different countries, particularly the United States and Mexico?

- What opportunities and constraints—challenges to the Church's social mission—emerging from national history, political traditions and culture, the institutional church, and development of civil society, are shaping the implementation of social justice teaching in each country?

In answering these questions, I found that the parish is the base cultural milieu where the Catholic social justice imagination is developed and implemented. Indeed a "from below" perspective brings the parish and the local community to the fore, because it is there that the hopes and aspirations for justice start. If they cannot emerge at this base level, how can the leaders really know what the people are experiencing in terms of the principles of social justice?

Four Approaches of the Catholic Social Imagination

In chapter 2 I posited that the Catholic Church's social justice doctrine is socially constructed, meaning that it is a doctrine that has developed as a reaction to social problems facing Catholics throughout the world. Those involved in the development in the doctrine believe that it is an affirmation of the scriptural and traditional principles of Christian charity and justice. Yet, unlike other doctrine that is nonempirically based, the social justice doctrine of the Church arises out of real life situations of poverty, violence, discrimination, hate, etc., which trigger a sense of injustice among those affected. What do Catholics do with that sense of injustice? That was the sociological question I sought to answer.

In both Mexico and the United States, I found that ordinary Catholics look at injustice in the world through a theological lens of sin and grace. Injustice is a reflection of sin in the world; justice manifests God's grace. According to the social doctrine, God's grace must be made manifest in human action as an unfolding of the reign of God in the world. Simply stated, good works produce a sense of heaven on earth. The principle of "structures of sin" recognizes that sin is a social reality that limits people's capacity to develop their potential. To change a structure of sin to a structure of grace requires the Catholic to move into these very structures and transform them. This clearly distinguishes Catholicism as a worldly religion, requiring its members to move their faith into the world.

At least four approaches derive from the primary integral-structural and church-world dynamics within the Catholic social imagination, and these approaches provide at least four logics to direct the Catholic social actor and community toward realizing social justice in the world. Figure 4 reframes my initial theoretical model of the Catholic social imagination to reflect this study's empirical findings.

THE INTEGRAL-CHURCH OR "ECCLESIAL" APPROACH

It is important to establish the theological and philosophical basis for the social doctrine, as was done in chapter 2, because I found that Catholics' entrance into social opportunity structures depended partly on their understanding of the Church in the world. So-called traditionalist Catholics in both countries who emphasize a future heaven attainable largely through belief in church doctrine and sacraments tend not to be involved in the work of the social doctrine, except in regard to sexual morality and family life. Actually, they see sexual morality and family life as belonging to the domain of moral theology rather than that of social theology. More complicated is the "ecclesial" orientation to the social doctrine, which takes the doctrine seriously but emphasizes its implementation within the Church itself as building an internal solidarity that will reflect outward to the world.

In Mexico, the Pastoral Social has provided a way to continue working out many of the ideas of theology of liberation and the *comunidades*

Church

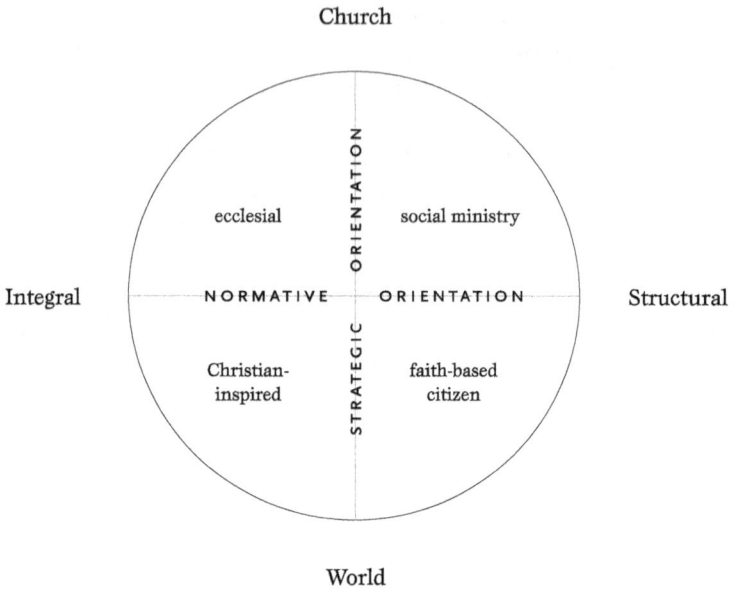

Integral

Structural

ecclesial

social ministry

NORMATIVE ─── ORIENTATION

Christian-inspired

faith-based citizen

ORIENTATION

NORMATIVE

STRATEGIC

World

Figure 4. Four approaches of the Catholic social imagination,
based on case studies of the U.S. and Mexican Catholic churches

eclesiales de base. In the Archdiocese of Guadalajara and other Mexican
dioceses, the Pastoral Social has become institutionalized through the
diocesan synod, a local council that brings the objectives of a diocese
into a canonical status. In Guadalajara this legal codification of the Pastoral Social played a critical role in keeping the objectives of social justice doctrine alive in the diocese despite changes in episcopal leadership.
Thus the archdiocesan offices of the Pastoral Social not only survive
changes in episcopal leadership but also have a sense of permanency in
the overall pastoral objectives of the local church, reflected in the fact
that the Pastoral Social is present in all the parishes of the archdiocese.
The archdiocesan weekly newspaper, *El Semanario,* contained a weekly
column focusing on different issues of Catholic social justice doctrine.
During 1999 and 2000, the newspaper carried many articles on citizen
responsibility to vote and even two columns related to the anti–domestic
violence act. However, those involved in the Pastoral Social were able to
reach only a certain threshold of activity in the archdiocese and were
not publicly involved in civil associations. Some members of the Archdiocesan Pastoral Social in Guadalajara and Mexico City were involved
in a parallel church life, meaning that they were not involved in a parish

but with others of like mind in Catholic religious life. They celebrated their own Masses on Sundays and weekdays with supportive clergy, who also provided other religious and spiritual support for them.

The institutional Mexican church exemplified the ecclesial approach, particularly in the pastoral letter *Solidaridad,* issued by the Mexican bishops to celebrate the Jubilee Year in 2000. As was shown in chapter 4, the Mexican bishops had an understanding of solidarity as a virtue, but they did not understand solidarity as an organizing principle for social change in civil society, nor did they understand the Church as a mediating institution in a larger organic solidarity with other institutional players in society.

I would contend that the ecclesial approach in Mexico can be deeply deceptive to people at the parish level, like the people of Las Pintitas. While they wish to be faithful Catholics, they do not know how to live out their social aspirations and their *inquietud* in the *plaza pública* without marginalizing themselves from the parish community or the diocese. Furthermore, since the departure of the Rev. Alberto Athié Gallo from the Conferencia Episcopal Mexicana in early 2000, the Pastoral Social in Mexico has been deemphasized through the reduction of personnel at the national level—staff who had coordinated key areas of human rights, migration, and indigenous rights for the Mexican church. All of these areas offered opportunities for the Mexican church to work with civil associations, thus moving it beyond the ecclesial approach. As the Mexican church continues this approach, I contend that it will continue to marginalize itself from civil society and see itself as an alternative to civil society. Its aggressive promotion of the new ecclesial communities as a parallel Catholic civil society is very much in keeping with the its earlier promotion of Catholic labor unions, Catholic Action, and the like. That kind of religious parallelism marked the Mexican Church's public life in the twentieth century because of historic barriers to entering Mexican public life. But despite the Church's new legal and institutional capacities since the constitutional changes of 1992, it appears that Catholic leaders continue to see the Church as a counterforce to *laicismo* and Mexican public culture.

The Las Pintitas parish is emblematic of good Mexican parishes seeking to implement social justice doctrine within the structure of the Pastoral Social and the other functions of the parish. But as I suggest in chapter 4, the Catholics of Las Pintitas can reach only a certain level of lay participation within their parish, and they do not have the capacity to move the Pastoral Social into civil society. Moreover, the actors of the civil sector in Las Pintitas are not part of the Church. Because of the historical division between Church and "society" per se, even though both sides have similar social goals and skills, they do not bring them together for the common good. Political culture constraints within both conservative Mexican Catholicism and liberal Mexican *laicidad* mean that each side is wary of the other, and the integration of faith and public life is further limited. So while the Las Pintitas Catholic social activists desire a different approach to effecting the social doctrine, they are much too restricted in the parish and loyal to church authority. Thus, they are forced to adapt to the ecclesial approach of the Catholic social imagination.

THE INTEGRAL-WORLD OR "CHRISTIAN-INSPIRED" APPROACH

The Catholics I found at the Instituto Mexicano de la Doctrina Social (IMDOSOC) found ways of creating alternative and parallel ecclesial spaces outside of the parish structure in order to be faithful Catholics while seeking social justice with a degree of freedom. They exemplify the Christian-inspired approach to the Catholic social imagination, because they emphasize the integral elements of social Catholicism but within independent civil society organizations. This approach could be taken up by the new ecclesial communities in Mexico as they develop a parallel Catholic civil society. For Church and society to come together for the common good in Mexico, it seems that both sides need to forge a new level of trust, producing goodwill.

People involved in IMDOSOC were the type of the new "Christian-inspired" Mexicans sought to bring their faith and values into the civil sphere but without Catholic identification. These are the actors like Manuel Goméz Granados who were formed in the Church and had hoped for it to join the *transición*. They remain very strong in their Catholicity and cultivate a specifically Catholic social imagination as the motivational force for structural change.

Among the many civil associations that I encountered in the United States, I cannot say that any of them were "Christian inspired" because of the Church's inability to create public structures for itself. Groups like Pax Christi and the Catholic Workers find it easy to identify themselves as Catholic. Organizations like Bread for the World and Habitat for Humanity that have a broad ecumenical membership base are more apt to be seen as "Christian inspired." They may attract Catholic members who do not want to be involved in a strictly Catholic organization.

Still, while these nondenominational U.S. organizations may be characterized as "Christian inspired," the term is used somewhat differently
from the way it is used in Mexico.

THE CHURCH-STRUCTURAL OR
"SOCIAL MINISTRY" APPROACH

Both in the United States and in Mexico, but particularly in the former,
there has been a significant professionalization of all functions of the
Church. As noted in chapter 3, the U.S. church has developed an extensive infrastructure of diocesan offices and parish equivalents that are
run by well-educated people. Because of this trend, Catholic social justice teaching has been transformed into a ministry at the various levels
of the U.S. church—parish, diocese, lay associations, schools, universities, and national offices. The ministry—particularly as carried out by
Catholic Charities—fulfills a specific function within the Church's life,
but it can operate without a great degree of integration with the other
functions. Further, sometimes the function can become disengaged
from the grassroots issues of the local community and may fulfill a service role without social activism.

In the United States, social justice ministry tends to be less integrated into parish life than is the Pastoral Social in Mexico. Not every
U.S. parish has a social justice function; those that do not have immediate needs to serve the poor and marginalized may not develop this ministry. Parishes that have a community-organizing component, such as
St. Anthony's in Oakland, are usually responding to needs of people in
their neighborhood. At the time of my study, no middle-class or affluent
congregations took part in Oakland Community Organizations. Moreover, parish organizational life in the United States is largely dependent
upon the pastor's vision and may undergo change when a new pastor
is appointed. Thus, some parishes have parish councils that include a
social justice ministry function and others do not. Even in a so-called
progressive diocese like Oakland, I found that parish organization was
highly dependent upon the pastor's leadership style. The diocese had
not called a synod, which meant that the functions of the diocese did
not have canonical status. Unlike Mexico, where the calling of a synod
has been more normative, since Vatican II few dioceses in the United
States have used the synod as a means to codify their pastoral objectives. Furthermore, the many elements of social justice ministry are
distributed among different offices, which appear not to have a common
or integrated vision. There are separate offices for prolife activities, the

Catholic Campaign for Human Development, Catholic Charities, Hispanic ministry, African American ministry, and so on. From the point of view of some St. Anthony social activists, the maintenance of separate offices projected an unclear vision of social justice ministry in the diocese, particularly when the offices seemed to be in competition for recruiting lay ministers from the parishes and securing resources for their work. In addition, the U.S. Catholic Church's organizational functions are not organized top to bottom around theological functions, as is the Mexican church's Pastoral Conjunto.

The social ministry approach requires remaining institutionally tied to the Church in the life of a parish, a diocese, and the national church and at the same providing services that address structural injustices. In the United States, social justice ministry provides opportunities for increased participation of the laity in important offices of the institutional church. The vast majority of men and women employed or volunteering in offices that direct the efforts of the CCHD, Catholic Charities, social justice ministry, Hispanic ministry, African American ministry, gay and lesbian ministry, etc., are laypeople. It is not uncommon to find the social justice ministers involved in civic associations or social movements representing the parish, diocese, or the national church. They can cooperate with other civic actors because the Catholic Church can be considered part of civil society. The U.S. bishops' letters on the economy and on peace exemplified this approach at the national level of U.S. civil society—particularly given the role the documents played in national public policy debates.

This has not been the case in Mexico. In the Archdioceses of Guadalajara and Mexico City, the various functions of the Pastoral Social are headed by priests assisted by dedicated laypeople, but the laity are not given functional authority in the ministry. Furthermore, the Mexican social justice ministers do not cooperate with other actors in civil society as representatives of the Church. The Church does not consider itself an actor in civil society, nor do actors in the civil sphere consider the Church a partner or stakeholder. To the contrary, the Mexican church is seen by civil society actors as more like a political party or the state, as having an unequal power relationship with civil society. As noted in chapter 4, this was particularly borne out in the counterforce behavior of the archbishop of Guadalajara and his intervention in the popular initiative process advocating the anti–domestic violence act in the state of Jalisco.

THE STRUCTURAL-WORLD OR
"FAITH-BASED CITIZEN" APPROACH

In the United States, Catholics' freedom to participate as Catholics in civil society allows for an approach to social justice doctrine implementation that is presently unavailable in Mexico. As noted in chapter 3, the U.S. Catholic community has had many "Catholic moments" for social justice teaching. Also, Catholic Americans have generated a large independent infrastructure of social institutions for their religious and social purposes that have evolved into cooperative institutions in a pluralistic society.

Acknowledging the temptation to idealize the U.S. situation, I believe that this national opportunity structure does provide a distinctive approach to social justice implementation by Catholic social activists. This "faith-based citizen" approach has a structural-world orientation, allowing Catholics to be public Catholics in civil society and to bring their distinctive theological language and ideas into civil discourse on social justice in the United States and the world. This approach enables clergy, religious, bishops, and the laity to bring their faith-based values into the public square without having to either represent the institutional church or social justice ministry or mask these values as "Christian-inspired." In this way the Catholic social doctrine becomes mediated in U.S. public life and contextualized within U.S. civil culture and discourse.

Since 1969, the Catholic Campaign for Human Development has helped generate a national institutional church culture to legitimize this faith-based citizen approach. As well, the Jubilee Year events of Jubilee Justice and Encuentro 2000 held in Los Angeles provided a large cultural framework within which the Catholic social justice citizen approach finds space as a legitimate approach alongside the ecclesial and social justice ministry approaches to implementing the Church's social doctrine in society. Thus, Catholics involved in Catholic Workers, Pax Christi, Bread for the World, Habitat for Humanity, the anti–death penalty movement, the United Farm Workers Union, School of the Americas Watch, Catholic Peace Fellowship, and other movements see themselves as part of the Church's social mission. As well, Catholics involved in community organizing and other social projects and causes can experience their activities as being within the mission of the Church. Members of all these groups are involved in civil society as citizens who bring their faith-based values to their associations and other actors in the civil sphere.

AT THE MARGINS APPROACH

Catholic social actors like Esther and Carlos of Guadalajara often find themselves as bifurcated social Catholics, with one foot in civil society and the other in the Church. It's a clumsy walk, and the foot in the Church often trips. Many people in organizations such as IMDEC, DEMOS, and CEMEFI get tired of walking like this and make the painful decision to leave the Church behind in their quest for social justice.

These are the actors like Carlos Núñez Hurtado, Efrén Orozco Orozco, Vicente Arredondo Ramírez, and Jorge Villalobos Grzybowicz, who were formed in the Church and had hoped for it to join the *transición*. While all of them consider themselves Catholics, they have joined civic associations to realize their aspirations for social justice in Mexico. But they are not "public Catholics" like Cesar Chavez, William F. Buckley, or Mario Cuomo. They felt that the institutional church, particularly at the parish level, was not supportive of their efforts. Through their move to the civil sphere in the 1970s and 1980s, they helped form Mexico's new civil society, which has become the space for the deeply felt *inquietud* of educated, middle-class Mexicans. They do not see the Catholic Church as a player in the quest for social change in ordinary urban Mexico.[13] These actors and others like them in urban social change organizations formed a significant base of nonpartisan citizen actors in the Amigos de Fox, which became the backbone of Vicente Fox's successful presidential campaign. The task that lies ahead for them is to implement the *transición* as an ongoing civil society that keeps the "social" and "civil" independent of political or religious domination in Mexican public life.

In the United States, increasing numbers of Catholic social activists have become marginalized because of their positions regarding what Pope Benedict XVI calls "ethical relativism" regarding reproductive rights, gay rights, women's roles in the institutional church, and other social questions on which the Church has taken strong positions based on the natural law. Groups such as Catholics for a Free Choice, Dignity, New Ways Ministries, the Rainbow Sash Movement, and the Women's Ordination Conference have been forced to meet outside of church facilities because of their so-called heretical positions regarding women's and gay rights in society and within the Church. In spite of attempts by many of the Church hierarchy to expel these social activists, they remain steady in their Catholic identity and Catholicity—but most often outside the institutional church. In many dioceses, organizations like Voice of the Faithful, organized in Boston in the early 2000s to promote due process for victims of clergy sexual abuse, and A Call to Action, organized to address the Church's governance and institutional practices and demanding transparency and due process, have also been excluded or marginalized.[14]

Marginalized social Catholics generally take the structural-world orientation and faith-based disciple approach of the Catholic social imagination and consider themselves "progressive Catholics." But there are also a small number of self-proclaimed "traditionalist Catholics" who feel that the social doctrine of the Church was part of a modernist agenda to reconcile the Church with the world. For them, use of modern scientific scholarship within the practice of theology—which the social doctrine does with its theological reflection on events in the post-biblical world—is highly suspect. Traditionalists argue that Vatican II was a heretical council because the Vatican Council had introduced the new liturgy and the use of the vernacular and produced the Declaration on Religious Liberty, which allowed the Catholic Church to enter fully into ecumenical dialogue and cooperation. Because of their rejection of Vatican II and subsequent church teaching, their understanding and acceptance of the social doctrine is limited to pre–Vatican II doctrinal development.

Working Out the Catholic Social Imagination

In developing the above four approaches of the Catholic social imagination, I have relied on the social opportunity structure theory introduced toward the end of chapter 1. The basic idea of this theory is that ideas and action are part of a social context and outside ideas and action cannot be realized without certain openings or constraints in the social milieu. Each of the above approaches represents certain opening or constraining elements coming from within the Church itself or from the larger society.

Each approach also draws on a particular repertoire of cultural skills, attitudes, imagination, discourse, habits, rituals, etc., that create a specific cultural milieu—its Catholicity or Catholic identity—for implementing the social doctrine. Thus, each of the approaches represents a social justice cultural milieu or habitus with its own threshold of engagement with society that keeps the Catholic social imagination within its centralizing normative and strategic dynamics. If Catholics have access to an approach that can be realized within the civil and political opportunity structures of their country, then the Church's doctrine can penetrate these spheres to the level enabled by that approach. Thus, the "social" of Catholic social justice doctrine is present in degrees, depending on the threshold of the approach and how much actual resolution of social injustice it allows. Crossing the boundary can cause one's marginalization or bring a necessary end to a social imagination's identification with the Catholic Church—as experienced among both progressive and traditionalist Catholics.

The ecclesial approach provides the least potential for the doctrine to penetrate society, because it is the least *social* of the approaches, self-limited as it is to the institutional church. The ecclesial approach develops a sense of justice within the Church and seeks to transform society through the Church itself. The institutional Mexican Catholic Church—particularly in the largest urban dioceses—takes this approach in both its conservative and liberal interpretations. On the conservative side, the Mexican church sees itself as a self-contained community that has suffered at the hands of modernism and its political and cultural institutions. The Mexican church celebrates its martyrs of the Cristero movement as those who stood against that culture. On the liberal side, the Mexican church recognizes that it must be part of the changes in modern Mexican society, but positions itself "above" the Mexican culture. The Church must be a "light" or example for society; society cannot be transformed without the Church. The ecclesial approach is similarly employed by some U.S. parishes and dioceses that are led by neoconservative pastors and bishops.

The Christian-inspired approach is an alternative to the ecclesial approach in Mexico. The actors involved in this approach felt marginalized by the institutional church when they attempted to help open up social space within the Church for social activist laity and clergy. Given the inability for Catholics to be public Catholics, these activists, motivated by many principles of the social doctrine, have created alternative spaces that are inspired by their faith. Those taking this approach see their activity as an integration of faith and citizenship. Many social justice activists in the United States also take such an approach, but in Mexico this approach sometimes of necessity fostered a social justice milieu that was not connected to the institutional church.

The social ministry approach taken by both the U.S. and Mexican churches has allowed for the institutionalization of social justice doctrine within the functions of the Church. A conservative version of this approach is to teach the doctrine and organize various programs within the Church to distribute social welfare goods. A liberal version

helps the Church open itself to public education campaigns and legislative lobbying for health and welfare, human and civil rights, and issues
developing from "the signs of the times." Most social justice ministry
offices in the United States take both directions and can accommodate
a wide range of participants, while in Mexico the social justice ministry's mission is largely educational and motivational as it carries out
charitable services through parishes and dioceses. Mexican social justice ministers were often in conflict with the ecclesial approach of the
bishops, which led many of these actors to participating independently
in Christian-inspired activities in their communities.

Finally, the faith-based citizen approach can be an option only where
the Catholic Church participates in a religiously plural civil society and
allows its members to be public Catholics, as in the United States, Canada, Australia, the European Union, India, and South Africa. Those
taking this approach seek to articulate a critical Catholic social justice
discourse that will not only transform society but continue to raise questions about society through ongoing social justice commitments. This
approach is inherently social, because its location is civil society itself.
However, if the approach moves to the strictly political sphere, it stands
to lose its critical Catholic perspective. Activists of this sort may be engaged in political change but suspicious of the power that politicians
and political institutions wield; thus this type of activist prefers the
civil field, where citizen power can be leveraged to monitor the political
sphere. This approach is taken along the breath of the political spectrum
in the United States—conservative, moderate, liberal, progressive—and
helps illustrate the dynamic nature of the Catholic social justice citizen approach as a cultural force within American civil society.[15] Also
to be noted is that this approach is unlike the pre–Vatican II European
and Latin American development of "Catholic" trade unions, professional associations, and political parties as parallel religious responses
to social issues. Rather, the Catholic faith-based citizen approach seeks
to place Catholic social justice values within a pluralistic public space.

Because each approach is a type, it is possible for a person, a group, or
an association to employ a mixed approach to social justice implementation. This would be true of the mixed Christian-inspired/faith-based
citizen approach that the Oakland Community Organization and the
Pacific Institute for Community Organizing provide for their members.
These organizations sent their Catholic members into civil society to
obtain structural social change yet brought them back into the centralizing dynamics of the social justice teaching and provided religious renewal. In Mexico, people engaged in a mixed ecclesial/social ministry

approach in the various levels of the Pastoral Social and a Christian-inspired/social ministry approach among the independent Catholics working for Voces Unidas and the Alianza Cívica. However, because each approach has its threshold of social possibilities, a mixed approach can pose conflicts for activists who are moving forward in one approach and held back in the other.

Integrating Social Justice Doctrine and the Social Justice Cultural Milieu

The thirty-seven social justice principles identified in chapter 2 constitute an extensive menu for Catholic social justice actors to choose from for raising specific social issues within a Catholic context or for creating a theological ambience for their social organizations. In reviewing the theological content of various religious and civic actors and their organizations, I found that they chose to focus on certain principles in order to theologically tailor social justice activity. Because the doctrine had not been systematized during the time frame of my research, I did not encounter anyone trying to implement the full doctrine. Furthermore, each approach to social justice implementation had a particular theological flavor, falling under one or the other of the six functional types of social justice principles developed in chapter 2.

The *ecclesial approach* is distinguished by its emphasis on the Church itself as an organizing principle, as well as its understanding of the social order as corporatist in nature. It emphasizes the philosophical tradition of Catholic social justice teaching as rooted in the natural law, which it employs as its analytical framework. Given the emphasis on the Church, this approach sees the social actor's role as primarily exemplifying the moral norm of charity and the virtue of solidarity in service to the poor.

The *Christian-inspired approach* emphasizes solidarity as an organizing principle, as an analytical framework, and as a virtue. Solidarity is also appealed to in its call for liberation, particularly the liberation of women, indigenous groups, and minorities. Further, it stresses the social roles of the laity, political leaders, and workers in free association and equal participation. The approach works from the analytical frameworks of the signs of the times, local analysis, and solidarity. Human rights, the dignity of the human person, the dignity of work, religious freedom, and the common good are guiding philosophical principles that direct, inspire, and motivate social and political activity in civil society.

The *social ministry approach* is the most encompassing in terms of the integration of the thirty-seven principles into a cultural milieu, particularly since it emphasizes the educational dimension of imparting the principles at the various levels of the Church. In Mexico, this approach is highly flavored by the virtues of solidarity and the option for the poor and the marginalized, as well as the philosophical principles of the dignity of the human person, the dignity of work, liberation, and human rights. In the United States, social justice ministry is characterized by the social roles of church, lay, and political leaders both within the Church itself and in civil society. The social ministry approach employs the analytical frameworks of the natural law, the signs of the times, local analysis, and the structures of sin. Along these lines, the organizing principles of association and participation are emphasized in order to achieve the philosophical principles of the common good, social justice, the dignity of the human person, and the dignity of work. In pastoral letters, the U.S. bishops have underlined the virtues of the option for the poor and solidarity and the moral norms of social responsibility, peace, disarmament, and human and economic development. These values have become embedded in parish, diocesan, and national social justice ministry programs.

The *faith-based citizen approach* is guided by the independent social roles that Catholics play in the civil sphere to express their faith and values. In general, the "faith-based" sense of this approach draws from the philosophical principles of social justice, the common good, the dignity of the human person, human rights, and freedom of religion; the organizing principles of association, participation, and solidarity; the moral norms of charity and social responsibility; and the virtues of friendship and solidarity. This approach is taken in the United States by a variety of activists but has not been developed in Mexico.

What motivates the more liberal or progressive activists of this approach are the virtues of solidarity and the option for the poor and the vulnerable and marginalized, as well as the moral norms of social responsibility, the just wage, peace, disarmament, human and economic development, and liberation. Liberals and progressives use the analytical frameworks of the signs of the times, local analysis, the structures of sin, and solidarity, guided by the philosophical principles of commutative and distributive justice, the dignity of the human person, the dignity of work, human rights, and freedom of religion. More conservative activists are motivated by the moral norms of charity, duty, responsibility, and family life, as well as the virtues of solidarity and friendship, particularly as developed by John Paul II. Conservatives are oriented in their social analysis by the natural law and by the organizational principles of the Church, subsidiarity, and the market economy, as well as by the philosophical principles of the natural law, private property rights, the dignity of the human person, and the nature of government as constitutional and limited. Thus, what clearly distinguishes the conservative and liberal Catholic faith-based citizen activists in their use of the principles is the conservative emphasis upon the natural law, family life, the limited role of the State, private property rights, charity, and duty and the liberal emphasis upon solidarity as an analytical and organizing principle, the option for the poor and the marginalized, liberation, human and economic development, the just wage, the signs of the times, local analysis, and the structures of sin. As well, there are "seamless garment" Catholics who seek to unite the liberal and conservative sides of "faith based."

In the case of the principle of solidarity, because there are five distinctive approaches to its interpretation, its discourse can be very confusing within the Church. In the United States, a conservative faith-based citizen working for a prolife organization will be thinking of Pope John Paul's sense of solidarity as a virtue, while an anti–death penalty activist will more than likely take a liberationist or philosophical approach to the concept. Yet at a big national event such as Jubilee Justice, *solidarity* was used in general in its labor-related and philosophical sense of bringing people together for the common good. The different meanings of the term are not contradictory, but because it has a range of nuanced meanings, a united discourse regarding solidarity cannot be assumed. In Mexico, the discourse of solidarity is more problematic. In Mexican public life, *solidarity* clearly implies a labor orientation toward socialist yet corporatist social organization, while ecclesial actors use *solidarity* in its Catholic sense (popularized by Pope John Paul II) as a virtue. There is little in common between these two versions of solidarity, especially in their applied sense in Mexico. I found that Mexican Christian-inspired activists tried to steer clear of both the traditional political and Catholic approaches to solidarity and ended up drawing from the liberationist and philosophical approaches to generate a new public discourse. Interestingly, given that the sociological approach to solidarity is the oldest and most rationalized, I did not find any actors in the United States or Mexico employing its analytical breakdown of mechanical, diffuse, and organic solidarity. Figure 5 summarizes the general strategic directions of the Catholic social imagination in Mexico and the United States.

Church

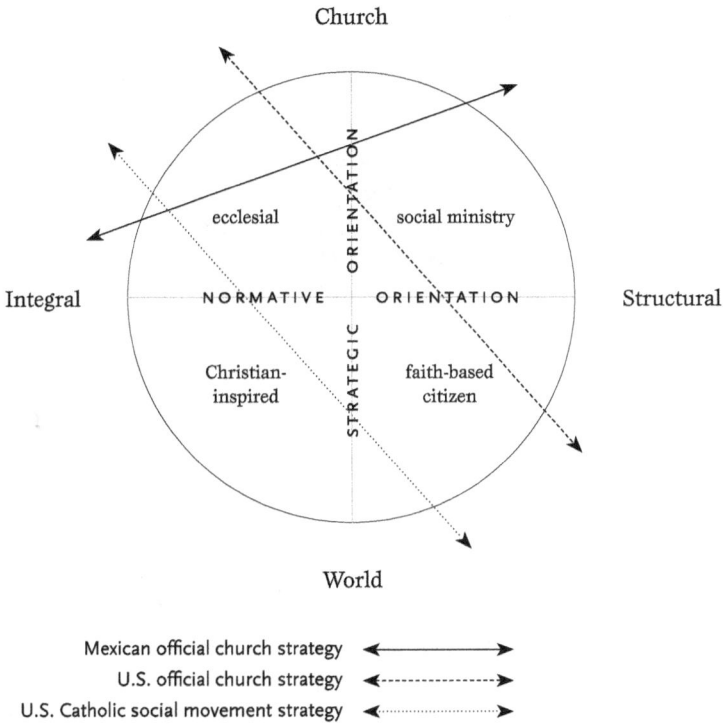

Mexican official church strategy   ←——————→

U.S. official church strategy   ←- - - - - - - - - - →

U.S. Catholic social movement strategy   ←·············→

Figure 5. Four strategic approaches of the Catholic social imagination in Mexican and U.S. churches

Locating the Social of Social Justice in the U.S. and Mexican Catholic Churches

Implementing Catholic social justice doctrine is a highly complex operation for the international church. I have shown in the cases of the United States and Mexico that the social doctrine's implementation is contingent upon the social opportunity structures available. In both countries these opportunity structures are opened or constrained by three key social forces: the political history of each country and the resulting national political culture; each country's religious history and its development of participatory opportunities within the liturgy, ecclesial structures, and independent church-related associations for the laity since Vatican II; and the historical development of a free civil society in each country, allowing religious actors to take their faith and values into the public square as both "Catholic" and "citizen."

My analysis has shown that the *social* implementation of the doctrine has at least four distinct approaches that represent an ideal-typic Catholic social imagination and provide different thresholds for translating the doctrinal principles into social justice attitudes and behaviors. The ecclesial approach is the least social, primarily because it limits the doctrine to the religious sphere, a theological understanding of the Church as an encompassing community and institution for values and action. In the ecclesial approach, the Church understands itself as parallel to society: the society is expected to become more Catholic simply because church members are mirroring charity for society. Thus, social justice is a justice within the Church. The Christian-inspired approach provides a high threshold for social justice to unfold, but it limits Catholic social justice doctrine to generic principles for civil society. Because of this, the development of a Catholic infrastructure for social justice is limited. This is social justice outside the Church. The social ministry approach provides a wide vehicle for developing the principles within the Church and has potential to equip Catholics for social action in civil society. This approach has different social thresholds, dependent upon how the local or national church allows programs to develop beyond ecclesial structures. In its most restrictive interpretation, this is a social justice within the Church; in its more open interpretation, it produces social justice within and outside the Church. The faith-based citizen approach provides the possibility for both significant Catholic doctrinal penetration into society and a high degree of independent social participation and association in civil society.

In regard to locating the social in Catholic social justice, then, the lowest degree of the social is offered in the ecclesial approach, while the highest degree is offered in the Christian-inspired and Catholic social justice citizen approaches. Theoretically, the lowest degree of Catholicity is presented in the social ministry and faith-based citizen approach, while the highest degree of Catholicity is theoretically offered by the ecclesial and Christian-inspired approaches. Again, theoretically the lowest degree of possibility of actual change in society is in the ecclesial and Christian-inspired approaches, while the highest possibility is in the social ministry and faith-based citizen approaches. But these theoretical predictions must be tempered by awareness of the dynamic quality of the Catholic social imagination as a normative-strategic space that constrains and opens each approach as Catholic social actors engage with each.

Because of the long historical development of civil society, the tradition of separation of church and state, and the development of high degrees of lay participation in its ecclesial structures, the U.S. Catholic Church has been able to integrate the Church's social justice doctrine into its ministerial life and into structures that allow the clergy and laity to move the doctrine into U.S. public life. Most important, the U.S. theological tradition and infrastructure have developed a contextual interpretation of the doctrine marked by themes of biblical justice and option for the poor. This interpretation has helped the bishops develop national and local programs such as the Catholic Campaign for Human Development to be mechanisms for social change in civil society and have influence for long-term institutional changes. The U.S. church has allowed a flourishing social justice cultural milieu to develop, based on lay participation in the liturgy, educational opportunities, contextual theology, a vast independent Catholic infrastructure of educational institutions, publishing houses, newspapers, magazines, and associations, and social movements developed from the doctrine. The social justice cultural milieu allows a wide range of activities—from conservative to progressive—to bring a public Catholicism to U.S. civic and political life.

The Mexican Catholic Church has a complex history in relation to the state, civil society, and the Church itself. The Constitution of 1917 laid down a strict separation of church and state that resulted in the marginalization of religion in public life, thus limiting the Church to develop public services for education, health care, and information. That limitation also explains why civil society in Mexico has until recently developed very little and gives credibility to Alexis de Tocqueville's understanding of religion as the "first institution" in civil society.[16]

Vatican II ushered in reform in the Mexican Catholic Church, marked by the development of ecumenism, liberation theology, and the *comunidades eclesiales de base*. However, in the 1980s a restorationist and neoconservative approach to Church life, led by the episcopal appointees of the apostolic nuncio Archbishop Prigione, systematically dismantled most of the reforms and oriented the Church toward the ecclesial approach to social justice doctrine and church life. The surviving Pastoral Social, as a function of the Church's mission, has attempted to integrate many of the elements of liberation theology with the social doctrine and the teachings of Pope John Paul II during his four visits to Mexico. However, the Mexican church has not supported a contextual theological interpretation for the doctrine, due to low theological production and the lack of a broad theological infrastructure. Similarly, there has been a low national identity in pastoral programs.

In Mexico, the widespread attitude of *no se meta en la política* (don't meddle in politics) limits the imagination regarding how the doctrine can move outside the Church into the civil sphere rather than the political sphere. This problem exists because of limited experience with an independent civil society. Catholic activists who wanted to be involved in social change prior to 1992 felt marginalized by the Church and ended up starting their own social justice associations, which became the backbone for the new civil society that emerged in the 1990s and opened space for the *transición* to occur. Indeed, this new civil society led by many Christian-inspired activists helped elect Fox as the first nonapparatus Mexican president, a president of the *transición*. Fox's election opened the possibility for a shift in the relationship between the Catholic Church and the state apparatus, but as he concluded his term of office, this possibility had not materialized. If the many Mexican activists taking the social justice ministry approach were allowed to create independent civil associations, it might be possible for the Church to develop new attitudes and opportunities for an emergent public Catholicism. However, because an overall social justice cultural milieu has yet to develop in the Mexican church and openings for a public Catholicism are still all too few, this transition will most probably be slow and incremental.

A Faith That Does Justice?

This study aimed to look at the many levels of the institutional Catholic church and ways that its members attempt to implement their religion's social justice doctrine in two countries. Over the course of five years I wandered far and wide in both the United States and Mexico to get involved directly with ordinary Catholics in their parishes and with diocesan organizations, local civil society associations, and national religious and civil associations seeking to implement the doctrine. My research has been experientially driven and either suffers or benefits from the participant-observer methodology I employed.

A good many fine historical and sociological studies published in the United States (and cited in my footnotes) have provided an empirical basis for many of my assertions. In Mexico, however, there are very few studies of the modern institutional church and few avenues for generating social data. Therefore, to get a broad overview of the social justice situation and generate an analytical framework, I compared the religious and civil institutions described in this study. I was extremely fortunate to mount this study during the preparations for the Jubilee Year and during the Jubilee events in both countries, since the international church itself provided a framework of social justice events that national churches were requested to implement in their own ways. Future research on the institutional church in Mexico should prove to be very fertile, given the changes in Mexican political culture and society that began in the era of *transición* to civil society and democratic political life.

As I reflect upon the hundreds of civic meetings, liturgies, demonstrations, and city council meetings I attended and the homes and offices I visited, I am most inspired by the ordinary men and women who have made decisions to move their faith into civic and political action. These people, especially the poor citizens of the San Antonio in Oakland and Las Pintitas in Guadalajara, were markedly different from those around them, because they had experienced an awakening, a *despertar,* regarding their lives as Catholics. Their social conversion required them to help create heaven on earth; the Jesus of their faith had to be incarnated in their local community. What motivates a person to leave home to attend endless planning meetings and work with people who would ordinarily not be one's friends? For the subjects of this study, Catholic social justice doctrine generated a rationale and motivation to leave home and go to the town square or *plaza pública.* For them, Catholics should be in the world, bringing their faith to the public square and creating the common good.

A faith that does justice? Yes and no. Yes, the Catholic Church provides variegated approaches to implement its social doctrine with a dynamic and complex Catholic social imagination. After seeing a Catholic social justice activist from a poor community actually win school reform, help obtain a supermarket for low-income elderly people in a government housing project, or help pass the first citizen initiative in Mexican history to address domestic violence, one can only say yes, there is a faith that does justice. These are social justice goods that affect everyday life. Without these kinds of social changes, the quality of life would remain low.

But the Catholic Church's social justice teaching faces many challenges. In particular, many of the activists I encountered have asked, what about justice in the Church itself? It's one thing to fight for racial, gender, and economic justice outside the Church, but what about discrimination against women in the Church, and what about the low wages the Church pays its clergy, nuns, lay teachers, janitors, and lay ministers in both the United States and Mexico? These questions are particularly pointed when asked of the ecclesial approach to social justice: how can people believe that the Church is a just institution and "a light to the world" when it lacks procedures for due process for clergy, laity, and theologians, is often not accountable for its finances, and keeps women from entering the priesthood and the hierarchical leadership? Catholics at every level in both the United States and Mexico are asking themselves these questions. The traditional excuse that "the Church is not a social institution" is increasingly under fire, due to civil complaints regarding sexual abuse by the clergy and civil rights abuses that have proliferated in the Church. As the U.S. clergy sexual abuse crisis unfolded, it took civil authority to bring the hierarchy of the Church to justice for the victims of the personal crimes of priests, brothers, nuns, and bishops.[17] But both conservative and liberal Catholics are asking themselves larger questions of the institutional church—questions about such as due process, transparency, priestly celibacy, and the natural law premises of the social doctrine and morality. These Catholics will not allow themselves to be forced out of the Church and do not see themselves as marginal—particularly when they can wield the power of the purse to catch the attention of Church authority.[18]

Indeed Catholics have a powerful and complex social imagination that operates in a wide social space both in the Church and in the world. As Roman Catholicism continues to grow in a complex global society, we can expect that the Catholic social imagination will play a significant role in shaping social justice possibilities in the face of increasing income disparities, social inequalities, political crises, migration, and other experiences of injustice. The Catholics I encountered in Oakland and Guadalajara will continue to ask themselves, "What would *Cristo encarnado* do?"

Appendix A ✚ Principles of Catholic Social Justice Doctrine: Sources from Papal Encyclicals and Documents of Vatican II

All the sources cited in this list can be found at the Vatican's website: www .vatican.va/holy_father/index.htm. The listing was compiled with reference to the following works devoted to the social doctrine of the Catholic Church: O'Brien and Shannon 1977; Jacobo 1997; Massaro 2000, pp. 78–79, 167; O'Brien 1991, pp. 13–24; Iriarte 1995, pp. 114–15; Williams and Houck 1993.

Analysis in Light of the Gospel and Social Teaching

As in the case of the natural sciences, the Church has confidence in this research also and urges Christians to play an active part in it. Prompted by the same scientific demands and the desire to know man better, but at the same time enlightened by their faith, Christians who devote themselves to the human sciences will begin a dialogue between the Church and this new field of discovery, a dialogue which promises to be fruitful. Of course, each individual scientific discipline will be able, in its own particular sphere, to grasp only a partial—yet true—aspect of man; the complete picture and the full meaning will escape it. But within these limits the human sciences give promise of a positive function that the Church willingly recognizes. They can even widen the horizons of human liberty to a greater extent than the conditioning circumstances perceived enable one to foresee. (*Octogesima Adveniens,* no. 40)

Application of Church's Teaching to the Temporal Order

In regard to the Church, her cooperation will never be found lacking, be the time or the occasion what it may; and she will intervene with all the greater effect in proportion as her liberty of action is the more unfettered. Let this be carefully taken to heart by those whose office it is to safeguard the public welfare. Every minister of holy religion must bring to the struggle the full energy of his mind and all his power of endurance. Moved by your authority, venerable brethren, and quickened by your example, they should never cease to urge upon men of every class, upon the high-placed as well as the lowly, the Gospel doctrines of Christian life; by every means in their power they must strive to secure the good of the people; and above all must earnestly cherish in themselves, and try to arouse in others, charity, the mistress and the queen of virtues. (*Rerum Novarum,* no. 63)

Association

In the last place, employers and workmen may of themselves effect much, in the matter We are treating, by means of such associations and organizations as afford opportune aid to those who are in distress, and which draw the two classes more closely together. Among these may be enumerated societies for mutual help; various benevolent foundations established by private persons to provide for the workman, and for his widow or his orphans, in case of sudden calamity, in sickness, and in the event of death; and institutions for the welfare of boys and girls, young people, and those more advanced in years. (*Rerum Novarum,* no. 48)

Common Good

But if the question be asked: How must one's possessions be used?—the Church replies without hesitation in the words of the same holy Doctor: "Man should not consider his material possessions as his own, but as common to all, so as to share them without hesitation when others are in need. Whence the Apostle with, 'Command the rich of this world . . . to offer with no stint, to apportion largely.'" (*Rerum Novarum,* no. 22)

Depoliticization of the Church

In turn, where the principle of religious freedom is not only proclaimed in words or simply incorporated in law but also given sincere and practical application, there the Church succeeds in achieving a stable situation of right as well as of fact and the independence which is necessary for the fulfillment of her divine mission. This independence is precisely what the authorities of the Church claim in society. At the same time, the Christian faithful, in common with all other men, possess the civil right not to be hindered in leading their lives in accordance with their consciences. Therefore, a harmony exists between the freedom of the Church and the religious freedom which is to be recognized as the right of all men and communities and sanctioned by constitutional law. (*Dignitatis Humanae,* no. 13)

Development as a Word for Peace and Order

When we fight poverty and oppose the unfair conditions of the present, we are not just promoting human well-being; we are also furthering man's spiritual and moral development, and hence we are benefiting the whole human race. For peace is not simply the absence of warfare, based on a precarious balance of power; it is fashioned by efforts directed day after day toward the establishment of the ordered universe willed by God, with a more perfect form of justice among men. (*Populorum Progressio,* no. 76)

Dignity of the Human Person

Labor, as Our Predecessor explained well in his Encyclical, is not a mere commodity. On the contrary, the worker's human dignity in it must be recognized. It therefore cannot be bought and sold like a commodity. . . . Everyone understands that this grave evil which is plunging all human society to destruction must be remedied as soon as possible. But complete cure will not come until this opposition has been abolished and well-ordered members of the social body—Industries and Professions—are constituted in which men may have their place, not according to the position each has in the labor market but according to the respective social functions which each performs. (*Quadragessimo Anno,* no. 83)

One of the salient features of the modern world is the growing interdependence of men one on the other, a development promoted chiefly by modern technical advances. Nevertheless brotherly dialogue among men does not reach its perfection on the level of technical progress, but on the deeper level of interpersonal relationships. These demand a mutual respect for the full spiritual dignity of the person. Christian revelation contributes greatly to the promotion of this communion between persons, and at the same time leads us to a deeper understanding of the laws of social life which the Creator has written into man's moral and spiritual nature. (*Gaudium et Spes,* no. 23)

Disarmament

Hence justice, right reason, and the recognition of man's dignity cry out insistently for a cessation to the arms race. The stock-piles of armaments which have been built up in various countries must be reduced all round and simultaneously by the parties concerned. Nuclear weapons must be banned. A general agreement must be reached on a suitable disarmament program, with an effective system of mutual control. (*Pacem in Terris,* no. 112)

Economic Development and Justice

History shows with ever-increasing clarity that it is not only the relations between workers and managers that need to be re-established on the basis of justice and equity, but also those between the various branches of the economy, between areas of varying productivity within the same political community, and between countries with a different degree of social and economic development. (*Mater et Magistra,* no. 122)

Economic Aid to Poorer Countries by Wealthier Ones

Today we are facing the so-called "globalization" of the economy, a phenomenon which is not to be dismissed, since it can create unusual opportunities for greater prosperity. There is a growing feeling, however, that this increasing internationalization of the economy ought to be accompanied by effective international agencies which will oversee and direct the economy to the common good, something that an individual State, even if it were the most powerful on earth, would not be in a position to do. In order to achieve this result, it is necessary that there be increased coordination among the more powerful countries, and that in international agencies the interests of the whole human family be equally represented. It is also necessary that in evaluating the consequences of their decisions, these agencies always give sufficient consideration to peoples and countries which have little weight in the international market, but which are burdened by the most acute and desperate needs, and are thus more dependent on support for their development. Much remains to be done in this area. (*Centesimus Annus,* no. 58)

Family Life and Marriage

Thus the family, in which the various generations come together and help one another grow wiser and harmonize personal rights with the other requirements of social life, is the foundation of society. All those, therefore, who exercise influence over communities and social groups should work efficiently for the welfare of marriage and the family. Public authority should regard it as a sacred duty to recognize, protect and promote their authentic nature, to shield public morality and to favor the prosperity of home life. The right of parents to beget and educate their children in the bosom of the family must be safeguarded. Children too who unhappily lack the blessing of a family should be protected by prudent legislation and various undertakings and assisted by the help they need. (Gaudium et Spes, no. 52)

The first and fundamental structure for "human ecology" is the family, in which man receives his first formative ideas about truth and goodness, and learns what it means to love and to be loved, and thus what it actually means to be a person. Here we mean the family founded on marriage, in which the mutual gift of self by husband and wife creates an environment in which children can be born and develop their potentialities, become aware of their dignity and prepare to face their unique and individual destiny. But it often happens that people are discouraged from creating the proper conditions for human reproduction and are led to consider themselves and their lives as a series of sensations to be experienced rather than as a work to be accomplished. The result is a lack of freedom, which causes a person to reject a commitment to enter into a stable relationship with another person and to bring children into the world, or which leads people to consider children as one of the many "things" which an individual can have or not have, according to taste, and which compete with other possibilities. (*Centesimus Annus,* no. 39)

Freedom of Religion

A sense of the dignity of the human person has been impressing itself more and more deeply on the consciousness of contemporary man, and the demand is increasingly made that men should act on their own judgment, enjoying and making use of a responsible freedom, not driven by coercion but motivated by a sense of duty. The demand is likewise made that constitutional limits should be set to the powers of government, in order that there may be no encroachment on the rightful freedom of the person and of associations. This demand for freedom in human society chiefly regards the quest for the values proper to the human spirit. It regards, in the first place, the free exercise of religion in society. This Vatican Council takes careful note of these desires in the minds of men. It proposes to declare them to be greatly in accord with truth and justice. To this end, it searches into the sacred tradition and doctrine of the Church—the treasury out of which the Church continually brings forth new things that are in harmony with the things that are old. (*Dignitatis Humanae,* no. 1)

Friendship

But, if Christian precepts prevail, the respective classes will not only be united in the bonds of friendship, but also in those of brotherly love. For they will understand and feel that all men are children of the same common Father, who is God; that all have alike the same last end, which is God Himself, who alone can make either men or angels absolutely and perfectly happy; that each and all are redeemed and made sons of God, by Jesus Christ, "the first-born among many brethren"; that the blessings of nature and the gifts of grace belong to the whole human race in common, and that from none except the unworthy is withheld the inheritance of the kingdom of Heaven. "If sons, heirs also; heirs indeed of God, and co-heirs with Christ." Such is the scheme of duties and of rights which is shown forth to the world by the Gospel. Would it not seem that, were society penetrated with ideas like these, strife must quickly cease? (*Rerum Novarum,* no. 25)

Government Is Constitutional and Limited

The protection and promotion of the inviolable rights of man ranks among the essential duties of government. Therefore government is to assume the safeguard of the religious freedom of all its citizens, in an effective manner, by just laws and by other appropriate means.

Government is also to help create conditions favorable to the fostering of religious life, in order that the people may be truly enabled to exercise their religious rights and to fulfill their religious duties, and also in order that society itself may profit by the moral qualities of justice and peace which have their origin in men's faithfulness to God and to His holy will. (*Dignitatis Humanae,* no. 6)

Human Rights

Once this is admitted, it follows that in human society one man's natural right gives rise to a corresponding duty in other men; the duty, that is, of recognizing and respecting that right. Every basic human right draws its authoritative force from the natural law, which confers it and attaches to it its respective duty. Hence, to claim one's rights and ignore one's duties, or only half fulfill them, is like building a house with one hand and tearing it down with the other. (*Pacem in Terris,* no. 30)

Just Wage as Family Support

Let the working man and the employer make free agreements, and in particular let them agree freely as to the wages; nevertheless, there underlies a dictate of natural justice more imperious and ancient than any bargain between man and man, namely, that wages ought not to be insufficient to support a frugal and well-behaved wage-earner. If through necessity or fear of a worse evil the workman accept harder conditions because an employer or contractor will afford him no better, he is made the victim of force and injustice. (*Rerum Novarum,* no. 45)

If a workman's wages be sufficient to enable him comfortably to support himself, his wife, and his children, he will find it easy, if he be a sensible man, to practice thrift, and he will not fail, by cutting down expenses, to put by some little savings and thus secure a modest source of income. Nature itself would urge him to this. We have seen that this great labor question cannot be solved save by assuming as a principle that private ownership must be held sacred and inviolable. The law, therefore, should favor ownership, and its policy should be to induce as many as possible of the people to become owners. (*Rerum Novarum,* no. 46)

Liberation Based upon Church's Social Teaching

Having said this, we rejoice that the Church is becoming ever more conscious of the proper manner and strictly evangelical means that she possesses in order to collaborate in the liberation of many. And what is she doing? She is trying more and more to encourage large numbers of Christians to devote themselves to the liberation of men. She is providing these Christian "liberators" with the inspiration of faith, the motivation of fraternal love, a social teaching which the true Christian cannot ignore and which he must make the foundation of his wisdom and of his experience in order to translate it concretely into forms of action, participation and commitment. All this must characterize the spirit of a committed Christian, without confusion with tactical attitudes or with the service of a political system. The Church strives always to insert the Christian struggle for liberation into the universal plan of salvation which she herself proclaims. (*Evangelii Nuntiandi,* no. 38)

The Market Economy's Proper and Legitimate Role

It would appear that, on the level of individual nations and of international relations, the free market is the most efficient instrument for utilizing resources and effectively responding to needs. But this is true only for those needs which are "solvent," insofar as they are endowed with purchasing power, and for those resources which are "marketable," insofar as they are capable of obtaining a satisfactory price. But there are many human needs which find no place on the market. It is a strict duty of justice and truth not to allow fundamental human needs to remain unsatisfied, and not to allow those burdened by such needs to perish. It is also necessary to help these needy people to acquire expertise, to enter the circle of exchange, and to develop their skills in order to make the best use of their capacities and resources. Even prior to the logic of a fair exchange of goods and the forms of justice appropriate to it, there exists something which is due to man because he is man, by reason of his lofty dignity. Inseparable from that required "something" is the possibility to survive and, at the same time, to make an active contribution to the common good of humanity. (*Centesimus Annus,* no. 34)

Option for the Poor

On the other hand, the right of having a share of earthly goods sufficient for oneself and one's family belongs to everyone. The Fathers and Doctors of the Church held this opinion, teaching that men are obliged to come to the relief of the poor and to do so not merely out of their superfluous goods. If one is in extreme necessity, he has the right to procure for himself what he needs out of the riches of others. Since there are so many people prostrate with hunger in the world, this sacred council urges all, both individuals and governments, to remember the aphorism of the Fathers, "Feed the man dying of hunger, because if you have not fed him, you have killed him," and really to share and employ their earthly goods, according to the ability of each, especially by supporting individuals or peoples with the aid by which they may be able to help and develop themselves. (*Gaudium et Spes,* no. 69)

Option for the Vulnerable

It is in fact the weakest who are the victims of dehumanizing living conditions, degrading for conscience and harmful for the family institution. The promiscuity of working people's housing makes a minimum of intimacy impossible; young couples waiting in vain for a decent dwelling at a price they can afford are demoralized and their union can thereby even be endangered; youth escape from a home which is too confined and seek in the streets compensations and companionships which cannot be supervised. It is the grave duty of those responsible to strive to control this process and to give it direction. (*Octogesima Adveniens,* no. 11)

Participation

The consciousness of his own weakness urges man to call in aid from without. We read in the pages of holy Writ: "It is better that two should be together than one; for they have the advantage of their society. If one fall he shall be supported by the other. Woe to him that is alone, for when he falleth he hath none to lift him up." (*Rerum Novarum,* no. 50)

Among the basic rights of the human person is to be numbered the right of freely founding unions for working people. These should be able truly to represent them and to contribute to the organizing of economic life in the right way. Included is the right of freely taking part in the activity of these unions without risk of reprisal. Through this orderly participation joined to progressive economic and social formation, all will grow day by day in the awareness of their own function and responsibility, and thus they will be brought to feel that they are comrades in the whole task of economic development and in the attainment of the universal common good according to their capacities and aptitudes. (*Gaudium et Spes,* no. 68)

Peace

Everyone must sincerely co-operate in the effort to banish fear and the anxious expectation of war from men's minds. But this requires that the fundamental principles upon which peace is based in today's world be replaced by an altogether different one, namely, the realization that true and lasting peace among nations cannot consist in the possession of an equal supply of armaments but only in mutual trust. And We are confident that this can be achieved, for it is a thing which not only is dictated by common sense, but is in itself most desirable and most fruitful of good. (*Pacem in Terris,* no. 113)

Private Property Rights

Private ownership, as we have seen, is the natural right of man, and to exercise that right, especially as members of society, is not only lawful, but absolutely necessary. "It is lawful," says St. Thomas Aquinas, "for a man to hold private property; and it is also necessary for the carrying on of human existence." (*Rerum Novarum,* no. 22)

Role of the Laity

In the developing nations and in other countries lay people must consider it their task to improve the temporal order. While the hierarchy has the role of teaching and authoritatively interpreting the moral laws and precepts that apply in this matter, the laity have the duty of using their own initiative and taking action in this area—without waiting passively for directives and precepts from others. They must try to infuse a Christian spirit into people's mental outlook and daily behavior, into the laws and structures of the civil community. Changes must be made; present conditions must be improved. And the transformations must be permeated with the spirit of the Gospel. (*Populorum Progressio,* no. 81)

"Signs of the Times" as Basis of Social Analysis

To carry out such a task, the Church has always had the duty of scrutinizing the signs of the times and of interpreting them in the light of the Gospel. Thus, in language intelligible to each generation, she can respond to the perennial questions which men ask about this present life and the life to come, and about the relationship of the one to the other. We must therefore recognize and understand the world in which we live, its explanations, its longings, and its often dramatic characteristics. (*Gaudium et Spes,* no. 4)

Social Justice

But not every distribution among human beings of property and wealth is of a character to attain either completely or to a satisfactory degree of perfection the end which God intends. Therefore, the riches that economic-social developments constantly increase ought to be so distributed among individual persons and classes that the common advantage of all, which Leo XIII had praised, will be safeguarded; in other words, that the common good of all society will be kept inviolate. By this law of social justice, one class is forbidden to exclude the other from sharing in the benefits. Hence the class of the wealthy violates this law no less, when, as if free from care on account of its wealth, it thinks it the right order of things for it to get everything and the worker nothing, than does the non-owning working class when, angered deeply at outraged justice and too ready to assert wrongly the one right it is conscious of, it demands for itself everything as if produced by its own hands, and attacks and seeks to abolish, therefore, all property and returns or incomes, of whatever kind they are or whatever the function they perform in human society, that have not been obtained by labor, and for no other reason save that they are of such a nature. (*Quadragesimo Anno,* no. 57)

Social Order

Because order, as St. Thomas well explains, is unity arising from the harmonious arrangement of many objects, a true, genuine social order demands that the various members of a society be united together by some strong bond. This unifying force is present not only in the producing of goods or the rendering of services—in which the employers and employees of an identical Industry or Profession collaborate jointly—but also in that common good, to achieve which all Industries and Professions together ought, each to the best of its ability, to cooperate amicably. And this unity will be the stronger and more effective, the more faithfully individuals and the Industries and Professions themselves strive to do their work and excel in it. (*Quadragesimo Anno,* no. 84)

Social Responsibilities of Christians

Men are by nature social, and consequently they have the right to meet together and to form associations with their fellows. They have the right to confer on such associations the type of organization which they consider best calculated to achieve their objectives. They have also the right to exercise their own initiative and act on their own responsibility within these associations for the attainment of the desired results. (*Pacem in Terris,* no. 23)

Solidarity

All Christians must be aware of their own specific vocation within the political community. It is for them to give an example by their sense of responsibility and their service of the common good. In this way they are to demonstrate concretely how authority can be compatible with freedom, personal initiative with the solidarity of the whole social organism, and the advantages of unity with fruitful diversity. They must recognize the legitimacy of different opinions with regard to temporal solutions, and respect citizens, who, even as a group, defend their points of view by honest methods. Political parties, for their part, must promote those things which in their judgement are required for the common good; it is never allowable to give their interests priority over the common good. (*Gaudium et Spes,* no. 75)

Solidarity as a Virtue

It is above all a question of interdependence, sensed as a system determining relationships in the contemporary world, in its economic, cultural, political and religious elements, and accepted as a moral category. When interdependence becomes recognized in this way, the correlative response as a moral and social attitude, as a "virtue," is solidarity. This then is not a feeling of vague compassion or shallow distress at the misfortunes of so many people, both near and far. On the contrary, it is a firm and persevering determination to commit oneself to the common good; that is to say to the good of all and of each individual, because we are all really responsible for all. (*Sollicitudo Rei Socialis,* no. 38)

The State in the Economy: What Is Reasonable Intervention?

The foremost duty, therefore, of the rulers of the State should be to make sure that the laws and institutions, the general character and administration of the commonwealth, shall be such as of themselves to realize public well-being and private prosperity. This is the proper scope of wise statesmanship and is the work of the rulers. Now a State chiefly prospers and thrives through moral rule, well-regulated family life, respect for religion and justice, the moderation and fair imposing of public taxes, the progress of the arts and of trade, the abundant yield of the land—through everything, in fact, which makes the citizens better and happier. Hereby, then, it lies in the power of a ruler to benefit every class in the State, and amongst the rest to promote to the utmost the interests of the poor; and this in virtue of his office, and without being open to suspicion of undue interference—since it is the province of the commonwealth to serve the common good. And the more that is done for the benefit of the working classes by the general laws of the country, the less need will there be to seek for special means to relieve them. (*Rerum Novarum,* no. 32)

Structures of Sin

The "structures of sin" and the sins which they produce are likewise radically opposed to peace and development, for development, in the familiar expression Pope Paul's Encyclical, is "the new name for peace." (*Sollicitudo Rei Socialis,* no. 39)

Man receives from God his essential dignity and with it the capacity to transcend every social order so as to move towards truth and goodness. But he is also conditioned by the social structure in which he lives, by the education he has received and by his environment. These elements can either help or hinder his living in accordance with the truth. The decisions which create a human environment can give rise to specific structures of sin which impede the full realization of those who are in any way oppressed by them. To destroy such structures and replace them with more authentic forms of living in community is a task which demands courage and patience. (*Centesimus Annus,* no. 38)

Subsidiarity

The supreme authority of the State ought, therefore, to let subordinate groups handle matters and concerns of lesser importance, which would otherwise dissipate its efforts greatly. Thereby the State will more freely, powerfully, and effectively do all those things that belong to it alone because it alone can do them: directing, watching, urging, restraining, as occasion requires and necessity demands. Therefore, those in power should be sure that the more perfectly a graduated order is kept among the various associations, in observance of the principle of "subsidiary function," the stronger social authority and effectiveness will be the happier and more prosperous the condition of the State. (*Quadragessimo Anno,* no. 80)

Work and Its Dignity

The following duties bind the wealthy owner and the employer: not to look upon their work people as their bondsmen, but to respect in every man his dignity as a person ennobled by Christian character. They are reminded that, according to natural reason and Christian philosophy, working for gain is creditable, not shameful, to a man, since it enables him to earn an honorable livelihood; but to misuse men as though they were things in the pursuit of gain, or to value them solely for their physical powers—that is truly shameful and inhuman. (*Rerum Novarum,* no. 20)

Workers' Participation in the Life of Their Industries

The Church has no models to present; models that are real and truly effective can only arise within the framework of different historical situations, through the efforts of all those who responsibly confront concrete problems in all their social, economic, political and cultural aspects, as these interact with one another. For such a task the Church offers her social teaching as an indispensable and ideal orientation, a teaching which, as already mentioned, recognizes the positive value of the market and of enterprise, but which at the same time points out that these need to be oriented towards the common good. This teaching also recognizes the legitimacy of workers' efforts to obtain full respect for their dignity and to gain broader areas of participation in the life of industrial enterprises so that, while cooperating with others and under the direction of others, they can in a certain sense "work for themselves" through the exercise of their intelligence and freedom. (*Centesimus Annus,* no. 43)

Worker's Labor and Its Priority in Economics

Thus, the principle of the priority of labour over capital is a postulate of the order of social morality. It has key importance both in the system built on the principle of private ownership of the means of production and also in the system in which private ownership of these means has been limited even in a radical way. Labour is in a sense inseparable from capital; in no way does it accept the antinomy, that is to say, the separation and opposition with regard to the means of production that has weighed upon human life in recent centuries as a result of merely economic premises. When man works, using all the means of production, he also wishes the fruit of this work to be used by himself and others, and he wishes to be able to take part in the very work process as a sharer in responsibility and creativity at the workbench to which he applies himself. (*Laborem Exercens,* no. 15)

Workers' Rights to Organize

The most important of all are workingmen's unions, for these virtually include all the rest. History attests what excellent results were brought about by the artificers' guilds of olden times. They were the means of affording not only many advantages to the workmen, but in no small degree of promoting the advancement of art, as numerous monuments remain to bear witness. Such unions should be suited to the requirements of this our age—an age of wider education, of different habits, and of far more numerous requirements in daily life. It is gratifying to know that there are actually in existence not a few associations of this nature, consisting either of workmen alone, or of workmen and employers together, but it were greatly to be desired that they should become more numerous and more efficient. We have spoken of them more than once, yet it will be well to explain here how notably they are needed, to show that they exist of their own right, and what should be their organization and their mode of action. (*Rerum Novarum,* no. 49)

Appendix B ✠ Research Sites and Instruments

During my research period, from 1997 through 2001, I employed two primary sociological methods: ethnography and interviews. The ethnographic research required participant observation in many venues. Typically I traveled to Mexico for three months of research and then back to the United States for three months. My longest period of continuous research in the United States was in Oakland for eleven months in 1997 and 1998. In Mexico, my longest periods were five months in Guadalajara in 1999 and five months in Mexico City in 2000.

Research Sites

The following were the ethnographic research sites of this study.

UNITED STATES
- Oakland, California, 1997–2000: Participation in the ongoing community organizing of Oakland Community Organizations (OCO) at St. Anthony Catholic Parish. This entailed attending monthly local organizing committee meetings, Sunday Mass, monthly meetings with the pastor and the assigned community organizer, area and citywide rallies, and related meetings with organizers of the Pacific Institute of Community Organizing (PICO).
- Ponchatoula, Louisiana, 1997: Attended a five-day intensive national leadership training offered by PICO National.
- Washington, D.C., 1999: During a one-month period I observed the work of the Catholic Campaign for Human Development of the United States Catholic Conference.
- Los Angeles, California, 2000: Participated in the Jubilee 2000 events sponsored by the National Conference of Catholic Bishops.

MEXICO
- Guadalajara, 1999: Participated in a four-week leadership training program held quarterly for NGO directors offered by the Instituto Mexicano de Desarrollo Comunitario (IMDEC).

- Guadalajara, 1999–2001: Participated in the Archdiocese of Guadalajara's Pastoral Social at three levels—parish of Las Pintitas, vicariate, and diocesan-wide. Attended weekly parish meetings and monthly vicariate and deanery meetings, consulted with the pastor and associate pastor, and met with the archdiocesan executive personnel on an ongoing basis. Assisted with food banks, fundraising, and worship services and visited many homes for cultural and religious celebrations.
- Guadalajara, 1999–2000: Participated in Voces Unidas, an NGO coordinated by IMDEC that organized the campaign against intrafamily violence.
- Oaxaca and Chiapas states, 2000: Participated in a one-month human rights fact-finding trip organized by the Archdiocese of Guadalajara.
- Mexico City, 1999–2000: Participated in events and trainings sponsored by the Instituto Mexicano de la Doctrina Social.
- Mexico City, 1999–2000: During a one-month period I observed the work of the Pastoral Social Nacional of the Mexican Bishops' Conference. As well, I participated in the events organized for Jubilee 2000, particularly the national Social Justice Week.

In the course of the ethnographic research I conducted 98 (51 United States, 47 Mexico) complete interviews that have been used as a basis for ethnographic observation, as well as for direct opinion and point of view of the social actors observed. The interview schedule that was followed appears below. Each interview took from 60 to 90 minutes to conduct. All interviews were taped with permission of the subject under the condition of anonymity. Only those who gave express permission to use their names have been quoted by name. The interviews were not quantified for this study: I cannot claim to have gathered a random or representative sample of Catholic social actors, particularly since my subjects are all social activists in their particular community or work.

Male = M
Female = F
Young adult (18–30) = Y
Adult (30–55) = A
Senior (55+) = S

UNITED STATES (TOTAL: 51 INTERVIEWS)

OCO-PICO Leaders, Oakland, California (9)

- national director, Oakland: M, S
- national consultant, Irvine: M, A
- OCO director, San Diego, M, A
- OCO community organizer: F, A
- OCO community organizer: F, A

- OCO community organizer: F, Y
- OCO community organizer: M, A
- community organizer, San Diego: M, Y
- community organizer, San Diego: F, A

OCO Local Leaders at St. Anthony Parish (11)

- pastor: M, A
- lay leader: M, A
- lay leader: M, A
- lay leader: F, S
- lay leader: F, S
- lay leader: F, S
- lay leader: F, A
- lay leader: F, A
- lay leader: F, Y
- lay leader: F, A
- lay leader: F, A

Other PICO Affiliated in San Diego, California (5)

- pastor, San Diego: M, A
- lay leader: F, S
- lay leader: M, A
- lay leader: F, A
- lay leader: F, A

Other PICO Affiliated in Orange, California (4)

- lay leader: F, S
- lay leader: M, A
- lay leader: F, A
- lay leader: F, A

Theologians (12)

- theologian, Fordham University, New York: M, S
- theologian, Weston School of Theology, Cambridge. Mass.: M, A
- theologian, Boston College: M, A
- theologian, Georgetown University, D.C.: M, S
- theologian, Georgetown University, D.C.: M, S
- theologian, St. Louis University: M, S
- theologian, Woodstock Center, D.C.: M, S
- theologian, Catholic Conference, D.C.: M, S
- theologian, Catholic Conference, D.C.: M, A
- theologian, Jesuit School of Theology, Berkeley: M, A
- theologian, Jesuit School of Theology, Berkeley: M, S

- theologian, Jesuit School of Theology, Berkeley: M, S
- theologian, Jesuit School of Theology, Berkeley: F, S

Catholic Campaign for Human Development, Washington, D.C. (9)

- national executive director: M, S
- education specialist: F, A
- education specialist: M, A
- economic development specialist: M, A
- field representative: M, A
- field representative: M, A
- field representative: F, A
- field representative: M, A
- development specialist: F, Y

MEXICO (TOTAL: 47 INTERVIEWS)

Pastoral Social, National, Mexico City (6)

- national executive director: M, A
- director, Caritas Mexico: M, A
- director, migration: F, A
- director, education: M, A
- director, indigenous: M, A
- director: F, A

Pastoral Social, Archdiocese of Guadalajara (7)

- bishop, liaison: M, A
- executive director: M, A
- deputy director: F, A
- priest coordinator, workers: M, A
- priest coordinator: M, A
- legal outreach: M, Y
- editor: M, A

Pastoral Social, Local Parish and Vicariate in Guadalajara (12)

- pastor: M, S
- associate pastor: M, A
- vicar of area: M, S
- lay leader: M, S
- lay leader: M, A
- lay leader: M, Y
- lay leader: F, S
- lay leader: F, S
- lay leader: F, A

- lay leader: F, A
- lay leader: F, A
- lay leader: F, Y

Instituto Mexicano de Desarrollo Comunitario, Guadalajara (6)

- founder: M, S
- executive director: M, A
- trainer: M, A
- trainer: F, A
- publications: F, Y
- publications: M, Y

Instituto Mexicano de la Doctrina Social, Mexico City (3)

- executive director: M, A
- editorial director: M, A
- editor: F, Y

Voces Unidas, Guadalajara (5)

- leader: M, A
- leader: M, A
- leader: M, A
- leader: F, A
- leader: F, A

Theologians (5)

- Jesuit Philosophy Center, Guadalajara: M, S
- Jesuit Philosophy Center, Guadalajara: M, S
- Jesuit Theological Center, Mexico City: M, S
- Jesuit Theological Center, Mexico City: M, S
- Worker Reflection Center, Mexico City: M, S

National Civil Society Leaders, Mexico City (3)

- executive director, CEMEFI: M, A
- executive director, DEMOS: M, A
- executive director, Centro Linda Vista: M, A

Interview Questions for Activists

Name / *Nombre*
Position / *Posición*
Institution / *Institución*
Location / *Lugar*

Clergy/*Clérigo* _____ Religious/*Religioso* _____ Lay/*Laico* _____
Age/*Edad*
Curriculum vitae?
Date of interview / *Fecha de entrevista*
Interview location / *Lugar de entrevista*
Explain goals of the interview. OK to quote what is said?
Permission to tape interview?

1. Your intellectual, activist, or pastoral contributions related to social justice organizing. Recollections of your formation in social justice, personal motivating factors for your involvement, activities or organizations involved in, your primary contribution to social justice.
   Favor hablar de sus contribuciones intelectuales, activistas, pastorales en cuanto a justicia social. Recuerdos de su formación en justicia social, factores personales que motivaron su compromiso, actividad, y activismo, y su contribución principal a justicia social.

   A. Recollections of your formation and development related to social justice concerns or activities from family, education, causes
      Recuerdos de su formación and desarrollo en la justicia social, de la familia, educación, causas, etc.

   B. Personal motivating factors for involvement in social justice
      Factores de motivación personal para su compromiso con la justicia social

   C. Activities or organizations related to social justice that you belong to
      ¿En cuales actividades y/o organizaciones participa relacionadas a la justicia social?
      1.
      2.
      3.
      4.
      5.

   D. How would you like people to remember your contribution to social justice—your primary contribution?
      ¿Cómo le gustaría que la gente recordara su contribución a justicia social—sus aportes principales?

2. What you think have been the major religious (theological, spiritual, etc.) contributions to and/or shifts in social justice activity since Vatican II in the United States?
   ¿Cuáles cree que sean las contribuciones principales (teológicas, litúrgicas, espirituales, etc.) de la actividad de justicia social a partir del Concilio Vaticano II en México?

    A. Theological contributions / *Contribuciones teológicas*

    B. Practical contributions / *Contribuciones prácticas*

    C. Other / *Otras*

3. What do you see as the particularly religious characteristics of social justice organizing and/or action in PICO and/or the local organizing group [e.g., OCO]?
   ¿Para usted, cuáles son las características religiosas de justicia social en su actividad o ministerio en [Pastoral Social, IMDEC, IMDOSOC, etc.]?

4. What you believe to be the successes and challenges for social justice organizing or activism in the United States—in general and in your particular ministry/position?
   ¿Qué opina que sean los éxitos y los retos de las actividades de justicia social en México—en general y en su posición o ministerio personal?

    A. Successes/*Éxitos*

    B. Challenges/*Retos*

[Summary of interview / *Resumen de la entrevista*]

5. Anything else?
   ¿Alguna otra cosa que desea comentar?

Interview Questions for Social Justice Theologians and Strategists

Name of respondent
Present position
Institution
Location
Clergy _____ Religious _____ Lay _____
Age
Curriculum vitae?
Date of interview
Interview location
Explain goals of the interview. OK to quote what is said?
Permission to tape interview?

1. Your intellectual or pastoral contributions to social justice theology. Recollections of your formation in social justice, personal motivating factors for your involvement, activities or organizations involved in, your primary contribution to social justice.

A. Recollections of your own formation and development related to social justice concerns or activities from family, education, causes

B. Personal motivating factors for involvement in social justice

C. Activities or organizations related to social justice that you belong to
1.
2.
3.
4.
5.

D. What do you believe to be your primary contribution(s) to social justice theology or activity?

2. What you think have been the major contributions to and/or shifts in social justice theology since Vatican II in the United States—theological, practical, etc.?

A. Theological contributions

B. Practical contributions

C. Other

3. What you believe to be the future challenges for social justice theology in the United States, in general and in your particular ministry/position?

A. In general

B. In your particular position or ministry

4. *For Jesuits only:* What do you believe to be particular Jesuit characteristics of social justice theology and/or action in the United States?

5. Anything else?

Chapter One

1. For the complete documentation of the proceedings of the Second Vatican Council, see Abbott 1966.
2. John Paul II 2000.
3. Bunson 1999, p. 345.
4. Bunson 1999, pp. 268–74.
5. The classic scriptural reference to the division between Church and world is Mark 12:17: "Give to the emperor the things that are the emperor's, and to God the things that are God's." Scripture quotations, unless otherwise noted, are from the New Revised Standard Version of the Bible (NRSV), copyright 1989 by the Division of Christian Education of the National Council of the Churches of Christ in the USA.
6. The scriptural texts regarding jubilee are Leviticus 25:8–12, Isaiah 61:2, Jeremiah 29:11, and Luke 4:18–19.
7. John Paul II 1999.
8. See in particular the sociological accounts of American Catholic culture in Greeley 1977; Greeley 1991; Greeley 2000.
9. Tracy 1981.
10. In social movement literature, social or political actors who test the boundaries are known as "insurgents," but I do not think that the use of that term is helpful in this study. Nor is *dissident* helpful, because I found that many Catholics who are testing boundaries do so in a prophetic way: they do not want to leave the institutional church but attempt to call the Church back to its stated mission. Therefore I avoid using a heuristic category for these persons. I prefer to draw from my ethnographic situations and interviews to let the actors give their own account of their social imagination and use their own labels or descriptive terms to define their situation.
11. Besides NAFTA, 1994 was also the beginning of the indigenous rebellion in the state of Chiapas and the collapse of the peso. At that time

many urban Mexicans, particularly those in social justice organizations, began to mobilize solidarity committees and to push for a greater role for civil society in the creation of Mexican social policy. See Tello Diaz 1995; Tangeman 1995; Fox 1996; Bilello 1996.

12. Hispanics constituted an estimated 17.92 million (29 percent) of the 62.01 million Catholics of the United States in 1999. They are the fastest-growing ethnic group of the U.S. Catholic community. See Bunson 1999, pp. 449–57.

13. The theme of atonement that marked the Jubilee Year emerged from a parasacramental understanding of reconciliation for sins by individuals that are construed as "structural sin." This was a major contribution by John Paul II to the principles of Catholic social teaching (John Paul II 1988). In my case studies I will analyze the importance of atonement in statements of the national bishops' conferences. Cardinal Law resigned his office in December 2002.

14. Pseudonyms will be used for some of the activists I interviewed in the course of my research.

15. Throughout this work I will use the term *ministry* for the work of Catholic activists who see themselves as practicing a full-time vocation in social justice. The term has become an ordinary one in the United States.

16. For brief histories of U.S. Catholics and social issues, see Ahlstrom 1972 and Curran 1982.

17. The key social justice pastoral letters by U.S. bishops in the 1980's were developed in a national consultation process involving theologians, academic specialists, and "listening sessions" involving ordinary Americans. See National Conference of Catholic Bishops 1983 and 1986.

18. Anderson 1995.

19. See Alinsky's key works regarding citizen empowerment in the United States: Alinsky 1989a and 1989b.

20. Coleman 1998.

21. Pacific Institute for Community Organizations 1997.

22. Byron 1989.

23. Wood 1995.

24. "Diane" is the pseudonym of a local lay activist in her forties. She is fluent in Spanish and English and is often asked to interpret at OCO meetings. As a schoolteacher, she is one of the few professionals in the local community. Because of this, she is a key bridge person who can relate to the immigrants of the parish and to public officials.

25. "Scott" is the pseudonym of a professional community organizer in his thirties. He has a bachelor's degree from an elite East Coast college, where he was a student activist. All his professional work has involved community organizing. He learned Spanish during his time at OCO.

26. Coleman 1991b.

27. Semana Pastoral Social Nacional can be translated as "National Week of Social Ministry."

28. For three days delegates were divided into small groups to discuss challenges to social justice ministry at the local, diocesan, state, regional, and national levels. The results of these discussions were to be given to the Mexican bishops so that they could "listen" to the concerns of Mexican priests, religious, and laypeople. Father Gallo himself told me that this event was designed to resemble the listening processes used by the U.S. Catholic bishops.

29. Archbishop Thuân delivered a similar address at the U.S. Encuentro 2000. In February 2001, he was named a cardinal by Pope John Paul II.

30. McCarrick was named archbishop of Washington, D.C., in January 2001, and in February 2001 he was named cardinal by Pope John Paul II.

31. The following journalistic accounts review this history: Alonso 2000 and Agencias Mexicanas 2000.

32. Rafael is a pseudonym for a staff member of an agency of the Conferencia Episcopal Mexicana. He, his wife, and their three children live in Mexico City.

33. A critical shift in Mexican political culture, particularly a disillusionment with the Partido Revolucionario Institucional (PRI), the sole ruling party in modern Mexican history, began in 1968. That year the Olympics were held in Mexico City, and students took to the streets in protests against social injustices. Government leaders feared that the demonstrations would embarrass Mexico as a modern and democratic country. A major demonstration at the Plaza de Tlatelolco in Mexico City was suppressed by police forces, resulting in the deaths of more than five hundred people. This massacre signaled the beginning of the *inquietud* marking Mexican political culture and a weakening of the PRI's control. See Poniatowska 1971; Bartra 1982b and 1992; Braun 1997.

34. Blancarte 1992, 1995a, and 1996.

35. For analyses of the importance of public religion and public Catholicism, see Casanova 1994 and Garrett 1989. During Fox's 1999–2000 presidential campaign as a candidate of the Partido Acción Nacional (PAN) and the Partido Verde (PV), he was regularly criticized in leading newspapers and periodicals for "waving the banner of Guadalupe" and "undermining *laicismo*." He was the first presidential candidate since 1917 to participate in religious services and receive Communion. He has written of the importance of his Catholic faith in his autobiography: see Fox Quesada 1999.

36. For a discussion of the development of *laicismo* in Mexican history, see Basave Fernandez del Valle 1990; Blancarte 1994a and 1996.

37. For an analysis of the distinction between "freedom of religion" and "freedom of belief," see Blancarte 1991 and 1995b.

38. Garcia Ugarte 1993b.
39. Camp 1997.
40. Ellacuría 1975; Eagleson and Scharper 1979; Dussel 1981; and Ellacuría and Sobrino 1993.
41. The Plan Pastoral or Pastoral Conjunto was developed after Vatican II as a strategic organizing principle by the CEM to divide pastoral functions among theological dimensions of baptism.
42. Steidlmeier 1984.
43. Bartra 1987.
44. Between 11 February and 16 July 1858, Mary, identifying herself as the Immaculate Conception, allegedly appeared eighteen times to Bernadette Soubirous outside the village of Lourdes, France. People began to be healed of physical infirmities at the grotto and spring of the apparition site. Lourdes has become the premier Marian shrine for physical healing, and the 11 February feast day of Our Lady of Lourdes was designated as a key Jubilee Year festival day.
45. Elena is this leader's actual name.
46. Paulo Freire instituted this now widely used pedagogy for literacy while working with illiterate peasants in northeast Brazil in the early 1960s. His philosophical premise was that people must be conscious of the words they use. Words must not "come from above" but from the people themselves. His primary text explaining this philosophy is Freire 1970.
47. See Núñez H., Fals Borda, and Caruso 1990.
48. René de Dios 1999.
49. See, in particular, Morris 1984; Snow et al. 1986; Morris and Mueller 1992; Calhoun 1994; McAdam, McCarthy, and Zald 1996.

Chapter Two

1. For general overviews of the notion of "social capital" and its religious capacity in the United States, see Espinosa, Elizondo, and Miranda 2005; Formicola, Segers, and Weber 2003; Verba, Schlozman, and Brady 1995; Warren 1998; Wuthnow 2004; Wuthnow and Evans 2002.
2. In contrast to the U.S. studies of religious capital, Mexican analysts of religion have largely focused upon historical studies of the Catholic Church; see Blancarte 1993; Camp 1997; García Ugarte 1993a and 1993b; Tangeman 1995.
3. Interestingly, in the United States bishops, theologians, and activists prefer the term *teaching* over *doctrine*. In chapter 3 I will explore this distinction among U.S. Catholics and the reason this is the American preference.
4. For U.S. and Mexican studies of the development of the social doctrine, see Blancarte 1995; Coleman 1991b; Curran 1982 and 2002; Curran and

McCormick 1999; Instituto Mexicano de Doctrina Social Cristiana 1989; Jacobo M. 1997; Massaro 2000.

5. For case studies of the social doctrine in the United States and Mexico see Blancarte 1995a and 1996; Briseño Chávez 1993; Camp 1997; Casanova 1994; Cuneo 1989; Dillon 1999; Levine 1992; Massaro 1998; Warren 2001; Weigert and Kelley 2004; Wood 2002.

6. For a historical review of the Church's reaction to the Enlightenment, see Wolin 1960, pp. 286–350, and Vidler 1964.

7. For a review of the history of the Church's historical relationship to liberal democracy, see Sigmund 1993, pp. 51–72, and Coleman 1991a, pp. 2–4.

8. See McBrien and Attridge 1995; McBrien 1994.

9. For a review of the religious reaction to Adam Smith and economic liberalism and the Catholic Church's and Protestant churches' responses to modernism and liberalism, see Troeltsch 1981, pp. 644–50.

10. For a comprehensive review of the results of Trent, see O'Malley 2000b.

11. Ibid.

12. The suppression of the Jesuits from 1773 to 1811 was premised upon the Jesuits' enculturation of national and local practices and traditions into the theology and practice of Trent, particularly in China, Japan, and Latin America. As well, the Jesuits had developed new interpretations of political philosophy that allowed regicide in the case of an unjust ruler. In moral theology, the Jesuits had developed a sophisticated methodology of casuistry, a pragmatic approach to the moral life and its principles. See the essays regarding Jesuit cultural and scientific contributions in O'Malley 1999.

13. For a brief review of the issues that let up to Vatican I and the consequences of the council, see O'Malley 2000a.

14. For a review of the effects of the globalization of the papacy, especially under John Paul II's papacy, see Dulles 2000.

15. Weber 1946b, p. 284.

16. The idea of a developmental doctrine comes from the theology of nineteenth-century English cardinal John Newman (Newman 1989). In sociology the idea of the "social construction of reality" is based upon a phenomenological transference of ideas and values to action that becomes structured. See Berger and Luckmann 1966.

17. Byron 1998.

18. The need for a systematic social justice doctrine has been articulated in, for example, O'Brien and Shannon 1977, pp. 11–43, and Speiker 1998.

19. I use "declaration" because it has been used in various documents of the modern Church to state the Church's position on moral and social justice questions.

20. The fact that the Catholic Church can actually change its position on social issues such as slavery, usury, women's rights, and birth control is historically analyzed by legal historian and jurist John T. Noonan in Noonan 2005.

21. Boileau 1998, p. 11 (emphasis added).

22. Up to the current time, critique of the natural law and its application to social justice teaching has come primarily from U.S. Catholic social ethicists. See Curran 1982.

23. John Paul II clearly has steered the Church toward the singular philosophical approach of the natural law for moral theology. See John Paul II 1993.

24. For references to the *Compendium,* see Pontifical Council for Justice and Peace 2005.

25. Hollenbach 1979 and 1988.

26. Habermas 1984, p. 42.

27. See "Discourse Ethics: Notes on a Program of Philosophical Justification" in Habermas 1990, pp. 43–115. Discourse ethics, according to Habermas, works by a principle of universalization in which "only those norms may claim to be valid that could meet with the consent of all affected in their role as participants in a practical discourse" (ibid., p. 197).

28. Ibid., p. 79.

29. Cohen and Arato 1992, pp. 376–77.

30. Miller 1999, p. 6.

31. For a history of the term *social justice* in relation to other understandings of justice in the Catholic Church, see Kettern 1998, pp. 85–101.

32. Cohen and Arato 1992, pp. 376–77.

33. My argument is similar to Catholic social ethicists' contention that there is not a specific "Catholic" or "Christian" social ethics, but a common social ethics to which Catholics bring their faith perspective and values. See Hollenbach 1979; Winter 1966; Curran 1982.

34. For a case study of the prolife movement in the Catholic Church, see Cuneo 1989.

35. Drinan 2000.

36. John Paul II wanted the Congregation of the Faith to issue a "social justice catechism" similar to the *Catechism of the Catholic Church,* issued in 1993. In chapters 4 and 5 I will show how the U.S. and Mexican bishops have selected from the social justice menu to issue pastoral statements.

37. O'Malley 2000a.

38. Curran 1990, pp. 155–78.

39. For a discussion of *sensus fidelium* and reception, see Mahoney 1987, pp. 207–10, 259–99.

40. For analyses of the foundations of charity, ethics, and justice as key to the Church's social tradition, see Troeltsch 1981, pp. 133–38; Theissen 1978 and 1992; Stark 1996.

41. For descriptions of the basic elements of the natural law, see Mahoney 1987, pp. 77–83; Kettern 1998, pp. 86–92.

42. For the text of *Rerum Novarum* and all other papal encyclicals, consult the Vatican Web site. Documents are listed under each pope's names at www.vatican.va/holy_father/index.htm.

43. Sources for this inventory of the principles of the social doctrine are O'Brien and Shannon 1977; Jacobo M. 1997; Massaro 2000, pp. 78–79, 167; O'Brien 1991, pp. 13–24; Iriarte 1995, pp. 114–15; Williams and Houck 1993. For complete texts, see the Vatican Web site for each pope's encyclicals: www.vatican.va/holy_father/index.htm.

44. United States Catholic Conference 2000.

45. Pontifical Council for Justice and Peace 2005.

46. For a review of the history of the writing of the encyclical, particularly the formation of a Catholic social movement and key bishops and theologians involved in the formulation of the principles in *Rerum Novarum,* see Murphy 1991, pp. 1–26; Coleman 1991a, pp. 25–42.

47. For a historical understanding of John Paul II's philosophical contribution to Church doctrine, see Curran 2005 and Weigel 1999.

48. For a general sense of John Paul II's social philosophy—apart from his encyclicals—see John Paul II and Messori 1994.

49. Social theologians have suggested that a failure to integrate spirituality and social justice remains a deficiency in the teaching. See Connolly and Land 1977; Steidl-Meier 1984; Haight 1985; Dorr 1991; Casaldaliga and Vigil 1994.

50. This distillation is based on recurrent themes in post–Vatican II social encyclicals that are further developed in other documents of the Vatican, national bishops' conferences, and theological writing. The tables of contents of works by social justice theologians reveal these recurring themes as evidence of the role of the encyclicals and the *Catholic Catechism.* I will review this issue in chapters 3 and 4 when I discuss national theology and social contexts.

51. For a discussion of analytical sociological language and its tropes and the issue of constitutive language, particularly in the sociology of Durkheim, see White 1978, pp. 21–22.

52. Durkheim 1984, p. xxx.

53. Lukes 1985, p. 351.

54. Ibid., p. 353.

55. Durkheim 1984, p. 61.

56. Ibid.

57. Ibid., p. 85.

58. Ibid., p. 87.

59. Durkheim 1986.

60. Lukes 1985, p. 158.

61. "Collective sense" refers to what Steven Lukes cites as the Durkheimian notion of "conscience collective." With mechanical solidarity, "the social molecules . . . could only operate in harmony in so far as they do not operate independently," while with organic solidarity "society becomes more capable of operating in harmony, in so far as each of its elements operates more independently" (ibid., p. 148).

62. Aron 1970, p. 17.

63. Durkheim 1984, p. 123.

64. Introduction by Robert N. Bellah in Durkheim 1973, p. xxv.

65. Ibid.

66. Ibid., p. xxvi.

67. Parsons 1977, p. 31.

68. Leon H. Mayhew, introduction to Parsons 1982, pp. 38–39.

69. Ibid., p. 209.

70. Ibid., pp. 206–7.

71. Hollenbach 1979, p. 157.

72. Ibid., p. 162.

73. Coleman 1991a, p. 32.

74. Ibid.

75. Curran 1982, p. 109.

76. Ibid.

77. Ibid., p. 110.

78. Quoted in Hollenbach 1979, p. 157.

79. Hollenbach 1994–95, p. 20.

80. Hollenbach 1979, p. 162.

81. Ibid., p. 165.

82. John Paul II 1988, n. 38.

83. See a thorough discussion of the background to John Paul's theological and moral understanding of solidarity in Bilgrien 1999, pp. 63–77.

84. John Paul II 1991, n. 13.

85. Ibid., n. 41.

86. For background on John Paul II's philosophical training and its influence on his papal teaching, see Weigel 1992 and 1999.

87. Bilgrien 1999, p. 79.

88. United States Catholic Conference 2000, p. 472.

89. Ibid., p. 471.

90. Ibid.

91. Ibid.

92. Ibid., article 1945, p. 472.

93. Ibid., article 1936, p. 470.

94. Ibid., article 1937, p. 470.

95. For histories of Catholic Action in Europe, Latin America, Australia, and the Philippines, see Alonso 1961; Bidegaín de Urán 1985; Civardi

and Martindale 1943; Michonneau and Meurice 1955; Poggi 1967; Sevilla 1953; Truman 1960.

96. These are the categories, borrowed from *Gaudium et Spes,* that the *Catechism* uses to delineate various kinds of inequality. Ibid., article 1935, p. 470.

97. Dussel 1981, pp. 324–25.

98. Gutiérrez 1973, p. 113.

99. Haight 1985, p. 21.

100. Ibid.

101. Ibid., p. 51.

102. Ibid., p. 161.

103. Sobrino 1993, p. 632.

104. Ibid., p. 633.

105. Ibid., p. 634.

106. Sobrino and Pico 1985, pp. 15–16.

107. McAuliffe 1993, p. 186.

108. Ibid., pp. 229–30.

109. Ibid., p. 230.

110. Pottenger 1989, p. 3.

111. Ibid., pp. 48–49.

112. Lamb 1982, pp. ix–x.

113. For a summary of how the hermeneutical circle is used by Juan Luis Segundo, see Pottenger 1989, pp. 59–61.

114. Violence and its institutionalization are emblematic of the "oppressor" or the enemy. Liberation theology has historically relied upon the analysis of Frantz Fanon, who popularized the oppressor-oppressed motif. For this history see ibid., pp. 146–52, and Dussel 1981, pp. 240–44.

115. The literature of liberation theology and liberationist solidarity is devoid of a discussion of institutions. Rather, great stress is placed on the social as social actors, groups, and movements. Spanish theologian Ignacio Ellacuría, one of the Jesuit martyrs in El Salvador, writes: "Just as it is the people of God who should have a priority in the Kingdom of God, and not a set of institutional superstructures that takes its place, likewise in this world's history it should be that social groups that carry the weight of history, and they should do so on their own" (Ellacuría 1993, p. 320).

116. For discussions of the importance of narrative, discourse, and language in relationship to action within pluralistic social contexts, see White 1978, pp. 1–23; Brown 1989, pp. 75–78; Habermas 1987, pp. 114–26.

117. Tracy 1981, p. 24.

118. I use *ideology* in this study to "refer to the set of beliefs, attitudes, standards of rationality, etc. that embody the basic values of some social group and that group's conception of the political order appropriate to those values." Definition in Bakhurst 1993, p. 192.

119. The concept of "Catholic imagination" was developed by sociologist Andrew Greeley to articulate the phenomenological development of sacramental Catholicism in the realms of art and music. By extension, I apply this idea to the realm of social justice. See Greeley 1981, 1991, and 2000.
120. Weber 1946a, pp. 327–28.
121. The classic sociological formulation of this method of social construction is found in Berger and Luckmann 1966.
122. The Jubilee Year events of 1999 to 2001 were organized by a special office of the Vatican headed by Cardinal Roger Etchegarry and posted on a special Web site sponsored by the Vatican. Each day of the Jubilee Year had a special purpose. For example, on 11 February, the feast day of Our Lady of Lourdes, the worldwide church celebrated a day for the sick. See www.vatican.va/jubilee_2000/jubilee_year/novomillennio_en.htm.
123. Mills 1959.
124. Max Weber famously developed the concept of "ideal type" in his study *The Protestant Ethic and the Spirit of Capitalism* by posing the thought experiment "What is the range of differences and similarities among Protestant sects?" in order to make analytical sense of "ascetic Protestantism." See in particular Weber 1992, p. 200, nn. 23–26 of chap. 2. follow this classical understanding of ideal type through my development of "ideal-typic Catholic social imagination" as a thought experiment regarding the range of behavioral possibilities for Catholic social doctrine.
125. Bourdieu 1990, p. 53.
126. I borrow the idea of "things" from Charles Lemert's introductory book to sociology: Lemert 2005.
127. *Integral* is used by the Church itself in describing its internal processes. The *Compendium of the Social Doctrine of the Church* employs *integral* throughout as a normative term: the individual Catholic is urged to integrate his or her life within the spiritual and organizational life of the Church. Pontifical Council for Justice and Peace 2005.
128. Swidler 1986, p. 273.
129. For a general understanding of these aspects of social movement theory see: McAdam, Tilly, and Tarrow 2001; Keck and Sikkink 1998.

Chapter Three

1. For depictions of pre–Vatican II U.S. cultural Catholicism and the changes following the council, see Dolan 1983; Dolan 1992, pp. 127–348; Dolan and Hinojosa 1994; Gillis 1999, pp. 68–94; Morris 1997, pp. 3–284; McGreevy 2003.
2. Morris 1997; McGreevy 2003.
3. See Dolan 1987, chap. 5, pp. 127–57.

4. On the history of the "Americanness" of the U.S. bishops, see Reese 1992, pp. 21–28. For discussions of parish life in the various U.S. regions and their common congregational model, see the essays in Dolan 1987.

5. For a discussion of Catholic institutional life in the United States, see Gillis 1999, pp. 261–66.

6. For a history of the impact of Catholic education on immigrants, see Dolan 1985, pp. 253–261.

7. For a broad review of the U.S. Catholic Church's lay and religious organizations see Gillis 1999, chap. 7, pp. 197–219.

8. For a discussion of the Americanization of the U.S. Catholic Church, particularly the way the Church integrated American institutional forms into its organization life, see Morris 1997, chap. 5, pp. 113–40.

9. For a history of Catholic parallel institutions and discrimination, see Dolan 1985.

10. The Catholic-American versus American-Catholic distinction is made in order to suggest that the primary identity of Catholics in the United States is U.S. citizens who bring their faith into their citizenship. They do not feel any contradiction between their citizenship and their faith; thus the United States does not have religiously oriented political parties like the Christian Democratic movements in Europe and Latin America. See Vidler 1964; Higgins and Bole 1993, pp. 43–78; Bole 1997, pp. 783–87. For a discussion of the dominant urban character of U.S. Catholicism and the types of issues urban Catholicism brings forth, see Morris 1997, pp. 141–64.

11. Catholics increased from a 14 percent share (10.7 million of 76.1 million) of the U.S. population in 1900 to a 22 percent share (59.1 million of 267.6 million) in 1998. For statistics on membership and institutional growth patterns in the U.S. Catholic Church, see Froehle, Gautier, and Center for Applied Research in the Apostolate (U.S.) 2000, pp. 3–19.

12. "Regency" is a period of from two to four years following philosophical studies. During this time the Jesuit scholastic usually does service work in a Jesuit high school, college, or parish. Upon completion of this service, the Jesuit scholastic begins his theological training.

13. Hollenbach 1979.

14. I was unsuccessful in obtaining interviews with any leading women theologians for this work. It is an unfortunate fact that in the United States there were fewer than five women Catholic social justice theologians whom I might have been able to interview.

15. A General Congregation is the highest deliberative body of the Jesuits. It is called by the Father General of the order in order to establish new policy. General Congregation 32 was held from December 2, 1974, through March 7, 1975. See Jesuits 1974–75.

16. The Woodstock Theological Center working group included Jesuits David Hollenbach (Christian social ethics), John R. Donohue (Bible), Avery Dulles (ecclesiology), William Dych (systematic theology), John Langan (philosophy), William Walsh (church history), Robert Roach (systematic theology), and John Haughey (Christology). The book is listed in my bibliography as Haughey 1977.

17. Hollenbach 1977, pp. 219–22.

18. Donohue 1977.

19. The following works reflect the Catholic American social justice discourse initiated by the essays in *The Faith That Does Justice:* Connolly and Land 1977; Finn 1990; Weigel and Royal 1993; Novak 1982, 1984a, 1984b, 1989; Gremillion 1976; Haughton and Stamps 1993; Holland and Henriot 1983; Steidl-Meier 1984; Stief 1987; Coleman 1991a and 1991b; Curran 1982; Hannafey 1993; Massaro 1998 and 2000; Royal et al. 1987; O'Brien 1991; Bilgrien 1999.

20. See the concluding essay, "Jesus as the Justice of God," in Haughey 1977, pp. 264–90.

21. See National Conference of Catholic Bishops 1983 and 1986.

22. For varying perspectives on this collaborative process, see National Conference of Catholic Bishops 1997; Mugavero 1989; Weigel 1982; Block 1986; Royal et al. 1987; Douglass 1986; Rasmussen and Sterba 1987; Gannon 1987; Hannafey 1993; Warner 1995.

23. See Dolan 1992, pp. 428–29.

24. See the sections on the arms race and disarmament (nos. 79–82) in *Gaudium et Spes* in Flannery 1992, pp. 990–94.

25. Byrnes 1991, p. 99.

26. National Conference of Catholic Bishops 1983.

27. Byrnes 1991, p. 106.

28. Jesuit sociologist and theologian John Coleman used the concept of "strategic theology" in theorizing how public theology can take shape in the U.S. church. Borrowing this concept from theologian John Bennett, Coleman says that "all theologies are to some extent strategic theologies. They give emphasis to the questions of a particular time and place and they seek to counteract what are believed to be the errors that are most tempting at that time." "My main interest," Coleman notes, "is uncovering a model for public theology that promises to have a strategic fit to the structural limits and possibilities of American Catholicism." See Coleman 1982, p. 131.

29. Henriot, DeBerri, and Schultheis 1999, p. 109.

30. National Conference of Catholic Bishops 1997, chap. 2.

31. Ibid., chaps. 2–3.

32. Henriot, DeBerri, and Schultheis 1999, pp. 120–29.

33. National Conference of Catholic Bishops 1997, pp. 3–12.

34. Ibid., chap. 4.
35. For a review of Catholic social programs in the United States, see Dolan 1985, chap. 12, pp. 321–46.
36. Walter Burghardt directs the Preaching the Just Word Program. See the program's Web site: www.georgetown.edu/centers/woodstock/pjw.htm.
37. John Padberg directs the Institute for Jesuit Sources at St. Louis University, which is the primary publishing house in the United States sponsored by the Jesuit Conference for Jesuit works.
38. Sins related to social injustice would include unjust discrimination in the workplace, usury, slavery, cheating, paying unjust wages, and the like For a discussion of the place of sin in Catholic social justice teaching, see Merkle 1994.
39. See Bellah et al. 1985.
40. I came to this conclusion after doing an extensive search for uses of the term *solidarity* by U.S. writers. See Palacios 1997.
41. For a complete discussion of the moral formation, especially the moral aspects of nonviolence, of the civil rights activists see Morris 1984, pp. 158–62.
42. For a discussion of social gospel theology and the civil rights movement, see *ibid.,* pp. 96–99.
43. For a discussion of the long-term impact of the civil rights movement and religious and civic activism, particularly the way liberal black Protestants acquire civic skills, see Verba, Schlozman, and Brady 1995, pp. 243–47.
44. One of the key reasons the Rev. Martin Luther King Jr., was able to make a "leap" from his Baptist tradition of biblical justice was his exposure to and training at Union Theological Seminary in New York City in the "Christian realism" of U.S. theologian Reinhold Niebuhr, who integrated philosophical pragmatism and liberal democracy with scripture and Christian tradition. Niebuhr had been a tremendous influence on Myles Horton, the organizer of the Highlander Folk School, who was to play a key role in the training of the early civil rights activists, including King. Thus Niebuhr's theological influence, Highlander Folk School training, and biblical morality—plus other factors—helped form a new religious-ethical-political nexus that was able to surmount the ethical and analytical limitations of the Baptist tradition. See: Morris 1984, pp. 140–49. For a summary analysis of Niebuhr's contribution to liberal Protestantism and evangelicalism, see Mott 1993, pp. 97–112.
45. In this tradition I include both Protestant and Catholic congregations that draw upon this history.
46. West 1994.
47. For a discussion of the impact of the civil rights movement and its religious component upon U,S. social movements, see McAdam 1982; Morris 1984.

48. For a discussion of the low "integrative" sense of Catholic prolife activists, which limits the capacity for abortion to be included in the larger social justice agenda, see Dillon 1993.
49. See the website of the United States Catholic Conference: www.nccbuscc.org/depts.htm.
50. For a discussion of the influence of Cardinal Joseph Bernardin's concept of "seamless garment," see Warner 1995.
51. For a description of the politics of the prolife and prochoice movements in their U.S. context, see Ginsburg 1998.
52. See www.usccb.org/prolife/intro.htm.
53. For materials on the Catholic-oriented anti–death penalty argument, see the Web sites of Catholics Against Capital Punishment (www.igc.org/cacp) and the Catholic Campaign to End the Death Penalty (www.usccb.org/sdwp/national/deathpenalty/dppressrelease032105.shtml). In early 2005, the U.S. bishops decided to begin a national discourse against the death penalty based largely on the evidentiary and legal arguments promoted by secular activists. See Social Development and World Peace 2005.
54. Prejean 1994.
55. By "new" I mean that Prejean's book helped reinvigorate the existing anti–death penalty movement by providing it a spiritual basis.
56. Forest 1997, p. 310.
57. For a history of the Catholic Workers and their relationship to the American hierarchy, particularly Day's personal relationship to Cardinal Spellman, see Forest 1994.
58. For histories of the UFW, see Dunne 1971; Day 1971; Stief 1987; Matthiessen 2000.
59. For a history of the U.S. bishops' labor policy and the UFW, see Higgins and Bole 1993, pp. 81–108.
60. For discussion of the interrelationship of the UFW, Hispanics, and the Catholic Church, see Guerrero 1987; Skerry 1993; Gomez-Quinones 1990.
61. For background on the impact of Cesar Chavez's integration of religion, spirituality, and community organizing within the UFW, see Yinger 1975; Griswold del Castillo and Garcia 1995; Dalton 2003.
62. For discussions of the influence of Latinos and farm labor in the reinvigoration of U.S. organized labor, see NACLA 1996; Nissen 1999.
63. For a description of Roger Mahony's involvement in the history of the UFW, see Higgins and Bole 1993, pp. 90–107.
64. The U.S. bishops have had a wide range of individual opinions on social issues, particularly abortion, the death penalty, and economic issues. However, they are capable of reaching a consensus and then uniting behind their statements. See Reese 1992, pp. 143–86.
65. For a biography of Father Roy Bourgeois, see Hodge and Cooper 2004.

66. See School of the Americas Watch 2005.
67. For discussions of the role of civil disobedience in Catholic social justice, see the following biographies: Berrigan and Coles 2001; Berrigan and Nhââat 1973; Curtis 1974; Dalton 2003.
68. For a history of the development of Catholic lay-oriented charitable organizations such as the St. Vincent de Paul Society and the shaping of U.S. Catholic social justice, see Dolan 1985, pp. 323–46.
69. Bernadicou 1996.
70. "Public theology" in the United States as the integration of religious belief and social concerns has been examined in the following works: Hehir 1986; Garrett 1989; Brown 1986.
71. Hacala 1995.
72. Froehle, Gautier, and Center for Applied Research in the Apostolate (U.S.) 2000, p. 99.
73. Ibid., p. 98.
74. See report by the Interfaith Funders: Warren and Wood 2001.
75. Engel 1998.
76. Dolan 1992, pp. 369–71.
77. Interview with the Rev. Robert Vitillo, 11 April 1999.
78. Froehle, Gautier, and Center for Applied Research in the Apostolate (U.S.) 2000, p. 98.
79. Neuhaus 1996.
80. Calpotura 1998.
81. The CCHD appeal can be viewed in relation to other national appeals related to charity and mission in the U.S. Catholic Church, such as the annual collections for the missions sponsored for the Society for the Propagation of the Faith and the December appeal for the retirement fund for men and women religious. These other appeals, which are partly based on social justice principles, generally rely on messages emphasizing charity rather than structural change.
82. The figure of 18 million is based on the average Sunday Mass attendance in the United States. See Froehle, Gautier, and Center for Applied Research in the Apostolate (U.S.) 2000, p. 23.
83. St. Anthony's is the actual name of the parish, and Oakland Community Organizations (OCO) is the real name of the organization. Except for those of public figures whose statements I have taken from the public record, I have changed the names of the community organizers, priests, religious, and laypeople.
84. Warren and Wood 2001, p. 5.
85. Tocqueville 1995, 2:121.
86. Schorr 1998.
87. Actually PICO grew out of OCO's foundations as the first organizing committee in what would become the PICO network.

88. In 2001 PICO had eighty-five affiliate organizing committees in fifteen states. It estimated that there were approximately 360,000 members of the PICO network in local organizing committees like the St. Anthony's local organizing committee (LOC).

89. Pacific Institute for Community Organizations 1997, p. 5.

90. National trainings of key lay leaders are held in January of each year in Ponchatoula, Louisiana, and in July in Los Altos, California. The leaders in attendance are identified and recruited by local professional organizers with the help of pastors and other leaders. The tuition and transportation costs are provided by the local congregation and LOC.

91. Wood 2002, p. 58.

92. Alinsky 1989b, p. 155.

93. The concept of the organic intellectual was developed by Antonio Gramsci. He realized that every community has natural leaders that surface who are capable of mediating the real interests of those at the bottom in relation to the real class interests of those at the top. See Gramsci 1972, pp. 291–93.

94. Lloyd and Thomas 1998, p. 20.

95. Seligman 1992, p. 8.

96. Wood 2002, pp. 61–84.

97. Tocqueville 1995, 2:121.

98. Putnam, Leonardi, and Nanetti 1993.

99. Many of these demographic changes are noted in an ethnographic study by Russell Jeung, which was conducted in a neighborhood close to my field site: Jeung 2005.

100. The history of St. Anthony Parish is chronicled in Abeloe 1972.

101. The pastor explained to me that the pastoral model of cells was introduced into Vietnam by French clergy in the 1950s. All the members of a parish are organized into groups of ten. The pastor has a leadership core group of ten that branches out into cells of ten. Thus, everyone in the parish has a group to belong to. Directives go from the pastor down through the cells.

102. For a full history of PICO and OCO, see Pacific Institute for Community Organizations 1997.

103. Parishes are assessed a participation rate based on the number of parishioners in the local organizing committee. Parish dues account for approximately 25 percent of OCO's annual budget. The rest of the budget is raised from local foundations and the Catholic Campaign for Human Development.

104. As an ordained Roman Catholic priest, I made myself available to celebrate the 9:30 Mass as well as to officiate at Spanish-language weddings and quinceañeras.

105. For accounts of the U.S. use of saints and feast days for social purposes, see Dolan 1992, pp. 195–220.

106. See Elizondo 1997; Guerrero 1987; Rodriguez 1994.

107. Elizondo 1981, p. 112.

108. In later discussions with priests and lay pastoral workers in Mexico, they found the idea of using Guadalupe as a social justice icon odd. Indeed, I could find no written Mexican theological or pastoral works related to Guadalupe social interpretation. Guadalupe scholarship is confined to historical works on the apparition itself or devotional materials. For Mexican Catholics, Guadalupe is part of a religiocultural construction of permanent ritual and cultural processes attached to the feast of Guadalupe on 12 December and devotions carried on both publicly and privately, such as pilgrimages by dioceses to the Mexico City shrine. Deviation from these processes has been rare. Only since the 1990s have there been artistic reinterpretations of the Guadalupe image in Mexico, mostly by feminist painters who have drawn on the basic elements of the image to relate Guadalupe to ordinary life and feminist self-projections. However, ordinary Mexicans in both the United States and Mexico would find these interpretations offensive, simply because the revered image is being altered.

109. For histories of these Encuentro processes, see the Web pages of the office of Hispanic Affairs of the United States Catholic Conference: www .nccbuscc.org/hispanicaffairs/history.htm.

110. In a survey conducted at a 9:30 Mass attended by approximately six hundred adults, approximately 90 percent of the congregation responded that they were born in Mexico. Of these Mexicans, 60 percent were from the state of Michoacán, 20 percent from the state of Jalisco, and 20 percent from a variety of other states. Thus the immigrant parents attending the meetings described in this section came primarily from the rural and urban-edge (Guadalajara and Morelia) areas of central Mexico. This group correlates highly with Roger Bartra's depiction of the ' "urban campesino."

111. I did not interview these neophytes, so I do not know what they were thinking. After observing this group for over a year, I believe that these social behaviors are not natural behaviors in such a public space. One might think that these people have social skills in other parts of their lives, such as home and work. However, having observed this group's behavior in the church space as well, I believe that the Mexican urban campesino in the US goes to the public spaces of church and halls without expectation to socialize. Rather, church is a place to pray; the gym is a place to wait for one's children.

112. For a variety of analyses of the divisions within the Latino community and the future of Latinos in U.S. political culture, see Garza et al. 1992;

Hurtado et al. 1992; Oboler 1995; McConahay 1996; Espinosa, Elizondo, and Miranda 2005; Skerry 1993.

113. This term denotes the rural migrants to Mexican and United States cities since a major agricultural "restructuring" of Mexico began in the mid-1970s. Typically these migrants, even though they live in cities like Oakland, Los Angeles, Chicago, Guadalajara, or Mexico City, maintain their rural concepts of living, particularly living day by day and having just enough knowledge to keep one's job and survive in the city. See Bartra 1982.

114. For overviews of the Faith-Based Initiative and the challenges it presents to religion and U.S. public life, see Formicola, Segers, and Weber 2003; Ryden and Polet 2005; Wuthnow 2004.

115. The Bush Administration's use of the Faith-Based Initiative has had success at the rhetorical level with its claims that "religious organizations do a better job at charity" and "government shouldn't be involved in charity." Both these expressions misunderstand PICO's development of faith-based as an orientation that elicits the social values of religion as an impetus to move religious people to civic action and make public institutions work better—not to dismantle public institutions that serve the common good.

116. Greeley 1991.

117. "Cultural toolkit" is a term coined by sociologist Ann Swidler. See Swidler 1986.

118. Here I paraphrase many responses I heard from delegates following each liturgical event at Jubilee Justice and at Encuentro 2000.

119. The liturgy as a cultural site for events, rituals, teaching, devotions, symbols, etc., can be viewed in the overall study of ritual and its social components. To construct the idea of cultural milieu—particularly the idea that ritual helps "construct a persuasive and apparently logical body of discourse"—I am using ideas of ritual theory from Bell 1992 and Douglas 1973.

120. This is a phrase coined by the Jesuit German theologian Karl Rahner.

121. For a complete listing of lay development programs in the United States, see Froehle, Gautier, and Center for Applied Research in the Apostolate (U.S.) 2000, pp. 160–63, 191–201.

122. Ammerman et al. 1997, pp. 63–160.

123. The U.S. bishops have issued a statement on the obligation to vote during each presidential election season.

124. Quan 1999.

125. Schorr 1999.

126. Oakland Community Organizations 2005.

127. Pacific Institute for Community Organizations 1997.

Chapter Four

1. For a discussion of Mexico's ideologically driven parties, see Almeyra 2000; Bartra 1993, pp. 101–64.
2. See Fox's history in the corporate world in his autobiography: Fox Quesada 1999, pp. 36–47.
3. Rivera 2000 discusses the analysis by Soledad Loeaza, Mexico's foremost scholar of the PAN, of the support Fox has received from the middle class.
4. For a history of the PAN, see Loaeza 1999.
5. For a discussion of the cultural factors required for the *transición,* see Rivera 2000.
6. Leñero Otero 1999, pp. 49–78.
7. "Los Mexicanos aspiramos y merecemos vivir en la certeza de la legalidad en la que el ejemplo del Gobierno haga del orden legal una realidad cívica" (Milenio 2000).
8. There was a conspicuous absence of "Club of Rome" bishops. At one point during Fox's campaign he had said that the Catholic hierarchy acted just like the PRI party bosses—a statement that he later retracted, but one that many in the *oposición* fully understood.
9. Loaeza 2000.
10. See in particular Salcedo Padilla Jr. 2000.
11. Niebuhr 1952, p. 17. At the opening of the presidential campaign, Fox's children presented him with a banner of Our Lady of Guadalupe. Interestingly, members of the Club of Rome condemned his use of the religious banner during an election. Mexican campaign law expressly forbids the use of religious symbols, and PRI party officials were of like mind with the Club of Rome. Oddly, the feast of Our Lady of Guadalupe on 12 December is a national holiday. Given the response of the Club of Rome, Fox's opinion regarding the image of the hierarchy in Mexico comes as no surprise. See Noticias Mexicanas 1999 and González 1999.
12. "El corazón de la filosofía ignaciana radica en comprender que sólo se alcanza la realización personal sirviendo a los demás. La congregación se propuso la tarea de formar hombres y mujeres capaces de transformar la realidad y servir a los demás, filosofía que dejó una profunda huella en mi vida adulta y me llevaría después a trabajar para crear fuentes de empleo y oportunidades." Fox discusses the influences of Father Scheifler and the Jesuits in his autobiography: Fox Quesada 1999, pp. 34–36.
13. Almeyra 2000.
14. For a discussion of Fox's election as an "awakening," particularly for Mexico's political culture, see P. Muñoz 2000.
15. I will use the Spanish *laicidad* throughout because there is not an adequate English translation for the concept. For a summary of the reform laws, see Dussel 1995, pp. 70–71. In general, these laws began a process

of limiting the role of the Catholic Church in public, so that by the time of the 1917 constitution, which severely restricted the Church's rights and privileges, Mexicans were accustomed to governmental restrictions upon religion.

16. Gómez-Pérez 1997, pp. 293–94.

17. The historical development of church-state relations in Mexico has been widely studied. See Ricard 1966; Knight 1990; Garcia Ugarte 1993a and b; Blancarte 1993.

18. For the broad consequences of church-state separation in Mexico, see Blancarte 1994b and the essay by Carlos Alvear Acevedo in Dussel 1984, pp. 313–58.

19. For an explanation of the authority of the Asuntos Religiosos, see Castellá 1997.

20. Mexican Catholics have shown a dual and seemingly contradictory tendency to desire public practice their faith, especially in their popular religious devotions, but at the same time want to limit the role of the institutional Church in Mexico's public life. See Blancarte 1991, pp. 293–318. For a detailed history of the Cristero rebellion, see Meyer 1976.

21. See the reflections of Gabriel Zaid, Mexico's leading Catholic social critic, regarding this problem: Zaid 1997, pp. 14–71.

22. In this present work "Mexican Catholicism" is limited to the mainstream population of mestizos, who make up 90 percent of the population of 92 million, and excludes the Church's outreach to indigenous populations, particularly in the southern states of Chiapas, Oaxaca, Yucatán, the coastal states of Guerrero and Veracruz, and the northern state of Chihuahua. Since Vatican II, the Church has organized religious life among indigenous peoples in quite distinct ways, and so far the "indigenous inculturation process" has not affected the mainstream church.

23. This feature is listed based on my two years of participatory observation of parishes in Guadalajara and Mexico City. My search for studies on parish life in contemporary Mexico was not fruitful. I did not encounter any centers of parish research. The current interests of Mexican sociologists of religion revolve around studies of new sects, church-state relations, and topical studies related to education, culture, and indigenous issues.

24. See the studies of popular religion by Dorothy Tanck de Estrada, Antonio Rubial García, Thomas Calvo, Mario Humberto Ruz, Jesús Tapia Santamaría, and José Miguel Romero in Sigaut 1997.

25. Dussel 1984, pp. 325–41.

26. See Zaid 1997, pp. 56–61.

27. The idea of "integral-intransigent" is developed by Roberto Blancarte in Blancarte 2000, pp. 296–301. In terms of leadership and the Church's Roman orientation, it is important to note that the key way for a priest to become a bishop is to serve as rector of a seminary. And the two-

thirds of Mexican rectors have been educated in Rome. See Camp 1998, pp. 265–67.

28. Key works of liberation theology include Gutiérrez 1973; Ellacuría and Sobrino 1993; Sobrino and Ellacuría 1996; Sobrino 1993; Sobrino and Hernández Pico 1985; Segundo 1985.

29. The Congregation of the Doctrine of the Faith (CDF) issued a declaration stating its concerns regarding nonorthodox elements of liberation theology, particularly its use of Marxist social theory. After great protest from many Latin American bishops regarding the CDF's apparent heavy-handed attempt to quash liberation theology, Pope John Paul II himself intervened with another declaration on the original declaration. The pope's intervention actually served to legitimize basic principles of liberation theology, particularly its emphasis on the preferential option for the poor and marginalized. See Segundo 1985.

30. I asked many informants if they could point to any theological texts they used to cite the foundations of the Pastoral Social and the Pastoral Conjunto. They said that this theological reflection and practice had emerged in Mexico in the 1970s and has been developed as a widespread grassroots phenomenon, but they could not refer me to specific texts, conferences, or theologians for me to cite.

31. Catholic Church, CEM 2000.

32. Athié Gallo 1993.

33. In Mexican public life, which includes the arts, politics, and journalism, the Catholic priest is considered, at best, little more than a sacramental instrument and, at worst, little more than a poorly educated ecclesiastical hack. I encountered this attitude in any number of intellectuals when I asked about the role of priests in Mexican society. This is certainly the image of the priest in Graham Greene's *The Power and the Glory* and in comedic riffs by the Mexican actor Cantinflas. A hit movie of 2000, *La Ley de Herodes,* portrays a priest as a slovenly dressed and money-grubbing power broker, akin to the local PRI mayor. However, no one questions the power of the priest, especially in rural and poor communities and parishes, where the priest often functions as a religious cacique. Jesuit priests are exempted from the harsh portrayals, since in post–Vatican II Mexico they are identified with leftist causes and intellectual freedom—almost as if they had a counterchurch.

34. For a history of the *semana católica social* in Mexico, see Goddard 1994, pp. 5–17. For an account of the October 1999 meeting, see Concha 1999.

35. *Mestizaje* is a process of ethnic and racial integration. Mexico's government has promoted this process for official national identity building, or *mexicanidad,* so that all citizens of Mexico can identify with a common heritage. This policy has served mestizo Mexicans well, but indigenous peoples who have retained their ethnic distinctiveness are not so well

served by it. For analysis of the classic construction of Mexican *mestizaje,* see Vasconcelos 1948. For an explanation of the complexity of *mestizaje* in Mexican modernity, see Garcia Canclini 1990, pp. 69–73. Regarding emigration, see Concha 1999.

36. For a history of Father Maciel's alleged sexual abuses, see Torres Robles 2001, pp. 269–67.

37. For details of Athié's removal and its implications for the Mexican church, see A. Muñoz 2000.

38. Alisedo 1999.

39. Catholic Church, CEM 2000.

40. See especially Sicilia 2000.

41. The Mexican bishops can be divided into at least four groups: Club of Rome, "open," moderates, and progressives. See Aguirre 1999.

42. Munguía 2000.

43. For a discussion of the orientation and practices of the Club of Rome, see Aguirre 1999.

44. "El reto que me espera es enorme, porque los 40 años de don Samuel al frente de la diócesis dejaron huella. Pero finalmente los dos estamos inspirados por el Evangelio y sobre todo por el Concilio Vaticano II. De manera que tanto don Samuel, como sus colaboradores y yo, tratamos de ser fieles a lo que Dios nos pide. Y la tarea que me espera no será exclusivamente mía, sino de toda la comunidad" (quoted in Corro 2000).

45. Prigione was apostolic delegate during the period when the Mexican government did not have diplomatic relations with the Vatican. In 1992 Mexico and the Vatican established diplomatic relations, at which time Prigione was named papal nuncio.

46. "Cuando Prigione fue nuncio en México, dejó que sólo algunos grupos, algunos obispos, fueran los interlocutores privilegiados con los poderes políticos y económicos del país, con los que tendió alianzas. Y el propio Prigione encarnó, en cierto sentido, la figura del interlocutor solitario que negociaba directamente con Roma y con los poderes políticos de México" (Vera 2000).

47. See especially chap. 5, "The Path to Solidarity," in John Paul II 1999.

48. Catholic Church, CEM 2000, nos. 4–8.

49. The original Spanish: "En lo social, la educación de inspiración cristiana debe fomentar la participación, el diálogo, la inculturación, el cambio social, la inserción familiar y el cuidado del medio ambiente."

50. "Es tiempo de que los católicos mexicanos asumamos la propuesta del Papa de 'rehabilitar' integralmente la caridad, superando una visión inmediatista y superficial, para comprenderla y vivirla como el Don-virtud teologal por excelencia, que Dios hace de sí mismo en Cristo al creyente por medio de su Espíritu para que la Trinidad habite en él" (Catholic Church, CEM 2000, no. 214).

51. Ibid., no. 200.

52. Ibid., nos. 202–11.

53. "Se trata de un profundo anhelo de millones de mexicanos deseosos de crecer al interior de una cultura de la vida que fortalezca instituciones democráticas y participativas, fundadas en el reconocimiento de los derechos humanos y en los valores culturales y trascendentes de nuestro pueblo. Cultura e instituciones construidas con la participación solidaria de todos, que sean salvaguardadas por las organizaciones representativas y subsidiarias llamadas a crear las condiciones reales que permitan una vida digna para todos. Esto supone una educación integral basada en el respeto a la persona humana y a la cultura, que incremente la responsabilidad y participación ciudadanas" (ibid., no. 67).

54. The process of writing the bishops' letter is described in Alonso 2000.

55. For a Catholic analysis of the challenges the Church faces in articulating the social doctrine in Mexican culture, see Anaya and Acción Católica Mexicana 1987.

56. The idea of citizen discipleship has been developed in the United States as merger of citizen responsibility and practice with Christian social responsibility, particularly as learned in religiously inspired civic organizations such as Bread for the World, Habitat for Humanity, Pax Christi, and other organizations. See Coleman 1998.

57. Examination of the development of the CEBs in Mexico from the late 1960s through 1980 is available in Dussel 1984, pp. 378–421.

58. Freire 1970.

59. Gutiérrez 1973.

60. Dussel 1984, pp. 399–421.

61. See the special edition of *Proceso* on the Church in Chiapas: Alisedo 1999.

62. Freire 1970.

63. Núñez Hurtado 1996, p. 177.

64. The PRD of the state of Jalisco chose Núñez as one of the proportional congressional representatives the party could name based on its total vote count. He chose not to run for office or to be reappointed. Instead, in 1998 he accepted an offer from the Jesuit university of Guadalajara, the ITESO, to fill the Paulo Freire Chair of Educational Pedagogy, which he presently holds.

65. These elements are detailed in ibid., pp. 185–98.

66. IMDEC 1999. IMDEC has also produced training materials for groups to use. See Bustillos and Vargas 1988; Ponce et al. 1997.

67. "Una gama de criterios y de valores que puestos en juego permanente con el contexto y su dinámica cambiante día a día, establezcan, revaloricen y/o modifiquen las normas de comportamiento individual y social, manteniendo siempre el principio fundamental de poner al hombre y a la mujer en el centro del accionar social" (Núñez Hurtado 1998, p. 156).

68. All the names of the actors in this section are fictitious.

69. Father Tacho has participated in several IMDOSOC training courses in Mexico City as a representative of the Archdiocese of Guadalajara. During the meetings I attended where he was present, he used various resources from IMDOSOC, including educational games.

70. For discussions of the rural restructuring process in Mexico and its consequences for migration and poverty, see Delaunay 1999; Szasz Pianta 1993; and the essays in Cornelius and Myhre 1998. Specific problems related to the state of Jalisco and the metropolitan area of Guadalajara are discussed in Vázquez Rangel and Ramírez López 1995, pp. 177–89.

71. My research plan had called for living in the colonia, but after living a few days with a family, I realized that I would be more of a burden than a help to a family of poor means. The primary issues related to access to potable water and electricity for my computer. The local water needed to be decontaminated. My solution was to live in a Jesuit residence and commute to my research site, as I did in the United States.

72. *Ejido* property is land given by the federal government to indigenous people or to farmers. Much of Las Pintitas had been *ejido* property that was now being sold to the new urbano-campesinos settling in the colonia. However, selling such property requires extensive negotiation and agreement with the government, which provides the final deed of ownership. I accompanied Victor to two meetings to finalize his ownership of the property.

73. For a discussion of the role of the teacher as a community leader and model of *laicidad* in Mexico's public education system, see the essays in Loyo 1985.

74. Durkheim 1912, p. 251.

75. "Intrafamily violence" is similar to the American concept of domestic violence but expands the concepts to extended family households. The citizen initiative received attention in the Guadalajara press. See René de Dios 1999.

76. "Conjunto de significaciones sociales que permite y hace presente algo que no es, pero que en tanto futuro deseable es, y da sentido al discurso, a la acción y a las prácticas sociales, a la vez permite definir estrategias y prorizar relaciones" (Robles Gil 1998, p. 65).

77. For a complete description of Mexican *compadrazgo,* see the anthropological study of Hugo Nutini and his colleagues: Nutini 1984.

78. For further discussion of Mexican Civic Catholicism, see chap. 9 of Forment's anthropological study: Forment 2003, pp. 192–215.

79. For a discussion of prototypical Mexican political culture and its problems, particularly the challenges facing a true political transition, see Bartra 1996.

80. The notion of *senti-pensamiento* comes from Uruguayan writer Eduardo Galeano, who has resided in Mexico City over the past several years. He is a regular contributor to *La Jornada,* the leading progressive newspaper in Mexico.

81. "Por esto podemos pensar que el desarrollo del concepto de 'inteligencia sentiente' (únicamente conscipiente) . . . puede ofrecernos el fundamento para el desarrollo de otros aspectos más humanos de la cultura en los que los latinoamericanos podemos alcanzar altos niveles de adelanto. Por ejemplo, en lo estético, la capacidad imaginativa de nuestros novelistas y poetas ha roto la barrera de la dependencia literaria y del subdesarrollo. Si bien en el plano tecnológico y del 'know-how' vivimos un secular atraso fruto, entre otras cosas, de la extracción de nuestra riqueza, ello no quiere decir que lo mismo suceda en el nivel de la cultura artística o humanista" (Fernández 2000).

82. Núñez Hurtado 1998, pp. 293–96.

83. Octavio 1999.

84. The disillusionment can be measured to some degree if one looks at membership rosters of such groups as the Legionnaires of Christ and their lay component Regnum Christi, Opus Dei, IMDOSOC, Jesuit-affiliated human rights groups, and other kinds of social movements within the Mexican church. I could not find reliable statistics on how many Mexicans are involved in these organizations. But even if small (100,000 or so), this is an important sector of educated and committed members whom the Church is not wise to ignore.

85. Gramsci 1957.

86. Centro Mexicano para la Filantropía and Villalobos Grzybowicz 1998.

87. As a kind of clearinghouse for *asociaciones civiles,* CEMEFI is equivalent to the United Way in Mexico. CEMEFI was responsible for bringing together the leadership of more than fifty key Mexican civil associations to help president-elect Vicente Fox create a civic agenda for his presidency. See Ballinas 2000.

88. The founder of CEMEFI, Manuel Arango Arias, spoke to this issue at a conference entitled "La Revolución Ética en Acción" (The Ethical Revolution in Action) in May 1998. See Arango Arias 1998.

89. The English translation of this book has been published as *Amador;* see Savater 1994.

90. Statistics compiled from Bunson 1999, pp. 448–54, 478–79.

91. In fact, the directors of IMDEC, IMDOSOC, CEMEFI, and DEMOS at the time of my study were all former priests or seminarians.

92. Carta Paramétrica 2005.

93. This is terminology coined by Jesuit German theologian Karl Rahner.

94. For a discussion of the new ecclesial communities in Latin America and their effects on national churches, see Soneira and CEIL/CONICET 2002.

95. I was able to observe the development and execution of two *fiestas patro-nales*—one in Las Pintitas and the other in Uruapán—during the time of my research. Both were weeklong events organized by a committee of local business leaders who raised money to cover the costs for musicians, food, and decorations. A band can cost U.S. $5,000 for a week of music.
96. Bartra 1992.
97. Paz 1993.
98. The first Mexican hometown association in the United States was founded in 1965 in Los Angeles. The movement has grown particularly as migra-tion has become city and state specific for Mexican émigrés, such as people from Michoacán and Zacatecas moving to Illinois or Mixtecs from Oaxaca moving to Los Angeles. See Sullivan 2000; Velasco Ortiz 2005.
99. Catholic Church 2004, 3.3.
100. For both scholarly and journalistic descriptions of some of the new eccle-sial movements—particularly the Legionnaires of Christ and their lay movement Regnum Christi, Opus Dei, Focolare, the Neo-Catechumenate, and Communion and Liberation—and their influence upon the neocon-servative trends within the Catholic Church, see Allen 2005; Soneira and CEIL/CONICET 2002; Torres Robles 2001; Urquhart 1999; Urquhart and Catholics for a Free Choice 1997.

Chapter Five

1. Burghardt 1996.
2. Catholic Church, Congregatio pro Doctrina Fidei 2002, 2.2.
3. Pontifical Council for Justice and Peace 2005.
4. For example, both the Vatican and the U.S. Conference of Catholic Bish-ops has mounted campaigns against the legalization of homosexual unions: Catholic Church, Congregatio pro Doctrina Fidei 2003; United States Conference of Catholic Bishops 2003.
5. The 2004 victory of George W. Bush was significant for the Catholic Church because this was the first presidential election since exit polling in which a Republican presidential candidate captured more than 50 per-cent of the Catholic vote. According to *New York Times* exit polling, Bush won 52 percent of the Catholic vote—56 percent of white Catholics and 39 percent of Hispanic Catholics voted for him. This shift is attributed to the ability of the Republican Party to energize Catholics regarding pro-life issues while neglecting other social concerns related to the economy, education, housing, etc. See Davidson 2004; Filteau 2005.
6. Massachusetts was a primary site of the new neoconservative Catho-lic-Protestant partnership that developed to combat the right for homo-sexuals to marry. Members of the Coalition for Marriage included Mas-sachusetts Family Institute, Catholic Citizenship, Focus on the Family, Family Research Council, Alliance Defense Fund, Massachusetts Catho-

lic Conference, Massachusetts Knights of Columbus, Mass Citizens for Life. Traditional Values Coalition, and Catholic Action League. See www .preservemarriage.org/about_us.htm. In 2004 similar coalitions were formed in Arkansas, Georgia, Kentucky, Michigan, Mississippi, Montana, North Dakota, Oklahoma, Ohio, Oregon, and Utah. In all eleven of these states, voter initiatives against gay rights for marriage passed and helped in the reelection campaign of President George Bush. See Associated Press 2004.

7. For a detailed account of the Vatican's involvement in the diplomatic processes related to the Iraq war and the U.S. bishops' mild response to the U.S. invasion, see Allen 2004, pp. 313–78.

8. Committee on Women in Society and the Church 1994.

9. Palacios 2001.

10. Wood 2002; Dillon 1999; Greeley 2000.

11. For key trends in the development of leadership personnel in the U.S. and Mexican churches, see Bunson 1999; Camp 1997; Froehle, Gautier, and Center for Applied Research in the Apostolate (U.S.) 2000.

12. Studies examining the impact on parish life of mobility in the United States include Ammerman et al. 1997 and Dolan 1989. The study of parish life in Mexico has not developed as it has in the United States. I could not find a single published study on the relationship of parish life and lay development in Mexico.

13. The exception to this attitude can be seen in the Church's role in Chiapas, especially that played by Bishop Samuel Ruiz. See Tangeman 1995; Tello Diaz 1995.

14. Salt of the Earth News 2002.

15. For example, conservatives such as George Weigel of the Ethics and Public Policy Center in Washington, D.C., and the Rev. Richard John Neuhaus of *First Things* and progressives such as Sister Helen Prejean of the anti–death penalty movement and members of the Catholic Workers all easily move within U.S. civil society as public Catholics, using a similar "cultural toolkit" to leverage their citizen capacity, inspired by Catholic social justice teaching, to effect political change. Of course, what makes these actors different is what they choose from the menu of social justice teaching to emphasize for specific social issues.

16. Tocqueville 1995.

17. While the clergy sexual abuse crisis is an ongoing problem and story, the following accounts of the crisis have addressed the causes of the crisis and proposed solutions: Oakley and Russett 2004, pp. 136–52; Allen 2004, pp. 224–312; P. Steinfels 2003, pp. 40–67.

18. As the Church entered the new millennium several Catholic essayists have written reflections of the future of the Catholic Church: Wills 2000; Oakley and Russett 2004; P. Steinfels 2003; M. Steinfels 2004; Gibson 2003.

BIBLIOGRAPHY

Abbott, Walter M. 1966. *The Documents of Vatican II.* New York: Guild.

Abeloe, William N. 1972. "St. Anthony's Yesterday and Today." Oakland, CA: St. Anthony Catholic Parish.

Agencias Mexicanas. 2000. "La iglesia mexicana también pide perdón por sus errores." *Público* (Guadalajara), 25 March, Internet edition.

Aguirre, Alejandrina. 1999. "Las pugnas secretas de la iglesia mexicana." *Contenido,* May, pp. 48–53.

Ahlstrom, Sydney E. 1972. *A Religious History of the American People.* New Haven, CT: Yale University Press.

Alinsky, Saul D. 1989a. *Reveille for Radicals.* New York: Vintage.

———. 1989b. *Rules for Radicals: A Pragmatic Primer for Realistic Radicals.* New York: Vintage.

Alisedo, Pedro J. 1999. "Adiós a Samuel Ruiz: La diócesis indómita." *Proceso,* special ed. no. 4 (27 October): 4–64.

Allen, John L. 2000. *Cardinal Ratzinger: The Vatican's Enforcer of the Faith.* New York: Continuum.

———. 2004. *All the Pope's Men: The Inside Story of How the Vatican Really Thinks.* New York: Doubleday.

———. 2005. *Opus Dei: The First Objective Look behind the Myths and Reality of the Most Controversial Force in the Catholic Church.* New York: Doubleday.

Almeyra, Guillermo. 2000. "La artritis ideológica." *La Jornada* (Mexico City), 26 March, available at www.jornada.unam.mx/2000/03/26/almeyra.html.

Alonso, Arthur. 1961. *Catholic Action and the Laity.* St. Louis, MO: B. Herder.

Alonso, Rubén. 2000. "La agenda de la iglesia." *Público* (Guadalajara), 2 April, Internet edition.

Ammerman, Nancy Tatom, Arthur E. Farnsley II, Tammy Adams, Penny Edgell Becker, and Brenda Brasher. 1997. *Congregation and Community.* New Brunswick, NJ: Rutgers University Press.

Anaya, Ricardo B., and Acción Católica Mexicana. 1987. *Doctrina social de la iglesia y apostolado seglar.* Mexico City: Librería Parroquial de Clavería.

Anderson, George M. 1995. "The Campaign for Human Development's Twenty-fifth Anniversary." *America* 173, no. 8 (23 September): 6.

Arango Arias, Manuel. 1998. *La ética de la responsibildad social.* Mexico City: Centro Mexicano para la Filantropía.

Aron, Raymond. 1970. *Main Currents in Sociological Thought: Durkheim, Pareto, Weber.* New York: Doubleday Anchor.

Associated Press. 2004. "Voters Pass All Eleven Bans on Gay Marriage: Ballot Initiatives Pave the Way for New Court Battles." MSNBC, www.msnbc .msn.com/id/6383353/ (accessed 3 November).

Athié Gallo, Alberto. 1993. *El Tratado de Libre Comercio: A la luz de la opción cultural propuesta por la doctrina social de la iglesia.* Mexico City: Instituto Mexicano de Doctrina Social Cristiana.

Bakhurst, David. 1993. "Ideology." In *A Companion to Epistemology,* edited by Jonathan Dancy and Ernest Sosa. Cambridge, MA: Blackwell.

Ballinas, Víctor. 2000. "Critican ONG de exclusión en el diseño de programas para la niñez." *La Jornada* (Mexico City), 3 November, available at www .jornada.unam.mx/2000/11/03/037nlsoc.html.

Bartra, Roger. 1982a. *Campesinado y poder político en México.* Mexico City: Ediciones Era.

——— 1982b. *El reto de la izquierda.* México: Grijalba.

———. 1987. *La jaula de la melancolía: Identidad y metamórfosís del mexicano.* Mexico City: Grijalbo.

———. 1992. *The Cage of Melancholy: Identity and Metamorphosis in the Mexican Character.* Translated by Christopher J. Hall. New Brunswick, NJ: Rutgers University Press.

———. 1993. *Oficio mexicano.* Mexico City: Grijalbo.

———. 1996. *Las redes imaginarias del poder político.* Mexico City: Océano.

Basave Fernández del Valle, Agustín. 1990. *Vocación y estilo de México: Fundamentos de la mexicanidad.* Mexico City: Noriega Editores.

Bell, Catherine. 1992. *Ritual Theory, Ritual Practice.* New York: Oxford University Press.

Bellah, Robert N., Richard Madsen, William M. Sullivan, Ann Swidler, and Steven M. Tipton. 1985. *Habits of the Heart.* Berkeley: University of California Press.

Berger, Peter L., and Thomas Luckmann. 1966. *The Social Construction of Reality.* New York: Doubleday.

Bernadicou, Paul. 1996. "The Jesuit Volunteer Corps at Forty." *America* 175, no. 7 (21 September): 15–17.

Berrigan, Daniel, and Robert Coles. 2001. *The Geography of Faith: Underground Conversations on Religious, Political, and Social Change.* Woodstock, VT: Skylight Paths.

Berrigan, Daniel, and Hòanh Nhââat. 1973. *Contemplation and Resistance.* Nyack, NY: Hoa Binh.

Bidegaín de Urán, Ana María. 1985. *From Catholic Action to Liberation Theology: The Historical Process of the Laity in Latin America in the Twentieth Century.* Notre Dame, IN: Helen Kellogg Institute for International Studies.

Bilello, Suzanne. 1996. "Mexico: The Rise of Civil Society." *Current History* 95, no. 598 (February): 82–87.

Bilgrien, Marie Vianney. 1999. *Solidarity: A Principle, an Attitude, a Duty, or the Virtue for an Interdependent World?* New York: Peter Lang.

Blancarte, Roberto. 1991. *El poder salinismo e iglesia católica: ¿Una nueva convivencia?* Mexico City: Grijalbo.

———. 1992. *Historia de la iglesia católica en México.* México: Colegio Mexiquense, Fondo de Cultura Económica.

———. 1993. "Cristianismo y mundo moderno: Una relación ambigua." In *Problemas sociorreligiosos en Centroamérica y México,* edited by Rodolfo Casillas R., pp. 35–49. Mexico City: Facultad Latinoamericana de Ciencias Sociales.

———. 1994a. *Cultura e identidad nacional.* Mexico City: Consejo Nacional para la Cultura y las Artes, Fondo de Cultura Económica.

———. 1994b. *Iglesia y estado en México: Seis décadas de acomodo y de conciliación imposible.* Mexico City: Instituto Mexicano de Doctrina Social Cristiana.

———. 1995a. "La doctrina social católica ante la democracia moderna." In *Religión, iglesias y democracia,* edited by Roberto Blancarte, pp. 19–58. Mexico City: La Jornada, Centro de Investigaciones Interdisciplinarias en Humanidades, Universidad Nacional Autónoma de México (UNAM).

———, ed. 1995b. *Religión, iglesias y democracia.* Mexico City: Jornada Ediciones, Centro de Investigaciones Interdisciplinarias en Humanidades, UNAM.

———. 1996. *El pensamiento social de los católicos mexicanos.* Mexico City: Fondo de Cultura Económica.

———. 2000. "El catolicismo social en el desarrollo del conflicto entre la iglesia y el estado en el siglo XX." In *Catolicismo social en México: Teoría, fuentes e historiografía,* edited by Ramírez Ceballos and Alejandro Garza Rangel, pp. 287–311. Monterrey, México: Academia de Investigación Humanística, A.C.

Block, Walter. 1986. *The U.S. Bishops and Their Critics: An Economic and Ethical Perspective.* Vancouver, BC: Fraser Institute.

Boileau, David A. 1998. *Principles of Catholic Social Teaching.* Milwaukee, WI: Marquette University Press.

Bole, William. 1997. "Labor Movement and American Catholics." In *The Encyclopedia of American Catholic History,* edited by Michael Glazier and Thomas J. Shelley. Collegeville, MN: Liturgical.

Bourdieu, Pierre. 1990. *The Logic of Practice.* Stanford, CA: Stanford University Press.

Braun, Herbert. 1997. "Protests of Engagement: Dignity, False Love, and Self-Love in Mexico during 1968." *Comparative Studies in Society and History* 39, no. 3 (July): 511–59.

Briseño Chávez, Pedro. 1993. *Doctrina social cristiana, la cultura y los medios de comunicación masiva.* Mexico City: Instituto Mexicano de Doctrina Social Cristiana.

Brown, Richard Harvey. 1989. *Social Science as Civic Discourse: Essays on the Invention, Legitimation, and Uses of Social Theory.* Chicago: University of Chicago Press.

Brown, Robert McAfee. 1986. "Reinhold Niebuhr: His Theology in the 1980's." *Christian Century* 103, no. 3 (22 January): 66–68.

Bunson, Matthew, ed. 1999. *2000 Catholic Almanac.* Huntington, IN: Our Sunday Visitor.

Burghardt, Walter J. 1996. *Preaching the Just Word.* New Haven, CT: Yale University Press.

Bustillos, Graciela, and Laura Vargas. 1988. *Técnicas participativas para la educación popular.* Guadalajara, Jalisco, MX: IMDEC.

Byrnes, Timothy A. 1991. *Catholic Bishops in American Politics.* Princeton, NJ: Princeton University Press.

Byron, William J. 1989. "Empowerment and Progress in the Campaign for Human Development." *America* 160, no. 14 (15 April): 350.

———. 1998. "Ten Building Blocks of Catholic Social Justice Teaching." *America* 179, no. 13 (31 October): 9–12.

Calpotura, Francis. 1998. "Campaign for Human Development Dictates Right Turn to Community Organizers." *ColorLines* (Oakland, CA) 1, no. 2 (Fall), available at www.arc.org/C-Lines/CLArchive/CL1_2.html#issue.

Calhoun, Craig J. 1994. *Social Theory and the Politics of Identity.* Cambridge, MA: Blackwell.

Camp, Roderic Ai. 1997. *Crossing Swords: Politics and Religion in Mexico.* New York: Oxford University Press.

———. 1998. *Cruce de espadas: Política y religión en México.* Mexico City: Siglo Veintiuno Editores.

Capseta Castellá, Joan. 1997. *Personalidad jurídica y régimen patrimonial de las asociaciones religiosas en México.* Mexico City: Instituto Mexicano de Doctrina Social Cristiana.

Carta Paramétrica. 2005. "Confianza en instituciones." Mexico City: Carta Paramétrica.

Casaldaliga, Pedro, and Jose-Maria Vigil. 1994. *Political Holiness: A Spirituality of Liberation.* Maryknoll, NY: Orbis.

Casanova, José. 1994. *Public Religions in the Modern World.* Chicago: University of Chicago Press.

Catholic Church, Conferencia del Episcopado Mexicano. 2000. *Del encuentro*

con Jesucristo a la solidaridad con todos. Mexico City: Conferencia del Episcopado Mexicano, Ediciones de la CEM.

———. 2004. *The Eucharist, Light and Life of the New Millennium.* Guadalajara, Jalisco, MX: Conferencia del Episcopado Mexicano. Available at www
.congresoeucaristico.org/en/Index.html.

Catholic Church, Congregatio pro Doctrina Fidei. 2002. "Doctrinal Note on
Some Questions regarding the Participation of Catholics in Political Life."
Vatican City: Congregation for the Doctrine of the Faith.

———. 2003. "Considerations regarding Proposals to Give Legal Recognition
to Unions between Homosexual Persons." Vatican City: Congregation for
the Doctrine of the Faith.

Centro Mexicano para la Filantropía and Jorge Villalobos Grzybowicz, eds.
1998. *Directorio de Instituciones Filantrópicas.* 3rd ed. Mexico City: Centro
Mexicano para la Filantropía.

Civardi, Luigi, and Cyril Charlie Martindale. 1943. *A Manual of Catholic Action.* New York: Sheed and Ward.

Cohen, Jean L., and Andrew Arato. 1992. *Civil Society and Political Theory.*
Cambridge, MA: MIT Press.

Coleman, John A. 1982. *An American Strategic Theology.* Ramsey, NJ: Paulist.

———. 1991a. "Neither Liberal Nor Socialist: The Originality of Catholic Social Teaching." In *One Hundred Years of Catholic Social Thought,* edited by
John A. Coleman. Maryknoll, NY: Orbis.

———, ed. 1991b. *One Hundred Years of Catholic Social Thought: Celebration
and Challenge.* Maryknoll, NY: Orbis.

———. 1998. "Religion and Public Life: Some American Cases." *Religion,*
p. 155.

Concha, Miguel. 1999. "Semana Social Nacional." *La Jornada* (Mexico City),
3 November, available at www.jornada.unam.mx/1999/11/03/Concha.html.

Connolly, William J., and Philip S. Land. 1977. *Jesuit Spiritualities and the
Struggle for Social Justice.* St. Louis, MO: American Assistancy Seminar on
Jesuit Spirituality.

Cornelius, Wayne A., and David Myhre, eds. 1998. *The Transformation of Rural Mexico: Reforming the Ejido Sector.* La Jolla: Center for U.S.-Mexican
Studies, University of California at San Diego.

Corro, Salvador. 2000. "El sucesor de Samuel Ruiz se compromete: No vengo a
destruir, sino a complementar." *Proceso,* no. 1222 (1 April).

Cuneo, Michael W. 1989. *Catholics against the Church: Anti-abortion Protest in
Toronto, 1969–1985.* Toronto: University of Toronto Press.

Curran, Charles E. 1982. *American Catholic Social Ethics: Twentieth-century
Approaches.* Notre Dame, IN: University of Notre Dame Press.

———. 1990. "The Teaching Function of the Church." In *Moral Theology:
Challenges for the Future,* edited by Charles E. Curran. New York: Paulist.

———. 2002. *Catholic Social Teaching, 1891–Present: A Historical, Theological, and Ethical Analysis.* Washington, DC: Georgetown University Press.

———. 2005. *The Moral Theology of Pope John Paul II.* Washington, DC: Georgetown University Press.

Curran, Charles E., and Richard A. McCormick, eds. 1999. *The Historical Development of Fundamental Moral Theology in the United States.* New York: Paulist.

Curtis, Richard. 1974. *The Berrigan Brothers: The Story of Daniel and Philip Berrigan.* New York: Hawthorn.

Dalton, Frederick John. 2003. *The Moral Vision of Cesar Chavez.* Maryknoll, NY: Orbis.

Davidson, James D. 2004. "Red States, Blue States: It's about Religion." *Tidings* (Los Angeles), 12 November, available at www.the-tidings.com/2004/1112/Signs_text.htm.

Day, Mark. 1971. *Forty Acres: Cesar Chavez and the Farm Workers.* New York: Praeger.

Delaunay, Daniel. 1999. "La dimensión regional de la emigración mexicana hacia Estados Unidos." *Estudios Demográficos y Urbanos* 14:117–64.

Dillon, Michele. 1993. "Argumentative Complexity of Abortion Discourse." *Public Opinion Quarterly* 57, no. 305–14.

———. 1999. *Catholic Identity: Balancing Reason, Faith, and Power.* New York: Cambridge University Press.

Dolan, Jay P. 1983. *The Immigrant Church: New York's Irish and German Catholics, 1815–1865.* Notre Dame, IN: University of Notre Dame Press.

———. 1985. *The American Catholic Experience: A Social History from Colonial Times to the Present.* Garden City, NY: Doubleday.

———. 1987. *The American Catholic Parish: A History from 1850 to the Present.* New York: Paulist.

———. 1989. *Transforming Parish Ministry: The Changing Roles of Catholic Clergy, Laity, and Women Religious.* New York: Crossroad.

———. 1992. *The American Catholic Experience: A History from Colonial Times to the Present.* Notre Dame, IN: University of Notre Dame Press.

Dolan, Jay P., and Gilberto Miguel Hinojosa. 1994. *Mexican Americans and the Catholic Church, 1900–1965.* Notre Dame, IN: University of Notre Dame Press.

Donohue, John R. 1977. "Biblical Perspectives on Justice." In *The Faith That Does Justice: Examining the Christian Sources for Social Change,* edited by John C. Haughey, pp. 68–112. New York: Paulist.

Dorr, Donal. 1991. *The Social Justice Agenda: Justice, Ecology, Power, and the Church.* Maryknoll, NY: Orbis.

Douglas, Mary. 1973. *Natural Symbols.* New York: Random House.

Douglass, R. Bruce. 1986. *The Deeper Meaning of Economic Life: Critical Essays on the U.S. Catholic Bishops' Pastoral Letter on the Economy.* Washington, DC: Georgetown University Press.

Drinan, Robert F. 2000. "Zeal to End Death Penalty Growing." *National Catholic Reporter* 36, no. 32 (16 June): 18.

Dulles, Avery. 2000. "The Papacy for a Global Church." *America* 183, no. 2 (15 July): 6.

Dunne, John Gregory. 1971. *Delano.* New York: Farrar, Straus, and Giroux.

Durkheim, Émile. 1912. *The Elementary Forms of Religious Life.* Translated by Karen E. Fields. New York: Free Press.

———. 1973. *On Morality and Society: Selected Writings.* Edited by Robert N. Bellah, translated by Mark Traugott. Chicago: University of Chicago Press.

———. 1984. *The Division of Labor in Society.* Translated by W. D. Halls. New York: Free Press.

———. 1986. *Durkheim on Politics and the State.* Edited by Anthony Giddens, translated by W. D. Halls. Stanford, CA: Stanford University Press.

Dussel, Enrique. 1981. *A History of the Church in Latin America: Colonialism to Liberation, 1492-1979.* Grand Rapids, MI: Eerdmans.

———, ed. 1984. *Historia general de la iglesia en América Latina,* vol. 5, *México.* Mexico City: Ediciones Paulinas.

———. 1995. "La iglesia en el proceso de la organización nacional y de los estados en América Latina, 1830-1880." In *Estado, iglesia y sociedad en México, siglo XIX,* edited by Álvaro Matute, Evelia Trejo, and Brian Connaughton, pp. 63-80. Mexico City: Miguel Angel Porrua Grupo Editorial.

Eagleson, John, and Philip J. Scharper. 1979. *Puebla and Beyond: Documentation and Commentary.* Maryknoll, NY: Orbis.

Elizondo, Virgilio P. 1981. *La Morenita, evangelizadora de las Américas.* Liguori, MO: Liguori.

———. 1997. *Guadalupe, Mother of the New Creation.* Maryknoll, NY: Orbis.

Ellacuría, Ignacio. 1975. *Liberación: Misión y carisma de la iglesia latinoamericana.* Lima: Movimiento Internacional de Estudiantes Católicos and Juventud Estudiantil Católica Internacional, Secretariado Latinoamericano.

———. 1993. "Utopia and Prophecy in Latin America." In *Mysterium Liberationis: Fundamental Concepts of Liberation Theology,* edited by Ignacio Ellacuria and Jon Sobrino, pp. 289-327. Maryknoll, NY: Orbis.

Ellacuría, Ignacio, and Jon Sobrino. 1993. *Mysterium Liberationis: Fundamental Concepts of Liberation Theology.* Maryknoll, NY: Orbis.

Engel, Lawrence J. 1998. "The Influence of Saul Alinsky on the Campaign For Human Development." *Theological Studies* 59, no. 4 (December): 636.

Espinosa, Gastón, Virgilio P. Elizondo, and Jesse Miranda. 2005. *Latino Religions and Civic Activism in the United States.* New York: Oxford University Press.

Fernández, David. 2000. *Nuevos paradigmas para una educación humanista.* Tlaquepaque, Jalisco, MX: Instituto Tecnológico de Estudios Superiories de Occidente (ITESO).

Filteau, Jerry. 2005. "Catholic Polarization Reached New Peak in 2004 Election, Speaker Says." Catholic News Service, Washington, DC, 22 February.

Finn, James. 1990. *Private Virtue and Public Policy: Catholic Thought and National Life.* New Brunswick, NJ: Transaction.

Flannery, Austin, ed. 1992. *Vatican Council I: The Conciliar and Post Conciliar Documents.* Collegeville, MN: Liturgical.

Forest, James H. 1994. *Love Is the Measure: A Biography of Dorothy Day.* Maryknoll, NY: Orbis.

———. 1997. "The Catholic Worker Movement." In *The Encyclopedia of American Catholic History,* edited by Michael Glazier and Thomas J. Shelley, pp. 310–12. Collegeville, MN: Liturgical.

Forment, Carlos A. 2003. *Democracy in Latin America, 1760–1900.* Chicago: University of Chicago Press.

Formicola, Jo Renee, Mary C. Segers, and Paul J. Weber. 2003. *Faith-Based Initiatives and the Bush Administration: The Good, the Bad, and the Ugly.* Lanham, MD: Rowman and Littlefield.

Fox, Jonathan. 1996. "How Does Civil Society Thicken? The Political Construction of Social Capital in Rural Mexico." *World Development* 24, no. 6 (June): 1089–1103.

Fox Quesada, Vicente. 1999. *A Los Pinos: Recuento autobiográfico y político.* Mexico City: Océano.

———. 2000. "Comparté el poder y las responsibilidades." *Milenio* (Mexico City), 2 December, special insert.

Freire, Paulo. 1970. *Pedagogy of the Oppressed.* New York: Herder and Herder.

Froehle, Bryan, Mary L. Gautier, and Center for Applied Research in the Apostolate (U.S.). 2000. *Catholicism USA: A Portrait of the Catholic Church in the United States.* Maryknoll, NY: Orbis.

Gannon, Thomas M. 1987. *The Catholic Challenge to the American Economy.* New York: Macmillan.

García Canclini, Nestor. 1990. *Culturas híbridas: Estrategias para entrar y salir de la modernidad.* Mexico City: Grijalbo.

García Ugarte, Marta Eugenia. 1993a. "Iglesia y modernidad: Las trampas de la historia." In *Problemas sociorreligiosos en Centroamerica y Mexico,* edited by Rodolfo Casillas R., pp. 51–58. Mexico City: Facultad Latinoamericana de Ciencias Sociales.

———. 1993b. *La nueva relación iglesia-estado en México: Un análisis de la problemática actual.* Mexico City: Nueva Imagen.

Garrett, William Reace, ed. 1989. *Social Consequences of Religious Belief.* New York: Paragon.

Garza, Rodolfo O. de la, Louis DeSipio, F. Chris Garcia, John Garcia, and

Angelo Falcon. 1992. *Latino Voices: Mexican, Puerto Rican, and Cuban Perspectives on American Politics.* Boulder, CO: Westview.

Gibson, David. 2003. *The Coming Catholic Church : How the Faithful Are Shaping a New American Catholicism.* San Francisco: HarperSanFrancisco.

Gillis, Chester. 1999. *Roman Catholicism in America.* New York: Columbia University Press.

Ginsburg, Faye D. 1998. *Contested Lives: The Abortion Debate in an American Community.* Berkeley: University of California Press.

Goddard, Jorge Adame. 1994. *Influjo de la doctrina social católica en el artículo 123 constitucional.* Mexico City: Instituto Mexicano de Doctrina Social Cristiana.

Gómez-Pérez, Luis Ramos. 1997. "Escuela católica y sociedad a principios del siglo XX." In *La iglesia católica en México,* edited by Nelly Siguat, pp. 293–306. Zamora, Michoacán: Colegio de Michoacán.

Gómez Quiñones, Juan. 1990. *Chicano Politics: Reality and Promise, 1940–1990.* Albuquerque: University of New Mexico Press.

González, Gustavo R. 1999. "No usé la imagen de la Virgen para atraer gente." *Excelsior* (Mexico City), 13 September, Internet edition.

Gramsci, Antonio. 1957. *The Modern Prince and Other Writings.* New York: International.

Gramsci, Antonio. 1972. *Selections from the Prison Notebooks of Antonio Gramsci.* Edited and translated by Quintin Hoare and Geoffrey Nowell-Smith. New York: International.

Greeley, Andrew M. 1977. *The American Catholic: A Social Portrait.* New York: Basic Books.

———. 1981. *The Religious Imagination.* Los Angeles: Sadlier.

———. 1991. *The Catholic Myth: The Behavior and Beliefs of American Catholics.* New York: Collier.

———. 2000. *The Catholic Imagination.* Berkeley: University of California Press.

Gremillion, Joseph. 1976. *The Gospel of Peace and Justice: Catholic Social Teaching since Pope John.* Maryknoll, NY: Orbis.

Griswold del Castillo, Richard, and Richard A. Garcia. 1995. *César Chávez: A Triumph of Spirit.* Norman: University of Oklahoma Press.

Guerrero, Andrés G. 1987. *A Chicano Theology.* Maryknoll, NY: Orbis.

Gutiérrez, Gustavo. 1973. *A Theology of Liberation: History, Politics, and Salvation.* Maryknoll, NY: Orbis.

Habermas, Jürgen. 1984. *The Theory of Communicative Action.* Translated by Thomas McCarthy. Boston: Beacon.

———. 1987. *The Philosophical Discourse of Modernity: Twelve Lectures.* Translated by Frederick Lawrence. Cambridge, MA: MIT Press.

———. 1990. *Moral Consciousness and Communicative Action.* Translated by Christian Lenhardt and Shierry Weber. Cambridge, MA: MIT Press.

Hacala, Joseph R. 1995. "Working with the Poor." *America* 173, no. 17 (25 November): 20–21.

Haight, Roger. 1985. *An Alternative Vision: An Interpretation of Liberation Theology.* New York: Paulist.

Hannafey, Francis T. 1993. "The Principle of Participation in Economic Justice for All: Catholic Social Teaching and the U.S. Economy." Master's thesis, Jesuit School of Theology at Berkeley, CA.

Haughey, John C., ed. 1977. *The Faith That Does Justice: Examining the Christian Sources for Social Change.* New York: Paulist.

Haughton, Rosemary, and Mary E. Stamps. 1993. *To Do Justice and Right upon the Earth: Papers from the Virgil Michel Symposium on Liturgy and Social Justice.* Collegeville, MN: Liturgical.

Hehir, J. Bryan. 1986. "A Public Theologian." *Christianity and Crisis* 46:39–41.

Henriot, Peter J., Edward P. DeBerri, and Michael J. Schultheis, eds. 1999. *Catholic Social Teaching: Our Best Kept Secret.* 3rd revised and expanded ed. Maryknoll, NY: Orbis.

Higgins, George, and William Bole. 1993. *Organized Labor and the Church: Reflections of a "Labor Priest."* New York: Paulist.

Hodge, James, and Linda Cooper. 2004. *Disturbing the Peace: The Story of Roy Bourgeois and the Movement to Close the School of the Americas.* Maryknoll, NY: Orbis.

Holland, Joe, and Peter J. Henriot. 1983. *Social Analysis: Linking Faith and Justice.* Maryknoll, NY: Orbis.

Hollenbach, David. 1977. "Modern Catholic Teachings concerning Justice." In *The Faith That Does Justice,* edited by John C. Haughey, pp. 234–63. New York: Paulist.

———. 1979. *Claims in Conflict: Retrieving and Renewing the Catholic Human Rights Tradition.* New York: Paulist.

———. 1988. *Justice, Peace, and Human Rights: American Catholic Social Ethics in a Pluralistic World.* New York: Crossroad.

———. 1994–95. "Civil Society: Beyond the Public-Private Dichotomy." *Responsive Community* 5:15–23.

Hurtado, Aida, David E. Hayes-Bautista, R. Burciaga Valdez, and Anthony C. R. Hernandez. 1992. *Redefining California: Latino Social Engagement in a Multicultural Society.* Los Angeles: University of California at Los Angeles Chicano Studies Research Center.

IMDEC. 1999. *Memoria: Escuela Metodológica Nacional, Ciclo 1999.* 4 vols. Guadalajara, Jalisco, MX: Instituto Mexicano de Desarrollo Comunitario.

Instituto Mexicano de Doctrina Social Cristiana (IMDOSOC). 1989. *Manual de doctrina social cristiana.* Mexico City: IMDOSOC.

Iriarte, Gregorio. 1995. *Ética social cristiana: Guía para la formación en los valores éticos.* Mexico City: Ediciones Dabar.

Jacobo M., Heriberto, ed. 1997. *Doctrina social de la iglesia: De Leon XIII a Juan Pablo II.* Mexico City: Ediciones Paulinas.

Jesuits, Congregatio Generalis. 1974–75. "Documents of the Thirty-second General Congregation of the Society of Jesus." Washington, DC: Jesuit Conference.

Jeung, Russell. 2005. *Faithful Generations: Race and New Asian American Churches.* New Brunswick, NJ: Rutgers University Press.

John Paul II. 1988. *Sollicitudo Rei Socialis (On Social Concern).* Washington, DC: United States Catholic Conference.

———. 1991. *Centesimus Annus (One Hundredth Year).* Vatican City: Libreria Editrice Vaticana.

———. 1993. *Veritatis Splendor (The Splendor of Truth).* Washington, DC: United States Catholic Conference.

———. 1999. *Eclesia en América (The Church in America).* Washington, DC: United States Catholic Conference.

———. 2000. "Universal Prayer: Confession of Sins and Asking Forgiveness." Zenit News Service.

John Paul II and Vittorio Messori. 1994. *Crossing the Threshold of Hope.* New York: Alfred A. Knopf.

Keck, Margaret E., and Kathryn Sikkink. 1998. *Activists beyond Boundaries.* Ithaca, NY: Cornell University Press.

Kettern, B. 1998. "Social Justice: The Development of the Concept 'iusticia' from St. Thomas Aquinas through the Social Encyclicals." In *Principles of Catholic Social Justice Teaching,* edited by David A. Boileau. Milwaukee, WI: Marquette University Press.

Knight, Alan. 1990. *State and Civil Society in Mexico since the Revolution.* Austin: Mexican Center Institute, Latin American Studies, University of Texas at Austin.

Lamb, Matthew L. 1982. *Solidarity with Victims: Towards a Theology of Social Transformation.* New York: Crossroad.

Lemert, Charles C. 2005. *Social Things: An Introduction to the Sociological Life.* Lanham, MD: Rowman and Littlefield.

Leñero Otero, Luis. 1999. "La familia en el siglo XXI: El caso de México." In *Perspectivas y prospectivas de la familia en América del Norte,* edited by Manuel Ribiero Ferreira and Raúl Eduardo López Estrada. Léon, Guanajuato, MX: Facultad de Trabajo Social, Universidad Autónoma de Nuevo León.

Levine, Daniel H. 1992. *Popular Voices in Latin American Catholicism.* Princeton, NJ: Princeton University Press.

Lloyd, David, and Paul Thomas. 1998. *Culture and the State.* New York: Routledge.

Loaeza, Guadalupe. 2000. "Granito de Arena." *Reforma* (Mexico City), 5 December, p. 17.

Loaeza, Soledad. 1999. *El Partido Acción Nacional, la larga marcha, 1939–1994: Oposición leal y partido de protesta.* Mexico City: Fondo de Cultura Económica.

Loyo, Engracia, ed. 1985. *La Casa del Pueblo y el maestro rural mexicano.* Mexico City: Secretaría de Educación Pública.

Lukes, Steven. 1985. *Emile Durkheim: His Life and Work.* Stanford, CA: Stanford University Press.

Mahoney, John. 1987. *The Making of Moral Theology: A Study of the Roman Catholic Tradition.* Oxford: Clarendon.

Malaguti, Raffaella. 2000. "Italy PM Says Rome Gay Pride Rally 'Inopportune.'" Reuters News Service, 24 May.

Massaro, Thomas. 1998. *Catholic Social Teaching and United States Welfare Reform.* Collegeville, MN: Liturgical.

———. 2000. *Living Justice: Catholic Social Teaching in Action.* Franklin, WI: Sheed and Ward.

Matthiessen, Peter. 2000. *Sal si puedes (Escape If You Can): Cesar Chavez and the New American Revolution.* Berkeley: University of California Press.

McAdam, Doug. 1982. *Political Process and the Development of Black Insurgency, 1930–1970.* Chicago: University of Chicago Press.

McAdam, Doug, John D. McCarthy, and Mayer N. Zald. 1996. *Comparative Perspectives on Social Movements: Political Opportunities, Mobilizing Structures, and Cultural Framings.* New York: Cambridge University Press.

McAdam, Doug, Charles Tilly, and Sidney G. Tarrow. 2001. *Dynamics of Contention.* New York: Cambridge University Press.

McAuliffe, Patricia. 1993. *Fundamental Ethics: A Liberationist Approach.* Washington, DC: Georgetown University Press.

McBrien, Richard P. 1994. *Catholicism.* San Francisco: HarperSanFrancisco.

McBrien, Richard P., and Harold W. Attridge. 1995. *The HarperCollins Encyclopedia of Catholicism.* New York: HarperCollins.

McConahay, Mary Jo. 1996. "Latino Evangelicos This Year's Wild Card." *National Catholic Reporter* 32, no. 43 (11 October): 7.

McGreevy, John T. 2003. *Catholicism and American Freedom: A History.* New York: W. W. Norton.

Merkle, Judith A. 1994. "Sin." In *The New Dictionary of Catholic Social Thought,* edited by Judith A. Dwyer, pp. 883–88. Collegeville, MN: Liturgical.

Meyer, Jean A. 1976. *The Cristero Rebellion: The Mexican People between Church and State, 1926–1929.* New York: Cambridge University Press.

Michonneau, Georges, and R. Meurice. 1955. *Catholic Action and the Parish.* Westminster, MD: Newman.

Miller, David. *Principles of Social Justice.* Cambridge, MA: Harvard University Press, 1999.

Mills, C. Wright. 1959. *The Sociological Imagination.* New York: Oxford University Press.

Morales, Isidro, Guillermo de los Reyes, Paul B. Rich, and American Academy of Political and Social Science. 1999. *Civil Society and Democratization.* Thousand Oaks, CA: Sage Periodicals.

Morris, Aldon D. 1984. *The Origins of the Civil Rights Movement: Black Communities Organizing for Social Change.* New York: Free Press.

Morris, Aldon D., and Carol McClurg Mueller. 1992. *Frontiers in Social Movement Theory.* New Haven, CT: Yale University Press.

Morris, Charles R. 1997. *American Catholic: The Saints and Sinners Who Built America's Most Powerful Church.* New York: Times.

Mott, Stephen Charles. 1993. *A Christian Perspective on Political Thought.* New York: Oxford University Press.

Mugavero, Francis J. 1989. "Catholic Bishops' Work." *New York Times,* February 4, p. 14.

Munguía, Jacinto R. 2000. "Las hipótesis: ¿Quién envió a Sandri a México?" *Milenio,* March 6, p. 40.

Muñoz, Alma E. 2000. "Ordenan movimientos en la CEM; Removerán a Athié Gallo." *La Jornada* (Mexico City), 13 February, available at www.jornada .unam.mx/2000/02/13/pol3.html.

Muñoz, P., et al.. 2000. "Estas elecciones son el despertar de México, coinciden intelectuales." *La Jornada* (Mexico City), 3 July, available at www.jornada .unam.mx/2000/07/03/pol6.html.

Murphy, William. 1991. "Rerum Novarum." In *A Century of Catholic Social Thought,* edited by George Weigel and Robert Royal. Washington, DC: Ethics and Public Policy Center.

NACLA (North American Congress on Latin America). 1996. "On the Line: Latinos on Labor's Cutting Edge." *NACLA Report on the Americas* 30, no. 3 (November-December), available at www.nacla.org/issue_disp.php?iss=3013.

National Conference of Catholic Bishops. 1983. *The Challenge of Peace: God's Promise and Our Response; A Pastoral Letter on War and Peace.* Washington, DC: Office of Publication Services, United States Catholic Conference.

———. 1986. *Economic Justice for All: Catholic Social Teaching and the U.S. Economy.* Washington, DC: Office of Publishing and Promotion Services, United States Catholic Conference.

———. 1997. *Tenth Anniversary Edition of Economic Justice for All: Pastoral Letter on Catholic Social Teaching and the U.S. Economy.* Washington, DC: Office of Publication Services, United States Catholic Conference.

Neuhaus, Richard John. 1996. "The Testing of Trust." *First Things: A Monthly Journal of Religion and Public Life,* no. 66 (October): 76.

Newman, John Henry. 1989. *An Essay on the Development of Christian Doctrine.* Notre Dame, IN: University of Notre Dame Press.

Niebuhr, Reinhold. 1952. *Moral Man and Immoral Society: A Study in Ethics and Politics.* New York: Charles Scribner's Sons.

Nissen, Bruce. 1999. *Which Direction for Organized Labor?: Essays on Organizing, Outreach, and Internal Transformations.* Detroit: Wayne State University Press.

Noonan, John Thomas. 2005. *A Church That Can and Cannot Change: The Development of Catholic Moral Teaching.* Notre Dame, IN: University of Notre Dame Press.

Noticias Mexicanas. 1999. "Divide el clero el uso que dio Fox a la Vírgen." *El Universal* (Mexico City), 13 September, Internet edition.

Novak, Michael. 1982. *The Spirit of Democratic Capitalism.* New York: Simon and Schuster.

———. 1984. *Freedom with Justice: Catholic Social Thought and Liberal Institutions.* San Francisco: Harper and Row.

———. 1989. *Catholic Social Thought and Liberal Institutions: Freedom with Justice.* New Brunswick, NJ: Transaction.

Núñez Hurtado, Carlos. 1996. *Educar para transformar: Una perspectiva dialéctica y liberadora de educación y comunicación popular.* Guadalajara, Jalisco, MX: IMDEC.

———. 1998. *La revolución ética.* Guadalajara, Jalisco, MX: IMDEC.

Núñez Hurtado, Carlos, Orlando Fals Borda, and Arles Caruso. 1990. *Investigación participativa y educación popular en América Latina hoy.* Guadalajara, Jalisco, MX: IMDEC.

Nutini, Hugo G. 1984. *Ritual Kinship: Ideological and Structural Integration of the Compadrazgo System in Rural Tlaxcala.* Princeton, NJ: Princeton University Press.

Oakland Community Organizations. 2005. "Issue Areas and Highlights." www.oaklandcommunity.org/issues.html.

Oakley, Francis, and Bruce M. Russett. 2004. *Governance, Accountability, and the Future of the Catholic Church.* New York: Continuum.

Oboler, Suzanne. 1995. *Ethnic Labels, Latino Lives: Identity and the Politics of (Re)presentation in the United States.* Minneapolis: University of Minnesota Press.

O'Brien, David J. 1991. "A Century of Catholic Social Teaching." In *One Hundred Years of Catholic Social Thought: Celebration and Challenge,* edited by John A. Coleman. Maryknoll, NY: Orbis.

O'Brien, David J., and Thomas A. Shannon, eds. 1977. *Renewing the Earth: Catholic Documents on Peace, Justice, and Liberation.* Garden City, NY: Doubleday Image.

Octavio, Carlos. 1999. "Propuestas contra la violencia intrafamiliar." *El Semanario* (Guadalajara), no. 145 (14 November): 4.

O'Malley, John W. 1993. *The First Jesuits.* Cambridge, MA: Harvard University Press.

———. 1999. *The Jesuits: Cultures, Sciences, and the Arts, 1540–1773.* Toronto: University of Toronto Press.

———. 2000a. "The Beatification of Pope Pius IX." *America* 186–11.

———. 2000b. *Trent and All That : Renaming Catholicism in the Early Modern Era.* New York: Oxford University Press.

Pacific Institute for Community Organizations. 1997. "Reweaving the Fabric of America's Communities." Oakland, CA: PICO.

Palacios, Joseph M. 1997. "Solidarity: Organizing Instrument and Principle for Justice." Paper presented at Durkheim Conference, UCLA Center for the Study of Religion, Los Angeles, 8 May.

———. 2001. "Locating the Social in Social Justice: Social Justice Teaching and Practice in the American and Mexican Catholic Churches." Ph.D. diss., University of California, Berkeley.

Parsons, Talcott. 1977. *The Evolution of Societies.* Englewood Cliffs, NJ: Prentice-Hall.

———. 1982. *On Institutions and Social Evolution: Selected Writings.* Chicago: University of Chicago Press.

Paz, Octavio. 1993. *El laberinto de la soledad, postdata, vuelta a el laberinto de la soledad.* Mexico City: Fondo de Cultura Económica.

Pius XI. 1938. *On the Reconstruction of the Social Order (Quadragesimo Anno): Encyclical of His Holiness Pope Pius XI.* New York: America Press.

Poggi, Gianfranco. 1967. *Catholic Action in Italy: The Sociology of a Sponsored Organization.* Stanford, CA: Stanford University Press.

Ponce, Daniel, et al. 1997. *Una propuesta para fortalecer nuestros procesos institucionales.* Guadalajara, Jalisco, MX: IMDEC.

Poniatowska, Elena. 1971. *La noche de Tlatelolco.* Mexico City: Ediciones Era.

Pontifical Council for Justice and Peace. 2005. *Compendium of the Social Doctrine of the Church.* Washington, DC: United States Conference of Catholic Bishops Publishing.

Pottenger, John R. 1989. *The Political Theory of Liberation Theology: Toward a Reconvergence of Social Values and Social Science.* Albany: State University of New York Press.

Prejean, Helen. 1994. *Dead Man Walking: An Eyewitness Account of the Death Penalty in the United States.* New York: Vintage.

Putnam, Robert D., Robert Leonardi, and Raffaella Y. Nanetti. 1993. *Making Democracy Work: Civic Traditions in Modern Italy.* Princeton, NJ: Princeton University Press.

Quan, Carol. 1999. "A Resolution for High Achievement." *Oakland Tribune,* 5 January.

Rasmussen, Douglas B., and James P. Sterba. 1987. *The Catholic Bishops and the Economy: A Debate.* New Brunswick, NJ: Transaction.

Reese, Thomas J. 1992. *A Flock of Shepherds: The National Conference of Catholic Bishops.* Kansas City, MO: Sheed and Ward.

Ren, Zhuoxuan. 1975. *Inside Mao Tse-Tung Thought: An Analytical Blueprint of His Actions.* Hicksville, NY: Exposition.

René de Dios, Sergio. 1999. "Iniciativa de ley." *Público* (Guadalajara), 6 March, Internet edition.

Ricard, Robert. 1966. *The Spiritual Conquest of Mexico.* Berkeley: University of California Press.

Rivera, María. 2000. "Fox gobernará para la clase media: Loaeza." *La Jornada* (Mexico City), 13 July, available at www.jornada.unam.mx/2000/07/13/010n1gen.html.

Robles Gil, Rafael Reygadas. 1998. *Abriendo veredas: Iniciativas públicas y sociales de las redes de organizaciones civiles.* Mexico City: Convergencia de Organismos Civiles por la Democracia.

Rodríguez, Jeanette. 1994. *Our Lady of Guadalupe: Faith and Empowerment among Mexican-American Women.* Austin: University of Texas Press.

Royal, Robert, Peter L. Berger, John Joseph O'Connor, and Lay Commission on Catholic Social Teaching and the U.S. Economy. 1987. *Challenge and Response: Critiques of the Catholic Bishops' Draft Letter on the U.S. Economy.* Washington, DC: Ethics and Public Policy Center.

Ryden, David K., and Jeffrey Polet. 2005. *Sanctioning Religion? Politics, Law, and Faith-Based Public Services.* Boulder, CO: Lynne Rienner.

Salcedo Padilla, Jorge, Jr.. 2000. "Fox laico." *Reforma* (Mexico City), 5 December, p. 6.

Salt of the Earth News. 2002. "VOTF Banned in Boston—and Elsewhere." Chicago: Claretian Publications, October, available at http://salt.claretianpubs.org/sjnews/2002/10/sjn0210d.html.

Savater, Fernando. 1994. *Amador: In Which a Father Addresses His Son on Questions of Ethics.* New York: Henry Holt.

School of the Americas Watch. 2005. "What Is the SOA?" www.soaw.org/new/type.php?type=8.

Schorr, Jonathan. 1998. "General Terra Nova Test Scores Lower." *Oakland Tribune,* 29 September, p. A1.

———. 1999. "Six Charter Schools Set for Approval." *Oakland Tribune,* 8 April, A1.

Segundo, Juan Luis. 1985. *Theology and the Church: A Response to Cardinal Ratzinger and a Warning to the Whole Church.* Minneapolis: Winston.

Seligman, Adam B. 1992. *The Idea of Civil Society.* New York: Free Press.

Sevilla, Victor J. 1953. *A Guide to Catholic Action in the Philippines.* Pasay City, Philippines: Mindanao Times.

Sicilia, Javier. 2000. "El nuncio que se va, el club que se queda." *Proceso,* no. 1217, 26 February.

Sigaut, Nelly, ed. 1997. *La iglesia católica en México.* Zamora, Michoacán, MX: Colegio de Michoacán.

Sigmund, Paul E. 1993. "Catholicism and Liberal Democracy." In *Catholic Social Thought and the New World Order,* edited by Oliver F. Williams and John W. Houck. Notre Dame, IN: University of Notre Dame Press.

Skerry, Peter. 1993. *Mexican Americans: The Ambivalent Minority.* Cambridge, MA: Harvard University Press.

Snow, David A., Jr., E. Burke Rochford, Steven K. Worden, and Robert D. Benford. 1986. "Frame Alignment Processes, Micromobilization, and Movement Participation." *American Sociological Review* 51:464–81.

Sobrino, Jon. 1993. "Communion, Conflict, and Ecclesial Solidarity." In *Mysterium Liberationis: Fundamental Concepts of Liberation Theology,* edited by Ignacio Ellacuria and Jon Sobrino, pp. 615–35. Maryknoll, NY: Orbis.

Sobrino, Jon, and Ignacio Ellacuría. 1996. *Systematic Theology: Perspectives from Liberation Theology, Readings from Mysterium Liberationis.* Maryknoll, NY: Orbis.

Sobrino, Jon, and Juan Hernandez Pico. 1985. *Theology of Christian Solidarity.* Maryknoll, NY: Orbis.

Social Development and World Peace. 2005. "Catholic Bishops Launch Major Catholic Campaign to End the Use of the Death Penalty." Washington, DC: United States Conference of Catholic Bishops.

Soneira, Abelardo Jorge, and CEIL/CONICET (Centro de Estudios e Investigaciones Laboralests / Consejo Nacional de Investigaciones Científicas y Técnicas). 2002. "Los Movimientos Eclesiales y la Realidad Latinoamericana." Ciudad Virtual de Antropología y Arqueología, Recursos de Investigación. www .naya.org.ar/congreso2002/ponencias/abelardo_jorge_soneira.htm.

Speiker, M. 1998. "The Actuality of Catholic Social Doctrine." In *Principles of Catholic Social Teaching,* edited by David A. Boileau. Milwaukee, WI: Marquette University Press.

Stark, Rodney. 1996. *The Rise of Christianity: A Sociologist Reconsiders History.* Princeton, NJ: Princeton University Press.

Steidl-Meier, Paul. 1984. *Social Justice Ministry.* New York: Le Jacq.

Steinfels, Margaret O'Brien. 2004. *American Catholics and Civic Engagement: A Distinctive Voice.* Lanham, MD: Rowman and Littlefield.

Steinfels, Peter. 2003. *A People Adrift: The Crisis of the Roman Catholic Church in America.* New York: Simon and Schuster.

Stief, Ron Michael. 1987. "Farmworker Justice and Catholic Social Teaching." M.A. thesis, Pacific School of Religion, Berkeley, CA.

Sullivan, Meg. 2000. "Mexican Immigrants in U.S. Keep Close Ties with Their Hometowns." *USC Chronicle,* 17 April, available at www.usc.edu/dept/LAS/ pase/FRAMES/NEWS/rivera2000.htm.

Swidler, Ann. 1986. "Culture in Action: Symbols and Strategies." *American Sociological Review* 51:273–86.

Szasz Pianta, Ivonne. 1993. *Migración temporal en Malinalco: La agricultura de subsistencia en tiempos de crisis.* Mexico City: Colegio de México.

Tangeman, Michael. 1995. *Mexico at the Crossroads: Politics, the Church, and the Poor.* Maryknoll, NY: Orbis.

Tello Diaz, Carlos. 1995. *La rebelion de las cañadas*. Mexico City: Cal y Arena.

Theissen, Gerd. 1978. *The First Followers of Jesus: A Sociological Analysis of the Earliest Christianity*. London: SCM Press.

———. 1992. *Social Reality and the Early Christians: Theology, Ethics, and the World of the New Testament*. Minneapolis: Fortress.

Tocqueville, Alexis de. 1995. *Democracy in America*. New York: Everyman Library.

Torres Robles, Alfonso. 2001. *La prodigiosa aventura de los Legionarios de Cristo*. Madrid: Editorial Foca.

Tracy, David. 1981. *The Analogical Imagination: Christian Theology and the Culture of Pluralism*. New York: Crossroad.

Troeltsch, Ernst. 1981. *The Social Teachings of the Christian Churches*. Translated by Olive Wyon. Chicago: University of Chicago Press.

Truman, Tom. 1960. *Catholic Action and Politics*. London: Merlin.

United States Catholic Conference. 2000. *Catechism of the Catholic Church*. Vatican City: Libreria Editrice Vaticana.

United States Conference of Catholic Bishops. 2003. "Between Man and Woman: Questions and Answers about Marriage and Same Sex Unions." Washington, DC: Committee on Marriage and Family Life, United States Conference of Catholic Bishops.

Urquhart, Gordon. 1999. *The Pope's Armada: Unlocking the Secrets of Mysterious and Powerful New Sects in the Church*. Amherst, NY: Prometheus.

Urquhart, Gordon, and Catholics for a Free Choice. 1997. *Opus Dei: The Pope's Right Arm in Europe*. Washington, DC: Catholics for a Free Choice.

Vasconcelos, Jose. 1948. *La raza cósmica: Misión de la raza iberoamericana*. Mexico City: Colección Austral.

Vázquez Rangel, Gloria, and Jesús Ramírez López, eds. 1995. *Marginación y pobreza en Mexico*. Mexico City: Editorial Ariel.

Velasco Ortiz, M. Laura. 2005. *Mixtec Transnational Identity*. Tucson: University of Arizona Press.

Vera, Rodrigo. 2000. "'Golpe de estado' de la línea dura en la Conferencia Episcopal." Centro de Ciencias Investigaciones Interdisciplinarias, March.

Verba, Sidney, Kay Lehman Schlozman, and Henry E. Brady. 1995. *Voice and Equality: Civic Voluntarism in American Politics*. Cambridge, MA: Harvard University Press.

Vidler, Alex. 1964. *A Century of Social Catholicism*. London: Society for the Promotion of Christian Knowledge.

Warner, Michael. 1995. *Changing Witness: Catholic Bishops and Public Policy, 1917–1994*. Washington, DC: Ethics and Public Policy Center; Grand Rapids, MI: Eerdmans.

Warren, Mark R. 1998. "Community Building and Political Power." *American Behavioral Scientist* 42, no. 1 (September): 78–92.

———. 2001. *Dry Bones Rattling: Community Building to Revitalize American Democracy*. Princeton, NJ: Princeton University Press.

Warren, Mark R., and Richard L. Wood. 2001. *Faith-Based Community Organizing: The State of the Field.* Jericho, NY: Interfaith Funders.

Weber, Max. 1946a. "Religious Rejections of the World and Their Directions." In *From Max Weber: Essays in Sociology,* edited by H. H. Gerth and C. Wright Mills, pp. 323–59. New York: Oxford University Press.

———. 1946b. "The Social Psychology of the World Religions." In *From Max Weber: Essays in Sociology,* edited by H. H. Gerth and C. Wright Mills, pp. 267–301. New York: Oxford University Press.

Weigel, George. 1982. *The Peace Bishops and the Arms Race: Can Religious Leadership Help in Preventing War?* Chicago: World Without War.

———. 1992. *A New Worldly Order: John Paul II and Human Freedom.* Washington, DC: Ethics and Public Policy Center.

———. 1999. *Witness to Hope: The Biography of Pope John Paul II.* New York: Cliff Street.

Weigel, George, and Robert Royal. 1993. *Building the Free Society: Democracy, Capitalism, and Catholic Social Teaching.* Grand Rapids, MI: Eerdmans; Washington, DC: Ethics and Public Policy Center.

Weigert, Kathleen Maas, and Alexia K. Kelley. 2004. *Living the Catholic Social Tradition: Cases and Commentary.* Lanham, MD: Rowman and Littlefield.

West, Cornel. 1994. *Race Matters.* New York: Vintage.

White, Hayden. 1978. *Tropics of Discourse: Essays in Cultural Criticism.* Baltimore: John Hopkins University Press.

Williams, Oliver F., and John W. Houck, eds. 1993. *Catholic Social Thought and the New World Order.* Notre Dame, IN: University of Notre Dame Press.

Wills, Garry. 2000. *Papal Sin: Structures of Deceit.* New York: Doubleday.

Winter, Gibson. 1966. *Elements for a Social Ethic: Scientific and Ethical Perspectives on Social Process.* New York: Macmillan.

Wolin, Sheldon. 1960. *Politics and Vision: Continuity and Innovation in Western Political Thought.* Boston: Little, Brown.

Wood, Richard Lawrence. 1995. "Faith in Action: Religion, Race, and the Future of Democracy." Ph.D. diss., University of California at Berkeley.

———. 2002. *Faith in Action: Religion, Race, and Democratic Organizing in America.* Chicago: University of Chicago Press.

Wuthnow, Robert. 2004. *Saving America? Faith-Based Services and the Future of Civil Society.* Princeton, NJ: Princeton University Press.

Wuthnow, Robert, and John Hyde Evans. 2002. *The Quiet Hand of God: Faith-Based Activism and the Public Role of Mainline Protestantism.* Berkeley: University of California Press.

Yinger, Winthrop. 1975. *Cesar Chavez: The Rhetoric of Nonviolence.* Hicksville, NY: Exposition.

Zaid, Gabriel. 1997. *Tres poetas católicos.* Mexico City: Océano.

www.ingramcontent.com/pod-product-compliance
Lightning Source LLC
Chambersburg PA
CBHW022138020426
42334CB00015B/946